JOYCE

The Man, the Work, the Reputation

MARVIN MAGALANER
and RICHARD M. KAIN

JOYCE

The Man, the Work, the Reputation

COLLIER BOOKS
NEW YORK, N.Y.

This Collier Books edition is published by arrangement with the New York University Press

Collier Books is a division of The Crowell-Collier Publishing Company

First Collier Books Edition 1962

Hecho en los E.E.U.U.
Printed in the United States of America

Preface

WITH HIS first major work appearing on the eve of the First World War and his last on the eve of the Second, James Joyce has seemed a symptom and portent of our age. At the same time he has challenged and delighted readers, scholars, critics, and artists with his verbal magic and unique vision. If the discovery of Joyce has at times been a grim work in progress, it is also a fascinating search, a second Quest for Corvo, as the Dublin Joycean, Niall Sheridan, has suggested.

The authors of this volume feel that the time has come to appraise the position of Joyce in the modern world. Though it is manifestly impossible to cover all the relevant material, the volume may provide something for beginners and advanced Joyceans alike.

But if no single volume can say the last word about Joyce, our analyses of his works attempt merely to discover a way of approach to what he wrote, to suggest a method of reading Joyce that will be profitable and exciting. The elaborate paraphrase of a "skeleton key" is not needed to accomplish this, nor must critical exegesis exhaust the possibilities of every paragraph Joyce wrote. Yet, at the same time, we hope that the avenues opened by our exploratory analyses will lead easily to further, extended insights.

In similar fashion, we have not tried to do again the biography of Joyce. In a few pages, we discuss only those categories of Joyce's life in which there has hitherto appeared to be confusion. In "The Joyce Enigma" and "The Problem of Biography," we seek to identify the points of dispute, and, if we can, illuminate cloudy places. These chapters should be looked upon principally as points of departure for further investigation.

What, then, does the book do? It is the first extended treatment of the history of Joyce's critical reputation. Making use of hundreds of books and articles—many unavailable except in private collections here and abroad—it seeks to show what the twentieth century has thought of this strange Irishman over the years.

As a corollary to this broad treatment of Joyce's reputation, the book is able to bring together in one volume, for the first time, the best criticism available on each of Joyce's major works. This criticism, scattered in esoteric journals, little magazines, out-of-print books, rare collectors' items, and foreign periodicals, is often out of reach of the student. Such critical opinion and analysis, supplemented by our own researches, should offer a useful addition to the literature on Joyce.

We have tried to stress those aspects of his life and work often treated casually. That is why we allot so much space to the generally slighted short stories of *Dubliners*. That is why, for instance, we have included excerpts from Joyce's as yet unpublished letters and have given a large share of attention to the relationship of Joyce to the modern arts.

Many people have had a share in this book and deserve our warm thanks: the staffs of the New York Public Library, the National Library in Dublin, The Houghton Library at Harvard University, The Sterling Memorial Library at Yale University, The Lockwood Memorial Library at the University of Buffalo, and especially the generous staff of The City College Library in New York. We are extremely grateful to Miss Frances Steloff of the James Joyce Society and The Gotham Book Mart for her assistance; to Mr. John J. Slocum for many favors, among them allowing us to inspect early drafts of the *Dubliners* stories; to Miss Grace LeRoy of New York University Press for many valuable suggestions; to Mr. Herbert Cahoon, curator of autograph manuscripts at the Morgan Library in New York, and to Mr. Joseph Prescott of Wayne University, for willingness to share their wide knowledge of matters Joycean; and to Miss Harriet Weaver for allowing us to quote from Joyce's unpublished letters. We certainly owe a debt to numerous students who during the past ten years have followed with us the path of the young boy in North Richmond Street reflecting on the word "paralysis" to the eminence of the seer who envisioned the meeting of Anna Livia with the sea.

Here we would like to record separately several other debts.

—Marvin Magalaner to Professor William York Tindall of Columbia University, who bears no responsibility for this book as such, but whose constant enthusiasm for his subject, since 1942, has made his students eager to pursue studies in Joyce; to Dr. Arthur Zeiger and Professor John C. Thirlwall of The City College of New York for much valuable assistance in preparing the manuscript; and to the late Professor Theodore Goodman of The City College of New York, several of whose suggestions have been incorporated into the *Dubliners* chapter, but whose love for Joyce, good writing, and his students is too great for incorporation anywhere.

—Richard M. Kain to the late Nora Joyce, and Giorgio Joyce in Zurich; to Sylvia Beach, the late Eugene Jolas, Maria Jolas, and Lucy Léon in Paris; to Patrick Byrne, Constantine Curran, Oliver St. John Gogarty, Richard Hayes, Patrick Henchy, and W. B. Stanford in Dublin; to Frank Budgen in London and Harriet Weaver in Oxford; to A. M. Klein of Montreal; to George Antheil, Padraic Colum, Vivienne Koch, Harry Levin, Ellsworth Mason, William T. Noon, S.J., and James F. Spoerri. Recitation of these names brings to mind happy hours spent dining with Mrs. Joyce and her son at Joyce's favorite rendezvous in Zurich, The Kronenhalle; viewing the rhododendron on the Hill of Howth; gazing at the coigns of Kildare Street from the steps of the National Library; talking about Joyce in Parisian apartments and cafés, in Dublin pubs, and in classrooms at Northwestern University, Harvard, and the University of Louisville. My special thanks are due to Niall Sheridan, Herbert Cahoon, John Slocum, and Joseph Prescott for their careful reading of the manuscript, and to Ernest C. Hassold, chairman of the Humanities Division at the University of Louisville, whose vision of the role that creative scholarship can play in the advancement of culture prompted the award of a research grant for European travel and a leave of absence during which times the major portion of this work was completed. President Philip G. Davidson and the trustees of the University of Louisville have been most co-operative in making these arrangements. To Thomas Ware, whose patient clerical work was of invaluable assistance, and to my family, whose aid and forebearance exceeded the call of duty, my personal gratitude is great.

R. M. K.

M. M.

Acknowledgments

WE WISH TO THANK *The South Atlantic Quarterly, The University of Kansas City Review, The Arizona Quarterly,* and *The Philological Quarterly,* in whose pages sections of this book first appeared, for permission to quote from the original articles by Marvin Magalaner. Parts of the book were first presented, by Richard M. Kain, as addresses before the Modern Language Association of America, the Yale Graduate Club, The James Joyce Society, and at the opening of the James Joyce Exhibition at The Sterling Memorial Library of Yale University.

Acknowledgment is gratefully made to the following persons and organizations for their kindness in allowing us to use copyright material in this book:

Faber and Faber, Ltd. (London), for quotation from *Our Exagmination* (1929), by Samuel Beckett and Others; Richard V. Chase and *The American Scholar* (Autumn 1944), for "Finnegans Wake: An Anthropological Study"; *Partisan Review* (March-April 1941), for Eugene Jolas' article on Joyce; *Accent* (Winter 1944), for "First Flight to Ithaca," by Richard Levin and Charles Shattuck; The Viking Press, for James Joyce's *Dubliners* (1914), *A Portrait of the Artist as a Young Man* (1916) and *Finnegans Wake* (1939), as well as the Padraic Colum edition of James Joyce's *Exiles* (1951); the British Broadcasting Corporation, for several lines from a program entitled "Portrait of James Joyce," presented on the Third Programme, Monday, February 13, 1950, and later; Harcourt, Brace and Company, for Joseph Campbell and Henry Morton Robinson, *A Skeleton Key to 'Finnegans Wake'* (1944); *The Saturday Review of Literature,* for Oliver St. John Gogarty's "They Think They Know Joyce" (March 18, 1950), and Mary Colum's "A Little Knowledge of Joyce" (April 29, 1950); Jarrolds Publishers (London), for Gerald Griffin's *The Wild Geese* (no date); Methuen and Company, Ltd. (London), and P. S. O'Hegarty, for the latter's *A History of Ireland under the Union* (1952); Random House, Inc., for James Joyce, *Ulysses* (1934), for Samuel Butler, *The Way of All Flesh,* and for Sigmund Freud, *The Basic Writings of Sigmund Freud* (1938); the Houghton Library of Harvard University, which has possession of the report of the publisher's reader on Joyce's *Dubliners;* Doubleday and Company, for *Bad Boy of Music* (1945), by George Antheil, reprinted by permission of Doubleday and Company, Inc.; Vanguard Press, for *James Joyce: Two Decades of Criticism* (1948), edited by Seon Givens; Liveright Publishers, for *The Critical Game,* by John Macy (copyright R 1950, John Macy); *The New Republic* (January 3, 1934), for Malcolm Cowley's "The Religion of Art: Readings from the Lives of the Saints"; Mr. T. S. Eliot, for his permission to quote from "Ulysses, Order, and Myth," an essay which appeared first in 1923 in *The Dial;* Charles Scribner's Sons, for James G. Huneker's *Unicorns* (1917); Gerald Duckworth and Company, Ltd. (London), for Anton Chekhov, *The Black Monk* (1903), edited by R. Long; the Yale University Library, for permission to quote from a letter by George Russell and several letters by James Joyce, all of which are in the possession of the library; Mr. Diarmuid Russell, for permission to quote from a letter of his father, George Russell, to James Joyce; Mr. Hugh MacDiarmid and William Maclennon, Ltd. (Glasgow), for permission to quote from *In Memoriam James Joyce.* To New Directions for *James Joyce: A Critical Introduction* (1941), by Harry Levin, *Stephen Hero* (1944), by James Joyce, and *An Exagmination of James Joyce* (1939), by Samuel Beckett and Others. To the officers of the James Joyce Society for *Recollections of James Joyce by His Brother* (1950), by Stanislaus Joyce.

Contents

JOYCE

The Man, the Work, the Reputation

A nice collection could be made of legends about me. Here are some . . .

—*Letter of James Joyce to Miss Harriet Weaver, June 24, 1921, quoted with the permission of Miss Weaver.*

PART I

The Man

Chapter 1

The Joyce Enigma

THE DISCOVERY of Joyce is an unending quest. Though he may feel bewildered or exasperated by the obscurity of the text, the sensitive reader immediately notes a strange power, akin to that of great poetry. The hypnotic magic of the style and the widening implications of the story suggest the presence of genius. Here is a writer who must be heeded. This awareness deepens with each re-reading. Image and symbol haunt the memory; themes provide endless opportunity for speculation. For in the work of Joyce dream opposes reality and the inner life of the mind is juxtaposed against the external world. Man exists in present and past alike, and even as he enacts his own drama he relives that of mythical forebears.

Whatever be the final judgment, this work is obviously the product of a sensibility complex and original. The labyrinth was the author's own symbol of his technical cunning, for it was the creation of the mythological Daedalus, whose name Joyce adopted for his quasi-autobiographical artist. Rather than Shakespeare's figure of art as a mirror held up to nature, or Stendhal's modification of it in his defintion of the novel as a mirror that travels along a highway, one may suggest the best image for Joyce's art to be that of a many-faceted prism, catching half-lights and projecting magnified distortions. As the young Stephen Dedalus reflects on the nature of language during one of his meditative rambles in the *Portrait,* he uses prism and mirror as contrasting metaphors, the prism for "a language many-coloured and richly storied" and the mirror for "a lucid supple periodic prose."

Hailed as a champion of artistic freedom and a technical experimenter, Joyce came to be accepted as the characteristic creative genius of our time. His life provided an archetype of the modern artist's isolation and dedication, his works gave a series of portraits of the artist, and his career developed into a paradigm of the problems of expression. For like his avowed masters, Flaubert and Ibsen, he marked through

The notes to Chapter 1 begin on page 323.

his work successive stages in the exploration of diverse techniques. Techniques and styles indicate modes of perception, in that they reveal the outward view of the perceiving mind—expression—and reflect the incidence of experience upon the mind—impression. In Joyce's work, structure, symbol, and style vary as he proceeds from autobiography to symbolic narrative (from *Stephen Hero* to the *Portrait*), from the epiphany or revelation in the short stories of *Dubliners* to the epiphany in drama, and, finally from the montage of *Ulysses* to the dream-myth of *Finnegans Wake*. Yet what seemed bewildering or eccentric at first appearance has since become a logical development in regard to the relationships among his several works and with respect to contemporaneous experiments in the arts.

Joyce's biography has a neatness of pattern that would have delighted his Scholastic mind—twenty years in Ireland, the only life he ever incorporated into art; twenty years in middle Europe, the great creative period; and almost twenty years of international fame, living in Paris and writing his final testament. So too is his literary career Hegelian. The naturalism of *Dubliners* conceals its antithesis in symbolic detail: its fundamental realism is countered by the subjectivity of the *Portrait,* and the synthesis of *Ulysses* attains a precarious balance between naturalism and symbolism. Viewed from the vantage point of *Finnegans Wake,* however, the Joyce canon becomes a progressive extension of the poetic and connotative, reaching its culmination in a gigantic symbolist poem. Such is the progress denominated very cleverly by Joseph Prescott in an early essay where each stage in the career is headlined by the successive phrases, "In the beginning was the Word," "and the Word was with God," "and the Word was God." [1]

In regard to contemporary art, what seems merely a perverse evasion of responsibility on Joyce's part in his juxtaposition of the heroic and commonplace, or his apparently careless disregard of art in the confusion of detail, will upon closer inspection prove to be an early manifestation of what has by now become common. Whether it be better termed dissonance or discontinuity, the method denies the demands of classical decorum, rejecting the harmony of subject, style, theme, and tone. Thus the very nature of the technique invites a multitude of conflicting reactions, changing with each reader and each reading. And this play of ambiguity itself seems a perfect expression of the anxieties and uncertainties of modern man and becomes a starting point in the self-examining of the art medium and its value. So painters will paste such alien materials as scraps of newspaper or strips of wood on their canvases, laughing at both themselves and their public.

Joyce's influence on creative art was immediate and fruitful. His manner of vision fertilized the imaginations of his contemporaries, not only in literature, but in the arts of painting, music, theater, and dance. The action was reciprocal, of course, and many of the devices that startled the first readers of *Ulysses* have since been recognized as similar to the techniques of the motion picture or those of nonrepresentational art. Joyce seems to have derived from and in turn contributed to a style now widely recognized but not fully understood. To lay the groundwork for such an understanding would require no less than a conspectus of modern culture. It demands study of the vogue for Byzantine forms and the consequent decline in esteem for Renaissance masters. It leads to an appraisal of the influences of primitive art, psychology, and industrial materials and techniques. Above all, the definition of modern culture requires insight into metaphysical concepts of space, time, and motion. Such suggestions emerge from the scrutiny of Joyce the technician.

Even more tantalizing is the problem of ascertaining Joyce's implicit values. Naturalist, symbolist, Marxist, humanist, and linquist have threaded their diverse paths through the labyrinth. Each has returned with his quota of riches, but often with his own reflection. Consequently, to survey the literature about Joyce is to be introduced to what Marvin Magalaner has described as "a fascinating panorama not only of the literary thought but of the political, social, and ethical nuances of the twentieth century." Yet, as the wittiest of Joyce commentators, Den Haan, the Hollander, has said: "Joyce lived an enigma, died an enigma, and left behind enigmatic work." He seemed to Den Haan one who "always reserved the last laugh to himself," a man whose supreme joke was that he could be "the invisible man who was even able to make his invisibility invisible," sardonically driving generations of critics mad, dissecting the work, racking their brains, boxing each other's ears. It is understandable that many have voiced annoyance at the strategy of a writer who deliberately plays off key,[2] or who expresses his views and then evades responsibility for them by wishing them upon his characters or putting them "into some broadly inclusive frame of irony."[3] Carl Jung is less bitter in facetiously concluding his brilliant essay with the remark that he is "now getting along fairly well." In lighter vein, Brian Nolan suggests that Joyce's fascination may lie in "his secretiveness, his ambiguity (his polyguity, perhaps?), his legpulling." Which, of course, is very Irish, as is the characterization of the works as "a garden in which some of us may play."[4]

One might appear blasphemous in suggesting the dilemmas of Christology, and most would think the Hamlet problem of greater magnitude and interest. Yet it is with these classic inquiries that Joyce dares to identify his Stephen Dedalus. The heretics Stephen recalls were those who fell afoul of the emerging orthodox conception of Christ's nature; Stephen's own plight is echoed in the Shakespeare discussion of *Ulysses*. One might also recall the fictitious characters who narrate Swift's fables and parodies, the simple tradesman Drapier, the blunt seaman Gulliver, the astrologer Bickerstaff, the superficial Whigs, the pedants, the projectors, and the stupid hacks who make Swift's works masterpieces of ironical indirection.[5] Indeed, the defensiveness of Hamlet's motley and Swift's masks may throw some light on Joyce's apparent need to confess and to conceal what he is confessing. Here is the "enigma of a manner" that Joyce referred to in the yet unpublished essay of 1904, "A Portrait of the Artist," and that anticipates the well-known "silence, exile, and cunning" of Stephen. Joyce's undergraduate essay on the Irish Poe, James Mangan, shows how the artist, bearing his stigma of vision and his role as "a vessel of wrath," keeps his dreams to himself and adopts a "purely defensive reserve."[6] So through Joyce's works we see a series of portraits and caricatures, the earnest Stephen Hero, the dedicated artist Dedalus, the aloof and searching Richard Rowan of *Exiles*, the counterposed Stephen and Leopold of *Ulysses*, and the final pair, Shem the sham artist and Shaun the complacent burgher.

These ambiguous images reflect the ironic temper of current art. The oblique and the equivocal appeal to the skeptical mind, fearful of disillusion and hesitant of commitment. Self-doubt and denigration have proved congenial to the artist. Romantic irony enacts the drama of the artist and his inevitably uncomprehending public; it reflects the ambiguity of the conscious and subconscious selves; and it provides a means of dramatizing the roles of art as creation and representation. Thomas Mann and André Gide have similarly represented the artist as outcast, or as prevaricator, or as escapist. In a world of pragmatic and positivist orientation the artist secures a degree of safety in mockingly accepting the world's valuation rather than attempting to justify his way of life to an alien public.

Though personal motivations can only be surmised, the richness of Joyce's orientation is clear. As an apostate who never forgot the power or poetry of the Catholic church, an exile who in imagination never left Dublin, he carried within himself the tensions that create a complex art. His verbal mastery derives from an acute ear and inherent musical taste as well as from the verbal associations of scholar and linguist. Hence the paradoxes of Harry Levin, one of the most perceptive Joyceans, are not mere stylistic mannerisms. In the Mangan essay Joyce had defined the poet as "a mediator between the world of reality and the world of dreams"; his work has suggested the influences of the factual Defoe and the visionary Blake, upon whom the young writer lectured in Trieste. If these two worlds collide more often than they coalesce in the arts it may be as much the effect of our dichotomized society as of the author's inner conflict. Yet a deeper harmony can be sensed in this play of opposites, brilliantly described by Levin as the "dizzying shifts between mystification and exhibitionism, between linguistic experiment and pornographic confession, between myth and autobiography." For in *Ulysses* the regional becomes cosmic, the map of Dublin points to the myth of Homer, Irish disorder and misrule are disciplined under imposed Scholastic concepts, and the most Irish of writers emerges as a major figure in the European tradition.

But throughout Joyce remained Irish, a fact he could never forget and many of his countrymen could never forgive. Like his compatriots Swift and Yeats he never ceased to love his country, no matter how much he might revile it. In a land where Catholic puritanism has never been able to eradicate pagan fantasy, where sentiment and scorn cohabit, where joviality is enjoyed at funerals, where theosophy and Scholasticism flourish side by side, it is no wonder that a minor industry of explaining the Irish to the Irish has been cultivated by the Irish, the most recent examples being the works of Sean O'Faolain and Arland Ussher. Poets are often statesmen, and even scholars can be wits. Catholic and Protestant, rural and urban, devout and blasphemous, romantic and realistic, Ireland is a land of divisions. Even now the country is cut into two portions, a fact that did not escape Joyce's attention. Using a language borrowed from, nay, imposed by their conquerors, the Irish have brought the English tongue to its most melodious expression. The paradoxes of the country have become a staple of its wit, of which Oscar Wilde and Shaw have been the principal exporters. It is in Ireland that the bull is cultivated—"If you see seven cows lying down in a field, and one rises, it's an Irish bull"—and the pun is in its proper habitat.

How it must have delighted the author to see himself become a legend and to note the pictures presented by friends and enemies! To quote again the Dutch investigator of the enigma:

> One can well ask, who is he? An apostate, god, joker, a master, a writer of obscenity, a man of good will, a man of the Middle Ages, a Revolutionist, an admittedly embittered man, an embalmer or a producer of life. He is silent. I shall not serve.

In rapid succession they pass by, like images in a distorting mirror or quick-change mimics in a music hall. Are these reflections or mere ventriloquist's dummies, the japing clown of Gogarty, Rebecca West's tasteless sentimentalist, followed by the esoteric scholar of Gilbert, the metaphysician beloved by German critics, the Swiftian Joyce of Kain, Pound's cynic, and the playboy seen by Dublin commentators? Finally, with the recent Catholic interests in Joyce there begins to emerge a latter-day Aquinas who builds his moral criticism on theological foundations, realizing that liturgy is both "an order of knowledge and an order of grace." So far has criticism veered toward orthodoxy that Herbert Marshall McLuhan has recommended Austin Farrer's commentary on the Book of Revelation as an ideal introduction to Joyce's art.[7]

To quote the opening of *Finnegans Wake,* here surely is a "commodius vicus of recirculation." The rebel against ecclesiastical authority is almost becoming a Father of the Church. A valid query at this point is that of the permissible limits of interpretation. Certainly one of the marks of great art is its width of appeal, yet one may question whether aesthetic communication does not demand some restrictions of meaning, in order to avoid irresponsible equivocation by the author, or uncontrolled and purely adventitious associations by reader or critic. Ned Polsky has recently protested the sophistry of a criticism "which wrenches texts in an attempt to save all renegades for the religion of their fathers," such as making "a good Jew" of Franz Kafka or saving Joyce for the church even though *non serviam* scarcely means *credo.*[8]

If ambiguity and equivocation be one of the major critical problems aroused by the indirection of modern art, the degree of permissible intensive interpretation is another. Where is one to stop, in a symbolist work, in descending from the larger aspects of theme and situation to the minute details of particular words or even of initial letters? In the history of Joyce criticism one encounters such protests as that of Joyce's brother Stanislaus against the symbolic reading of *Dubliners.* So too has the Irish writer Frank O'Connor recently asserted that though Joyce convinces the reader "that he knows nothing at all," when you hear some of the farfetched explications "you are left with a feeling that you don't even want to know." [9]

Between literalism and free association lie the limits of responsible and relevant interpretation. Despite its extensive speculations on the nature of art, the new criticism has not yet defined these limits. One should not wish to restrict literature to an exact prosaic content (the fallacy of the paraphrase) nor to the author's stated intentions. It is certainly true that successive generations have found additional levels of meaning in the classics. Yet critics readily fall prey to Bacon's Idols of the Cave, in becoming so "attached to certain particular sciences and speculations" that they "distort and colour" their contemplations "in obedience to their former fancies." Such reading with a bias, be it religious, sociological, or psychological, is often ingenious and illuminating, but it proceeds by association and analogy far from the text. R. P. Blackmur has denominated this as tendentious criticism. Its method is one of infinitely extended deduction of meaning and implication or, in the words of a recent treatment of the subject, the exercise of "an immoderate wish to use all literature as documentation of hypotheses which have nothing to do with literature." [10]

An opposite practice is that of unrestrained induction, in which critics, like terriers in sand, dig deeper and deeper into the text until the surface disappears, or becomes a morass of cryptic clues. To remain on the immediate surface of a work of art is to deny its referential values and to fall into a servile and prosaic literalism. But the extremes of induction and deduction violate the integrity of the work as literature. Its meaning becomes of the order of philosophic abstraction, its content less humanly valuable and interesting. There is no substitute for the critic's tact and taste, based on his sense of relevance, his judgment of the distance and direction of suggestion appropriate to the given work, and his knowledge of the artist's individual temperament.

Rebellion against Victorian propriety and academic art has taken many forms. One of its aspects is the obscene. However, no phase of the Joyce story seems to be of less interest now than the question of the artist's license. Tolerance here may be the result merely of a growing indifference and laxity, rather than a considered facing of the question, which should have to reckon with the necessity for artistic freedom, the demands which depth psychology makes upon characterization, and the role of the subconscious in contemporary thought. Joyce was first hailed as a pioneer in flaunting bourgeois reticences, without any deep concern about whether his freedom had added any new domain in the realm of art. This, the fundamental attitude of *The Little Review,* has been succeeded by a complete disregard of the entire question.

Though modern writers and readers are inclined to laugh at the cry of alarm provoked by the first appearance of *Ulysses,* they would do well to remember that the freedom they now enjoy is due in large part to the acceptance of Joyce's work. At present we are more concerned with political than moral censorship, but the problem of moral censorship, though held in abeyance, is not solved. Old-fashioned as it might sound, Robert Lynd is wise in remarking that "disgust is merely the other side of good taste," without which we would not have civilization. Decency is more a matter of manners than of morals, he continues, and is dependent on the state of society. Thus improvements in sanitation render objects that "once were the comic contretemps of ordinary life" nothing more than "offensive irrelevancies." Lynd is amused at the "extreme antipuritans" with their "laughterless enthusiasm" for psychoanalysis. Indecency provides little food for the imagination, indeed may even put it into fetters, though it can be justified as an expression of a pessimism such as Baudelaire's. Many lesser men are mere "epicures of the unsavoury" or "scandal-mongers about the soul and body of man." In his essay of 1927 Lynd saw *Ulysses* as an attempt to enrich the loam by working the subsoil, but an attempt so extreme as to bury the soil and to leave "a vast waste in which the imagination starves." Eight years later he granted that Joyce was sincere, "in love with truth as he saw it, and no exploiter of obscenity for commercial ends." [11] Rather Joyce uses obscenities with the dispassionate indifference of an anthropologist, an observation which parallels Stuart Gilbert's justification of *Ulysses* on the grounds that since obscenity has its place in life, suppression would render the artistic picture incomplete. Certainly what might be considered pornography in Bloom's thought is clearly understood to reflect his emotional starvation. As for the tone of the entire work, Judge Woolsey, in lifting the American ban, considered it an honest psychological study, free of pornographic intent, its effect being tragic or "emetic" rather than aphrodisiac.

Mangan's obscure oriental and medieval lore, "embroidered as in a web," which "rapt him out of his time," is also curiously prophetic of the later Joyce. For if he be God's gift to English departments, as often alleged, curricular offerings will have to be modified. One of the major sources of difficulty is that the art stems not from the main streams of classical and Renaissance culture but from neglected tributaries of Scholasticism, theosophy, and symbolism. Such obscurity poses problems of the rivalry between creation and criticism in reader and artist. There is the specious delight in recognizing the obscure or esoteric, specious in that it is related less to imaginative perception than to the puzzle-solving instinct, not always free of *Schadenfreude* at having discovered something that another has missed. This, and the awe that the dim of mind feels for the master technician, are the vulgarities or fallacies of appreciation. The creator is not exempt from similar temptations. Joyce is not innocent of the sin of mechanical rather than imaginative development of themes. If the publicized six hundred rivers be found in the Anna Livia Plurabelle section of the *Wake,* could Joyce not as well have introduced as many flora, fauna, or anything else? Many commentators fail to note that there is little aesthetic value in comprehensiveness for its own sake. One also questions whether the purely accidental associations of the pun testify to more than the ingenuity of the perpetrator.

Were Joyce no more than the indefatigable magpie he is often described as being, his influence on contemporary literature would be slight. He would be ranked with the linguistic eccentrics, his books mere curiosities. The charges against "Ph.D. literature" would be fully applicable, and one should have to agree wholly with such an adverse criticism as that of Frank O'Connor, the complaint that the static nature of Joyce's material made it "responsive to endless technical development." Joyce accordingly treated it "rather as a professor than as an artist," and he seemed therefore to write only for the Ph.D. who could spend a lifetime deciphering his text.[12]

But literature is not a Rosetta Stone, and the true test of value is not obscurity. The vitality and imaginative energy that Joyce seldom fails to display, the richness of his insights, and the music of his style depend but little upon obscurity. O'Connor's prediction of a reaction against Ph.D. literature is probably justified. Joyce may suffer from such a reaction, but his contributions to literature are incontrovertible.

One must also realize that complexity may have an important place in some forms of artistic expression. It may contribute not only to a meaning that would be falsified by simplification but add to the tone of the discourse. Enough has been suggested here to indicate that the question is a complicated one of degree, relative to the level of the material, to the taste and education of the reader, but depending ultimately on the artist's creative imagination.

In tracing the relationship of *Finnegans Wake* to occult tradition, M. J. C. Hodgart admits that this tradition, "the attempt to prove that everything is symbolic of one comprehensive Whole," has often been close to mania, with its plays on words and numbers, its random associations, its continual allegorizing. Yet absurd as such fantasies are, English literature has had a long esoteric tradition, from medieval allegorizing to the metaphysicals and the romantics, which often achieves strikingly beautiful effects, as in Sir Thomas Browne. Nevertheless, the final assessment of Joyce's work will depend upon his rendition of "states of feeling."[13]

At once unique and universal, Joyce is personally present in all he wrote, yet his works are myths of our time. Whether modern, Irish, or Joycean—and it is all three—the text is full of perplexities. Realistic foreground and metaphysical essence, verbal detail and structural framework have inspired exegesis, speculation, even prophecy. Elucidation of the text leads to a search for the literary antecedents and personal tensions that lie behind the work. Cultural alienation as well as exile severed Joyce from the Anglo-Saxon tradition. Inherent predilections, reinforced by training, drove his thought into obscure by-ways of Scholastic logic. Yet even here Joyce is less the eccentric individualist than the forerunner of a modern return to Scholasticism, and once again the enigma seems to inhere as much in the crosscurrents of modern thought and the equivocal nature of contemporary art as in the author's orientation.

Joyce's art raises basic questions of communication—the limits of language, the role of expressive and imitative form, the scope of symbolism, the problem of obscurity. Immoderately attacked and praised, the author has undergone great vicissitudes in evaluation. His work, though centered upon one provincial background, concerns questions endemic to our time. An age that both desires and fears authority will respond to Joyce's treatment of the possibilities and limitations of allegiance—to church, state, family, art, or self. Among other modern issues may be enumerated the fragmentation and urbanization of culture, the decay of social institutions and the consequent alienation of man, the dichotomy of art and life, the problems of semantics and communication, relativity both psychological and metaphysical, and the relationship of myth, religion, and history to modern life.

The sensational public effect of the work raises problems of censorship. Its literary impact arouses speculation about whether it marks a dead end in fiction, an eccentric bypath, or a stimulus to further development. The final question is that of the author's nature, whether he be artist, cynic, humorist, or seer. To some the confusion will suggest a lack of final definition; to others this diversity highlights Joyce's importance as a voice of his age. No wonder then that since March 1918, when Buck Mulligan first appeared on the Martello Tower to usher readers of *The Little Review* into the world of *Ulysses,* the Joyce question has been central in discussions of modern literature. Innumerable reviews and articles have appeared; Slocum and Cahoon list 121 translations of Joyce into the major European tongues as well as into Japanese and Urdu; over 50 books and theses discuss the man and his work, in French, German, Dutch, Italian, Welsh, and Japanese, as well as in English. One must also include works on psychology, linguistics, philosophy, sociology, and cultural history. Yet so contradictory are the findings that one feels the pertinence of the cry in *Finnegans Wake:* "A hundred cares a tithe of troubles and is there one who understands me?"

Chapter 2

The Problem of Biography

AMONG CONTEMPORARY WRITERS in English, Joyce has had by far the lion's share of personal publicity. Even Hemingway, whose "death" recently evoked banner headlines usually reserved for armistices and murderers, has enjoyed long spells of comparative obscurity spent in the quiet of private life. Joyce's comings and goings, on the other hand, his private spats, his tastes in wines and opera, the shade of his trousers, the degree to which he perspired, his off-the-record judgments of the works of other artists—everything about him, in short —was fair game for the tabloid press, the austere academic journals, café gossip, and the inspired announcements of the faithful. Two full-length biographies, which appeared during his lifetime, added greatly to the store of information and misinformation concerning his every move. Swarms of interviewers, special correspondents, literary editors, cranks, and admirers descended upon the dignified figure, determined to break through his reserve. His life was most certainly not his own.

Yet, with all this glare from the spotlight of public notoriety, surprisingly little is really known about Joyce's personal life. Or perhaps so much is known that the true picture fails to emerge from a twisted mass of contradictory testimony. Even intimates, eyewitnesses, fail to agree on ostensibly undebatable points. Thus, the editor of a Parisian magazine, reporting on her first meeting with the novelist, recalls his "tall, painfully thin figure."[1] Aidan Higgins, on the other hand, knew him as a "half-blind *little* person" (italics mine) whose appearance might disappoint the expectant visitor.[2] Elliot Paul makes much of the fact that Joyce was a most fastidious dresser when he lived in Paris.[3] But, during this same period, composer George Antheil says, "Joyce wore white duck (despite the fact that white ducks are not worn in Paris, even in midsummer)."[4]

Perhaps more important that these discrepancies in mere physical description are the various versions of Joyce's atti-

The notes to Chapter 2 begin on page 324.

tudes toward his circle of acquaintances. His apparent aloofness has been quite differently interpreted, depending on whether the critic was friend or foe. So we have Margaret Anderson, the American editor who risked imprisonment to publish the episodes of *Ulysses,* finding that, under his reticence, Joyce was kindly, gentle, and fatherly, in spite of his suffering.[5] Djuna Barnes, writing for the gentle readers of *Vanity Fair* in 1922, agrees. He has, she discovers at their first meeting, the throat of a "stricken animal" and a head turned beyond disgust but not so far as death; "he is simple, a scholar, and sees nothing objectionable in human beings if they will only remain in their place."[6] The reader is never told what this place is.

Ford Madox Ford (then Hueffer) suggests that it may be that of abject worshiper: "Mr. Joyce seemed to take little share in the rough and tumble of the several vortices. As befitted the English writer of distinction, he sat as if wrapped in sacred shawls, a high priest on an altar at which one was instructed to offer homage."[7] Malcolm Cowley reiterates Joyce's lofty position but is not as charitable in assigning motives. He ascribes the unique niche that the Irishman occupied in Paris to a rather narrow "pride, contempt, ambition," found in his works and carried over into the life, consciously and arrogantly. Nor does he consider this "self-aggrandizement" justified by Joyce's personal myth—a blind, hypochondriac author who lived in cheap bourgeois hotels, with "no companions of his own intellectual stature, and associated either with family friends or else with admiring disciples. Except in matters concerning literature and the opera, his opinions were those of a fourth- or fifth-rate mind." Dissenting from the more favorable opinion of the Misses Anderson and Barnes, Cowley insists that Joyce is "inhuman and cold." It was, he says, "as if he had starved everything else in his life to feed his ambition . . . . selling youth, riches and part of his common humanity." Cowley leaves the interview chilled by the touch of "long, cold, wet-marble fingers."[8]

It is hard to reconcile attributions of inhumanity, hypochondria, and coldness with the more florid anecdotes told about the Joyce of the 1920's. Perhaps they should be prefaced with Joyce's own admonition to Frank Budgen in an unpublished letter: ". . . never believe anything an Englishman tells you in the press or an Irishman in a bar about me."[9] George Antheil, an American, tells how he and Joyce, driven on by their admiration for the music of Purcell, managed to crash three exclusive musicales sponsored by a French society woman before being discovered and unceremoniously ejected.[10] He tells too how Joyce contrived to get Adrienne Monnier, a literary friend whose austere manner of dress made her appear nunlike, to accompany him to the Moulin Rouge. Once there, Joyce was successful in convincing the *cocotes* who frequented the place that she was indeed a nun. His skill in deception, says Antheil, soon had them believing that the "nun" had been lured out of her convent and was now being spirited away to the United States for a gay time. So outraged was Joyce's audience at the Moulin Rouge that he and his companions had to escape before violence occurred.[11]

Reports of such undignified conduct are not limited to one source. Another American, Robert McAlmon, remembers meeting Joyce almost nightly in Paris for an aperitif and recalls fondly that the author "was ready to stay out all night . . . never ready to go home at any hour." "One night," McAlmon says, "he wept in his cups when telling of the fertility of his forefathers. . . . Joyce would sigh, and . . . swear that by the grace of God he was still a young man and he would have more children before the end."[12]

All critics agree that Joyce was a good husband and father and that he loved his home life. Few, however, concede that it constituted a suitable environment for an anti-Philistine author. Bourgeois, middle class in the extreme (representing everything that Joyce in his writing was not), its repugnant reality is usually captured by recalling the "roseate syphilis" or "green gangrene" wallpaper and the two "color-retouched photographs" of Joyce and his wife above the gas fireplace. Heavy plush chairs and an upright piano complete the picture. Some attribute the ugliness of his surroundings to his semiblindness. None have yet found fault with his hearing or reconciled the happy-husband theme with the evidence that Nora was "scolding him loudly for getting egg all over the bedspread and wondering audibly why in the world didn't he get up to work instead of sitting in bed all day writing."[13] Paradoxes abound in the study of Joyce's life.

The student who respects Joyce and admires his great talents may rightly have qualms about the relevance of these intimate details to a critical-biographical study. One advances to firmer ground by examining conflicting reports concerning the attitude of the writer toward his reading public. This is especially true in Joyce's case since, in almost all his works, he treats of the artist as a part of, and in opposition to, his society. His theme is aloneness, apartness, the need for communication. It is inconceivable that the attitudes which he ascribes to his characters should not have been colored by his own experiences in similar circumstances. It is worth while, then, to clear away some of the misconceptions that are current concerning Joyce's thinking.

The idea that Joyce was indifferent to his reading public is ridiculous. No artist spends almost forty painful years in an effort to say something with beauty and force while at the same time coolly rejecting an audience for his remarks. The real problem, of course, was to find readers sufficiently sophisticated and skilled to profit from their reading. On this count, Joyce was not enthusiastic, as this bitterly sarcastic (and unmailed) reply to a publisher's request for Joyce's endorsement of another writer's book clearly indicates:

> . . . the only things I can suggest as likely to attract the British reading public are a preface by Sir J. M. Barrie, author of My Lady Nicotine, opinions of the book (to be printed on the back of its jacket) from two deservedly popular personalities of the present day, such as, the rector of Stiffkey and the Princess of Wales and (on the front jacket) a coloured picture by a Royal Academician representing two young ladies, one fair and the other dark but both distinctly nicelooking, seated in a graceful though not unbecoming posture at a table on which a book stands upright, with title visible and underneath the picture three lines of simple dialogue, for example:
>
> Ethel: Does Cyril spend too much on cigarettes!
> Doris: Far too much.
> Ethel: So did Percy (points)—till I gave him ZENO.[14]

What, then, was a public brought up on this tripe to do when confronted with the difficulties of *Ulysses?* Margaret Anderson passes on Joyce's answer. Joyce, she says, "doesn't consider it a valid excuse for people to say they can't read him because he is too hard to understand. When he was a young man he wanted to read Ibsen . . . so much that he learned Norwegian. . . . He feels that people can make the same effort to read him."[15] When Joyce was not making extravagant demands on the time and attention of potential readers of his books (like the probably apocryphal pronouncement: "I spent seventeen years writing *Finnegans Wake;* I expect my readers to devote their lives to reading it"), he displayed a more normal anxiety at the task that he had laid out for them. He worried lest the public misunderstand his meaning. He was saddened, according to Maria Jolas, that the *Wake* was hardly noticed upon publication in 1939 because of the outbreak of war.[16] Thirty years earlier, he had been equally concerned, says his brother Stanislaus, lest, owing to their mundane subject matter, the ostensibly unspectacular short stories he was preparing should alienate readers. He often spoke at that time of the "two or three unfortunate wretches who may eventually read me." [17]

Joyce's attitude toward the professional reader—the journalist-critic, the publisher's reader, the fellow author—has been somewhat distorted by Herbert Gorman's attempt to make a martyr of the author of *Ulysses.* Confusing Stephen Dedalus' creed of "silence, exile and cunning" with the mature Joyce's anxious willingness to make a living and to get his works before an audience, Gorman paints the picture of an intractable artist, impervious to bad reviews, and lack of reviews, and numbed into insensitivity through frequent rebuffs from publishers.[18] Quite the reverse of this, Joyce was extremely eager for critical attention and for applause. He may write the publisher Grant Richards, in an important unpublished letter, "Critics (I think) are fonder of attacking writers than publishers; and I assure you their attacks on me would in no way hasten my death," [19] but in letter after letter to the same man, he speaks of his disappointment at not finding certain reviews among the clippings sent to him by Richards: "I shall . . . write to my brother and ask him to search the files . . . ." [20]

Like a normal human being, he worries about his reputation in the literary community. He speaks in an unpublished letter to Frank Budgen of Marcel Proust, saying almost in a tone of relief that he "cannot see any special talent" in the work of the Frenchman. He adds wistfully, "I think a fall of mine would not altogether disappoint some admirers. It seems to me I have made a bad impression here [in Paris]. I am too preoccupied (Bloomesque word) to rectify it." [21]

Certainly, when it was a question of pleasing publishers, or meeting their objections, Joyce went out of his way to come to a suitable agreement. The long account of the correspondence with Grant Richards concerning *Dubliners* (given by

Herbert Gorman) shows to what lengths he was willing to go. In one letter, which Gorman does not publish, the author even offers to omit five stories—one third of the entire collection—if the publishers will agree to the inclusion of a different, disputed story.[22] There are few writers who would make such an offer, and it should eradicate the vague, romantic notion of Joyce as the immovable rebel, unwilling to give an inch to the encroachments of Philistine conventions.

Critics are sharply divided on Joyce's relationship to Ireland. In this matter it is not possible to accept their judgments at face value. It is in the nature of things that Marxists should interpret his exile from Dublin's fair city in one way, that fervent nationalists should see it in another light, that Irish Catholics should place upon it still a third interpretation, and that most literary critics should see it in literary perspective.

Not even Joyce's words themselves, treasured and preserved and later recorded by his awed interviewers, may be accepted without question. It was a subject so close to the raw edges of the exile's nerves that he was often forced to hide his true feelings behind a conventional oath, a snarl, a bitter paradox, or a dignified understatement. If the words of Francini-Bruni, who gave up his friendship with Joyce to discredit him in public lectures, may be believed, the Irish exile thought poorly of his birthplace. He quotes Joyce as saying that "the Emerald isle is a field of thorns . . . . hunger, syphilis, superstition, alcoholism. Puritans, Jesuits and bigots have sprouted from it . . . . The Dubliner is of the mountebank race the most useless and inconsistent . . . . However Ireland is still the brain of the United Kingdom."[23] Perhaps to Djuna Barnes he came closest to a matter-of-fact statement, though it covers only a small part of the relationship: "The Irish are people who will never have leaders, for at the great moment they always desert them. They have produced one skeleton—Parnell—never a man."[24] Alfred Kerr describes vividly Joyce's reaction, during an interview, to the mention of the Irish. The author dropped his calm aspect and became sharp. The Norwegians expelled Ibsen, he recalled, and the Irish had never forgiven Joyce for painting certain types of his countrymen and the city of Dublin.[25] Revenge was the spur.

There was no reason, indeed, why Joyce should have remembered the Ireland he left behind with any pleasure. Even those who should have understood his feelings—the literary elite of Dublin—gave him no encouragement. If we may believe Stanislaus Joyce, the poet A. E. (George Russell) told him that his brother was a worthless cad and that starvation on the continent would do him good. In fact, says Stanislaus, when Joyce reported from Europe that he had found a job as teacher in the Berlitz schools, Stanislaus woke the poet after midnight to taunt him.[26] When Joyce worked at the library in Dublin, the staff did little more than tolerate him. The professors at the university regarded him with suspicion for his unorthodox behavior and his dangerous reading of authors like Maeterlinck and Ibsen. Religious authorities warned his favorite aunt, Josephine Murray, not to let her children fraternize with their strange cousin. And the "greats" of Ireland, George Moore and William Butler Yeats, though they may have recognized the genius in the youth, were puzzled and repelled by his attitude and behavior. This is not to say that Joyce was blameless or that he tried in any substantial way to alleviate the rapidly deteriorating situation. There is much biographical truth in the portrait of Stephen Dedalus in *Ulysses,* wandering from place to place in Dublin, seemingly doing his best to antagonize even those who are trying to be on his side. But his youthful arrogance does not change the fact that his memory of this period in his life was sad and bitter.

Critics have tried to read more than this personal bitterness into his voluntary exile. Marxists like D. S. Mirsky find that Joyce is an "apostate-emigrant." Being a member of the Irish intelligentsia, the author, according to this theory, was lost in Ireland because that country did not have an industrial bourgeoisie for the intelligentsia to represent. Thus, people of Joyce's stamp "could have no base, and . . . had to be 'expatriated.' "[27] Intense Irish nationalists enjoy picturing Joyce in headlong flight from his birthplace in order to avoid military involvement and the duties of militant citizenship, like the Easter Rising of 1916. What they often fail to realize is that Joyce has done more to enhance the reputation of modern Ireland internationally than all the brave soldiers of Ireland—and has probably suffered more in the process.

Yet, in spite of all this, in spite of the unpleasantness of personal reminiscences, Joyce apparently never lost his affection for—and certainly not his interest in—his own city. A group of his Irish friends have testified unanimously to this. Con Curran relates:

> Ah yes, over and over again, of course, seeing him in later years, and asked [*sic*] him when he was coming back to Dublin, his invariable reply was: "Have I ever left it?" His love of Dublin was as great as his friendship for the people he knew in his youth in Dublin. To be a Dubliner of his generation was the passport to his house in Paris, or wherever he lived, in his later years.

Another tells how

> If you asked him if he'd see anybody, his first question was always: "Do they come from Dublin?" And if they came from Dublin he would always see them . . . . his wife told me that his room was always full of Dublin papers, and I remember once a friend arriving from Dublin and Joyce spent the whole evening arguing whether the price of bread had gone up or down, because the friend said it had gone up and Joyce maintained that it hadn't.[28]

Literary critics with no ax to grind are content to accept the fact that Joyce *did* leave Dublin and that his permanent exile *did* produce prodigies—some feel, truly great prodigies—of literary effort, which no modern Irishman who has stayed at home has yet produced. These critics would undoubtedly second the fervent opening of the prayer by Trinity College's Sir John Mahaffy, while objecting to its conclusion: "Thank God, they have both cleared out of Dublin [Joyce and George Moore], but not before they had squirted stink like a pair of skunks on all the decent people. . . . It's an ill bird that fouls its own nest. James Joyce is a living argument in defence of my contention that it was a mistake to establish a separate university for the aborigines of this island—for the cornerboys who spit into the Liffey." [29]

How may the bewildered student account for the widely divergent judgments expressed by competent scholars, people who were intimately acquainted with Joyce and his affairs, and ranking novelists like Arnold Bennett and Virginia Woolf, who disagree sharply concerning their Irish colleague? There is, of course, the fact that Joyce has been dead only twenty-one years. Even before his death he had attained the status of a myth, as had Odysseus in his lifetime. His premature attainment of mythical proportions without the usual time lag to allow for appropriate public reception of the myth has encouraged confusion. The whole truth about the mythical hero cannot be told because his contemporary subordinates in the story are still very much alive—not only alive but embroidering the Joyce myth with their own designs, shaping to their own ends, or to what they think would be Joyce's ends, the very myth of which they are a part. Such unorthodox practice, engaged in on a wholesale basis, must result in contradictions. It has meant the quite understandable suppression of important but embarrassing correspondence, some unwillingness to admit to the charmed circle of initiates those less fortunate than themselves, and a very human attempt to cash in on the notoriety of the leader. It has also meant, up to this time, the appearance of only one real biography—and that by a close friend of Joyce, supervised and censored by Joyce throughout.

Organizations devoted to the study of, and the dissemination of information about, important writers perform a serious and worthwhile function. The Browning and Tennyson we know today are what they are to us partly because their legend and their works were interpreted and given shape and context by members of "societies" established in their name. It is debatable, however, whether these poets have not suffered, as well as profited, at the hands of their over-enthusiastic admirers. The repugnance with which Tennyson was viewed during the Edwardian age and down even to the nineteen forties may well have been the sharp reaction to having a literary god foisted upon a new generation of less devout worshipers.

Adherents of the Joyce-as-deity school, for all their considerable value, have done harm in the long run to their hero. True, they have brought together Joyceans to talk, to marvel, to project books, to plan exhibitions, and to afford an in-person view of great-ones-who-knew-the-master. But they have, at the same time, distorted the emphasis from the works (and why else is Joyce remembered?) to the eccentricities of an all too human being. Publications of such groups are quaint and biographically interesting, but they skirt the significant all too often. They brook no real and basic criticism of Joyce, as man or author, allowing only mention of trivial foibles recalled wistfully with an expression halfway between a smile and a sigh. Tempest-in-teapot controversies generated by such an obviously cultist environment lend no honor to Joyce's name and no light to biographical scholarship. An article in *The New York Times* attacks Peter

Kavanagh for attacking Joyce "so viciously and unjustifiably, that I attacked him [Kavanagh] and we haven't spoken since . . . . We just slaughtered Kavanagh. He could not answer. He was beaten to a pulp." In a letter to the newspaper, Kavanagh replied that he "never attacked James Joyce or his works. . . . What I did attack—and what turned my hearers . . . puce with anger—was the cult of Joyce, the devotees who worship the dead Master with the insane fury of the possessed. Joyce was sane enough: it is his commentators who are mad." The rebuttal, heavy with the weight of six outstanding American Joyceans, is reminiscent of a religious affirmation or a political credo: "We attended the meeting of the James Joyce Society . . . at which Dr. Peter Kavanagh spoke and confirm that Dr. Kavanagh violently attacked Joyce and his works as reported . . . ." [30] Without going into the rights and wrongs of the situation, one can see the danger and the damage, certainly unmerited by the dead author, to Joyce's reputation among neutral readers of the *Times*. The same kind of danger, now dissipated, once threatened Joyce from his closest "friends," the extreme avant-gardists of the *transition* group under Eugene Jolas, who, after the excitement of the publication of *Ulysses,* declared "The Revolution of the Word" and implicated the innocent Joyce in outlandish literary excesses. But that story is better saved for the discussion of the *Wake*.

The problem of Joyce's biography is further complicated by frequent excursions into print of Joyce's personal enemies. Safe from personal rebuttal by the dead artist, bristling Dubliners like Oliver St. John Gogarty are doing their utmost to prove that Joyce's fame is an unfortunate mistake. One cannot blame Gogarty, the model for Buck Mulligan in *Ulysses,* for wanting to get even with the eccentric youth who shared his Martello Tower and later revealed him in literature at his Shaun-like worst. Yet there should be a difference between legitimate revelation of Joyce's weaknesses, literary and personal, and the actual attempt to write off the entire career of the most exciting and influential novelist of this century as "a gigantic hoax . . . one of the most enormous leg-pulls in history." [31] People who have read the sermon on Hell in *A Portrait,* or the ending of "The Dead," or "Proteus" in *Ulysses* need no reassurance that Gogarty's condemnation is extravagant. Nevertheless, the fact that it is there and must be taken into account, if only to be discarded, serves to cloud the biographical horizon. And the fact that no proof is offered makes difficult a point-by-point refutation.

This does not prevent Mary Colum from leaping into the breach with a spirited defense of Joyce as a serious artist and an equally lively attack upon Gogarty for the "misinformation" in his article. She complains that, although Gogarty met Joyce only once after his twenty-second birthday, he has made readers think he was an intimate of the mature novelist. Thus "he has succeeded in placing all over the country in strategic positions attacks and misinformations about Joyce, his family, his friends, his readers, and his work." [32] Mrs. Colum proceeds to detail Gogarty's inaccuracies in scathing understatement and effectively demonstrates the paucity of fact in his broadside attacks. It should be stressed that even Joyce's firmest supporter acknowledges his humanity and fallibility as person and artist. The objection is to groundless criticism of the man.

Mention of some of the inaccuracies in this one Gogarty article will indicate the difficulty that the student of Joyce may encounter through indiscriminate acceptance of "expert" criticism: Gogarty attributes the publishing difficulties of *Dubliners* to the wrong publisher, he misquotes a line from one of Joyce's books, he calls one female critic "Mr.," he confuses the name and the nationality of Joyce's patron, and so on through a long list of small but significant errors.[33]

Irish literary friends and enemies of Joyce, on one issue at least, are united. They feel, with some heat, that no biographer or critic has a right to speak of Joyce authoritatively unless he himself is a product of Dublin, preferably of 1904 vintage. Gogarty avers: "When I read those who although they have never been in Dublin set themselves up as 'guides to Joyce' or as masters of 'The Master,' I feel sorrow for their ignorance and then anger at their presumption." [34] And Padraic Colum, than whom Joyce has no more sincere booster, has been heard to say that to know Joyce one must know Dublin. These people have a point. Certainly it would not do to write a definitive biography of Hardy without spending time on his health, or of Faulkner without examining Yoknapatawpha County's acres. But no critic would insist that a capable job might not be done by an Englishman on Faulkner or an American on Hardy. Similarly, for Joyce, what may be lost in terms of the feel for the local argot may be compensated for by detachment and scholarship, the first impossible for the native Dubliner, the second too often considered unnecessary in dealing with the rowdy boy down the street. It is interesting that even among Irish critics the expatriates almost alone have dealt with their famous problem child.

There is a middle group of Irish intimates of Joyce, represented, for instance, by J. F. Byrne, the Cranly of *A Portrait,* whose biographical information has been valuable but who have distorted the emphasis of their contributions. Byrne's autobiography, *Silent Years,* illustrates this tendency. From the point of view of the Joyce scholar, it is valuable for its picture of elementary school life in the 1890's; for its account of how Joyce came to give the name Cranly to Byrne; for a visit to the famous number seven Eccles Street, which turns out to have been Byrne's home for a number of years. The book sets straight several details of Joyce's brief flirtation with a career in medicine. Yet, when it comes to the subtle, symbolic undercurrents of Joyce's autobiographical novels, Byrne appears wholly innocent of any insight, even when he himself, as Cranly, is immediately concerned. He makes no reference to his role as Judas or as John the Baptist—both strongly hinted at in *A Portrait.* Instead, he devotes a long section of presumably literary criticism to the discovery of an error in Joyce's mathematics in the Ithaca episode of *Ulysses.* And of serious disagreements with his now famous friend he gives only a suggestion, feeling, apparently, that the time has not yet arrived for the full biographical story. That such books are appearing at all is a hopeful sign for the future biographer.[35]

It must be remembered, moreover, that Joyce himself unwittingly added to the possibility of biographical chaos by creating such a vivid fictional counterpart of himself as Stephen Dedalus. In his own mind at least a tenuous connection existed, for as early as 1903 he was signing his early versions of stories from *Dubliners* with the pseudonym "Stephen Daedalus."[36] Though he later realized that too often fact was confused with fiction, Joyce with Dedalus, he tried in vain to insist upon the fallacy of equating the two. He reminded Frank Budgen, who reminded his readers, that the Stephen of *A Portrait* and *Ulysses* was a sketch of the artist *as a Young Man.* The reminder, however, has been little heeded. Just as Byron, in spite of his denials, will be remembered always as Childe Harold, even the mature Continental artist, James Joyce, is fated to immortality as the priggish aesthete of fiction. Many biographical critics, blinded by their idea of what Stephen should be and do and say, have found what they were looking for in his creator.

A further and somewhat similar difficulty that comes from accepting semiautobiographical fiction as autobiographical fact lies in Joyce's method of constructing his main characters. Like many writers, he found it valuable to use the strict and narrow facts of his own life and those of his family enriched but often sharply modified by factual material from the careers and the writings of others with whom he might have felt a kind of spiritual kinship. Yet since his borrowings are often not explicitly admitted in his ostensibly autobiographical fiction, the reader can hardly be blamed for ascribing to Stephen-Joyce and to the other characters in the novels personality traits that they may not, in actuality, have possessed.

It is possible to point out rather clearly how this tendency to borrow alters, even if only slightly, the view we get of many of Joyce's protagonists. It can be shown that Stephen, in *A Portrait,* is what he is partly because Joyce wished to present him as a literary counterpart of Claude Melnotte, the hero of Bulwer-Lytton's play, *The Lady of Lyons;* [37] or that Stephen inherits all the characteristics of Joyce's boyhood hero, James Clarence Mangan, as recorded in Mangan's painful fragment of autobiography—and that Stephen's father resembles Mangan's father more closely than he does Joyce's. One might even show Joyce's debt to Gerhardt Hauptmann's hero, Michael Kramer; and to Nietzsche's Zarathustra in fashioning a surrogate of himself, the unfortunate Mr. James Duffy of the short story "A Painful Case." [38]

I should like to develop here, in some detail, only one such literary-autobiographical borrowing—Joyce's almost certain debt to the nineteenth-century Irish poet, James Clarence Mangan.[39] Joyce contributed an essay on Mangan to the undergraduate literary review in 1902. In it, referring evidently to Mangan's recently published autobiographical fragments, Joyce tells how

> In a moment of frenzy he [Mangan] breaks silence, and we read how his associates dishonoured his person with their slime and venom, and how he lived as a child amid coarseness and misery and that all whom he met were demons out of the pit and that his father was a human boa-constrictor . . . .[40]

The fact that Joyce mentions the figure of the boa constrictor, taken directly from the poet's account of his life and found in none of the contemporary reviews or biographies, is strong evidence that the young novelist had seen Mangan's *Fragment of an Unfinished Autobiography*.[41] Since Mangan was one of Joyce's few heroes at this time, it is more than reasonable to suppose that he would have read the book when it was published, sold, and discussed in Dublin. It is also safe to assume that the young artist who, in 1902, was examining his own memories of childhood, preparatory to writing *Stephen Hero* and the later works, must have been startled by what he found in Mangan's book. For the picture of himself that Mangan paints is the picture of several of Joyce's autobiographical heroes and of young Joyce himself.

Mangan recalls that he sought relief from the ugliness of poverty and unpleasantness of family relations in "books and solitude." "I shut myself up in a close room; I isolated myself in such a manner from my own nearest relations, that with one voice they all proclaimed me 'mad.' " Later, he confides: "I loved to indulge in solitary rhapsodies, and, if intruded on upon those occasions, I was made very unhappy. I merely felt or fancied that between me and those who approached me, no species of sympathy could exist; and I shrank from communion with them as from somewhat [*sic*] alien from my nature . . . . It was a morbid product of . . . pride." He complains too of having to "herd with the coarsest of associates, and suffer at their hands every sort of rudeness and indignity . . . ."[42] The boy who feels this way is surely the boy of the story "Araby" and of Joyce's other autobiographical prose. The young narrator of "Araby" shuns people too and hides from his uncle and from his girl friend, who is identified only as "Mangan's sister." (The similarity in names is interesting though nothing would be gained from pushing too far a seeming coincidence.) The boy narrator cannot stand to be "jostled by drunken men and bargaining women." He ignores the sights and sounds of exterior reality and bears his "chalice safely through a throng of foes." He prefers the dark rooms of a lonely house to companionship and warmth. "The high cold empty gloomy rooms liberated me,"[43] he says. Like Mangan, he engages in solitary rhapsodies and is annoyed by interruption.

It goes without saying that this striking of Byronic poses, this unwillingness to herd with men, this adolescent desire to live a life apart did not originate with Mangan or with Joyce. Coleridge in his letters comments on his own romantic childhood—one that bears many resemblances to that of Stephen Dedalus. And Tennyson's moody ruminations in graveyards are well known. Joyce did not need to discover Mangan's autobiography to imitate the literary, romantic conception of childhood. But that he did discover it and use it seems evident from the parallel lines of development that both authors follow.

Thus, Mangan's preoccupation with romantic isolation and retreat to a dream world plays a large part in *A Portrait of the Artist*. Like young Mangan, Stephen Dedalus lives "in his imagination . . . through a long train of adventures" based on his reading. Mangan's boyhood feeling that other people were "alien from my nature" finds its counterpart in Joyce's description of Stephen's emotions:

> The noise of children at play annoyed him and their silly voices made him feel, even more keenly than he had felt at Clongowes, that he was different from others. He did not want to play. He wanted to meet in the real world the unsubstantial image which his soul so constantly beheld.

And where Mangan, from boyhood on, is haunted "by an indescribable feeling of something terrible . . . some tremendous danger," Stephen, even in the "sunbonnet" stage, feels "himself a gloomy figure amid the gay cocked hats." In later boyhood, he is happy "only when . . . far from them [people's voices], beyond their call, alone or in the company of phantasmal comrades." Even after Stephen has grown to manhood, the necessity for isolation bothers him as it does Mangan: "To merge his life in the common tide of other lives was harder for him that any fasting or prayer." [44]

It is impossible to know how much of Stephen Dedalus would have been differently presented if Mangan's autobiography had not caught Joyce's attention. Consequently, for those biographical commentators who insist upon too close identification of Stephen with Joyce, the risk of distortion and misrepresentation is considerable.

Compounding this biographical confusion is Joyce's deliberate projection, throughout his career, of successive images of himself as artist, images that are as much ironic distortions as reflections. His as yet unpublished essay of 1904, "A Portrait of the Artist," now in Miss Sylvia Beach's possession, begins with an incisive discussion of the difficulties of portraiture.

By means of his full treatment of the early Dublin years we are able to visualize the successive masks that the young Joyce adopted. The *Portrait* itself is a gallery of images—the shy schoolboy, subject to reverie yet capable of defying tyranny courageously; the sex-tormented adolescent; the religious devotee as narcissist; the arrogant artist seen half ironically in the conclusion of the book, but with full seriousness in *Stephen Hero*. As the images merge into one another, so the ideal changes—from Byron to Ibsen to Rimbaud. It was Stephen's preference for Byron that aroused Heron's antagonism in *A Portrait*. Stanislaus Joyce, who recalled the Byronic phase, found it followed by admiration for Shelley. A Shelleyan idealism colors the essay on Mangan, and Stephen cites Shelley for his concepts of the imagination and his vision of the cosmic spaces. While an undergraduate Joyce had attracted attention, both at home and in the college, as a disciple of Ibsen; in his essay "The Day of the Rabblement" he even dares to consider himself a successor. The torch, passed to Hauptmann, may be taken by the young acolyte—"the third minister will not be wanting when his hour comes."

Recollections by friends of the early years create the picture of a likeable student, serious but gay, a picture that seems confirmed by the tone of references to Joyce in *St. Stephen's,* the college magazine. In the June, 1901 issue we read of "Jocax, the prophet," who has "inveighed with wonted vehemence against his fellow members [of the Debating Society] for not understanding his sublimities." In December of the same year, Joyce being nineteen at the time, a facetious essay appeared, inspired by the "Rabblement" pamphlet. In mock-Elizabethan style the author protested against this "rebell" as an Italianate and corrupt influence, but the editor assures his readers that the *"dreadful Mr. Joyce* is quite a respectable person in private life." He is "the hatter" when he gives the paper on "Drama and Life" in March 1902 but is conceded to have reached "to no mean height of eloquence," though only the faculty sponsor, Magennis, could penetrate "the mist that overhung the writer's closing remarks." Even the caustic footnote in the Jesuit account of University College, *A Page of Irish History* (1930), grants Joyce a certain ability:

during his student days James Joyce was not taken seri-

> ously. It was understood that he had a weird sort of talent, but no one in the college seems to have guessed that he was destined to achieve almost world-wide celebrity.[45]

As "the mystic Jocax," the "dreaming one of Nola," "the Mad Hatter," or "*dreaming Jimmy,*" Joyce's reputation was already being created and his masks receiving amused attention.

Joyce was always preoccupied with "anti-selves," Hugh Kenner notes, the major roles being "the young Rimbaud in Dublin, a Svevo-like accountant of ethical balances in Trieste, and a pallid disciple of Huysmans and Lautreamont in Paris." These faces, those of Stephen, Bloom, and Shem, have their opposites. Lynch and Mulligan confront Stephen in *A Portrait* and *Ulysses;* Richard Rowan's opposite in *Exiles* in his own hidden side; Shem and Shaun provide a final music-hall variant of the conflicting ego and alter ego.

The main obstacle to understanding James Joyce, however, lies in the environmental circumstances of his childhood and adolescence and concerns chiefly his relationship to his nation. When Gabriel Conroy, in "The Dead," shouts at Miss Ivors, "I'm sick of my own country, sick of it," he is certainly speaking for Joyce as the author might have spoken at twenty-one. Stephen's remark, that Ireland is like the old sow that eats her farrow, reinforces the extravagant bitterness and dark hopelessness of his youthful feeling. Yet all evidence points to the Joyces as a particularly patriotic family and to young James as a fervent nationalist. The alteration in attitude from childhood to maturity must be sought in events rather than in an inexplicable change of personality.

Actually, the attitude is one of frustration—the frustration of "Araby" and "An Encounter" and "The Sisters," in which the search for a father and a secure fatherland is unsuccessful. This ingrained frustration may be traced to Joyce's ambivalent feeling for Parnell and for what he symbolized to the child and to the man. The knowledge of what was as a result of Parnell's downfall, and what might have been had his policy and influence prevailed, changes positive love of nation to active disgust and colors all subsequent decisions of the disillusioned artist. Further, the tangible results for Joyce and his family of Parnell's shifting fortunes blend into, and become identified with, the ebb and flow of Joyce's youthful patriotism. The outcome seems to be that Joyce finds it impossible to separate his attitude concerning his own fate from his feeling for Ireland and the symbol of Parnell. Though fragments of this national background of Joyce's youth have been examined by Gorman and by Robert Kelly,[46] the problem of biography requires another look.

The Joyce family had been for years a distinguished Irish clan. It had given its name to the famous "Joyce's Country" of Ireland and had supplied the Irish with their most distinguished political leader of the first half of the nineteenth century, Daniel O'Connell, the Liberator. Because of his connections, John Stanislaus Joyce, the Simon Dedalus of fiction, had a sinecure in the office of the Collector General of Rates so that he might uphold the gentlemanly tradition of respectability without the burden of work. In February 1882 Joyce was born into a family that had apparently hitched its wagon to the right political star. Parnell's superiority as a leader was acknowledged even by his enemies, and John Stanislaus might well have been on his way to a magistracy as a political hanger-on of the Great Man. The spirit of optimism, general throughout Ireland because of the failure of England's Coercion Bill and the immediate prospect of long-withheld Home Rule, brightened the Joyce household as well.[47]

Only three months after Joyce's birth, however, all was changed by the senseless murder of Lord Cavendish and his subordinate by patriotic extremists in Dublin's Phoenix Park. As a consequence, Joyce's early childhood was lived in an atmosphere of overwhelming coercion. England applied the screws:

> The ordinary processes of law were suspended, trial by Jury gave place to trial by Judges, who were given complete power to decide questions of fact . . . . The Viceroy was given power to suppress public meetings and . . . newspapers. Boycotting was declared illegal. . . . It was the complete Coercion Act. [48]

It may be objected that, serious as these punitive measures might have been for the adults of Ireland, they could have had no influence on a sensitive child under ten years of age. Yet, though it may be admitted that even a James Joyce of six or seven would have remained innocent of legal or political issues, he could not have been untouched by the spirit of the time, by the atmosphere at the dinner table (witness the

Christmas dinner scene in *A Portrait*), by the emotional reaction of his father to daily twists and turns of national politics. In Ireland, where small children re-enact scenes of national excitement rather than cops and robbers, Joyce had to be aware, even without *A Portrait's* red brush for Michael Davitt and green brush for Parnell, of the emotional complex that was Irish political life.[49]

To be aware of a national attitude at this time was to be aware of Parnell as hero. Just as small children loved or hated the myth of Franklin Roosevelt during the 1940's, without knowing the merits or demerits of N.R.A. or the recognition of Russia, simply because of the attitude to which they were exposed at home, at school, and in the play center, so young Joyce acquired his hero ready-made. Most young Irishmen, says Donat O'Donnell in *Maria Cross,* were drawn to Parnell, for in him the anticlerical, anti-British, and even anti-Victorian forces of the time were exemplified. The artist who was later to adopt Ibsen, Mangan, Sullivan, and Homer as heroes placed all his vague childhood longings for accomplishment in this bearded St. George, a St. George who fought the British dragon for Ireland. Religious tales may well have entwined themselves into the political myth until Parnell acquired attributes of Christ and his angels, struggling against evil in the world. If Gladstone could tell an interviewer in 1897 that "Parnell was the most remarkable man I ever met . . . . and the most interesting . . . . Parnell was supreme all the time,"[50] it is no wonder that to an unsophisticated child who looked to his father for a sense of values Parnell should have assumed superhuman proportions.

For young Joyce to have known even vaguely of the brave fight waged by The Chief to recover the political ground lost by the assassinations, so that by 1886 it was possible for Gladstone to argue seriously in Parliament for an Irish Home Rule Bill, was bound to make the aftermath of the Parnell affair shockingly bitter. Parnell's vindication during the libel trial of *The Times* was no preparation, even for hardened veterans in politics, for the fall which was to come just two years later over an issue that had nothing to do with the political well-being of Ireland. In the late 1880's his supporters still attributed to him the strength of lions. He had seemingly weathered every storm and come within hailing distance of securing a free Ireland. It appeared appropriately paradoxical, therefore, that his downfall should come, not at the hands of his English enemies in and out of Parliament, but through the manipulations of a political adventurer, Captain W. H. O'Shea, with whose wife Parnell had long been carrying on an affair. Named corespondent in the politically inspired divorce proceedings, Parnell, a proud figure to the last, maintained a silent aloofness. So strong was his position in Ireland that after the divorce trial and its attendant disclosures, he was elected unanimously by party heads as their leader. Only then were political lines drawn and the fight to depose him begun. Only then did T. M. Healy give vent to his real feelings of hatred for his superior—the sordid story of which nine-year-old Joyce told in his first published work, *Et Tu, Healy!* So Parnell was unceremoniously dropped by the very people whose cause he had brought to the edge of success. This was in December 1890. In the following year, Parnell died.

Repudiation and death, though not related in fact, were linked by millions of sentimental Irishmen like Joyce's father.

> —The story is very short and sweet, Mr. Casey said. It was one day down in Arklow, a cold bitter day, not long before the chief died. May God have mercy on him!
>
> . . . . Mr. Dedalus took a bone from his plate and tore some meat from it with his teeth, saying:
>
> —Before he was killed, you mean.[51]

A letter in *United Ireland* in January 1892 plays the same tune:

> If my boy ever rats on a man like Parnell . . . I believe I'll rise up out of my grave and disown him . . . .
>
> And now Parnell is dead. I cried and cried when I heard it . . . . they've broken his brave, iron heart, those miserable hypocrites and traitors . . . . he could have saved [notice the verb] us all . . . . But they killed him with their hatred, these middle class hypocrites, who only hated him because he loved the people so.[52]

The heat of controversy so affected the nine-year-old Joyce that, in *Et Tu, Healy!*, as his brother Stanislaus recalls, Parnell is

> likened to an eagle, looking down on the grovelling mass of Irish politicians from

"His quaint-perched aerie on the crags of Time
Where the rude din of this . . . century
Can trouble him no more." [53]

From the affair came Joyce's distrust of political matters and his eagerness to expose the falseness of oratorical bombast—explicitly illustrated by the Circe episode in *Ulysses* and by Shaun's speeches in *Finnegans Wake*. For a boy just entering adolescence, Parnell's death meant the death of national hope, unless a true successor could be found. Fifteen years later, in "Ivy Day in the Committee Room," it is clear that no such hero has arisen and that "the grovelling mass" is blindly tearing Ireland to pieces.

The sparkling Parnell era coincides for Joyce with his childhood period of familial love, social and financial security, and religious wholeness. Joyce's father, who "had a hairy face," and whose political fortunes fell with Parnell's, may sometimes have been confused, by the boy, with the bearded lion. Not long after the repudiation of Parnell, John Stanislaus starts his family on its nocturnal flights to avoid creditors. Parnell's loss of prestige in Parliament is matched by Stephen's feeling of inferiority when questioned about his father's affairs and the status of the family. Finally, the unity and strength of Stephen-Joyce's religious allegiance and inclination are shaken by the division he finds in his own home in the Parnell case. The Christmas dinner scene in *A Portrait* is ample evidence of his shock at the revelation that his two chief childhood authorities, his nurse and his father, might be at variance concerning the role of the church in political affairs. The frightening idea that the church might be wrong in an official action and a secular hero right must have been particularly influential at this point, when the church was still an abstraction and Parnell a very tangible and immediate god.

Lord Morely, commenting on Parnell's death, writes:

> I cannot explain it [the public outpouring of emotion] save by the intensity of countless private griefs and by the reactions of a general sense of consternation as at the happenings of something incredible and monstrous—that together create a sort of collective nerve tensity which carries individuals out and away beyond their normal depth. Certain it is that public sorrow in Ireland was manifest on a scale and to a degree unparalleled. . . . And the public

funeral in Dublin was an immense spectacle of human emotion . . . .[54]

Such a spectacle to a nine-year-old could have gone a long way toward deifying its principal figure. The insistent rumors that "Parnell was not dead but was seeking, through the device of a simulated decease, to start a fresh career elsewhere," [55] were certainly as important as Irish myth in bringing to birth Joyce's saga of Finn-Again, when the mature author came to construct his own religious pattern. But many years had to elapse between the fall of the hero and Joyce's attempt to put Humpty Dumtpy together again in the *Wake*. In the interim, Joyce's articles on Parnell in European newspapers and his occasional lectures on the subject showed that the national tragedy had not left his mind nor his heart. Maria Jolas has reported that, in later life, his interest in national and international politics was keen, possibly because during the war a shift in the political winds might have had personal consequences for him and his expatriate family.[56] During all his life, however, he sought to escape personal involvement in political affairs and to order his life around a more stable support—the private integrity of the artist inviolable by the whims of Healy or Quisling.

Recovery from this childhood wound was expensive. It required voluntary exile from Ireland. It meant insult from those who saw Francis Sheehy-Skeffington, Joyce's schoolboy friend, die violently but heroically in the Easter Rising in 1916 and who castigated slackers like Joyce for peaceful abstention. It undoubtedly had something to do with the stiffness that characterized Joyce's approach to new acquaintances and to popular causes. He had been burned once, at a sensitive age, and he intended to withhold giving himself completely to all but a few safe friends and to any movements. His reluctance, even after he had won fame as a writer, to become involved in the affairs of Ireland as Yeats had—Joyce adamantly refused the offer of a seat in the Irish Academy—though explicable on other grounds, may have been induced by fear that those who rise in Ireland are headed for a fall. Perhaps cyclical rise and fall in *Finnegans Wake* recall most obviously the pattern of Paradise lost and regained, but to Joyce, Parnell is as illustrative of the working out of the pattern as Adam. No public event in his life did more to color his personality and his work than Ireland's treatment of The Chief.

The final and most significant problem in Joyce's biography is to see plainly and unemotionally Joyce's place in or out of Catholicism. Even if the author had not made the religious crisis and aftermath the central issue of all his semiautobiographical works, it would have great importance in enabling the reader to understand a major contemporary writer. But Joyce's dramatization of his personal struggle makes the problem paramount.

Most critics agree with Gorman that Joyce's "Roman Catholicism is in his bones, in the beat of his blood, in the folds of his brain and he cannot rest until it is either removed or clarified . . . . it is there, twisted out of all resemblance to itself.[57] Few, however, agree on what this means. Reading the story of Stephen-Joyce's apostasy in *A Portrait*—especially the influence of the sermon on Hell—Thomas Merton experiences a strong impetus toward conversion *to Catholicism*.[58] For each critic who believes, like Elliot Paul, that Joyce enjoyed his status of nonbeliever, there is another who insists upon the anguish that his lack of belief caused Joyce. For each statement like Lloyd Morris' that Joyce may have eagerly wished to return to Catholicism,[59] there is a counterbalancing argument, such as the one put forward by Morris Ernst and based presumably on Joyce's own words, that the Irish author had never really left the church.[60]

While he lived, Joyce added greatly to the critical confusion. A wearer of many masks, especially when his deepest feelings were involved, he presented a deliberately ambiguous picture of his war with Catholicism. He could be, at one moment, the impudent gamin sticking out his tongue at the bishop —in this vein is the story told by his friends of the turn of the century about his seeking out innocent priests in the reading room of the National Library in order to deliver petty insults. Or, again, he might be the proud intellectual Stephen, rejecting in the lofty tones of Lucifer an oppressive domination that his spirit abhors. Or, as in *Stephen Hero,* his complaint might be delivered by Stephen, the social critic, in whose breast burns a fierce resentment against a religious system whose representatives pick their way with unmoved placidity among the "cringing warrens" of the poor. Or, finally, the author might appear as the caustic defiler of a proud and holy tradition in the obscene and blasphemous passages of *Finnegans Wake*. It is difficult to separate the author from his various poses, but the attempt is worth making.

As a child Joyce had the standard, normal Catholic upbringing of an Irish youngster of the 1880's. His good-tempered, pious mother personifies the strengths and weaknesses of Irish Catholicism during that period: her skill in music brought remarkable beauty to the middle-class suburban hearth; her deep religious sense, not so much a conviction as an intuition, gave her the emotional strength to compensate for physical weakness; her routine adherence to the demanding ritual calendar supplied a center of meaningful activity about which family life and religious hope might revolve. If she worried out loud, it was not about creditors or bedbugs—matters of immediate concern to Stephen Dedalus—but about the irreverence or profanity of her brood, the external signs of troubled spirits. From such maternal singleness of mind, one might have expected priests and nuns to come. One of Joyce's sisters did enter a religious order. And the stress on respectability through religious conformity brought Joyce very close to a Jesuit novitiate.[61]

Perhaps if his father had been less like the Martin Cunningham of *Ulysses,* a "good practical Catholic" in Bloom's words, Joyce might have followed the pattern of unquestioning belief his mother set for him. But first his father and then his intellect intruded upon comfortable acceptance. Whatever else religion may have meant to John Stanislaus, it meant a way of getting on in the world. There is every evidence on this score that Joyce's father and his counterpart, Simon Dedalus, were of one mind. The kind of religious education his children received was less important than the social and vocational contacts to be made while receiving it. "The Jesuits cater for the upper classes," says Mr. M'Coy in "Grace." Joyce's father was well aware of this distinction that set the order apart from the less respectable Christian Brothers. Perhaps the latter was all right for Paddy Stink, but for Stephen-Joyce it would be a Jesuit future. "They're the boyos have influence."[62]

This intrusion of a materialistic attitude into Joyce's religious environment served to reveal the obverse of the coin of his mother's piety. The idea that, in a practical sense, being "religious" might "pay" disturbed him when he was old enough to understand its implications. As a youth, he was idealistic enough to condemn tacitly any outward conformity to the demands of respectable religion when inner compulsion was lacking. In "Grace" he has only scorn for Kernan and his friends as they assume postures of deep piety in the Jesuit church while their minds and spirits are elsewhere. The care with which they kneel on handkerchiefs and protect their hats point up cuttingly the primacy of their material considerations. Young Joyce, observing Dublin folk and folkways, saw that religion was not always synonymous with belief. The caricature of Shaun is artistic expression of this discovery.

The biographer must return again and again to the Parnell affair. Though Joyce must have believed, before Parnell's repudiation, that not all Catholics embraced the church with like motives and equal depths of religious intensity, he had no reason to imagine this church as anything but an ideal, benevolent spiritual mother. The cruel shock of hearing the venerable institution denounced in blasphemous epithets as partisan, calculating, anti-Irish, parasitic, and worse in his own home, by people whom he had always supposed to know everything, made a deep impression. Though for several years there was outwardly little change in his attitude, the skepticism of his late adolescent years undoubtedly had its origin in just such unresolved dilemmas of childhood. In the restrictive atmosphere of Clongowes or Belvedere, there was little opportunity for an intellectual and emotional break with the forms and requirements of the faith. Not until his days at University College did Joyce reach the conclusions imparted to Cranly by Stephen in the *Portrait* dialogue.

That conversation shows the strength of the hold that the church still has over his mind, if not over his will. Though his adult decision is that "I will not serve," he admits freely that at school he did believe. His problem arose when he could not always "unite my will with the will of God." His fear now is not so much of damnation and punishment as of "the chemical action which would be set up in my soul by a false homage to a symbol behind which are massed twenty centuries of authority and veneration."[63] It is not a question of conversion *to* anything but rather the greater difficulty of having to surrender one sanctuary, through conscience, without being able to replace it immediately with another. Not until middle age when he is able to erect his obscure Viconian citadel does Joyce truly resolve his problem.

In considering the problem of biography, one must be impressed by the fact that, though hundreds of people have contributed their two or three pages of personal reminiscence, only one full-length biography exists. Though the reader may take his pick of extensive biographical accounts of Joyce's much less controversial contemporaries—Yeats, Henry James, Gide—only Herbert Gorman's biography of Joyce is available to those interested in the author of *Ulysses*. Potential biographers who came after Gorman were deterred, perhaps, by his status as official biographer, with an inside track to intimates of his subject and the approval and active help of Joyce himself in preparing his study. By the 1930's Joyce was sufficiently entrenched as a distinguished man of letters to be able to take a positive role in arranging details of operation for books about himself. In a letter to Frank Budgen (March 1, 1932), he tells his friend that Gorman and Golding are doing biographies and that Duff is writing a book about him. "Your [*sic*] will be the seventh book mainly about a text which is unobtainable in England."[64] He tells Budgen to see Stuart Gilbert's book and Paul Smith's key to *Ulysses* so that Budgen will not duplicate the work of the others. Joyce goes on to reject Budgen's request that he be allowed to use the Joyce-Budgen correspondence in his book because, as Joyce puts it, "this invades Gorman's ground." Budgen is given the right, however, to use the material of their correspondence provided that it is not published in quotation. This shrewd parceling out of his life and work to selected friends undoubtedly must have discouraged objective and unattached scholars from intruding while Joyce lived.

They were surely not deterred by the consideration that Gorman had already said all that could be said, for the limitations of his important contribution were immediately very evident. Though an unrivaled collection of source materials such as the citations from early notebooks, it provides no clues to Joyce's attitude toward Ireland, his religious position, or his mature aesthetic. The critics recognized that Gorman's attempt was far from the last word. Zabel found the biographer "obtuse" in dealing with such problems, and judged that the "rough, rapid, graphic, and gross" style "does not make one regret the absence of formal criticism . . . ."[65] The author "never fully emerges," Stonier complained, though this may be the fault of Joyce as much as of Gorman. The book "evades nearly all the issues" and is neither critical nor sensitive enough to appeal to those who already know Joyce, for much of the detail is "aimless local color."[66] *The Irish Times* also considered the portrait "negative and anaemic"; to Donagh MacDonagh, Gorman displayed "the most amazing lack of emotional or poetic perception" and portrayed "a completely externalized Joyce," utterly devoid of the spirit seen in his work:

> not for a moment the Stephen Dedalus who blows like a clear wind through even the most sordid passages of his saga, not for a moment the humorist whose laughter is everywhere in his work.[67]

Conal O'Riordan was amazed "that so long a book . . . should yet tell us so little of what is essential." The book has generally been considered sketchy, discursive, and badly written, though Louise Bogan found that the "devotion and naiveté of its author might make it better than the work of a "more detached and wiser man" in that he "lets through facts which might have been suppressed" by a more subtle mind.[68]

The most sustained and intelligent attack on Gorman's abilities as a biographer comes from Amsterdam, where J. Den Haan's long critical essay on Joyce, *Mythe van Erin,* appeared. After trying to categorize the major works touching on Joyce's life—those by Harry Levin, Richard M. Kain, and Herbert Gorman—he evaluates the latter book as the worst biography he has ever read, especially in those chapters dealing with the author's mature years. Den Haan attributes the trouble partly to the friendship between Joyce and his Boswell, partly to the personal attention that the novelist gave to the preparation of his own biography. The critic feels that Joyce deliberately enmeshed Gorman in a web of trivial personal details to distract him from writing of Joyce's friends and enemies in any specific and vital environmental context. The work becomes, in Den Haan's words, the history of Joyce's writing but not the history of the man himself. The critic notes in extenuation the fact that it is hard to write a biography about a living man, his family, and his acquaintances. He is amused, however, by the number who, spurred on by revelations of the subject himself, have succeeded only in chasing shadows obligingly set up for them by a serious-faced Joyce, grinning behind his mask.[69]

Most criticial readers find Gorman's emotional adulation distasteful. To the London *Times* his "ecstasy about his hero recalls the gentleman of Marie Lloyd's song of praise, 'Everything he does is so artistic.' " Joyce was regarded by another reviewer as "a sufficiently massive figure not to need inflating." In the biographer's reverent eyes, Joyce was always right and the world always wrong. The romantic cliché of the persecuted artist is always at hand, though, as Mary Colum remarked, Joyce "had good friends and wise appreciators."[70]

The "many raw, over-simple and stupid" attacks on Ireland were resented by *The Irish Times;* not only Ireland, but the Catholic church and the British Empire are excoriated "because they did not instantly adjust themselves when . . . Joyce and they were not completely in agreement" (March 22, 1941). Mary Colum also resented Gorman's attitude, that "of a prosecuting attorney," and stated that "his country did not do badly by him" in providing him with a superior education and a stimulating environment. One suspects, however much the observation is resented by idolators of Joyce, that much of Gorman's patronizing tone may be directly traceable to Joyce's own arrogance. The fact is that Dublin had been, since the mid-eighteenth century, more than a provincial city, and even today maintains much of the eighteenth-century tradition of polite learning. Though Trinity College, with Tyrrell, Lecky, and Mahaffy, maintained a prestige not equaled by Joyce's alma mater, University College prepared many who were destined to play important roles in modern Ireland. One of the sources of Joyce's antagonism may have been the fact that the Mulligans and Lynchs, despite their vulgarity, attained honors which he had failed to achieve.

But these are comparatively small matters. It took forty years from the turbulence of the spirit described in *Ulysses* to the relative calm of the *Wake*. Joyce's forty years of wandering in the wilderness were the direct consequence of the author's apprenticeship to maturity—his first two decades. No biographer has yet dealt satisfactorily with the shaping forces of this formative stage. Perhaps Richard Ellmann's projected biography of Joyce, based on exhaustive researches in Ireland and elsewhere, will supply the background for further study. At the moment, however, Joyce's biography is very much a problem—in fact, *the* problem of Joyce's scholarship.*

* Since these lines were written, Stanislaus Joyce's *My Brother's Keeper* and Richard Ellmann's massive and excellent *James Joyce* have supplied many of the answers to questions about Joyce's life.

PART II

The Work

Chapter 3

Poetry

PADRAIC COLUM, Oliver Gogarty, "John Eglinton," Constantine Curran, and others have made us familiar with the young man who, arrogant and shy, experienced the initiation into art described so romantically in *Stephen Hero* and the *Portrait*. One aspect of this orientation was scorn for those he considered his intellectual inferiors, another was fear, and still another was aspiration. A dedicated disciple of the religion of art, Joyce elaborated his aesthetic theories while he expressed his yearnings in limpid verses such as the literary villanelle in the *Portrait*. Colum and Gogarty recall his shy reading of these lyrics from beautifully inscribed sheets of vellum. Joyce's inherent musical taste and infallible ear produce an almost pure poetry, conventional in diction and imagery. Yet this limpid verse has an obviousness that often skirts perilously close to sentimentality. Rebecca West was delighted to discover what she felt to be mawkishness, delighted because she had finally come upon her key to Joyce—"a great man who is entirely without taste." And the ensuing argument she carried on with herself, trying to distinguish between art and sentimentality, covers almost two hundred pages of dodging and dividing, embracing and repelling. Such is the strange necessity of art, which gives the book its title. Louis Golding plays a variation upon this theme in his *James Joyce,* interpreting the poetry as an expression of the author's subconscious and repressed desire for beauty, the prose his stark awareness of the nightmare of life.

Arthur Symons served as literary agent for Joyce's early poetry, and in 1907, almost three years after the publisher's receipt of the manuscript, Joyce's first book appeared. A slender volume, *Chamber Music,* with its spinet on the title page, has until recently suggested the work of Elizabethan lutanists rather than the ironic dissonance of the later Joyce. The airs of the nineties and those of the Renaissance mingled in Yeats and Joyce alike. On that well-known early morning of June

The notes to Chapter 3 begin on page 327.

17, 1904, the muddled Stephen confesses admiration for Dowland, Byrd, and Bull. He hopes like Yeats to purchase a lute from Arnold Dolmetsch and, like Bloom, to arrange a tour. For the full story of Joyce's early poetry one may consult the edition of *Chamber Music* (1954) in which William York Tindall says everything that can be said and perhaps some things that cannot be said about the lyrics.

No sensational reception of *Chamber Music* could have been expected. The poetry is traditional in rhythm, image, and at least surface meaning. The most interesting early reviews are those by Symons and Thomas Kettle, the intellectual leader of Joyce's circle. Symons found the poems "tiny evanescent things" that evoked "not only roses in mid-winter, but the very dew of the roses." Slight yet perfect, they were like "ghostly old tunes . . . played on an old instrument." Kettle, who could recall Joyce as "wilful, fastidious, a lover of elfish paradoxes," the artist as a young man, thought "these delicate verses" completely traditional and literary, lacking any sense of modern problems. He too was reminded of "clear, delicate, distinguished playing of the same kindred with harp, with woods-birds, and with Paul Verlaine."[1]

The poems in *Chamber Music* have had an extensive musical career of their own, as the Slocum-Cahoon *Bibliography* indicates, the Eugene Goossens, Samuel Barber, and David Diamond settings being among the best known. Joyce wrote to the Dublin organist Geoffrey Molyneux Palmer, indicating that he hoped the composer would set them all to music, which was "partly my idea in writing," and admitting that "if I were a musician I suppose I should have set them to music myself."[2]

An important though unfortunately little known study of Joyce's poetry by John Kaestlin appeared in the Cambridge University undergraduate magazine, *Contemporaries,* in the summer of 1933. Kaestlin, who was the editor, warned against a facile surface reading of the poems as typically *fin de siècle.* Joyce's art, rather than reflecting the thin and popular emotionalism of the nineteenth century, is related to the painstaking workmanship of the medieval Scholastic mind. Even the Elizabethan song, which demands music, is less complete in itself than this verse. Though lacking philosophy or metaphysical content, the poems achieve a rare union of "harmonic purity and rhythmic freedom." The author, even in this earliest work, manifests his characteristic preoccupation with words and with linguistic discipline.

Though Joyce's later references to this poetry are slighting—"a young man's book," "a capful of light odes"—there is no external evidence to support Tindall's scatological reading, which may mar for many readers his otherwise excellent and thorough edition. No one has devoted more time and care than the editor to the history of the poems and their relationships to Yeats, Verlaine, the romantics, and the Elizabethan and Jacobean song writers with whom the poet Joyce is always linked. Yet to Tindall no gesture can be innocent, no attitude uncompromising; he sees chamber pots everywhere. Stephen Hero had noted his necessity "to express his love a little ironically," with the "modern note" represented by a "suggestion of relativity . . . mingling itself with so immune a passion."[3] But the relativity is, as the context shows, that of sensual passion contrasted with chivalric terminology, not of an obsessive concern with micturition.

One suspects some insensitivity in the description of these poems as an "amorous sandwich," but eyebrows are lifted still higher by this "water, water, everywhere" reading that always comes back to the archetypal squatting figure. It is true that many have suspected Joyce of having a "cloacal obsession," but the critic who sees evidence of this in everything he reads may well question his own interpretation. Is the "Figure in the Carpet" always the result of indiscretion or fixation? It is a little disconcerting, after all this symbol-counting and image-construing, to read in a note that the editor rejects one line of interpretation in most flippant terms:

> Stephen notes in *A Portrait* . . . that the symbols of the Holy Spirit are "a dove and a mighty wind," two of the important images of the poems. A little confused by this possibility, I prefer not to pursue it.[4]

On the basis of slight suggestion or association we are led into a labyrinth. Curves of the day lead to the seasons, colors almost make a spectrum, walking beside water "suggests separation from life," and thence to onanism, masochism, and urination as creative! The girl in the poems becomes not only the eternal feminine, but "the indefinite archetype, like Jung's anima, of all that man supposes, suggesting by turns the mistress, the mother, the church, Ireland, and maybe the soul itself." One recalls Corvick's remark in James's "The Figure in the Carpet" to the effect that "if he had had Shakespeare's own word for his being cryptic he would at once have accepted it" but that "we had nothing but the word of Mr. Snooks." We have the word of our editor that the glens around Dublin, "where lovers go," are fine "for other sports," "for letting hair down." In this forced facetiousness, even the conventional "wild wind" becomes "sexy."

It is true that Joyce was, like any vivacious and irresponsible Irishman, addicted to the questionable limerick and the mocking allusion. But those of his early poems that have survived are outspoken; there is no mistaking tone or intent.[5] The question also arises as of whether the artist's achievement is increased or diminished by a Freudian reading. Whether obsessive or infantile, such fixations contribute little that is of poetic value, whatever interest they may hold for students of psychopathology. Tindall feels that the poems "conceal too well" what they are attempting to reveal: "the form is inadequate for the burden it seems meant to carry." The critic seems bent upon destroying the suspicion of sentimentality that readers have always found in this verse. Thus the *Irish Statesman* considered this "most resolute and unabashed explorer of the crypts and sewers of the soul" to be at heart "a submerged sentimentalist."[6] An early review in the *New Republic* was closer, however, in seeing the basic formality and courtliness giving rise to "a sentiment so faint that it seems fairy-like, a madrigal from the stars."[7] Certainly the seriousness with which Joyce embraced his muse would indicate a more conventionally romantic interpretation, or rather one that qualifies without destroying romance. So John Anderson interprets the "I hear an army" poem as a contrast between the imagination of the lover and "the recognition of objectivity by wisdom" on the part of the poet.[8]

Though some reviewers felt that Tindall "argues plausibly" for the "chamber pot" reading and that "the most outrageous of his deductions is perhaps as likely as any of the lot," Horace Gregory, in an otherwise laudatory response, felt that "to speak too often of Joyce's 'cloacal obsession' does not disclose the secret of his genius." That secret is to be found rather in his almost infallible ear. If micturition be symbolic of creation, Anthony Kerrigan shrewdly remarked, why should the poet feel the terror of solitude? Would not an art, so self-bounded, be barren and onanistic?[9] The one virtue of such reading is to alert us to the antipoetic Joyce. As pure poet he always comes dangerously near the insipid. For not only is his verse devoid of meaning and color, as Levin observed, but it lacks reference to any concrete experience or any complex reaction; its flaccid nature constitutes one of the best arguments in support of our current demand for irony, tension, and ambiguity. By 1927, when the baker's dozen of later lyrics, *Pomes Pennyeach,* appeared, the grim drama of events had led men to discount "pure poetry," and Joyce himself had done much to arouse expectations of a more troubled music. Thus Zabel reflects the taste of our time in looking for poems that reflect "the tragic surge and wrath" of *Ulysses* or remind one stylistically of "the broken lights and dissonances" of the prose epic.[10] He found only two or three such poems, and though one could possibly double the number, his demurrer still stands. The contrast between Joyce the poet and Joyce the prose writer remains unsolved, despite the efforts of Tindall to bring them closer, nesting under the same innuendo.

The first poem, "Tilly," balances two contrasts, giving rise to a play of perspectives—on the one hand, the cattle drove's insensitivity and the doomed herd which is stupidly moving toward "home" and, as symbolic parallel, the flowering branch raised above their steaming heads. The storm at Fontana in which the "senile sea" thrashes against "crazy pierstakes" suggests the startlingly accurate etymologies of *Ulysses,* as Joyce uses the almost obsolete sense of "crazy" as "cracked." The apostrophe to the cathedral of night, with its "sindark nave" in which the "starknell" tolls for man, brings Baudelaire close to the Stephen who in *Ulysses* walks the strand meditating how he too was conceived, "Wombed in sin darkness." Ironic mockery of the speaker's emotion dominates the complex point of view in the "Memory of the Players in a Mirror at Midnight" as well as the simpler "Bahnhofstrasse," for the first contrasts the "Dire hunger" of love with its grimacing counterfeit by the actors and the second describes the eyes of the crowds on Zurich's principal thoroughfare as "signs that mock me as I go." Love as hunger and doom disturbs the broken lines of "A Prayer." In "Simples" one finds beneath the innocent picture of the child gathering flowers the foreboding that they may be "simples" or palliatives for her tragic future. It is a touching poem, and curiously prophetic of the sad destiny of Joyce's own daughter, now a mental invalid.

Possibly Joyce's finest poem is the "Ecce Puer," inspired by the coincidence of birth and death in the family, when the poet's father died within six weeks of the birth of his grandson. A good interpretation by L. R. Holmes traces the echoes of the Nativity and Crucifixion ("Ecce Homo," "child is born," "father forsaken," "forgive") as well as Lear's "joy and grief" and breathing on the glass—two instances of the father-child theme. Each individual re-enacts the Biblical story, with the ironic difference that each is both victim and persecutor.

> Each man both places and wears a crown of thorns, each of us crucifies and is crucified, each forsakes and is forsaken, and each must forgive much, just as each asks forgiveness.[11]

Holmes fails to notice the phrase "unclose his eyes"—the child's eyes blinded by original sin and also blind like Joyce's. This, with the "glass" of the third stanza, suggests the mirror of art, and Paul's "Now we see through a glass darkly" (the first Epistle to the Corinthians). But more important than the echoes is the counterpoint of joy and grief, birth and death, the darkness of the past and the light of a new world.

Chapter 4

Dubliners

THE DEVIOUS PATH that *Dubliners* traveled to eventual publication is almost legendary though the reasons for its difficulties are still obscure. When the manuscript of the original twelve short stories reached the publishing firm of Grant Richards in 1905, the publisher's reader submitted a quite favorable report. He found that Joyce portrayed Dublin "with sympathy and patience which equal his knowledge of . . . its idiom, its people, its streets and its little houses." The reader, probably Filson Young, found, moreover, "an order and symmetrical connection between the stories making them one book." And he praised Joyce's "truthfulness" and his "artistic sincerity [which] has been placed above other cries in the street."[1] On the basis of this favorable report, Richards accepted the book, entered into a contract with the Irish author, and even encouraged him to submit a draft of the long autobiographical novel that later became *A Portrait of the Artist*.

The difficulties that arose concerning publication began in May 1906. They are discussed in great detail in Gorman's biography and constitute, indeed, the most valuable section of the official "life."[2] In the long and painfully enervating correspondence reprinted there, one may easily see growing the myth of Joyce as exile, as alienated artist. His brush with morally sensitive printers, his disagreements with timid publishers, and his seemingly endless struggle against shadowy Irish nationalist and Irish religious forces, which, it is rumored, sought to keep him silent—these inconclusive skirmishes occupied his time and attention for a decade. Then, just as it seemed that the publication of *Dubliners* would never occur, the climate of opinion changed, Richards reentered the picture, and the book appeared in 1914 in England—and two years later in the United States.

It is probable that the reading public might have objected to *Dubliners* if it had appeared as planned in 1906. There

The notes to Chapter 4 begin on page 327.

seemed to be no plot to the stories. The Edwardian idea of style was apparently lacking. Nor had the episodes any obvious message or moral. To make matters worse, gross liberties seemed to have been taken with the proprieties of language. The book was strong medicine for those accustomed to James Stephens' sentimental novels of slum life in Dublin. Years earlier, George Russell (A. E.), editing an agricultural paper, *The Irish Homestead,* had written to Joyce for a possible contribution of fiction. In an almost rude letter, he asks: "Look at the story in this paper. . . . Could you write anything simple, rural . . . so as not to shock the readers. . . . It is easily earned money (£1) if you can write fluently and don't mind playing to the common understanding & liking for once in a way."[3]

Yet this was just what Joyce could not do, then or later. If *Dubliners* was to be "a chapter of the moral history of my country," and if Dublin had been chosen because it marked "the centre of paralysis," then it followed that the stories delineating such paralysis might have to deal clinically with evil, perversion, atrophy of powers, physical ugliness, and decay. There was no more impropriety in an artist's dealing with such subjects than in a surgeon's probing a cancerous organ. An unpublished letter from Joyce to Richards makes his position clear:

> I know that some amazing imbecilities have been perpetrated in England but I really cannot see how any civilized tribunal could listen for two minutes to such an accusation against my book. I care little or nothing whether what I write is indecent or not but, if I understand the meaning of words, I have written nothing whatever indecent in *Dubliners.*[4]

Never one for false modesty, the twenty-four-year-old Joyce informed his publisher, in another eloquent unpublished letter, of the high purpose behind his refusal to capitulate to editorial edicts on matters of style and content in *Dubliners.* He fights to retain certain disputed passages "because I believe that in composing my chapter of moral history in exactly the way I have composed it I have taken the first step toward the spiritual liberation of my country." He admonishes Richards: "Reflect for a moment on the history of the literature of Ireland as it stands at present written in the English language before you condemn this genial illusion of mine which, after all, has at least served me in the office of a candlestick during the writing of this book."[5] The first step on this road to supernatural regeneration was the clear recognition of the state of his country at its immediate worst. "I seriously believe that you will retard the course of civilization in Ireland," he tells Richards in 1906, "by preventing the Irish people from having one good look at themselves in my nicely polished looking-glass." To accomplish his end, he would use a "style of scrupulous meanness" and fill his books with "the odour of ashpits and old weeds and offal."[6]

Joyce's long delayed debut into the ranks of fiction writers was neither heralded in advance, as were his later works, nor met with undue attention. Of the early reviewers only Gerald Gould, in the *New Statesman* of June 27, 1914, remarked the entry of a "man of genius" with an original and mature attitude, though Gould felt that the achievement contained "a threat" of "a set mode of though rather than a developing capacity." For the rest, *Dubliners* attracted little more notice than would be claimed by any naturalistic work of the French school. To *The Saturday Review* Joyce seemed a victim of morbidity, cultivating a "diseased art" that "poisons the springs of one's thoughts" and leaves "no remembrance of beauty or grace, or even poetry." In similar vein the *Everyman* reviewer lamented Joyce's callousness and pessimism and wondered whether his undoubted abilities were merely those of "a genius that, blind to the blue of the heavens, seeks inspiration in the hell of despair." The writer for the Liverpool *Daily Courier* recognized, however, that though Joyce's verse could not have betokened anything "so sunless, searching and relentless," the beauty, strangeness, and power of the stories were undeniable.[7]

His emphasis on mood limits the success of his longer stories, *The Times* thought, for "the issue seems trivial, and the connecting thread becomes so tenuous as to be scarcely perceptible." *The Saturday Review* also sensed a tendency for the reader to become "lost in words" and to find the stories "a little pointless." The *Manchester Guardian* questioned whether "tragedies that are lived in an undertone" can be "whispered in art." The short pieces seem to succeed but in the longer stories "the whisper becomes monotonous."[8]

Ezra Pound regarded *Dubliners* more as an aesthetic charter of "prose free from sloppiness" than as a work of art. His essay in *The Egoist* hailed Joyce as one of the first writers in English to whom a connoisseur of French could turn without the feeling of having one's head "stuffed through a cushion." He does not veer to sentiment or fantasy nor escape to farce or horror; he "gives the thing as it is" and avoids "telling you a lot that you don't want to know." As a relief from the "rosy, floribund bore" of impressionism, and as a writer of "clear hard prose," Joyce occupies a high place among contemporaries.[9] If this seems something less than Joyce's due, we must recall that Pound championed Joyce not only with Harriet Weaver, and fought for the serial publication of the *Portrait,* but carried the banner to America through *The Little Review.* His letters to Amy Lowell, Harriet Monroe, Goldring, Mencken, Margaret Anderson, and John Quinn through the war years testify to his continuing interest, though his comments are scarcely penetrating—"damn well written," "a very fine piece of work" are typical summations. But the role played by Pound, Miss Weaver, Margaret Anderson, and others at this time is a matter of biographical rather than critical concern.

Later critics have had little to say about *Dubliners.* Reviewers hostile to the mature writings of Joyce often express an attitude of regret that he had ever pushed beyond the simplicity of the stories. Herbert Gorman offers a rather obvious critique of *Dubliners.* Harry Levin emphasizes the technique of revelation, the revealing nuance that Joyce calls the epiphany. Dominating the book, Professor Levin finds, is the mood of disillusion, expressed by a romantic irony where the intensity of emotion is contrasted with the vulgarity of its expression:

> The feeling is deliberately couched in a cheap phrase or a sentimental song, so that we experience a critical reaction, and finally a sense of intellectual detachment.[10]

Dissenting views of *Dubliners* have been rare. George Samson, who is so antipathetic to the moderns that one wonders why he should have been selected to discuss them in *The Concise Cambridge History,* concluded that Joyce's early works alone would leave him "an unimportant figure." A voice more worthy of respect, V. S. Pritchett, has considered most of the tales "awkward, provincial," recalling not the Russians but Gissing: "There is the same amateurishness of touch, the same self-pity."[11]

But beneath the "awkward" and faltering surface of his naturalistic dung heap, Joyce included much more than Grant

Richards found—much more than most sophisticated contemporary critics give him credit for. The symbolic content of *Dubliners,* what it suggests and insinuates, is far more damaging to the object of his attack than the flippant reference to Edward VII in one story or the hint of perversion in another. The irony of the decade of delay in publishing the book is that it was caused by petty differences of opinion concerning what was proper. During all that time, nobody objected to the much more explosive symbolic content because nobody recognized its presence. This esoteric content may be more effectively presented, however, after Joyce's relationship to the modern short story has been establishd.

The short story form, as we know it, is very young, dating back to the middle years of the nineteenth century. Before that time, a short story was simply a story that was not long. The developments which were to change the short story from the status of truncated novel to that of a highly specialized artistic form came not from England or Ireland but from Russia, France, Germany, and America. England, where tastes in the nineteenth century ran to bulk, and standard novels to three heavy volumes, was hardly in a position to effect a revolution in reading tastes. Circulating libraries encouraged the triteness and artificiality of the ordinary novel. They helped to prevent literary reform. Finally, as H. E. Bates points out in his excellent discussion of the problem, explicit moralizing and preaching and the taboo on honest discussion of sex in literature robbed the English novel of the elements that might have produced a new view of the short story. Such writing impelled a large audience to reject the very qualities on which modern short stories depend for their effect.[12]

The conventions of this heavy English novel had, for instance, ruled out impressionist narration, with its accompanying gaps in temporal and spatial arrangement of episodes, it had discouraged any but the most obvious symbolic representations, and it had by its example relegated the quality of poetic concentration to disuse. It is impossible to imagine a story like Joyce's "The Sisters" lacking these attributes and yet retaining much of the power that resides in it.[13]

Joyce's kind of short story begins, perhaps, with Gogol, whose quiet, intense characters have become the norm in modern tales. The profusion of detail, the ugliness yet warmth of the subject, the handling of ordinary lives of ordinary civil servants are common to both writers. (Notice the resemblance of Gogol's copyist, Akaky Akakyevitch, to Farrington of Joyce's "Counterparts.") Both Gogol and Joyce looked at commonplace people and found within them such powerful internal conflicts that there was no reason to seek material elsewhere.

Critics of *Dubliners* most frequently cite Chekhov and Maupassant as Joyce's models. Louis Cazamian finds the stories in the tradition of the latter.[14] In his book on Joyce, Louis Golding agrees.[15] Allen Tate and Mary Colum see at work the influence of Maupassant's teacher, Flaubert.[16] The frequency of such claims merits examination.

Joyce and Maupassant are really quite different in their approach to the short story. In that genre, the Frenchman is usually the celebrator of violent emotion, passion, love, undying hate; of flamboyant, startling action: dueling, rape, brutal murder, assassination. Joyce, on the other hand, seldom raises his voice as he examines the less overt manifestations of human behavior: the inhibitions, the frustrations, and the disappointments of the ordinary person. The conclusion of a story by the French writer finds the lives of his characters sharply altered in a very obvious way: in "The Vendetta," the widow Saverini returns peacefully to her home after seeing to it that her enemy has died a bloody death; the vicious Prussian officer in "Mademoiselle Fifi" lies stabbed to death while his murderess flees to safety; the noisy athlete in "The Duel" destroys himself rather than risk the disgrace of failure. In just the opposite way, Joyce gains his effects. It is the shock of having nothing happen, overtly at least, that brings home sharply the emptiness of the lives that he reveals. In "Two Gallants," a gigolo tries to wheedle a coin from his servant girl companion and is successful. Chandler, of "A Little Cloud," dreams of escape from narrow family problems and a debilitating suburban life, but realizes that such escape is impossible. Joyce's stories are keyed to the tempo of routine middle-class life, while Maupassant usually selects the extraordinary moment in an ordinary existence.

To maintain the interest of his readers in story after story whose center is sensuous animal passion, Maupassant must supply an artificial device, the trick ending. This he does with great skill; yet artful contrivance does not entirely make up for the profusion of artificial jolts that he uses to give point and climax to his tales. Joyce would never ask his readers to accept, as the Frenchman does, a series of extremely unlikely actions leading up to a melodramatic denouement.

Joyce's brother Stanislaus, while agreeing that his brother admired Maupassant, remembers that Joyce criticized him for being too concise, for his "insistent wish to define things in a phrase," and for his brutality in judging the fictional characters he had created. His "characters seem to rise to a momentary interest only to fall back again into banality." In Joyce's writing, on the other hand, Stanislaus finds everyday life foremost, "and the incident, in itself so slight . . . serves only to illuminate a certain moment of the everyday life. Judgment is always supended. . . ."[17]

Other points of difference in technique may easily be adduced. Maupassant is not especially interested in symbolic presentation. He usually tells his story in a flat, clean, clear, brittle, and totally admirable way, presenting his account on the realistic level only. Joyce was not content to stop at this point. Edmund Wilson puts emphasis on another difference—the difference between poetry and prose.[18] It is unfair, of course, to speak of the sound and rhythm of Maupassant's writing in translation, but even in its French original, his prose is only prose, simple and lucid. Joyce's short stories carry a ryhthm and cadence, however, rarely found in short stories. It is unnecessary to quote the melodious final paragraph of "The Dead" to indicate Joyce's superiority in writing musical prose. In short, Joyce may have learned a great deal about fictional technique from reading Maupassant, but there is little evidence in *Dubliners* to show that he made use of it in his own work. We know from Gorman that Joyce devoured "several volumes" of Maupassant,[19] but differences in temperament, habits of life, and approach to art would not have been conducive to Joyce's finding the influence he needed in this pupil of Flaubert.

It is quite a different matter with Chekhov—and a much more difficult one. Perhaps Joyce did not know of the existence of the Russian while *Dubliners* was in preparation, for Chekhov's reputation was scarcely international in the early years of the twentieth century. Very occasionally, in the 1890's, an English translation of one of his stories would appear in *Temple Bar* or elsewhere.[20] And *The Fortnightly Review,* which ran Joyce's review of Ibsen, did publish two of Chekhov's stories (1903 and 1906), but there is no certainity that Joyce ever saw them.[21] It is very likely, however, that he did see a collection of Chekhov's stories called *The Black Monk,* published in London in 1903, with an introduction by an Irishman, Robert Long.[22] It contained, among others, "The Black Monk," "In Exile," "Rothchild's Fiddle," "Sleepyhead," and "Ward No. 6." That a man interested in significant Continental literature, and especially in the short story, would have been unaware of this revolutionary publication is hard to believe.

Both writers tried in their stories to represent the flat surface and the twisted core of life. The visible portion of the iceberg was to be reproduced faithfully and with acute sensitivity to realistic detail. The smell of the peasantry, their wretched cottages, their brutality to servants or to horses—the daily affairs of life—were to be sketched with stark and unremittant fidelity. Joyce demanded that his pictures of middle-class politicians at work, or Irish priests, or tea salesmen, be accurate and immediately recognizable. But both artists recognized, in addition, the key role in life played by less material, less tangible elements in the human personality. At a time when it was not popular to plumb beneath the surface, they acquiesced in the artistic necessity of considering in their stories the great mass of iceberg under water—the hopes, the dreams, the self-deceiving illusions, the unconscious motivations, and the contradictions of the emotional life. Because both Joyce and Chekhov understood that the delineation of life required consideration of the whole iceberg, their stories have distinctive similarities. The discovery by both artists that the tension set up between life-as-it-is and life-as-it-should-be constitutes "the story" provides them with a common theme.[23]

Chekhov uses this motif most notably in "Ward No. 6." The creeping paralysis of small-town officialdom wears down the ambitions and distorts the mind of the local doctor until he finds stimulation only in conversation with a village madman and is himself adjudged insane. Joyce employs the split between illusion and reality throughout *Dubliners,* recognizing no explicit demarcation between them.

It is most certainly present in "Araby," where the exotic Oriental motif is deliberately employed so that it may be contrasted with the banal reality of the salesgirl's flirtatious interlude and the bareness of the darkened suburban bazaar. When Maria, the laundress, sings in the quavering voice of an elderly spinster of how "I dreamt that I dwelt in marble halls," the theme is reiterated. It is equally apparent in Gabriel Conroy, in "The Dead," who, in spite of constant self-examination, fails to see himself as others see him. The revelation of all the shifting undercurrents to such a personality would have been impossible for most writers in the short story, which demands brevity and yet completeness. Joyce and Chekhov were probably best fitted, fifty years ago, to show the way.

All novelists, of course, deal in some way with the struggle of the individual against the world and against his inner self. But Joyce and his Russian counterpart are alike in more specific ways. They are concerned with the same kinds of characters and situations. Avoiding Maupassant's overt action, they deal, as Matthew Josephson has pointed out, with "people who find themselves in a trap, or a 'box' . . . who plan to escape. . . . But nothing happens, or at least nothing happens as they planned. . . ."[24] To mention Joyce's main characters is to establish a gallery of thwarted escapees: Farrington, Eveline, Gabriel, Little Chandler, the boy in "An Encounter," and Polly Mooney's husband.

When a writer depicts life in realistic detail, he must be careful not to suggest artificiality by arranging his plot so that the details are too pat, too obvious and artful, for that is not how events seem to happen in life. Maupassant, with his structural hardness, his fixed opening and trick closing, disregarded that modern dictum. Chekhov made it his trademark. He felt that "a story should have neither beginning nor end." Like Joyce, he preferred to seem "inconclusive." That is one of the reasons why the reader does not have to stretch his imagination too far in going from *Dubliners* to *A Portrait*. Joyce's characters and situations extend themselves far beyond the pages on which they actually appear and take on an independent life of their own. What happened to them before they walked across the stage and what will happen after the curtain descends are important to the reader. "Ivy Day in the Committee Room" ends on an anticlimactic, inconsequential remark. "Grace" closes in the middle of a sermon. The ending of "Clay" skirts the irrelevant as Chekhov's "Vanka" does, the one with a remark about Balfe's music, the other with a dog wagging his tail.

The objectivity and impersonality of the two writers have often been misunderstood and ascribed to a lack of warmth and human understanding. Joyce and Chekhov have been pictured as unconcerned scientists, toying with their human specimens as with an exhibit under a microscope. But this appearance of hardness and detachment is a deliberate device of writers who felt intensely the pity and terror of the situations and the people whom they created, and yet could not trust themselves to write without restraint of what was closest to them. An air of distance and matter-of-factness, even in recounting emotionally gripping events, would produce, they felt, more powerful effects.

Chekhov speaks for his own, and surely for Joyce's pratice, when he lays down rules for the tone of a literary work: "The only defect . . . is the lack of restraint, the lack of grace. . . ." And again, "when you depict sad or unlucky people and want to touch the reader's heart, try to be colder—it gives their grief, as it were, a background, against which it stands out in greater relief." Finally, "You must be unconcerned when you write pathetic stories. . . . The more objective, the stronger will be the effect."[25] This is a rather crude expression by Chekhov of what later became Stephen's aesthetic theory. Ideally, the artist, "like the God of the creation, remains within or behind or beyond or above his handiwork, invisible, refined out of existence, indifferent, paring his fingernails." Like Joyce, Chekhov felt that "Subjectivity is a terrible thing. It is bad in this alone, that it reveals the author's hands and feet."[26] Both artists are alike in their ability to keep their hands and feet out of the picture.

Frequent parallels between the factual details of Chekhov's stories and of Joyce's demand more detailed treatment than can be offered here. It must serve now merely to point out the resemblance of the madman, Ivan Dmitritch, in "Ward No. 6" to Stephen Dedalus. Their families suffer financial reverses, they teach school at starvation wages, their mothers die. Chekhov's description of Dmitritch parallels that of Stephen, detail by detail:

> Never . . . had he had the appearance of a strong man. He was pale, thin, and sensitive to cold. . . . His disposition impelled him to seek companionship, but thanks to his irritable and suspicious character he never became intimate with anyone, and had no friends. Of his fellow-citizens he always spoke with contempt, condemning as disgusting and repulsive their gross ignorance and torpid, animal life. He spoke in a tenor voice. . . . However he began a conversation, it always ended in one way—in a lament that the town was stifling and tiresome, that its people had no high interests, but led a dull, unmeaning life. . . . Of woman and woman's love he spoke passionately. . . . But he had never been in love.[27]

Other instances of fictional resemblances abound. One might show how, in spirit at least, Gabriel Conroy is like the Greek Master of "The Man in a Case," who tries to ward off all the dangers of existence by physical shields—galoshes, preoccupation with ancient books, umbrellas—and finally, in his coffin, is thoroughly protected from natural hazards. Or how the hotel bedroom scene in "The Dead," in which Gabriel sees his real aging appearance in the mirror, finds its counterpart in Chekhov's "The Lady with the Pet Dog." In both tales the critical moment of revelation is rendered through the device of looking into a mirror to glimpse reality through the illusion. Whether or not Joyce knew Chekhov's work is fascinating speculation, but that they had much in common, artistically, is unquestionable.

Young Joyce probably learned about another Russian, Turgenev, from another Irishman, George Moore. In *Impressions and Opinions* (1891), Moore had lauded "Turgueneff" for his sketches, in which "the slightest events are fashioned into marvellous stories." These he hailed because they were "absolutely new in form as in matter. . . ." Each of the twenty-five stories in *A Sportsman's Sketches* is capable of independent existence.[28] But like the stories in *Dubliners,* Turgenev's simple sketches produce the over-all affect of a corrupt, dying, despairing country whose inhabitants are trapped in a system of their own making. Each story breathes that "special odour of corruption" that Joyce tried so hard to get in his own book. Yet it is probable that Turgenev's work came to Joyce at second hand through Moore's *The Untilled Field,* published in 1903.[29] In this volume of stories, the spirit and method of the Russian was successfully applied to Irish subjects. Moore too had found in the everyday concerns of petty folk a larger symbolic meaning, which carried beyond the characters to indict a whole nation.

Though Joyce could learn little from the diction and style of Moore, he may have picked up and used several themes that pervade *The Untilled Field*. Moore is fond of stressing the great influences of the none too scrupulous members of the clergy, the ignorance of the ordinary Irishman, and the necessity of flight by emigration. In "The Exile" a man must make up his mind to be either a priest or a policeman. The qualifications for the job seem to be very much the same in both professions. Joyce's "Grace," as we shall see, suggests a similar theme. Moore's descriptions of the priest's house and of the youth's rejection of priesthood in this story remind one of "The Sisters." Further, the dozing priest in Moore's "Patchwork," "huddled in his armchair over the fire . . . the cassock covered with snuff . . . and the fat, inert hands," suggests Father Flynn. Whatever Joyce in his formative stage may have learned from Moore, he had only ridicule for Moore's refined, artificial style in later novels like *The Lake*.

The sources of Joyce's realism in *Dubliners* are difficult, and perhaps unnecessary, to trace. In spite of Mary Colum's emphasis on the relationship, he is no closer to Flaubert than most of the young writers of his day in English who admired what the better realists were doing and who sought to emulate their integrity in careful documentation and observation of the facts of life. From reading "A Simple Heart," Flaubert's chief contribution to the realistic short story, Joyce could have learned what every realist had to say—not only the Goncourts in *Germinie Lacertoux* (1864) and Zola in *Germinal* but even George Moore in *A Mummer's Wife*—that there are servants and masters in an unequal world, that scullery maids are notoriously faithful to their employers, that the lives of the poor are ugly and wretched but that love, even when unmerited, may justify existence. In Flaubert's effective story, Joyce could have found the surface hardness and objectivity, in the face of terrible disclosures, that later distinguish his own short stories. Also, his strong bent for ironic fictional conversations may possibly derive from Flaubert's *Bouvard et Pécuchet*.[30]

In this novel Flaubert deals with the level of society that Joyce considered his special province: the middle-class civil servant, the bourgeois salesman, shopkeeper, or clerk. He sees them very much as Joyce sees them, in their monotonous sameness, dressing alike, acting alike, thinking alike. The interminable account of matters on which Bouvard and his associate agree covers several volumes: "Mais la banlieue, selon Bouvard, était assommante par le tapage des guinguettes. Péuchet pensait de même."[31] It is but a step to the ironic conversations of similar small men in Joyce's "Grace."

> "I haven't such a bad opinion of the Jesuits," he said. . . .
> "They're the grandest order in the Church, Tom," said Mr. Cunningham. . . .
> "There's no mistake about it," said Mr. M'Coy, "if you want a thing well done and no flies about, you go to a

Jesuit. . . ."

"The Jesuits are a fine body of men," said Mr. Power.[32]

The tone that Flaubert took toward his environment, especially in *Madame Bovary,* creeps also into the work of his disciples and reaches its zenith in Joyce. Hard to define, it is perhaps a romantic debunking of a romanticism that has lost its power and needs pitilessly to be exposed. By displaying coldly a product of bouregois education, bourgeois social standards, and bourgeois monetary vulgarity, he is able to convey to his audience the tragedy implicit in the gap between small-town reality and romantic illusion. The former brings death; the latter financial and social success. This hiatus between reality and illusion, as has been pointed out, is essentially Joyce's subject matter, and the trapped people of Dublin, educated by the priests, provincial in outlook, are his equivalents for the Flaubertian characters. The boy in "Araby," whose disillusion derives from his sudden realization of the difference between romance and reality, is a minor Madame Bovary.

Something should be said of the degree of accuracy of Joyce's naturalistic details in *Dubliners.* While there is no special virtue in slavish adherence to truth of environmental background, in a creative work, at the same time, Joyce's fidelity to the facts of Dublin as a physical entity should be recognized. Though the contest itself may not be the center of interest in "After the Race," it is exciting to recognize that not only did such a race take place but that young Joyce was commissioned to cover a like event for the local newspaper. His very pedestrian and uncomfortable account of it, unsigned, and in the form of an interview with the driver of one of the racing cars, has recently been found.[33] Again, Joyce sets one of his most memorable scenes in *Dubliners* in Corless' restaurant, where Little Chandler is made to feel more and more an outsider, a frustrated provincial, by his successful, cosmopolitan friend, Gallaher. It has often been assumed that, for this scene at least, the writer had created the setting from his imagination. Yet examination of *Thom's Official Directory of . . . Ireland* for 1896 shows this item: "Corless, Thomas, wine merchant and proprietor Burlington dining rooms, 24, 26, and 27 St. Andrew Street" and later reference to the place as "Burlington Restaurant and Oyster Saloons." Since Joyce writes that "People went there after the theatre to eat oysters and drink liqueurs," it is reasonable to suppose that once more he preferred to deal, like Zola, with a maximum of observable fact in his fiction.

The surface resemblance of the stories in *Dubliners* to some naturalist fiction has too often led to indiscriminate labeling of the book as a product of Zola's movement. It does indeed seem to conform to many of the criteria of naturalism that Vernon Parrington suggests: objectivity in the spirit of the scientist, frankness, an amoral attitude toward material, and a bias toward pessimism in selecting characters and the details of environment. Yet what he designates the vital principle of naturalism, its philosophy of determinism, seems quite unimportant in Joyce's stories.[34] Not one of his characters may be accused of being a mere economic or social puppet, going through the motions of living so that the scientist-author may pull the strings and observe and record the results of his experiments in the area of heredity or environment.

Nor can it truly be alleged that Joyce's adherence to the tenets in Parrington's list of naturalist charcteristics is more than superficial and accidental. Even Zola, the expounder of the gospel of scientific objectivity, found himself taking sides and becoming, in spite of himself, partisan to a cause. There is no doubt that he stands with Etienne in *Germinal* forcefully taking a position on the social system of the future, as he speaks darkly but exultantly of the "black avenging army, germinating slowly in the furrows. . . ." Similary, through the smoke screen of random conversation in "Ivy Day in the Committee Room," one can see without difficulty the figure of the author condemning, cursing, comparing, hoping—though not a word of direct comment is recorded, certainly, with regard to frankness, he possesses all the qualifications of the naturalist group, but, in addition, he has, in *Dubliners*, a sense of refined reticence not available to Zola and his circle, who were forced to shock in order to dramatize their revolutionary position in nineteenth-century letters. As for Joyce's pessimism in selecting characters and setting, his position was determined for him by the only life he knew—a sordid, poverty-ridden, monotonous day-by-day existence in a city whose former greatness seemed in eclipse. Zola may have chosen his battleground, but Joyce was forced to fight on the streets of his home neighborhood. Paradoxically, however, Zola traveled to the scene of action of whatever novel he was preparing in order to do justice to his subject; while

Joyce, in order to work with artistic vision, had to separate himself physically from those scenes with which he was most deeply concerned as man and artist. Perhaps distance was for the Irish writer a necessary condition for the task of transforming living people and oppressive environment into mysteriously symbolic ingredients of literature. For, from first to last, Joyce was primarily a symbolist writer.

By nature and upbringing Joyce found himself drawn to presentation through indirection. From early childhood, his mind had been alert to hidden meanings—to the significance, for instance, of the maroon brush for Michael Davitt and the green for Parnell. The symbolism of wine and wafer in the sacrament had thrilled him in his school days. The hidden fullness of details of the mass attracted and frightened him by their power. Allusions to the inexpressible, clothed in images of Mary, the Sacred Heart, or the dark flames of Jesuit Hell, were his daily intellectual and emotional fare. There is much of the symbolist in every Catholic Irishman. Unlike most of them, however, Joyce put the technique to work in his books.

Like many distinguished contemporary writers—Eliot, Pound, Yeats—Joyce found what he needed in Dante. The familiar story of Dante and Beatrice, lovers on a spiritual plane, becomes a symbol of the unrealizable in an imperfect world. From Dante's quest too may have come additional support for the familiar theme of the symbolic quest in *Ulysses* and in the first few stories of *Dubliners*. In addition, much of the symbolism of Hell that appears impressively in *A Portrait* and unobtrusively in *Dubliners* is colored by Dante's classic representation.

Joyce came to maturity as a new wave of organized symbolism was making itself felt in English-speaking countries. Only Swinburne and a handful of Englishmen had previously recognized the importance of Baudelaire's strange poems and tortured pronouncements. Rimbaud was just a name to many literary people outside France. Arthur Symons's *The Symbolist Movement in Literature* (1899) gave formal standing to these foreigners. But earlier than that, according to William York Tindall, Joyce had turned to them because they gave him a way to express reality.[35] By suggestion, by mysterious images rich in symbolic associations, the reader might be made to feel the truth about Dublin, a truth deeper than any based on a lengthy, factual, naturalist survey. That Joyce had earlier experimented with symbolic indirection in his poetry has already been demonstrated in what has been said of *Chamber Music.*

When Joyce turned from poetry to short fiction, he had before him the example of Yeats's early prose—filmy, misty, strangely spiritual and beautiful short stories. Because he admired so much the artistry behind them, Joyce committed several of them to memory and studied their technique.[36] Yeats's stories, like Chekhov's, deal almost poetically with the thin line that separates illusion and reality, spirit and matter, natural and supernatural. His "The Tables of the Law" tells of the quest of a man to achieve a mystical and direct communion with the powers above. He fails utterly, for he has ignored and alienated himself from the real world, thinking that he can create beauty in a void. He decides that only by tracing himself the human pattern of sin and redemption, only by intercourse with God's world on earth, can he hope to encounter reality. His misfortune, and he knows it, is that he is so far removed from the things of the world that he is unable to sin.

The suggestive details—the symbolism—of the story probably interested Joyce much more than the familiar romantic theme. In the first paragraph, the quester, Aherne, is asked why he has at the last moment before ordination refused "the berretta."[37] As the question is asked, Aherne raises a glass of wine, but, without drinking, he replaces it on the table "slowly and meditatively" and holds it there. It is a safe bet that Joyce was aware of the symbolic rejection of priesthood in this action. The acceptance or rejection of priesthood becomes, in fact, an important symbolic situation in "The Sisters," in *A Portrait,* and certainly in *Ulysses.* Other suggestive details give evidence of how Yeats and Joyce manipulate symbols. Aherne's predilection for the painters of the Sienese school because they "pictured not the world but what is revealed . . . in . . . visions" is a symbolic reflection of his own character. Knowing this circumstance, the reader has no need of two or three pages of discursive exposition.

Yeats's story is heavy with additional symbolic details, which Joyce appears to have stored up for future use. There is the narrow door that leads to Aherne's chapel, the six "unlighted" candles on the altar, and the secret book of Joachim of Flora, whose writings receive mention in the "Proteus" episode of *Ulysses.* In the story too are traces of the French symbolists. The confusion of senses in the final wild scene is familiar. "Faint figures robed in purple, and lifting faint torches with arms that gleamed like silver," burning gum, a "heavy purple smoke" might well have satisfied Rimbaud in his days as magician and alchemist. Finally, the "great bird made of flames," recalling the phoenix, the Holy Spirit, and Joyce's birds (especially in "An Encounter"), is as mysteriously symbolic as Baudelaire's albatross or Mallarmé's troubled swan.

From Yeats's stories Joyce learned how realistic detail could be wedded to symbolic evocation, how an insinuation could be more forceful than the statement of a fact. He saw the strength that derived from effective presentation of visions. These visions, dreams, or reveries dot the pages of his prose, with one significant difference. Yeats will present a delicate hint of the supernatural but is not content to leave it at that. He is more analytical of his visions, more discursive, and wonders: "I do not know if they were demons or evil spirits." Joyce lets the reader wonder. But Joyce appears to adopt Yeats's habit of associating with the dead and the spiritual a mélange of sensuous impressions. What the boy narrator of "The Sisters" smells and tastes and hears is given great stress as he kneels before the dead priest. The odor of wet ashes, the faint music, the rustle of funereal garments herald the vision of Stephen's dead mother throughout *Ulysses*.

Yeats impressed Joyce with the importance of symbol in a story. But Joyce worked out his own technique and called it *epiphany*. He explains it in *Stephen Hero*. Stephen Dedalus chances to hear snatches of a trivial, flirtatious conversation on a Dublin street. Inexplicably, it makes a deep impression on him, and he thinks of "collecting many such moments together in a book of epiphanies. By an epiphany he meant a sudden spiritual manifestation, whether in the vulgarity of speech or of gesture or in a memorable phase of the mind itself."[38] To explain still further, Joyce must give Stephen's well-known analysis of the qualities of beauty: first, to be beautiful a thing must have wholeness, that is, it must be seen as separate from all other things. Second, it must have harmony, or symmetrical balance of part with part within the framework of the thing. Finally, and most important, it must have what he calls radiance. This radiance or whatness or *quidditas* is apparent in a work of art "when the relation of the parts is exquisite, when the parts are adjusted to the special point [so that] we recognize that it is *that* thing which it is. Its soul, its whatness, leaps to us from the vestment of its appearance. The soul of the commonest object, the structure of which is so adjusted, seems to us radiant. The object achieves its epiphany."[39] This is a rather complicated way for Joyce to say that he would present beauty in symbolic form. In essence, it may be put thus: radiance equals epiphany equals symbol. He sees epiphany as a device of expression that, perfect in its wholeness and harmony, will show forth in an instant of illumination a meaning and significance greater than the words in another combination would carry. Thus, clay may be clay, but in Joyce's short story it becomes, through skillful arrangement of the total pattern, symbolically representative of impending death, and hence it lends meaning to the otherwise trivial narrative.

Perhaps the best approach to the symbolic meaning of the stories in *Dubliners* is through scrutiny of the first story, "The Sisters." Fortunately, three versions of the story are available for study. The earliest, Joyce's contribution to George Russell's *Irish Homestead,* runs to about sixteen hundred words (half the size of the final version) and is little more than a record of a rambling conversation or two, with incidental description of several Dublin slum dwellers. It is signed "Stephen Daedalus."[40]

The story tells of a boy, Stephen perhaps, whose elderly friend, the Reverend James Flynn, lies dying. The lad maintains a vigil on the sidewalk below. But death occurs when the child is not present, so he hears of the event from grown-ups at supper. The next morning he visits the priest's house. He thinks of the old man, feeble, waking to talk occasionally to the little boy or to complain of his needs to his two sisters, Nannie and Eliza. On the evening of the same day, the boy comes with his aunt to pay formal respects to the dead man. They kneel with deaf Nannie at the coffin, then make small talk about the priest's life. The sisters speak of his life as "crossed," his attitude "disappointed." They date this attitude to the time he dropped and shattered a chalice. This accident is supposed to have affected his mind so that he would laugh to himself in his dark confessional. This draft of the story shows the young Joyce at his blunt, unsubtle worst. An intermediate version of the story, in the collection of John J. Slocum, apparently represents an attempt by Joyce to revise the *Homestead* story.[41] In it Joyce is at work refining his diction, reworking tenses, economizing on superfluous words, making it a neater piece. What he adds to it to bolster its symbolic content will be dealt with shortly.

The final *Dubliners* version of "The Sisters" is to the *Homestead* draft what *A Portrait* is to *Stephen Hero*. The quantity of information in the latter may be greater, but there is more artistry in the former. We learn in the *Homestead* story that Cotter is "the old distiller" and that he owns "prize setters." In *Dubliners* we must assume his occupation from his "talking of faints and worms." In the former we find that Nannie "is almost stone deaf"; we learn of her deafness in the final version when all those who talk to her raise their voices. In the short interval between first and last drafts, Joyce had learned to use the symbolist technique of expression through suggestion rather than through explicit telling. Joyce had lengthened the story to almost twice its original size. He had also shifted the emphasis from the sisters to the boy and his environment.

What, specifically, has been added? Joyce had promised earlier to write of the moral paralysis of his country. In this final version he reveals that the priest's malady is paralysis, a word that "sounded to me like the name of some maleficent and sinful being. . . ." Thus, at the beginning of the narrative, the author associates the priest with paralysis, sickness, and vague evil. The dreams and visions of the symbolists also come into play. After death, the "grey face of the paralytic" appears before him, apparently trying to "confess" a sin.

The problem of the relationship of the boy to the priest becomes complicated in the *Dubliners* version. By trying to confess to the lad, Father Flynn shows that he considers Stephen's role a priestly one. After all, the old man has trained him in Latin, in the catechism, and in performing some of the ceremonies of the priesthood. Yet the boy resists: "The duties of the priest toward the Eucharist and . . . confessional seemed so grave to me that I wondered how anybody had ever found in himself the courage to undertake them." Nor can he perform his functions as a Catholic communicant, much less those of priest-confessor. Kneeling with the rest of the mourners at the bier, he "pretended to pray but . . . could not. . . ." In the same way, Stephen, in *A Portrait*, kneels silently while Uncle Charles prays aloud, for the boy can respect, "though he did not share, his piety." Later, offered wine and crackers by the sisters, he hesitates to take the wine and refuses the crackers. So much space is given to the details of the offer, omitted completely from the *Homestead* version and merely mentioned in a sentence in the intermediate draft, that the question arises of Joyce's intention to express symbolically here the boy's hesitation to accept "Communion." Considered from the point of view of Joyce's biography or Stephen's spiritual history, the episode seems significant.

At the time when Joyce was turning his obvious first version of the story into the very delicately symbolic story that we have today, his mind was full of his involuntary conflict with the national religion. Behind him lay his rejection of the life of a Jesuit; immediately before him were the many vital decisions that had to be made: to leave Ireland, to refuse to conform to religious ritual observances, to enter a frightening profession. That the shock of such a conflict was tremendous is clear from Joyce's inability to forget his period of mental strain and emotional turmoil. A man whose life was the literature he created might well have attempted to project his conflict in his short story.

The Father Flynn whose shadowy essence dominates the revised story appears to be illustrative of the, to Joyce, decaying Irish Catholic God. Being a part of the paralyzed Irish environment, the Deity of the church is also paralyzed. With care, Joyce carries through the analogy, not made in the *Homestead* version, in all details. Paralysis, it will be recalled, reminds him of the word "simony." Not only does the church suffer from physical paralysis, but morally it is sick, if the perversion theme may be transferred—as it must be—from the man to the church. (In the specific context of this story, simony may be involved simply in the superior relationship of Flynn to the boy, since the Catholic church defines simony as any exchange of spiritual for temporal things. It can take the form of having the applicant pay homage, "which consists in subserviency, the rendering of undue services.") And much is made of the advisability of keeping the younger generation, represented by the boy narrator, away from the perverted influence of Irish religion, which has "smiled continually" but has been guilty of awful sins.

True, Father Flynn, a surrogate for the Deity, has made friendly overtures to Stephen, as to Joyce. It was possible to rouse him from his "stupefied doze," says Joyce, in a tone reminiscent of Gautier and the early Eliot, by bringing him a contribution of snuff. But so weak and enervated is the old

God that "his hands trembled" and the gifts of snuff sprinkled through his fingers and "gave his ancient priestly garments their green faded look. . . ." Yet the father figure had done something for the boy: ". . . taught me to pronounce Latin properly . . . explained to me the meaning of the different ceremonies of the Mass . . . amused himself by putting difficult questions to me. . . ." The old man had ended by trying to make a priest of him and had succeeded in scaring the boy with the awful solemnity of a priest's functions.

Perhaps his spiritual superior might have convinced the boy if he himself had not been so inept in carrying out his own priestly functions. Had not Father Flynn dropped and broken the chalice? Had he not crushed this symbol of spiritual responsibility? Even in death the coffined priest lies silently, "his large hands *loosely* retaining a chalice [italics mine]." An indication of how important Joyce considered this chalice symbol is its evolution from draft to draft. In the first version, the priest grasps a rosary, in the second a cross; but Joyce saw in time the artistic rightness of placing in the dead man's hand what, as a living man, he could not hold.

The stage is set now in the story for presentation of the boy's symbolic reluctance to accept the ceremonies of his former faith. He cannot pray; he delays drinking the wine and refuses the wafers offered to him by the sisters. The role of Nannie and Eliza assumes an importance that the merely realistic part they play does not apparently justify. After all, Joyce, who took great pains with his story titles, did call the story "The Sisters." They do not represent nuns. As nurses, who minister to the wants of Father Flynn (the God of the church on earth), they may play the symbolic part of priests. As one of their functions is the bestowing of Communion, Joyce has the two sisters offer "Communion" to the unwilling boy. Significantly, the *Homestead* draft makes no mention of food and drink offered to the guests. In the intermediate version, one line is devoted to the offering: "We, as visitors, were given a glass of sherry each." But not until the final version does Joyce spend half a page describing the details of the proffered "Communion." All along, he seems to be groping toward inclusion of this symbolic situation, without grasping yet its full significance.

Taking the sisters as priestly figures helps to give consistency to the details of the story. Nannie is deaf, as in Joyce's opinion the average priest was deaf to the words and needs of docile parishioners. Nannie leads the prayers at the bier of the dead father. Her voice is audible above the voices of the others. Both sisters apparently offer "Communion." Both point out rather weakly the virtues of the impotent, feeble Father Flynn. Throughout the story, too, there is an air of disappointed expectancy as the living await a sign, a voice, a sound from the dead figure of the Catholic faith. As must happen, however, "there was no sound in the house: and I knew that the old priest was lying still in his coffin. . . ."

Critics have almost universally dismissed all the stories in *Dubliners* except "The Dead" as trivial sketches—and let it go at that. Too few have seen the trouble that Joyce took to give more than a surface meaning to his seemingly transparent, harmless stories. Yet even in the fragile narrative of "An Encounter," a richness of symbolic content is evident.

The main outlines of the story are simple and ordinary. Three boys, weary of the unromantic life of schoolboys, decided to play truant for one day and to make an excursion to the old Pigeonhouse Fort. One loses his courage and backs out, leaving the narrator and Mahony to go together. The former, his mind full of "penny dreadful" notions of what adventure and adventurers should be, watches wide-eyed on the docks to catch a glimpse of foreign sailors, whose eyes, he has been led to believe, will be green. He is disappointed. But later in the afternoon, the two boys fall in with an elderly pervert whose strange conversation they do not quite understand although it makes them uneasy. The narrator suddenly discovers with a shock that the rheumy eyes of their unwholesome acquaintance are "bottle-green." "I turned my eyes away." The boys, worried by the tone of his conversation, depart hurriedly.

The dead and inconclusive note on which the story and the quest for adventure end is, of course, deliberate. The attempt of the boy in "The Sisters" to find a spiritual father and a calling had resulted in rejection and almost in revulsion. The expectation of discovering romance and adventure in Dublin must end in more than frustration—in a souring of childhood dreams of glamour and love. This happens also to the adolescent narrator in "Araby," and his youthful exuberance is permanently dampened.

The theme of escape receives its first treatment from Joyce in "An Encounter." The three conspirators plan "to break out of the weariness of school-life for one day at least" by playing hooky in the freedom and privacy of the isolated Pigeonhouse. Perhaps significantly, the boy who withdraws from the adventure has parents who "went to eight-o'clock mass every morning" and a brother who is preparing for the priesthood. He is not present to share their disillusion on the docks nor does he wander with them into an open field where their quest for adventure, and a father, is gratified and rebuffed.

The perverted old man whom they encounter—a symbol of love turned sour in the enervating Dublin climate of fifty years ago—bears an interesting resemblance to Father Fynn. Both are old men, the decay of their physical being indicated by reference to Flynn's "big discoloured teeth" and to the anonymous old man's mouth in which there were "great gaps . . . between his yellow teeth." Joyce speaks too about Flynn's "ancient priestly garments," which have a "green faded look"; and of the other old man: "He was shabbily dressed in a suit of greenish-black. . . . He seemed to be fairly old. . . ." Both men enjoy the companionship of children and delight in initiating them into mysterious rites—Flynn in describing the intricacies of the Catholic Mass, the other in detailing the ceremony of whipping a miscreant boy. "He described to me how he would whip such a boy as if he were unfolding some elaborate mystery." Flynn is a symbol of impotent God, and the boys call the pervert a "josser," pidgin English for "God." The old man's voice grows "almost affectionate" as he strives to win the love that he can seemingly never attain, for his distorted revelation of it serves merely to alienate those to whom it is revealed. In much the same way, Father Flynn, by harping on the complexities of his office, alienates the boy whom he most wishes to convert. Though both old men seem to covet the father role, and though the child in both stories craves a father, father and son seem incompatible. Not until *Ulysses* will father and son attain even partial compatibility.

The boys in "An Encounter" never do reach their destination, the Pigeonhouse, in the filthy slum of Ringsend. This structure, erected far out on a breakwater in Dublin Bay, once a "watch house, store house and place of refuge for such as were forced to land there by stress of weather," later a fort, and finally a power station supplying light to the vicinity, is symbolically too far away from the young adventurers to fulfill for them any of its functions.[42]

At least one of the functions of the symbol is religious. His mind fascinated by correspondences, Joyce saw many literary possibilities in the Pigeonhouse. "Pigeon" brought to mind "dove" and dove recalled the Holy Ghost. When Stephen, in the "Proteus" episode of *Ulysses,* sees the Pigeonhouse, he says to himself cryptically, *"Que* [*sic*] *vous a mis dans cette fichue position?"* and responds, *"C'est le pigeon, Joseph."*[43] Later it becomes clear that these words are supposedly exchanged by Joseph and the Virgin Mary on the matter of Mary's baffling pregnancy. In a blasphemous verse, also, Christ, the speaker, stresses the same circumstances:

> I'm the queerest young fellow that ever you heard,
> My mother's a jew, and my father's a bird. . . .[44]

The Pigeonhouse, then, is identified in Joyce's mind with the "father" of Christ and with fathers in general. In its towerlike proportions, it may also be a rather trite phallic symbol of fatherhood. The boy narrator, moreover, being an orphan, seeks in this quest a father. The ironies are multiple. The boys choose this retreat because they are sure that their teacher, Father Butler, will not interrupt their fun, for a Dublin priest (a father) would have no reason to visit the Pigeonhouse, the temple of the Holy Ghost. Furthermore, though attracted toward the Pigeonhouse-Holy Ghost-father symbol, the boys amuse themselves by shooting birds with Mahony's catapult. They succeed only in poisoning the springs from which their desires arise. Instead of a father, a sterile pervert greets them. Their quest fails, for they are unable to reach the house of the Dove, of the father.

A strong case may be made for the presence in all of the stories of *Dubliners* of symbolic strands that help to tie together the seemingly discrete details of each and operate beyond that to leave in the awareness of the reader a sense of vital interconnection among the stories. David Daiches recognized early the power of this symbolic fabric but did not choose to demonstrate in any detail how it operated within a specific narrative. William York Tindall has been concerned also with symbolic pattern in Joyce's fiction. He has, however, given only perfunctory attention in his writing to analysis of the narratives in *Dubliners.* Close elucidation of the text of the stories to make clear their meaning would consume more space than this book can allot to them, yet some idea of fruitful lines of investigation may be suggested.

In "Araby," for which Cleanth Brooks has provided a good explication, exile and the illusion-reality motif are given early treatment by young Joyce.[45] He portrays the bright flame of the boy narrator's hope against a dreary and sordid backdrop to foreshadow its inevitable disappointment. The boy lives, symbolically, on a dead-end street. The neighborhood is decaying: "odours arose from the ashpits," and a discarded rusty bicycle pump lies hidden in untended shrubbery. In this unprepossessing environment, a sensitive boy feels the first stirring of love for the younger sister of his playmate. Why Joyce does not name the girl specifically, beyond calling her "Mangan's sister," is a problem. Perhaps it is to render more ideal this object of an almost spiritual love that he prefers to keep her Christian name anonymous. Or perhaps there is a relationship here between the romantic Irish poet, James Clarence Mangan, whom Joyce so much admired in his essay of 1902,[46] and the girl who symbolizes the acme of romance and poetry. That he should be the spiritual companion of Mangan may not be too far-fetched, since Joyce says in his essay on the poet: "The world, you see, has become somewhat unreal for him. . . . How will it be for those dreams which, for every young and simple heart, take such dear reality upon themselves? One whose nature is so sensitive cannot forget his dreams in a secure, strenuous life." And the anonymity of the girl may be further explained by a remark in the same essay that the faces of Laura and Beatrice "embody one chivalrous idea, which is no mortal thing, bearing it bravely above the accidents of lust and faithfulness and weariness. . . ."[47] It does not matter what one calls Mangan's sister: she is the imaginary Mercedes of *A Portrait;* she represents all the things that Dublin does not.

When books fail to provide relief from the oppressive atmosphere, he is drawn to the girl, who attracts him with the "soft rope of her hair," as with a noose. He is torn between a natural predilection for escape to the solitude of his romantic dreams, on the one hand, and the necessity of compromising with the world of reality in which his ideal love moves. For her the narrator is willing to go through the mundane motions of requesting a few shillings, taking a train ride, and so forth, in order to enjoy the ideal beauty promised in the name "Araby." The romance that the name breathes is synonymous for him with the romantic dreams he harbors of his future with the girl. But the disappointment that actuality holds out for those who expect too much is harsh.

Reality provides no fabulous wonderland. The end of the

journey and the object of the quest is a makeshift bazaar—and the narrator arrives too late, just as it is closing for the night. In the same way, the boys in "An Encounter" find their trip to the Pigeonhouse blocked by approaching night. The narrator remarks, "I recognised a silence like that which pervades a church after a service," as he finds that "the greater part of the hall was in darkness." It is the darkness of his own street, especially of the deserted house of the priest, which is mentioned at the beginning of the story. It is the darkness of his lost religion. Bitter in his disappointment, the boy snatches at the one consolation that remains to him—the chance to buy for Mangan's sister a trinket in one of the booths still open. Here, however, the imagined rebuff of the indifferent salesgirl and the fragments of a particularly pointless and flirtatious conversation of this woman and her male companion bring him up sharply and show him the falsity of the entire situation in which he is involved. He learns from this epiphany that reality never comes up to life's promise.

In some ways, the Araby bazaar suggests the church and is its symbol. The narrator's quivering eagerness to reach it, his willingness to overcome material obstacles for the joy of attaining his destination, has religious fervor. But the worldly, the trivial, the gross await him at journey's end. The glowing colors with which idealists surround spiritual objects fail to appear. Again, Joyce seems to be saying, the quest for the father, for the Church, has been thwarted by reality. The bazaar turns out to be just as cold, as dark, and as man-made as the gloomy house of the dead priest on his own street. It is almost empty, too, and the only activity going on is the counting of the day's receipts. "The light," says the narrator, "was out." Suggestion through symbols again in this story reveals much more than the "plot" seems to supply.

"Ivy Day in the Committee Room," written before the end of 1905, deals with political decay in Dublin. Against a backdrop of Ireland's political glory in the days of Parnell's ascendancy, Joyce projects his narrative of the decay of contemporary political institutions and politicians. This juxtaposition of the old and desirable with the new and reprehensible in Dublin's political life is a favorite modern technique. Joyce found it especially workable here, as he did on a much larger scale late in *Ulysses*. He sets the time of the story as an anniversary of the death of Parnell, symbolic of the death of principle and moral righteousness in government and the rise of factionalism based on self-interest and mean expediency. By selecting his anniversary, the author is able to focus the reader's attention on both periods at once and thus heighten the meanness by keeping constantly before him the memory of former selfishness. In much the same way, Yeats speaks of "romantic Ireland" as "dead and gone," placing it with the patriot "O'Leary in the grave."[48]

In terms of simple narrative, the story is colorless enough. A group of petty ward workers and political canvassers meet in a bare, hired room and speak of their day's success in rounding up votes for their candidates. Their reminiscences of better days gone by, their backbiting and small jealousies, and their remarks on the campaign—in short, their whole conversation—*is* the story. Though their talk wanders from topic to topic, casually, and appears aimless and undirected, actually it is carefully regulated. So is the descriptive comment by the author. Several of the themes need a closer look.

Constant stress is placed, throughout the story, on the age-youth, father-son motif, which was to concern Joyce so strikingly in his later writings. The replacing of the older generation by the new, which in one sense should be heralded joyously as a sign of progress and fulfillment, is treated dolorously by the exiled artist. This is ironic in a story whose title mentions the ivy, symbol of regeneration. For Joyce can find no encouragement in the rising generation of which he is a member. "Old Jack," with his "old man's face," entitled by his seniority to veneration and respect, is given scant consideration by the young men. Mr. Henchy alone makes the conventional murmur, "O, don't stir, Jack, don't stir," when the old man rises, but Joyce is quick to add that Henchy "sat down on the chair which the old man vacated." Jack discourses at great length upon the worthlessness of his own child, who, in these dissolute times, "goes boosing about." Plaintively he asks, "What's the world coming to when sons speaks [*sic*] that way to their fathers?"

The dependence of son on father is constantly reiterated. Their employer, the candidate from the Royal Exchange Ward, "Tricky Dicky Tierney," is held up to ridicule because his "little old father kept the hand-me-down shop in Mary's Lane." Shortly after that, talk centers on Joe Hynes, who has just left the little circle of politicians. Someone suggests that Joe is a spy for the rival camp. " 'His father was a decent respectable man,' Mr. Henchy admitted. 'Poor old Larry Hynes! Many a good turn he did in his day! But I'm greatly afraid our friend is not nineteen carat. . . .' " Even the teen-agers are flippant and disrespectful to their elders. Mr. Henchy, seeking the support of one youngster, is told: ". . . when I see the work going on properly I won't forget you, you may be sure." The politicians find, when the seventeen-year-old boy who delivers their drinks accepts and drains one of the bottles, that in drink begins the corruption of youth—yet they do not appear to recognize or decry their own major part in this corruption. When the lad leaves, muttering thanks for his drink, the fatal act is laconically recorded: " 'That's the way it begins,' said the old man. 'The thin edge of the wedge,' said Mr. Henchy."

Whatever the reason, the young men of Ireland are not prepossessing. They seem to have been born old. Joyce describes Mr. O'Connor significantly as a "gray-haired young man" and bestows upon him a "face disfigured by many blotches and pimples." He is no more attractive mentally than physically. Lazy, slow-witted, he twice rolls the tobacco for a cigarette "meditatively," but it is only "after a moment's thought" that he "decided to lick the paper." Like Lenehan, of "Two Gallants," he seems able only to agree with remarks made by others and seldom has the inspiration or initiative to make an original statement. Ireland is a country of old men (no matter what their chronological age), of ugly and stupid souls from whose efforts, or perhaps lack of effort, little in the way of spiritual or material regeneration may be expected. It is, in fact, a kind of Hell, peopled by small-time politicians, renegade priests, and sinful youngsters.

"Ivy Day in the Committee Room," to emphasize this point, carries a heavily weighted structure of Hell symbolism. It seems inconceivable that so disciplined a writer as Joyce would mention maybe a score of times the fire, smoke, cinders, and flames on the hearth of the committee room simply to tell the reader that the room contained a fire. These numerous references to the environment of Hell, in the moral context of the story and of the volume, are not the only evidence. They are reinforced by certain seemingly casual remarks, figures of speech, and imagery to which the conventional Christian description of Hell is central. Their profusion implies an impossible series of coincidences or, more probably, a deliberate attempt to evoke in the reader the idea that political Dublin is Hell.

The first sentence introduces the motif: "Old Jack raked the cinders together with a piece of cardboard and spread them judiciously over the whitening dome of coals." Throughout the story, he continues to nurse the fire, fanning it into bright flame when it suits Joyce's purpose to have the room revealed in the glare. By this device, the reader discovers "a leaf of dark glossy ivy in the lapel" of one of the men, which "the flame lit up." The Parnell motif of regeneration is thus introduced against a background of fire. It is interesting to note, too, that, when Mr. Hynes enters the fire-lit room, he asks, "What are you doing in the dark?" Joyce makes it plain that the fire, at that moment, is still burning. Perhaps he is picturing the fire of Hell, as he does in the sermon in *A Portrait,* as flame which, "while retaining the intensity of its heat, burns eternally in darkness."[49]

Continuing the Hell motif, Mr. Henchy refers to the candidate whom they represent and from whom they draw a salary as a "Mean little schoolboy of hell." Also, when the group greets another canvasser coming in to report, its spokesman addresses him: "Hello, Crofton! . . . Talk of the devil." Can it be significant too that the politicians are not able to gain access to their drinks without the aid of the fire, which causes the corks to fly out with an empty "pok"? Frank O'Connor's ingenious explanation for the noisy succession of "pok" sounds is that they represent what has become of the traditional gun salute to Parnell as statesman-hero in the Dublin of "Ivy Day."

It would be strange if, in Joyce's Hell, as in Dante's, there were no sinful clerics. The desire to have an important segment of Dublin life, the priest, represented in the Committee Room calls for the contrived entrance of Father Keon to the fireside circle. The priest is looking for Mr. Fanning, the campaign treasurer, who is not present. He leaves, and that is all there is to the incident. His appearance and departure do, it is true, provide food for half a page of cynical discussion on Keon's clerical status and means of livelihood. He may be, as Stanislaus Joyce believes, an unfrocked clergyman, or perhaps he still retains his clerical authority. But Joyce's displeasure is plain. The priest is "very thick" with the treasurer and spends much time in pubs with him. This blend of religion, drink, and politics qualifies the priest for a place in the Hell of the Committee Room.

The author's descriptive comments support such an assignment. "A person resembling a poor clergyman or a poor actor appeared in the doorway . . . it was impossible to say whether he wore a clergyman's collar or a layman's. . . ." In a story about Parnell there is an obvious double meaning to these seemingly innocent lines; Joyce is pointing up the thin line that separates, or does not separate, the religious from the secular in his Dublin. He is stirring up the raging controversy over the right of the Catholic clergy to take part in influencing a state election. The priest admits, indeed, that he has come to see the treasurer of a political group on a "little business matter." This admission is especially damning since the whole incident of Keon's brief appearance follows immediately a discussion of Irish traitors like the infamous Major Sirr who would "sell his country for fourpence." Joyce's conversational narrative only *seems* to wander in "Ivy Day."

The decade or so that had passed since the death of Parnell had dissipated all but the last vestiges of the enthusiasm for a cause which his presence generated. The question of money for political services rendered is paramount: "Has he paid you yet?" is repeated in various guises until it becomes deliberately annoying. Mr. O'Connor voices the favorite sentiment of the group when, speaking of Tierney, he says, "I wish he'd turn up with the spondulics." The shoe boy will sell his vote for money. Father Keon goes into conference with the treasurer. The candidate himself evades his proper obligation by putting off questions concerning payment. Graft, it is hinted, plays a large part in the election of city officials. And those municipal officeholders are judged not by their actions in government but by the shabby display that they make: "What do you think of a Lord Mayor of Dublin sending out for a pound of chops for his dinner? How's that for high living?" A far cry from the steadfast single-mindedness of the Parnell era, at least when the earlier period is seen through the roseate haze of time and a national myth.

With Hynes's reading of his almost doggerel poem commemorating Parnell's death, Joyce gets his chance to sum up implicitly the contrast between the glory that had been and the present tawdry circumstances. The reading of the sincere but poetically decayed poem that seeks in vain to recapture that fleeting glory is another good example of epiphany. What could have been a lame and sentimental ending becomes, through a fine balance of parts and proper timing, a moving symbol of decay.

The poem, neither better nor worse than many of the patriotic journalistic pieces in Duffy's *Nation,* and according to Stanislaus Joyce a parody on Joyce's first published work, *Et Hu, Healy!*, is poor poetry, questionable politics, and sentimental rhetoric. That its effect should be powerful, in spite of these defects (or maybe because of them), is testimony to the strength of the Parnell legend. Joyce might well have had in mind such an audience as his own father, Mr. Casey, or his uncle, heartbroken, frustrated followers of their "dead king." Beyond the political implications, the poem is also indicative of the decay of taste in aesthetics, in religion, in journalism that prevailed, or so he felt, in Joyce's Dublin. It is what makes old Jack, a representative of a happier day, exclaim: "God be with them times! . . . There was some life in it then."

There is some evidence of social decay—and the cheapening of personal relationships—in "Ivy Day," but Joyce chose to concentrate his attention on this strain of Ireland's paralysis in stories like "Two Gallants" and "Clay."

The story "Clay" shows most clearly the operation of symbolism on several levels simultaneously.[50] Though a quick reading may deceive the reader into thinking that the sketch concerns nothing more than the frustrated longings of a timid old maid for the joys of life, a husband, children, and romance, careful examination leads to discovery of interesting patterns. All the social relationships in the story, for instance, are awry. Maria should be married but is not. Alphy and Joe, though brothers, fight continually. Mrs. Donnelly strives to keep peace in the family by calming her drunken husband. The laundresses quarrel often. The saleswoman in the cake shop is impudent to the most inoffensive of customers. The young men on the tram will not rise to give her a seat. And even the innocent children are half accused of stealing the missing cakes. Through this maze of human unpleasantness moves the old maid, Maria, a steadying and moderating influence on all those who have dealings with her.

Her role as peacemaker is stressed. In the Protestant laundry, she "was always sent for when the women quarrelled over their tubs and always succeeded in making peace." Her employer compliments her on her ability as mediator: "Maria, you are a veritable peace-maker." Her calm moderation alone keeps Ginger Mooney from using violence against the "dummy who had charge of the irons." "Everyone," says Joyce, "was so fond of Maria." And rightly so. Her tact prevents a family quarrel over the loss of a nutcracker when she quickly says that "she didn't like nuts and that they weren't to bother about her." Though she does not wish a drink of wine offered by Joe, she "let him have his way." Maria's function as peacemaker, dovetailing as it does with a great many other details of the story, suggests the hypothesis that Joyce intended to build up a rough analogy between the laundry worker Maria and the Virgin Mary. Along certain lines, the relationship is fairly obvious.

Maria, of course, is a variant of the name Mary. Certainly there is nothing subtle about the associations that the name of the main character evokes. The Virgin is well known for her role as peacemaker, for the invocations to her, especially by women, to prevent conflict. Accordingly, she is invoked ("sent for") whenever the laundresses argue and she "always succeeded in making peace." Without her restraining and comforting influence, much more violence would occur. There is surely a suggestion of the church in Maria, for, like Mrs. Kearney and the two sisters, she offers a form of Communion to the women by distributing the barmbracks (raisin bread) and beverage.

Carrying the analogy further, Joyce makes much of the fact that Maria is a virgin. At the same time, and this is significant, she has children, though they are not born from her womb. "She had nursed . . . [Joe] and Alphy too; and Joe used often to say: 'Mamma is mamma but Maria is my proper mother.' " There would seem to be no reason, in a very short story, to quote Joe directly here unless more was intended by the author than the bare statement that Maria had aided his mother in bringing up her sons. There are additional Biblical parallels too. In the Gospel according to Luke, it is Elizabeth who announces to Mary that she is blessed and will have blessed offspring. Interestingly enough, in "Clay" it is Lizzie (Elizabeth) Fleming, Maria's co-worker in the laundry, who "said Maria was sure to get the ring and, though Fleming had said that for so many Hallow Eves, Maria had to laugh and say she didn't want any ring or man either. . . ."

Other similarities crowd in to lend support to the idea. Maria works in a laundry, where things are made clean; Mary is the instrument of cleansing on the spiritual plane. All the children sing for Maria, and two bear gifts to her on a Whitmonday trip. That one gift is a purse has ironic meaning in Joyce's mercenary Dublin. The laundress finds her appearance "nice" and "tidy" "in spite of its years," perhaps a circumspect way of saying that, after centuries, the freshness of Mary as a symbol is still untarnished. On the other hand, Maria finds on the tram that she is ignored by the young men and in the bakeshop treated insolently by the young girl. Only the elderly and the slightly drunk treat her with the respect which she enjoys but which she is too timid to demand. The meaning for Joyce of this situation needs no spelling out. The fact, finally, that Maria gets the prayer book, in the game of the three dishes, and is therefore slated to enter a convent and retire from the world is additional evidence of the author's symbolic intent.

Joyce is not content, however, with working on this single level. He has accomplished one purpose. Just as in *Ulysses* the juxtaposition of the heroic age and the human—of wily Odysseus and sly Leopold Bloom—serves to point up the contrast between the glory that was Greece and the mundane sphere that was Dublin for the artist of 1900, so the superimposition of modern Maria upon the ancient and venerable symbol of Mary is aesthetically effective. Now he goes a step beyond.

The story, originally entitled "Hallow Eve," takes place on the spooky night of the thirty-first of October, "the night set apart for a universal walking abroad of spirits, both of the visible and invisible world; for . . . one of the special characteristics attributed to this mystic evening, is the faculty conferred on the immaterial principle in humanity to detach itself from its corporeal tenement and wander abroad through the realms of space. . . ."[51] Putting this more bluntly than Joyce would have wished, Maria on the spirit level is a witch on this Haloween night, and as a traditional witch Joyce describes her. "Maria was a very, very small person indeed but she had a very long nose and a very long chin." To fix this almost caricature description in the minds of his readers, the author repeats that "when she laughed . . . the tip of her nose nearly met the tip of her chin." And two sentences further on, he reiterates the information for the third time, and for a fourth before the story is through. The intention is very plain. In addition to these frequent iterations, Joyce's first sentence in "Clay"—and his story openings are almost always fraught with special meaning—discloses that this was "her evening out." By right it should be, for witches walk abroad on Allhallow Eve. In itself, however, implying that the old woman is a witch is of minor significance. It derives fuller meaning from the illusion-reality motif.

This motif is central to the story, gives it, in fact, its point.

Halloween is famous for its masquerades, its hiding of identities of celebrants, conjuring tricks, illusions of goblins and ghosts—in other words, famed for the illusions that are created in the name of celebrating the holiday. It is a night on which it is hard to tell the material from the spiritual, witch from woman, ghost from sheeted youngster. On this night, things are not what they seem.

In the first paragraph, Joyce touches gently upon the motif more than once. Maria's work in the kitchen is done. Barmbracks have been prepared. It is legitimate to wonder whether the baking was done in accordance with this Irish custom: unmarried girls would knead a cake "with their left thumbs. . . . in mute solemnity; a single word would have broken the charm and destroyed their ardent hopes of beholding their future husbands in their dreams after having partaken of the mystic 'dumb-cake.' "[52] The finished barmbracks "seemed uncut; but if you went closer you would see that they had been cut into long thick even slices and were ready. . . . Maria had cut them herself." The contrast between the illusion of wholeness and the reality of the actual slices is given prominent mention only because it belongs within the larger framework of the motif. Also, in the same paragraph, the cook delights in the cleanliness of the big copper boilers in which "you could see yourself," another reference to illusion, possibly connected in Joyce's mind with the Allhallow Eve custom of looking into a mirror to see one's future husband.

In other respects, also, the spirits are at work in this story. Things, as things, lose their materiality and become invisible. At least they are missing and cannot be found. The plum cake disappears. "Nobody could find the nutcrackers." Finally, Joe trying to locate the corkscrew, "could not find what he was looking for." Maria herself is ambiguous, sometimes more a disembodied spirit than a person. Her body, though it exists, is "very, very small," and a hearty burst of laughter grips her "till her minute body nearly shook itself asunder." On this night she is able to get outside her body, almost, and look at it objectively: "she looked with quaint affection at the diminutive body which she had so often adorned . . . she found it a nice tidy little body."

It is in dreams, however, that Maria is able to put the greatest distance between illusion, namely, the love and adventure which have never entered her life, and reality, the drab, methodical existence of a servant in a laundry. Or if not in dreams, in the reverie induced by a dream song, "I dreamt that I dwelt in marble halls." The whole story builds up to this central split, at which point all the minor examples of the thin line between fantasy and actuality attain meaning and stature. In these rich and sensuous lines, sung in a "tiny quavering voice" by Maria, are packed the antitheses to the frustrating life of the average Dubliner. Mary in contemporary life has decayed in scope to Maria and is no more imposing a spiritual figure than a witch on a broomstick. The marble halls have been converted into laundry kitchens. Most tragic of all, there is no one in the world to whom the old maid can, with truth, sing "that you loved me just the same." In Maria's rendition of the song, she inadvertently omits the second and third stanzas and carelessly sings the first verse twice. Joyce emphasizes that "no one tried to show her her mistake." Little wonder that her audience remains tactfully silent about these missing verses:

> I dreamt that suitors sought my hand
> That knights on bended knee,
> And with vows no maiden heart could withstand,
> They pledged their faith to me.
>
> And I dreamt that one of that noble band
> Came forth my heart to claim,
> But I also dreamt, which charmed me most,
> That you loved me still the same.

Maria's error is probably attributable to an emotional block that prevents her from giving voice to remarks so obviously at variance with the reality of her dull life. Leopold Bloom suffers a similar lapse when of Boylan's affair with Molly he speaks of "the wife's admirers" and then in confusion adds, "The wife's advisers, I mean."[53]

Joyce's decision to change the title of the story from "Hallow Eve" to "Clay" shifts the emphasis from the singing of the song to the ceremony of the three dishes. This familiar Irish fortunetelling game requires blindfolded players to select from a group of traditional objects the one which, so the story goes, will be symbolically revelatory of their future life. Poor Maria puts her fingers into a dish which the thoughtless children have jokingly filled with clay. She is to get neither the prayer book (life in a convent) or the ring (marriage). Death is her fate. There is a subdued shock when even the insensitive people present at the Halloween party realize the symbolic significance of selecting clay as an omen of things to come. Joyce, leaving nothing to chance, has earlier prepared the reader for the symbolic action by showing that Maria is half in love with easeful death: "She had her plants . . . and she liked looking after them. She had lovely ferns and wax-plants. . . ." The emblems of the Virgin Mary, it is interesting to note, are unlike the others, late-flowering plants and late-blossoming trees.

Joyce was a very young writer when he wrote "Clay." He seems uncertain where to place the emphasis, and perhaps he allows too many motifs, even though a tenuous connection among them does exist, to deflect from the central point of his narrative. Perhaps he has not sufficiently reinforced the relationship between the witch and the Virgin, though the history of the church holiday actually establishes all the parallel background he needs: the day set aside in honor of saints (like Mary) by Boniface IV has had its eve perverted by celebrants to the calling forth of witches. The two supernormal female figures, the saint and the witch, share this holiday. The writer who was soon to wrestle with the intricacies of interlocking symbolic levels in *Ulysses* was in "Clay" learning his trade. The result is a much more complicated story than commentators in the past have discovered.

In the B.B.C. magazine, *The Listener* (March 25, 1954), Stanislaus Joyce takes issue with such "scientific" explication of the early works of his brother as has been attempted in this chapter. He attacks particularly an "American critic," undoubtedly Magalaner, who "finds in the short story 'The Clay' [*sic*] three levels of significance on which Maria is successively herself, a witch, and the Virgin Mary." He continues:

> Though such critics are quite at sea, they can still have the immense satisfaction of knowing that they have dived into deeper depths than the author they are criticising ever sounded. I am in a position to state definitely that my brother had no such subtleties in mind when he wrote the story. In justice, though, I must say that exaggerations like those I have mentioned are not typical of American criticism . . . .[54]

This type of personal-acquaintance criticism is understandably dangerous. What family of a deceased writer has not felt that blood relationship and lifelong closeness afforded deeper insight into the writer's work than detached criticism could? This is a natural and healthy family tendency; yet the results, as evidenced in authorized biographies and critical studies by sons and grandsons and nephews of nineteenth-century literary greats, are generally regarded with amusement or dismay by today's scholars. One should respect such prime sources of biographical information, but, at the same time, one may suspect critical judgments enunciated by such sources as the last word, on, say, literary symbolism.

Stanislaus Joyce admits that *Ulysses* was "intended by its author" to have "various levels of significance." One wonders whether, if Joyce had not "leaked" his intention to Stuart Gilbert and others, Stanislaus would not be insisting equally on the "pernicious" quality of explications of that novel. It is very difficult to be sure of Joyce's intentions in his poetry and short stories, as it is in *A Portrait*. Eugene Jolas records how "Joyce blanched" when Jolas guessed merely what the title of *Finnegans Wake* was to be. "Ah, Jolas, you've taken something out of me," was the author's sad reply.[55] It is quite possible that the earlier Joyce might have been toying with the idea of multiple symbolic levels in the works before *Ulysses* without discussing his unformulated plans with his younger brother.

Much more compelling than these vague speculations is the internal evidence of the early works themselves. In *A Portrait*, after building up the image of Cranly as a schoolmate on one level, and on another as John the Baptist, Joyce finally tells the reader specifically, and with no chance of misinterpretation, that Cranly is "the precursor." Had he not stated his intention on almost the last page of the book, it is reasonable to assume that Stanislaus Joyce might have resisted such a farfetched interpretation bitterly. It should be remembered that the Cranly-John parallel was being worked in by Joyce very shortly after the time that *Dubliners* was completed. Or consider once again, for a moment, "The Sisters," which the present writer was fortunate enough to examine in its three successive drafts. Either Joyce is losing his aesthetic sharpness and his sense of economy and proportion as the drafts progress or he is incorporating at least one important page that can be justified on no other ground than its symbolic significance. Stanislaus accepts in "Grace" the presence of a parody structure of the *Divina commedia,* apparently because Joyce told him that it was there, but he would probably ridicule the reliance of "Araby" on Dante's *Vita nuova.*

Our position is, in short, that nobody, not even a brother, is "in a position to state definitely" that a writer did not have certain "subtleties in mind" when he wrote this or that work. He may express his disbelief—and his closeness to the writer entitles his opinion to be considered seriously—but he should not seek by fiat, as Thomas Gradgrind does in Dickens' *Hard Times,* to stifle the faculty of wonder and speculation in readers.

For "The Background to 'Dubliners,' " supplied by Stanislaus Joyce in this article, all students should be grateful, though again they may quarrel with his interpretation of the significance of the facts. He explains that he and his brother James were the adolescent adventurers of "An Encounter" and that the events of the story really happened. Mr. Duffy, of "A Painted Case," is Joyce's idea of what Stanislaus would become in middle age. Stanislaus tells us that Joyce got most of the factual information about committee rooms and politicians from him, for Stanislaus once worked as clerk for a municipal candidate. Most of the article concerns the origin of "The Dead."*

This final story in *Dubliners* represents Joyce's most highly developed and artistic use of the short story medium and of symbols prior to *Ulysses.* Much of the impressiveness of the story comes from its noble theme, easier to feel than to identify precisely. David Daiches defines it as "a man's withdrawal into the circle of his own egotism, a number of external factors trying progressively to break down the walls of that circle . . ." and the final breaking down from within and within.[56] Stanislaus Joyce speaks of "The Dead" as "the final chorus of the book . . . a story of ghosts, of dead who return in envy of the living. . . ."[57] Finally, Allen Tate, in his most discerning analysis of the novelette, calls it a treatment of the "great contemporary subject: the isolation and frustration of personality."[58] All these attempts at definition are necessarily

* William York Tindall's *The Literary Symbol* (New York: Columbia University Press, 1955), contains an excellent, concise explication of "The Dead" (pp. 224-28). Tindall's analysis agrees at most points with the one presented below but includes, in addition, new corroborative insights.

inconclusive because what Joyce is saying cannot be fixed in a formulated phrase.

The death motif may be said, however, to stand out above the others in importance, for it supports all the other themes. It is puzzling how a critic can have been so insensitive to the pervasiveness of imagery of death in the story as to say, "there is only one dead person in it and he is not mentioned until near the end. That's the kind of trick an Irishman . . . would play on us. . . ."[59] Equally undiscerning is the remark of another critic that the artistic purpose of giving in detail the long description of the dinner party is simply to make Gabriel Conroy wait longer for his wife's love in their hotel room.[60] The many pages, apparently of prelude to the main action, must have their full exposition, partly to allow presentation of Gabriel's reactions to different situations but mainly to give the author scope to develop his motif of death.

Though the story takes place at Christmas time, when the mind is turned to birth and beginnings, the air of deadness and decay in the description of the "gaunt house" and of its ancient owners, the two maiden aunts of Gabriel (and of Joyce), penetrates the surface warmth and lushness of the special banquet preparations. Hints of the faded glory of family fortunes and the frankly faded inhabitants of the mansion add to the impression that the reader is watching the stiff gyrations of long dead souls.

The dead overshadow much of the conversation at the party and after, with emphasis on the fact of human forgetfulness of those who die. In lighthearted jest, when he wishes to eat his dinner undisturbed, Gabriel asks that the guests "kindly forget my existence"[61] for a few minutes. Ironically, these words take on a deeper meaning later when a chastened Gabriel sees unmistakably that that is exactly what will happen to him, to everyone, eventually. When the talk turns to opera singers and musicians of an earlier day, "Tietjens, Ilma de Murzka, Campanini, the great Trebelli," the younger guests cannot recall even the names of the great:

> 'For me,' said Aunt Kate, . . . 'there was only one tenor. . . . But I suppose none of you ever heard of him.'
>
> . . . . 'His name,' said Aunt Kate, 'was Parkinson. I heard him when he was in his prime . . . .'
>
> 'Strange,' said Mr. Bartell D'Arcy. 'I never even heard of him.'[62]

Then the conversation veers to an order of Trappist monks,

who sleep in their coffins "to remind them of their last end." The party over, and transportation home being the problem, they speak of "The never-to-be-forgotten Johnny," their father's dead horse, whom Mr. Browne has already forgotten. The tenor Bartell D'Arcy sings of "The Lass of Aughrim" in words which tell that "My babe lies cold." Gabriel communes with the dead by nodding at and saying good-by to the statue of Daniel O'Connell, as the cab drives by the figure of the deceased liberator. These frequent references to the dead are crystallized in three ways in the novelette: in Gabriel's after-dinner speech, in his wife Gretta's story of Michael Furey, and in the symbol of the snow.

Gabriel's speech concentrates on the relationship of past and present, accentuating, as do most of the stories, the bleak contrast. His hope that "in gatherings such as this" will be kept alive "the memory of those dead and gone great ones whose fame the world will not willingly let die"[63] sounds hollow, coming after the section in which the guests fail to recall the great singers of a few short years earlier. In such tragic ironies as this "The Dead" is steeped. The speaker waxes eloquent upon the "sad memories" of "absent faces" but philosophizes bravely that one must not brood over the dead. "Therefore, I will not linger on the past." Before the night is over, a shade from the past will return to haunt him, to destroy the complacency of his marriage relationship and to give him a lesson in false egocentricity.

The memory, stronger than a ghost, of Michael Furey, evoked for Gretta Conroy by a ballad, is the final shock that the tottering ego of Gabriel cannot bear. That a dead boy, one who worked "in the gasworks," should alter even slightly the relationship between his wife and himself is unthinkable at first. But then, beside this figure of romance that Gretta's meager description conjures up, he sees himself as "a ludicrous figure . . . a nervous, well-meaning sentimentalist. . . ."[64] What the successive but petty assaults upon his ego of Lily's rebuff, Miss Ivors's insulting banter, and even his wife's evasion of his attentions have failed to accomplish entirely this crowning defeat has brought about. The skill with which Joyce handles the dramatization of the Michael Furey episode has been analyzed acutely by Allen Tate.

The aftermath of his wife's disclosure is a period of severe soul-searching by Gabriel, who has never before been able to decide what his wife was a symbol of. Now he realizes that she stands for romance, a romance denied to their marriage by his stodginess and fussiness, the concrete expressions of an overweening ego. "So she had had that romance in her life: a man had died for her sake. It hardly pained him now to think how poor a part he, her husband, had played in her life."[65] His aging appearance gives him reason to shudder at the thought of slowly fading and withering "dismally with age." Rather than that, he wishes to become a shade "boldly" as the young Michael had, "in the full glory of some passion." The wide difference between Furey's love and the lust which he himself has felt earlier in the evening comes to disturb his peace. But most disturbing of all the sensations that beset him is the consciousness of his own loss of identity in a "dissolving and dwindling" world. Like Michael Furey, of whose very existence he had been unaware two hours earlier, he too is drifting slowly toward impalpability, toward oblivion.

Joyce, sometimes directly, often symbolically, extends his remarks on the meaning of death beyond *Dubliners* to the later books. Young Stephen, thinking of his own illness and of Parnell's death, in *A Portrait,* ruminates:

> But he had not died then. Parnell had died. . . . He had not died but he had faded out like a film in the sun. He had been lost or had wandered out of existence for he no longer existed. . . . not by death, but by fading out in the sun or by being lost and and forgotten somewhere in the universe![66]

With much less naïveté, mature Leopold Bloom thinks of Parnell at Dignam's funeral: "Gone at last. People talk about you a bit: forget you. Don't forget to pray for him. Remember him in your prayers. Even Parnell. Ivy day dying out. . . ."[67] It is Stephen Dedalus himself who puts his finger on the theme of the Gabriel Conroy story. Discussing his theory of Hamlet in the library episode of *Ulysses,* the Irish Telemachus, "with tingling energy," demands: "What is a ghost? . . . One who had faded into impalpability through death, through absence, through chance of manners. . . . Who is the ghost from *limbo patrum,* returning to the world that has forgotten him?"[68]

As the symbolic representation of oblivion and death, the figure of the snow plays its part. Joyce's use of the snow as symbol throughout the story is perhaps the main reason why the narrative rises above the commonplace of realistic portrayal and assumes a poetic cast. His use of the snow symbol, furthermore, changes at various stages of the tale, making for a fuller utilization of the possibilities of the universal image. Gabriel is introduced to the reader as he is "scraping the snow from his goloshes." "A light fringe of snow lay like a cape on the shoulders of his overcoat." He is thus physically covered with the cold substance, and in his own words, "I think we're in for a night of it." The initial impression one gets of the protagonist is of a man overly concerned with protecting himself and his possession, namely Gretta, from the snow by an excess of outer clothing, mufflers, and the ever-intruding galoshes. " 'Goloshes!' said Mrs. Conroy. 'That's the latest. Whenever it's wet underfoot I must put on my goloshes.' " If this oversolicitousness to avoid sickness and worse be coupled with the fact that cold and snow are universally accepted as concrete representations of death, may it not be said with justice that Gabriel's attempt to ward off death is the symbolic keynote of the beginning of the story?

Conversely, Gabriel's petty attempts to keep himself and his loved ones from all contact with living nature may certainly be interpreted as a desire to shun life. Excessive care for outer garments, insistence upon galoshes, a wish to escape contact with water, snow, cold air—all these point to a desire to avoid what life in this world offers. As Tindall has pointed out, Joyce has used this water (snow)-life symbolism often enough to leave no doubt of its applicability here.[69] In *Chamber Music* it is used in a general sense. The uncle of the boy narrator in "The Sisters" advises cold baths (contact with life) for the secluded, introverted "Rosicrucian," his nephew. Stephen, in *A Portrait*, enjoys watching his companions swim, but, being an exile from direct contact with life, will not enter the water himself. In *Ulysses*, Stephen speaks of his fear of the water and will not, in fact, take a bath more than once a month.

Joyce's most unambiguous example of this symbol at work is the mysterious "chap in the macintosh," who, unknown to the other mourners, attends Dignam's funeral. He comes uninvited. He is characterized only by the macintosh which he wears—a garment whose purpose is to keep off from the body any contact wtih water (life). Thus, he represents death. Bloom senses this: "Mr Bloom stood far back, his hat in his hand, counting the bared heads. Twelve. I'm thirteen. No. The chap in the macintosh is thirteen. *Death's number* [italics mine]. Where the deuce did he pop out of?" In many ways, the shadowy man in *Ulysses*, whose macintosh has the same symbolic value as Gabriel's galoshes, is the antithesis of the ambiguous Good Samaritan in "Grace." The latter, though he also enters the group of bystanders, unknown and unheralded, immediately calls for water. He uses his good offices to bring the dazed Tom Kernan back to life.

In "The Dead," as the action proceeds and Gabriel meets rebuff after rebuff to his powerful but nervous egocentricity, the life-death ambiguity seems to resolve itself. The alteration is reflected in his new attitude toward snow and cold. In a passage undoubtedly of more than passing descriptive importance since the author repeats it in substance twice, this change is recorded: "How pleasant it would be to walk out alone, first along by the river and then through the park! The snow would be lying on the branches of the trees and forming a bright cap on the top of the Wellington Monument. How much more pleasant it would be there than at the supper-table!" In the second reference to the snow outside, which occurs just before he makes his after-dinner address, he thinks of people "standing in the snow . . . gazing up at the lighted windows. . . . The air was pure there. In the distance lay the park where the trees were weighted with snow. The Wellington Monument wore a gleaming cap of snow. . . ."[70] Now, if we extend the figure of snow as death, it would appear that Gabriel, without knowing it perhaps, is little by little seeking the purity and peace of a death and oblivion which, physically, he actively rejects. But why the mention of the monument? It is, of course, a prominent landmark of Dublin. More than that, however, the monument is eminently, if somewhat tritely, suitable as a phallic symbol in the context of the narrative, just as Nelson's pillar is phallic in the "Aeolus" episode of *Ulysses*. Like Dylan Thomas, though with no such formal system as basis, Joyce is always equating love and death in his Dublin. It is quite probable that Gabriel's unconscious longing for snow-death should be bound up with his recollection of the phallic symbol of sexual love, now covered with a cap of cold, bright snow. This phallic identification seems especially likely since Joyce, in *Finnegans Wake,* makes use of the "big Willingdone mormorial tallowscoop" in Phoenix Park with similar intent.[71]

Before the heat of Gabriel's lust, the cold disappears on the journey to the Gresham Hotel. Gabriel thinks only of Gretta and his need for her. His feverish mood is soon dispelled by the story his wife tells of early love and Michael Furey. In bed, he feels that his "soul had approached that region where dwell the vast hosts of the dead." It is when he feels "his own identity . . . fading out into a grey impalpable world . . . dissolving and dwindling" that the snow image reasserts itself and overwhelms everything else in sameness and death. "He watched sleepily the flakes, silver and dark, falling obliquely against the lamplight. The time had come for him to set out on his journey westward." Here the identification of snow with death is explicit. And still the snow continues to fall "faintly through the universe and faintly falling, like the descent of their last end, upon all the living and the dead."[72] Bloom puts it simply, "No one is anything."

Beneath this blanket of snow-death, all men lose their identities, or, to put it another way, all identities are of similar appearance. Beneath it, Gabriel's selfishness is smothered and his personality may emerge anew. "In 'The Dead,' Joyce is attempting to show the change from a wholly egocentric point of view, where you regard the world as revolving round yourself to a point of view where your own personality is eliminated and you can stand back and look disinterestedly on yourself and on the world. . . ."[73]

Joyce's handling of the snow, both as descriptive detail and as symbol simultaneously, is one strong reason for the success of the story. Recognizing that the snow changes from a "hostile force of nature" at the beginning to a "symbol of warmth, of expanded consciousness," which he equates to Gabriel's breaking out of his own ego, Allen Tate, in his analysis, lets it go at that.[74] Undoubtedly he is correct. The question is whether he has said enough.

"The Dead" proved to Joyce that he had carried his kind of short story as far as it would go. He had outgrown a form that he had developed to a high point of excellence. He needed more spacious fields in which to roam than those afforded by the limited area of the short story or even of the novelette. Though he had tried to stick with the prose form which had, in his own opinion, served him well, and had even tried to send Mr. Bloom into the literary world as the Mr. Hunter of a short story, he was discerning enough to see that he was getting beyond the scope of contributions to *The Irish Homestead*. Like Yeats, like Eliot, without abandoning the advantages of the outgrown form, he was able to extract from it what he needed and to build on it a new and different kind of novel that was to travel far beyond Dublin, or even Europe, to astonish the world.

The most interesting item of criticism which has thus far appeared on *Dubliners* tries to prove that *Dubliners* is, in fact, *Ulysses* in miniature—or at least an early attempt by Joyce to superimpose the heroic framework of the *Odyssey* on the epiphanies of paralyzed Dublin. Richard Levin and Charles Shattuck make an elaborate case for this "First Flight to Ithaca."[75] Proceeding from Joyce's remark that he had first thought of the title "Ulysses at Dublin" for his volume of short stories and from his insistence that the order of the stories be undisturbed by editors, the collaborators find the first half of the *Odyssey* echoed in the tales, with "The Dead" an analogue of the final scene.

Since the essay is available in the Givens collection, it is necessary here only to sample the method. The commentators mention "Clay" as one of the simplest, and it will be appropriate to consider it. The visit of the laundress Maria to the family of her former employer on Allhallows, with her choice of the saucer of clay and her pathetic song, "I dreamt that I dwelt in marble halls," constitutes one of the most successful scenes in *Dubliners*. One would doubt that Odysseus's descent into Hades was prefigured, though the occasion and the suggestions of the prophecy suggest it. Like Ulysses, Maria has been separated from loved ones. Her fears that Joe might be drunk parallel his concern over the journey. She is encouraged by the matron (Circe), and departs in the rain, as Ulysses did in tears, on a train (ship), in two journeys, carrying food offerings and arriving in the rain. Joe, the man of the house in which Maria used to work, as the only male in the story must do "multiple symbolic duty" as Agamemnon, Minos, Achilles, Ajax, and Tantalus. Both Maria and Ulysses are greeted on arrival; both have failed in a duty (to bring the plum cake, to bury Elpenor), but both receive portents of the future. Maria's song, "a most ingenious Odysseyan recall," expresses the mood of Ulysses at the end of his visit.

This rather farfetched, though possible, Homeric interpretation has been much pursued but little commented upon in print. Students seem unwilling to take a position with regard to its thesis: that Dubliners contains "far more obvious and far greater concentration of Homeric references than . . . *Ulysses*."[76]

The authors of the article are rightly careful not to insist upon too rigid a parallel relationship between the events of the *Odyssey* and those described in *Dubliners*. Even Stuart Gilbert's painstaking analysis of Homeric parallels in *Ulysses*, carried out with Joyce's active co-operation, did not go that far. But Levin and Shattuck do suggest "that Joyce was operating under some structural compulsion more exacting than any he chose to reveal" in planning and executing the contents and order of the volume of short stories. They base their contention not only on Joyce's predilection for the wily Greek as hero but primarily upon "Clues . . . in his correspondence with his prospective publishers: in his insistence upon printing certain 'objectionable' stories, or, if they be omitted, upon stating in a preface that the 'book in this form is incomplete'; in his insistence that the stories be printed in an exactly specified order . . . ."[77]

There exists, however, an unpublished letter from Joyce to publisher Grant Richards that casts considerable doubt upon the strength of evidence based on this line of investigation. On May 20, 1906, Joyce sent to the publisher one of a long series of letters calculated to lessen the differences between them concerning the suitability for inclusion of certain words and phrases in the offending manuscript of *Dubliners*. "I have agreed," says Joyce, reasonably, "to omit the troublesome word in *Two Gallants*. To omit the story from the book would really be disastrous. It is one of the most important stories in the book." So far, the quotation would seem to bear out the contention of Shattuck and Levin that Joyce was fighting to retain Homeric parallel structure. The very next sentence, however, seems conclusively destructive of that hypothesis. Joyce continues, "I would rather sacrifice *five* of the other stories (which I could name) than this one."[78] It seems distinctly unlikely that, if "structural compulsion" were the spur, the author would be offering flatly to eliminate one third of the entire completed volume of fifteen stories. Yet there is little doubt, in the context of the letter, that the offer is genuine and sincere. "Two Gallants," the story for which Joyce is willing to make the sacrifice, moreover, is finally published by him out of the normal sequence of its Homeric counterpart—"the only violation of Homeric order in the book."[79]

This is not to say that the entire thesis of the article is disproved by a sentence but simply that its validity must be based on other grounds. It is dangerous to ascribe to Joyce a consistent pattern of analogy in any book. As William York Tindall and Richard Ellmann have indicated, Joyce seldom has any intention of creating continuous allegorical or analogical representations.[80] Instead, painting in bold strokes, he may portray Stephen Dedalus as possessing, for the moment, Christlike attributes, or the narrator of "Araby" as Telemachus. But even in *Ulysses,* his most obvious and ambitious excursion into structural parallels, the result is deliberately ragged and imperfect, for prodigious talent is disdainful of artificial barriers.

The attempt of the authors of "First Flight to Ithaca" to demonstrate such structural compulsion leaves them frequently embarrassed at the necessity of explaining discrepancies in emphasis, tone, order, and detail on the basis of Joyce's artistic intention. Such an argument leads to the practice of pointing out parallels triumphantly where the details fit and of having to discover convenient but inconclusively established stylistic devices at work (*i.e.*, deflation, inflation, paradox, and so forth) to explain inconvenient lapses in the pattern. Yet even if the presence of Homer in *Dubliners* is dubious, the thought that it may possibly be there is salutary, for it acts as a caution to those who consider the short stories too slight and flimsy to merit detailed study.

If additional evidence were required to prove the complexity and depth of young Joyce's creative imagination at the time he was writing *Dubliners,* one has only to compare the sprawling manuscript of the autobiographical novel that he had gotten under way by 1906 with the modified and refined *Portrait of the Artist* that was its end product.

Chapter 5

A Portrait of the Artist as a Young Man

FROM ITS FIRST APPEARANCE, the *Portrait* was recognized as a work of genius, the finest of the contemporary confessional novels. The courage of the author, his fresh style, his uncanny psychological insight, his command of dialogue marked him as the most promising novelist of his generation. In view of the timidity of the English printers, it is surprising that Joyce was so widely accepted. The book had appeared in *The Egoist* from February 16, 1914, to September 1, 1915. Miss Harriet Weaver, sponsor of Joyce and an editor of the magazine, told of the difficulties of securing an English printer.[1] The result was that after publication in New York in 1916, American sheets were bound and issued in England in 1917.

Of course there were those who lamented Joyce's addiction to the "revolting by-paths" of naturalism, though conceding his "undoubted power."[2] He seemed "unpleasantly precocious," his work "A Study in Garbage," "A Dyspeptic Portrait," the pageant "of a tortured liver," the coarseness of which mars its "uncommon beauty, descriptive power and insight"; it is "Realism Run to Seed," a "brilliant and nasty variety of pseudo-realism."[3] Yet even these opponents conceded the power and skill of the novelist. Possibly the most characteristic reaction is that of *The Irish Booklover,* which lamented the fact that "a master of a brilliant descriptive style" and one as skilled in dialogue "as any living writer" should so "jar on one's finer feelings:"

> Oh! the pity of it. In writing thus is he just to his fine gifts? Is it even wise, from a worldly point of view . . .? Above all, is it Art?[4]

Few were as unperceptive as the reviewer for the *Knickerbocker Press,* who "could not tell what he was driving at" and who was so "intensely" bored as to conclude that the book "as a whole means nothing." *The Bellman* mocked it as an example of the confessional novel, wherein the hero,

The notes to Chapter 5 begin on page 331.

"moody, sensitive, pessimistic and a trifle daft . . . in a vain and tortuous search for the thing he should do, does an amazing number of things . . . he should not do—arguing, from start to finish, on all conceivable subjects." This type of novel is "no better in an Irish guise than it has been in any other."[5] Yes, it can still be as entertaining to quote the more extreme blunders now as it was for *The Egoist* editors in 1917, classifying them under such headings as DRAINS ("we feel he would be really at his best in a treatise on drains") or OPPORTUNITIES OF DUBLIN (Ernest Boyd's complaint that Joyce was blind to the better side of the city). *The Irish Booklover's* questions concerning the advisability of writing esoterically was captioned WISDOM. *The Sphere*—ADVANTAGES OF IRISH EDUCATION—had promised to find half a dozen graduates of Clongowes Wood, including Sir Arthur Conan Doyle, who have become "most conventional citizens of the Empire."[6] It is entertaining, but it perpetuates one of our most sentimental myths—that of the misunderstood genius, mocked in the marketplace.

More frequent was the recognition of genius. The Italian critic Diego Angeli, whose comments Joyce himself translated for *The Egoist,* characterized Joyce as "a new writer with a new form" and with "new aims" that make the work "the first streak of the dawn of a new art."[7] Others noted that his "extraordinary gifts," originality "almost to the extent of appearing foolish," mark Joyce as "amongst the few great masters of analytic reminiscence."[8] His originality is found to be "almost overwhelming"; the work "would give distinction to any list of contemporary fiction in any country"; particular scenes—the Christmas dinner, the sermon—are "comparable with the best in English literature."[9] The *New Statesman* found that "Nobody is surprised to find all writing London talking about this book." Joyce is "already known as a finished artist," and the dialogue, descriptions, and images make the *Portrait* "the most exquisite production of the younger school" and, indeed, "the most authentic contribution to English literature" in some time.

Joyce's uncompromising sincerity was almost universally noted. The author W. N. P. Barbellion exclaimed in his diary, "James Joyce is my man . . . a writer who tells the truth about himself." He admired the "candour and verisimilitude" and added, "I wish I could discuss James Joyce with someone." Joyce's "naked truthfulness," "sincere intent" and "unconquered though ingrowing and indeterminate idealism," and "fine Irish veracity" make the work "terribly honest," "one of the most remarkable confessions outside Russian or French literature."[10]

The author's psychological vividness is no less remarkable; indeed, *Medicine and Surgery* found it the most striking of the book's many qualities. For as "a close and searching study of mental processes" it is "of surprising worth," revealing "a man's life such as you know . . . to be true." The author is "not only a writer of the first rank but an analyst of human character whose knife is dexterously handled." The surgical metaphor will recur in reviews of *Ulysses;* it gives rise to a debate that still continues. J. C. Squire rather inconsistently accused him of an olfactory preoccupation—he "can never resist a dunghill"—and yet found his detachment "almost inhuman." A more reasonable resolution of the inconsistency was that of *The Irish Times,* which suspected that "undoubtedly a personal animus" lay "behind the author's ostentatious detachment." The fact that the tone is "so uniformly depressing" makes one doubtful of the book's veracity, but Stephen is a type "unfortunately common to Dublin," and the book's value lies in its "extraordinary power in presenting a real problem." In his taste for the unpleasant, Joyce has an "almost Russian naïveté." Even Zola, with his "keen pig's nose," only registered nasty smells, but Stephen actually liked them, *The Dublin Review* noted.[11] H. G. Wells also found "a cloacal obsession," though it did not prevent him from praising the work. It is Well's phrase, incidentally, that Joyce answers in *Ulysses,* where Professor MacHugh links Roman and English imperialism in that they bring to every conquered shore sanitary conveniences.[12]

Joyce's break with the church came in for its share of attention. *The Catholic World* found occasion to moralize on the hero's apostasy, though it granted the book's vividness. The "irresistible effect of sharp, first-hand reality" is acknowledged. The hero himself is an enigma, with the main contrast that of a "manner of self-sufficiency and cold acuteness" joined to a basic "irrationality of motive." Stephen's self-love finally leads to a paradoxical conclusion, causing "this apostle of self to speak of finding freedom when he has left truth at home."[13] The indictment is not so unsympathetic as it might seem. Joyce later called Frank Budgen's attention to his own ironical treatment of Stephen: "Some people . . . forget that it is called *A Portrait of the Artist as a Young Man.*"

Most early readers took Stephen's troubles seriously and

identified him with the author as a "man of a soul," possessing, as Ernest Boyd wrote, "an uncontrolled horror and detestation of the circumstances which moulded and governed his life." His idealism is "unconquered though ingrowing and indeterminate"; he is, in the words of the *Manchester Guardian,* a "Sensitivist," who, though helpless, is "keenly concerned for intellectual experience and for a faith" and who is unique among modern heroes in having "a genuine sense of sin." Though supine, Stephen carries within himself the possibility of conquering his weaknesses, in which case a man and an artist would emerge "from the lounger."[14]

Francis Hackett and Ernest Boyd approached the novel from their own experience of Irish life. To Hackett its significance was in disposing of the myth of Irish wit and irresponsibility and in revealing "the inevitable malaise of serious youth" with "tenacious fidelity." Boyd termed it "the chronicle of a soul stifled by material and intellectual squalor" but thought it unfair to the finer aspects of Dublin life. For the problem is basically that of the lower middle-class Catholic:

> Culture for him is represented by the pedantries of mediaeval metaphysics, religion by his dread of hell. Left to drift abjectly between these extremes Stephen Dedalus disintegrates. . . .

American readers likewise felt it a valuable portrait of the true Irishman, "proud, critical, idealistic, hating everything English" or, as another reader put it, "strange, proud, imperious, secret and, subtle-minded."[15] Joyce's Dubliners are "people under a blight" having "something of the frowsiness, the shabbiness, the dirtness of Dublin"; the same critic had "never seen a religion so unspiritually presented":

> The author knows the theology but if there's any soul in it I cannot discover it.[16]

James Gibbons Huneker saw Joyce's affinities with Chekhov, Maupassant, and Huysmans but found him "an Irishman, who sees the shining vision in the sky." Yet he is "too Irish to be liked by the Irish."[17] Though chary of direct expression, Joyce reveals "the greatest contempt for a social organization which permits so much vileness to flourish"; he explains "how we breed and develop our Stephen Dedaluses, providing them with everything they crave, except the means of escape from the slime which envelops them." The book is "redolent of the ooze of our shabby respectability, with its intolerable tolerance" of such conditions. H. G. Wells found it to be "the most living and convincing picture . . . of an Irish Catholic upbringing," whereas Padraic Colum saw more sensitively the essential Catholicism of Joyce's mind:

> Even in the way the book is written there is something to make us think of the Church—a sense of secrecy, of words being said in a mysterious language, of solidity breaking into vision.[18]

The newness of the words, the freshness of the style caught the attention of most critics. *The Scotsman* noted Joyce's mastery of hypnotic suggestion, "a rare skill in charging simple forcible language with an uncommon weight of original feeling." Joyce has surpassed *Dubliners* in "the genius which welds naturalism, realism, and the imaginative." The prose has such mastery that "even his most casual descriptions haunt the mind." As a stylist he is almost unequaled, particularly for his sentences "with many facets, transparent, full of meaning."[19]

Ezra Pound emphasized the authentic economy of Joyce's style, "the nearest thing to Flaubertian prose" in current English, with no padding of "pages of slosh." There is a curiously "seductive interest" in such "clear-cut and definite sentences." Even the seemingly objectionable has its aesthetic purpose:

> I have yet to find in Joyce's published works a violent or malodorous phrase which does not justify itself not only by its verity but by the heightening of some opposite effect, by the poignancy which it imparts to some emotion or to some thwarted desire for beauty.[20]

Joyce, "the best prose writer of my decade," joined Wyndham Lewis and Eliot in making "the most important contribution to English literature of the past three years," indeed, as author of one of the few works that show creative invention.[21]

In Mencken's characteristically trenchant words, "a Joyce cult now threatens," following the rage for Dunsany. The Irish have contributed to the stodginess of English literature "a gypsy touch, a rustic wildness, a sort of innocent goatishness." One of the first to remark the music of the Anglo-Irish idiom, Mencken found that any page of Synge or Dunsany shows "how they have retaught the tone-deaf Sassenach how to write *pour le respiration et pour l'oreille.*" The magic of their imagination is seen in the contrast between Dunsany, where "A deer cavorts in the forest, a horn winds, it is the springtime of the world," and Phillpotts, who "suggests a cow munching alfalfa in a stall." The *Portrait,* "sure in its effect and original in its method," is "new both in plan and in detail."[22]

The ideas behind this newness appear to have come upon Joyce rather suddenly, for the early draft of *A Portrait* shows little of the imaginative daring of the final version. Published as *Stephen Hero* in 1944, the manuscript that survives deals only with Stephen's life after he has entered University College. It includes, therefore, merely the ground covered by the final chapter of the *Portrait.* Yet, even from the fragment that remains, it is easy to see how much more conventional, discursive, explicit, and unsubtle is the early draft as compared to the latter. Theodore Spencer, the editor of the manuscript, has described clearly the specific differences—changes from one draft to the other that show Joyce's increasing awareness of the value of concentration, impression, symbolic suggestion, and, for want of a more appropriate term, musical prose.

If the *Stephen Hero* manuscript had been published unrevised by its author, it might well have been titled *A Photograph of the Artist as a Young Man,* for in it is not the essence of Stephen-Joyce distilled from autobiographical chaos but a series of candid camera shots from the author's album. These, presented in frankly polemical prose, retain intact, as do photographers' proofs, the unretouched awkwardnesses of life, interesting and meaningful, but not yet subject to the restraints and modifications of patterned art. One incident seems as important as the next—a walk with Maurice, the death of Isobel, charades at the Daniels. And each receives the full treatment, the copious development it might have expected from Dickens or Dreiser—or from a disinterested photographer taking somebody else's wedding photographs.

In this early draft, also, Joyce had not yet given himself over to the impressionist technique that so distinguishes *A Portrait.* He still introduces each new character in his fictional autobiography with ample, conventional descriptive words. Those characters who fail to impinge themselves with sufficient force on the delicate recording apparatus of Stephen's consciousness are not allowed, in *Stephen Hero,* to become vague shadows, colorless backdrop for the protagonist. Later, in the *Portrait,* all such people, even Emma, lose their characteristics as human beings to become fixed as a gesture, a distinctive phrase, a provocative foil surrounding Stephen and becoming the external instrumentality of his actions. Thus, the teacher of Gaelic hardly exists for the reader of *A Portrait*. But in the early manuscript he is introduced with all the fanfare of John Galsworthy introducing Soames Forsyte or Thomas Mann describing Frau Consul Buddenbrook:

> The teacher was a young man in spectacles with a very sick-looking face and a very crooked mouth. He spoke in a high-pitched voice and with a cutting Northern accent. He never lost an opportunity of sneering at seoninism and at those who would not learn their native tongue. He said that Beurla was the language of commerce and Irish the speech of the soul and he had two witticisms which always made his class laugh. . . . Everyone regarded Mr. Hughes as a great enthusiast and some thought he had a great career before him as an orator. . . . he often spoke but as he did not know enough Irish he always excused himself at the beginning of his speech for having to speak to the audience in the language of the . . . "Spiritual Saxon." At the end of every speech he quoted a piece of verse. . . .[23]

This introduction of the unimportant Mr. Hughes continues for many lines beyond this excerpt and reveals Joyce, in the tradition of *Dubliners,* still in the "telling" stage. This stage is, of course, of great importance to scholars of Joyce in filling in gaps in biography and autobiography, but it represents to Joyce's *Portrait* what detailed pencil sketches are to the finished painting of a master.

Harry Levin believes that the whole manuscript of *Stephen Hero* came to about one thousand pages. Indeed, the fragment of the final chapter of *A Portrait* that survives in the early manuscript is about as lengthy as the entire published *Portrait*—five chapters in all. Like Thomas Wolfe, though without the help of a fatherly editor, Joyce had to learn to prune, to cut, to distill the essence from the words that flooded to his pen. Even Joyce remarked of *Stephen Hero:* "What rubbish it is."[24]

But *A Portrait,* as eccentric as it may have seemed to critics during the early years of this century, could not lightly be dismissed as trivial. Trying to make something of it, however, proved as difficult then as reading the *Wake* is today. Attempts in various magazines demonstrate the plight of reviewers. It is "rather a study of a temperament than a story." Making "no coherent whole," the book is "almost a literary curiosity"; realism is blended "with a hazy impressionism which leaves the reader constantly uncertain whether he is being given an account of an actual happening or . . . of a phantom passing through the brain of Stephen." Yet, ventures another writer, "when you understand what he is doing it is very easy to follow and very fascinating." Unity is attained "less by the sustained sequence of his ideas than by the pregnancy of the individual utterances."[25]

Francis Hackett attributed the work's vividness to its subjectivity, the art of "communicating the incidents of Stephen's career through the emotions they excited." Not by an even lighting, but by fitful illuminations, is the meaning revealed; to use the metaphor of a Liverpool reviewer:

> A book which flashes its truth upon one like a searchlight, and a moment later leaves the dazzled reader in darkness.[26]

Stephen's mind is a mirror that intensifies as it reflects and gives to his experiences "the unwilled intensity of dreams." And the seemingly "hither-and-thither" method becomes "a complete and ordered thing" because of the "subtle sense of art" that has worked "amidst the chaos."[27]

Joyce must be understood as an impressionist or postimpressionist. In Diego Angeli's perceptive review, which may have been inspired by Joyce, just as the critiques of Budgen, Gilbert and the *transition* group were, it is pointed out that attackers have missed "the subtlety of the psychological analyses" and the "value of certain details and certain sudden arrests of movement." The work should "break down the tradition of the six shilling novel"; its "brushwork . . . reminds one of certain modern paintings in which the planes interpenetrate and the external vision seems to partake of the sensations of the onlooker."

With the natural advantage of forty years of further development in the technique of the novel, the modern critic is well able to understand and sympathize with those who tried to cope with *A Portrait* before 1920. Realism blended "with a hazy impressionism" was unexpected. When an author like Joyce began by revealing specifically the intimate details of his childhood, the reader was prepared for straight documentation in the Zola manner. And, to be sure, the book contained a careful record of actual names, dates, and places in the approved naturalistic way. Students at Clongowes Wood during Joyce's time had, indeed, included Roche, Saurin, Cecil Thunder, the MacSwiney brothers, and even Wells, who had shouldered Stephen into the ditch. Paddy Rath and Rody Kickham had dined in the refectory with Stephen, and "one of the best [cricket] partnerships was J. M. Magee, captain 1891-92 and Mr. William Gleeson, S.J.," the latter being the master in charge of flogging miscreants. In fact, so precise is Joyce's description of his days at school that "the Spaniard who was allowed to smoke cigars" may be identified as José Arana y Lupardo of Bilbao, Spain, a student at Clongowes from 1890 to 1892, and the "little Portuguese who wore the woolly cap" as Francisco da Silva Ruas, a later registrant.[28]

The reviewers could understand all this. They could also handle satisfactorily such frankly hazy works as Yeats's *Shadowy Waters* or Maeterlinck's *Pelléas et Mélisande*. But a combination of the implicit and the explicit, the realistic and the impressionistic/symbolic raised obstacles. How justify the great gaps in the narrative from the statement of the moocow theme in sentence one to the playground scene at Clongowes, years later, on page two? Or the fusion into one elusive ideal love of the images of mother, Eileen, Mercedes of the Monte Cristo story, "the beautiful Mabel Hunter," and the rest? Or the pervasiveness of green and red all through the first chapter—in the brushes, the geography book with "earth green and the clouds maroon," the holly and ivy at Christmas time, and Dante "in a maroon velvet dress and with a green velvet mantle . . . walking proudly and silently past the people who knelt by the waters' edge."[29]

The realist-impressionist novel seemed strange and daring in 1918. That all action, even the most realistic situations, should be sifted ostensibly through the consciousness of the protagonist before being transferred to the page by the author meant an alteration in the task of the reader. The author, no longer omniscient and omnipresent, was now bound to record only what impressed itself as significant on the mind and emotions of his central character. If that meant a gap of three years here, five years there, in the action, so be it. The author had to restrain his wish to tell all, to aid his audience with Dickensian asides. He had to become in theory merely the instrument of the hero he had created. Actually, it goes without saying, the success of each such experiment in fiction varied directly with the skill and the sensitivity of the author in manipulating his protagonist so that, out of the welter of raw impressions that go into making an existence, the novel should highlight those best calculated to provide significant fictional form. It was Joyce's talent to do this surpassingly well.

The method of impressionism may be dangerous in its tendency to encourage vague outlines and absence of clear pattern. If the consciousness of a human, and therefore imperfect, protagonist is to be taken as the touchstone of relevance in a fictional work, then the work may theoretically wander as far afield in its structure and substance as the vagaries of its fallible hero. To replace the comfortable, traditional mold of chronological narration of objectively recorded events, the author must find a device which, while it does not violate the impressionist stream, will provide a measure of cohesion, continuity, and firmness in which discrete impressions merge to become pervasive themes.

Joyce's device in *A Portrait* is the motif—the expressive reiteration of an action, a situation, or a speech, which eventuates in the emergence of a significant pattern of meaning or feeling essential to the unity of the novel. Sometimes the motif is scarcely noticeable, and yet it operates below the threshold of awareness. At other times the motif may be insistently present in the consciousness of the reader (*i.e.*, the red and the green imagery of the first chapter) without the reader knowing precisely what to make of the theme or what to do with it.* Certain motifs, finally clear in their significance, frequent in their occurrence, need little critical exegesis to be felt and understood by the average reader.

Hugh Kenner, in his excellent article, "The Portrait in Perspective," points out that the motifs introduced on the first page or so of the book contain the germ of all that Joyce

* William York Tindall's book, *The Literary Symbol,* contains a brilliant analysis of Joyce's method of using symbols and "relatively unassigned and unattached images that concentrate feeling at important points." Professor Tindall illustrates his point (pp. 78-86) with special reference to *A Portrait.*

had to say in *A Portrait* and in each of his subsequent novels.[30] To trace one of these motifs in its various appearances through the book should demonstrate its value in cementing together the often discontinuous narrative blocks.

Joyce introduces the motif on page two:

When they were grown up he was going to marry Eileen. He hid under the table. His mother said:

—O, Stephen will apologise.

Dante said:

—O, if not, the eagles will come and pull out his eyes.—

Pull out his eyes,
Apologise,
Apologise,
Pull out his eyes.[31]

Thus, even in early childhood, Stephen is revealed as guilty of an unspecified crime possibly related to sex (". . . he was going to marry Eileen") or to religion (Eileen is a Protestant) or simply to disobedience of constituted authority (his mother and his governess). Authority demands that he admit the alleged error of his way or suffer the painful consequences. In this first reference to the motif, as Kenner mentions, Prometheus is undoubtedly suggested: first, because of his awful torment at the hands of the authority he had defied (Stephen's eyes are more vulnerable than his liver, so the Promethean punishment undergoes alteration); second, because in stealing fire from the gods, Prometheus performs literally Stephen-Joyce's later act of taking creative inspiration from its mysterious source. So much for the initial statement of the motif.

Only two paragraphs later, a variation of the motif is presented. Stephen, at Clongowes, is questioned by an older boy, Nasty Roche:

What is your name?

Stephen had answered: Stephen Dedalus.

Then Nasty Roche had said:

—What kind of a name is that?

And when Stephen had not been able to answer Nasty Roche had asked:

—What is your father?

Stephen had answered:
—A gentleman.
Then Nasty Roche had asked:
—Is he a magistrate?[32]

This sharp question and answer routine, suggesting in its definiteness a familiar catechism, reinforces the motif of apology for a hazy guilt that outsiders feel Stephen ought to exhibit. Always troubled by questions about his father in later boyhood, he is even at this early period brought to the point at which he must remain silent or confess that his father is not what he might be—a keenly felt reflection on the young boy himself. It is interesting, considering Joyce's care in selecting names for his characters, the Roche ("rock," in French) may well represent the church here putting the questions—and a "Nasty" Roche at that.

Several pages further on, Stephen again feels a sense of sin and guilt when questioned by Wells on whether he kisses his mother every night before he goes to bed. The "other fellows" laugh when he says that he does and redouble their laughter when, in confusion, he says that he does not. Once more, the little boy feels guilty when society singles him out for questioning, scorn, and ridicule. He "blushed under their eyes" and wondered, "What was the right answer to the question? He had given two and still Wells laughed." In the climactic scene of Chapter 1, Stephen is questioned by Father Dolan, here the actual representative of the Catholic Church, and then punished for a crime of which he is innocent—a crime, to reinforce the motif, that involves punishment for having weak eyes. When summoned from his seat in the classroom to be beaten by Dolan, Stephen stumbles, "blinded" by fear and haste. At the blow of the pandybat upon his hand, "A cry sprang to his lips, a prayer to be let off. But . . . he held back the hot tears and the cry that scalded his throat." Stephen, the embryo artist and rebel, will not "Apologise" even when the world seeks to "Pull out his eyes." Stephen kneels on the floor, ironically out of fear and pain inflicted by the father rather than from adoration. He has not knuckled under to the pressures of his hostile environment.[33]

Numerous further instances of the prevasiveness of this motif might be adduced, but two or three additional examples should suffice. In high school at Belvedere, Stephen's schoolmates twit him about his ascetic ways, his father, and his girl friend. When he does not readily confess his latest love affair, he is playfully hit with Heron's cane until he jestingly recites the *Confiteor* to the reiterated beat of the admonition, "Admit." These same "friends" belabor him, more in seriousness than in jest, for refusing to allow, in a literary catechism, that "Byron was no good." Again he is tormented, like St. Stephen by the mob, for sticking to his beliefs. Again, the refrain is "Admit." To avoid an open clash, he is forced to confess his error in theology on an English composition, when questioned by Mr. Tate. Most dramatic, perhaps, is Stephen's confession to the old priest of his sins of the flesh—a terrified outburst occasioned by the long, dreadful sermon on Hell, which develops in macrocosm the motif of "Apologise/Pull out of eyes" enunciated in microcosm at the beginning of *A Portrait*.[34]

With powerful motifs such as this—or the theme of mother-lover-church or exile and flight or the religion of art and the dedication of the artist—running through the book to give it substance and form, there is little need for the step-by-step nursing that Galsworthy or Arnold Bennett so skillfully supplied for their readers. Relatively few in *A Portrait,* and comparatively simple, these themes increase and multiply, twine and intertwine, to form the narrative meshes of *Ulysses* and the *Wake*. The intellectually apprehended motifs of his *Portrait* become the elaborate musical and rhythmical and multi-leveled symbolic fabric of Joyce's maturer works.

Yet it is not too much to say that even in *A Portrait,* as in *Dubliners*—both preparatory exercises for the books to follow—the author left little to chance. The marks of his consummate control are evident in every line. From the name of Betty Byrne (compounded of Elizabeth as mother of John the Baptist and of Byrne, real name of Cranly, who in *A Portrait* is identified as the precursor)[35] to the characterization of Simon Moonan as today, no name or fact seems too unimportant to escape Joyce's obsession for total relevance. One case in point demonstrates how this compulsion may work toward the strengthening of a key motif.

Near the end of Chapter 2 of *A Portrait,* Joyce makes the offhand remark that with "the money of his [school] prizes," Stephen Dedalus "led a party of three or four to the theater to see . . . *The Lady of Lyons*."[36] This is the first and last mention of Bulwer-Lytton's play in the book, although the name of the main character of the romance appears once, two pages farther on.[37] A synopsis of the plot of this casually mentioned play gives little hint of the use to which it is to be put by

Joyce. Pauline Deschappelles, a proud beauty, scorns marriage for money or for the sake of acquiring a title. Her rejected suitors plot to humble her by tricking her into marriage with a social inferior, Claude Melnotte, the son of a gardener. Melnotte, just returned from Paris where his father's legacy has allowed him to learn Latin, dancing, fencing, and the other arts, is the darling of the village. Though he wears fine clothes and looks like a prince, he hides his love for Pauline because he is conscious of his social handicap as a gardener's son. He watches his unattainable heroine from afar, sends her flowers anonymously, and finally dares to send her his poetry, which she rejects violently.

Insulted, Claude joins the conspiracy to force Pauline to wed beneath her station. She falls into the trap, but before the marriage his true love for her makes him unwilling to carry the plot to its end. His cohorts, the rejected suitors, insist, and the two are joined. Pauline discovers the fraud, spurns his attentions, and is allowed to retain her virtue. After several further turns of the plot, Claude goes off to battle to forget his part in the shameful affair. He returns rich and powerful several years later to find Pauline about to marry one of the suitors in order to save her father from bankruptcy. Having made his fortune in the wars, Claude is able to pay the debt, save his love from a fate worse than death, take revenge on the wicked suitors, and carry off the prize as the curtain comes down.

This is as unlikely a story with which to fortify a motif as one can find for an author who, above all, abhorred the sentimental and the banal. But just as Joyce found use in the Nausicaä episode of *Ulysses* for such a mood as a foil for the contrasting mood of Leopold Bloom, so in *A Portrait* Bulwer-Lytton's play has its appropriate place.[38]

Joyce had used the motif of the unworthy adolescent lover before in the "Araby" story of *Dubliners*.[39] There the boy narrator watches his beloved from afar, not daring to submit the ideality of his illusion to the soiled world of reality. In that story also there is the desire to bear gifts to his love—to seek adventure so that he may be worthy. In "Araby" Joyce hints at the ideal love of Dante for the ideal abstraction of Beatrice.

In *A Portrait,* the motif suggested by *The Lady of Lyons* is subordinate to, but on a plane parallel with, the theme of *The Count of Monte Cristo*. The latter serves as one of the unifying threads of the impressionist narrative. Its motif deserves separate treatment, which cannot be offered here except in brief allusion. Stephen is shown poring over a "ragged translation of *The Count of Monte Cristo,*"[40] which stamps firmly in his mind the "figure of that dark avenger" and of his secret lover, Mercedes, always pictured thereafter as standing in a garden. Stephen's adolescent identification with this avenging shadow, with this heroic lover-adventurer, leads to childish fantasies in which he sees himself a dignified and proud lover, able to refuse with haughtiness and restraint the tribute of Mercedes, "who had so many years before slighted his love." He revels in his imaginary response, "Madam, I never eat muscatel grapes."[41] The restlessness induced by the drab routine of growing up in Dublin sends him "wandering in the evening from garden to garden in search of Mercedes."[42]

The reinforcement of the Monte Cristo theme by *The Lady of Lyons* motif is clear. In both, and for all of Joyce's adolescent heroes, there is the unapproachable heroine against a background of gardens and flowers; the lover whose sense of inferiority prevents him from speaking out; the eventual acquiring of polish, of Continental culture and wealth (or the hope of such acquisition); the turning of the tables that gives the mature lover the opportunity to show his true worth by rescuing the now chastened heroine from difficulty and to "play the dark avenger" to his enemies.

It is obvious that Joyce expected such parallels as have been pointed out to be apparent to his readers. Both the play and the book enjoyed wide popularity among the middle classes in the nineteenth century. An indication of his being able to take this for granted is offered by the casual mention of Bulwer-Lytton's hero, Claude Melnotte, with no further reference to the source from which the hero was being drawn:

> Only at times, in the pauses of his desire, when the luxury that was wasting him gave room to a softer languor, the image of Mercedes traversed the background of his memory. He saw again the . . . garden of rosebushes . . . and he remembered the sadly proud gesture of refusal which he was to make there, standing with her in the moonlit garden after years of estrangement and adventure. At those moments the soft speeches of Claude Melnotte rose to his lips and eased his unrest. A tender premonition touched him of the tryst he had then looked forward to and, in spite of the horrible reality which lay between his hope of then and now, of the holy encounter he had then imagined at

> which weakness and timidity and inexperience were to fall from him.[43]

It is also apparent how inextricably bound up are the two motifs in Joyce's own mind, so that Melnotte and Monte Cristo are interchangeable symbols of a state of feeling.

These "soft speeches" of Claude Melnotte offer considerable further reasons for Joyce's selection of *The Lady of Lyons* as the play to which Stephen, in *A Portrait,* should take his parents and friends. Claude's mother in the play, suspicious of her son's cultural acquisitions from the Continent and of his unorthodox artistic bent, nags him constantly to abandon the ways of the artist and return to honest, normal, lucrative pursuits:

> Leave glory to great folks. Ah! Claude, Claude! Castles in the air cost a vast deal to keep up! How is all this to end? What good does it do thee to learn Latin, and sing songs, and play on the guitar, and fence and dance, and paint pictures? All very fine; but what does it bring in?[44]

Though slightly more florid than the speeches of Stephen's mother, bidding him beware of dangerous authors like Ibsen and urging him to accept a job in Guinness's respectable brewery, these quoted remarks in the play must have carried a familiar note to mother and son. And Claude's "soft" answer is, though embroidered and dated, what we should have expected Stephen to say.

> Wealth! wealth, my mother!—wealth to the mind—wealth to the heart—high thoughts—bright dreams—the hope of fame—the ambition to be worthier to love Pauline.[45]

Melnotte's passion for Pauline follows the same pattern as Stephen's for his succession of dream lovers. First he wrestles with an inferiority complex: "Even from this low cell, poverty,—I lift my eyes to Pauline and forget my chains." Then follows the association of the loved one with flowers. "Thou knowest not that for the last six weeks I have sent every day the rarest flowers to Pauline; she wears them. I have seen them on her breast. . . ." Finally, emboldened by apparent success, Melnotte, like Stephen, composes poetry for the lady: "I have now grown more bold—I have poured my worship into poetry—I have sent my verses to Pauline—I have signed them with my own name."[46] Moreover, while Stephen ordinarily does not take overt action to achieve his aim in love, and therefore feels himself defeated, Melnotte, because he takes the step, is rejected utterly.

Yet, despite Joyce's deliberate emphasis on these superficial similarities, Stephen certainly is following a path basically different from the one traversed by such romantic heroes as Melnotte. The irony of the surface comparison, as Professor Charles Anderson has pointed out to the present writer, is underlined by the dissimilar character of their respective dream worlds. Melnotte can push his luck, can hope eventually to get the girl of his feverish dreams, the *ne plus ultra* of his worldly hopes. For Stephen the dream world is dissipated even as it takes form. The woman figure, whether Mercedes or another, is unattainable both as a flesh-and-blood person and as symbolic representation of the church, beckoning him to intimate communion through the sacramental "muscatel grapes," which he must refuse.

Melnotte, Dante, Stephen, Joyce, Monte Cristo—all these figures merge at times, at other times stand apart and operate separately to achieve the literary ends of the author. The story of Stephen's boyhood could have been told without the frequent iteration of parallel motifs. The recognition of such motifs, however, affords to the reader a control of the narrative, both intellectual and emotional, impossible in single-leveled fiction. Understanding this, Joyce strives to make every word count, both for itself and for the surrounding context.

Such intensive verbal concentration, however, has meant a quarter century of neglect of the real meaning of *A Portrait*. Early commentators like Gorman hailed it as the pioneer in "impartial recording of the subconscious mind." But Gorman accepts it as entirely autobiographical and values it solely on the basis of realistic accuracy. To Charles Duff the *Portrait* and *Dubliners* "pale into insignificance" in relation to the later work. Louis Golding found only "a sense of prelude," and though he reads it largely for autobiographical detail, he notes Joyce's use of motif.

It was not until Joyce's death, and the subsequent assessment of his entire career, that the novel was more fully understood. Harry Levin's study[47] relates the autobiographical novel to the tradition of European realism, and its offshoot in the story of the artist, where Mann, Proust, and Gide make significant contributions. Symbolism enters by way of Stephen's name, as protomartyr and as the mythical experimenter with flight and creator of the labyrinth.

An artist of Joyce's artistic precision would naturally select a name for his main character with special care. The appropriateness of the name Stephen Dedalus has many times been commented upon, but the choice bears further emphasis. Joyce's view of the artist as isolated and exiled, misunderstood by his neighbors and consequently vilified by them, would have made the association with St. Stephen—martyred and stoned to death by a mob—a natural one, even without the further reinforcement afforded by the location of Stephen-Joyce's school on St. Stephen's Green. But Joyce needed more than the association with a misunderstood martyr. "Daedalus" suggested Dedalus and the hero of *A Portrait* and *Ulysses* was clothed in a fabulous name, suggestive of his classical-Christian background. Now, implicit in the name alone, the protagonist became the mythical artificer, the wise father as well as his inexperienced son. Where Daedalus had created wings with which to escape from the labyrinth on the island of Crete, Stephen Dedalus would seek escape as a creator of art, would fly like Keats on the wings of poesy, beyond the nets that another island had thrown up to keep her sons ever imprisoned in the maze of contemporary Dublin. If anyone doubted the autobiographical implications for Joyce, he would have only to note the pseudonym Joyce signed to his early *Dubliners* stories in *The Irish Homestead,* a combination of Christian martyr and hawklike artist—"Stephen Daedalus."

Since the whole book points toward the selection of a calling by the hero—to enter the church and celebrate the soul or to leave it in favor of the celebration of the things of this world in art—the dramatic resolution of that conflict is made the high point of the novel. Here, near the end of the fourth chapter, the storm abates. The sin and guilt of an insecure childhood and a fear-ridden adolescence, the failure of the strict regimen of forced piety and devotional rituals (Chapter 3) are, at least for the time being, no longer important considerations for the young man who now knows what he wants. At this point, at which his main interest is no longer the art of religion but the religion of art, the realistic and symbolic levels of the narrative achieve their most obvious union. "Now, at the name of the fabulous artificer, he seemed . . . to see a winged form flying. . . . What did it mean? Was it a quaint device opening a page of some medieval book of prophecies and symbols . . . a symbol of the artist . . . ?" Now he crosses, really and symbolically, a succession of bridges over Dublin streams as, significantly, "A squad of Christian Brothers" crosses in the opposite direction. And as he crosses "the bridge over the stream of the Tolka," he can turn his eyes "coldly . . . towards the faded blue shrine of the Blessed Virgin." In his determined mood, he requires only a sign, not heavenly this time, that his new faith in profane creation is justified. Such assurance is offered to his eager being by the appearance of the girl on the beach.[48]

The sense of joy in his new vocation and the sense of beauty of the episode—the crucial event of the book—is rendered in prose of rhythmic and euphonic loveliness, as rare and fragile as the incident it describes. As Stephen walks along the beach anticipating the revelation, he is "alone and young and wilful and wildhearted, alone amid a waste of wild air and brackish waters and the seaharvest of shells and tangle and veiled grey sunlight. . . ." The girl, when she appears, exudes a fragile beauty that draws from the hero "an outburst of profane joy." "Her bosom was as a bird's, soft and slight, slight and soft as the breast of some darkplumaged dove. But her long fair hair was girlish: and girlish, and touched with the wonder of mortal beauty, her face."[49] It is as if Joyce's (and Stephen's) elation with the calling of art had spilled over to bathe the objective statement of the transition in an exemplifying glow. This is one reason why the last chapter of *A Portrait,* devoted to the formation of Stephen's intellectual attitudes—mainly the aesthetic—often appears anticlimactic and fragmentary. That Joyce planned it that way in anticipation of its function as a bridge to *Ulysses* is certain. But for the reader concerned only with *A Portrait* there is a question of artistic symmetry and shape in Chapter 5 that seems to have no ready answer. One may speak of the power of deflation, of the frustrating close, of the staccato entries on the last pages as balanced by the babyish prose of the first section. The fact remains that after Chapter 4 *A Portrait* apparently runs steadily downhill. Yet the motifs require the final chapter for their culmination and for the establishment of the bridge to *Ulysses*. This may help to explain the unusual amount of "talk" and of explicit intellectual conceptualizing near the end of *A Portrait*.

An exciting explanation of the symbolic meaning of

Chapter 5 is offered by C. G. Anderson, who reads it as an allegory of the betrayal, Crucifixion, and Resurrection of Christ, with Stephen representing "the poet as God—creator, redeemer, and priest." Joyce, says Anderson, gives us the key by identifying Cranly as John the Baptist and hinting at his additional roles of Judas and Satan. If Daedalus is a symbol of the Father and Creator, then Stephen, his son, takes on Christlike proportions. Once the reader gives assent to this emerging religious pattern, the rest follows easily. The final chapter becomes the story of Christ as artist, crucified by family, nation, and church. Fried bread and tea become the Eucharist, the box of pawn tickets is the tabernacle, and the act of Mrs. Dedalus in washing Stephen's ears and head may stand for the washing of Christ by the faithful Magdalene. Anderson goes on to show the organic importance of the hymns mentioned and sung in the chapter; he brings to light traces of the Last Supper, the judgment of Christ by Pilate (Stephen by McCann), and the Crucifixion of Stephen-Christ on the library steps as Emma-Mary stands by in the rain.[50] If one reads the chapter in such a way—and knowledge of the way in which Joyce wrote makes the interpretation more than plausible—there is a temptation to assign the deeper, symbolic climax to the final rather than to the penultimate chapter.

Hugh Kenner, following Levin, sees chains of association not only within the book itself but images that are extended and fulfilled in Joyce's later works:

> . . . the *Portrait* is important not only as an independent work of art but also as a demonstration that the intricate analogical simultaneities of *Ulysses* and *Finnegans Wake* are not irresponsibly excogitated from esoteric reading, but grow out of Joyce's persistent contemplation of intense psychological experience.

Kenner's brilliant elucidation of these analogies must be considered by all who wish to know the root of Joyce's linguistic virtuosity. Moreover, he demonstrates that Stephen's development in each of the five chapters is dialectical; in each stage of his career the young artist triumphs over one obstacle only to reach an unstable equilibrium that must be resolved at the next stage. But when Kenner argues that Stephen is ultimately "insufferable," an "indigestibly Byronic hero," that the fundamental mode is one of irony, one is likely to question the reading. However, Joyce's remarks to Frank Budgen about the title, *"as a Young Man,"* come to mind again and one sees in the Stephen of the *Portrait* something of an anticipation of the proud, humorless, ineffectual character in *Ulysses*.[51]

Following Kenner, Dorothy Van Ghent shows that the interior monologue is ideally adapted to the subjective novel. Stephen's main physical activity is walking. His environment becomes an ever-widening circle of contact with reality; it is paralleled by his mental activity of linking phrases and impressions into large and more coherent wholes.[52] The coalescing of vision and reality occurs in the epiphany, or symbolic showing forth.

There are many types of epiphany, as Irene Hendry has shown. The simplest is the final, integrating episode or situation of the *Dubliners* stories which can also be found in the stories of Chekhov or Mansfield. Of the three terms that Stephen borrows from Thomism, *integritas* or "wholeness," *consonantia* or "symmetry," and *claritas* or "radiance," which in the early *Stephen Hero* draft is linked to the essential "whatness" or thing-in-itself (the *quidditas*), this simple form lacks wholeness and whatness. Revelation without a narrative base, the lyric or subjective vision, is seen in the sudden awareness of birds in flight or a girl on the shore. Here the meaning must be understood through the identity with the character himself. The etherealization of the background characters who appeared in realistic detail in the *Stephen Hero* draft, the conception of characters as essences, is carried out by Joyce's linguistic virtuosity, "the vehicle of the radiant esthetic experience itself." Here is pure *quidditas,* heightened by auditory effect. The fourth, most impersonal type is the physical detail—pandybat, ashplant—that, superficially resembling traditional or Freudian symbolism, is closer to Christian emblematic iconography. Moreover, each work becomes one large epiphany and each is a stage in "a vast Human Tragedy, an epiphany of all mankind"; that is the entire canon.[53]

The distinction of the three qualities of integrity, consonance, and radiance is central to Stephen's aesthetic theory. These qualities correspond to the three levels of apprehension —sensation, analysis, and comprehension—as they do in Aquinas.[54] Indeed, the articles of the learned doctor themselves are labyrinths of objections, counterobjections, and conclusions, providing, as McLuhan has said, "rich esthetic satisfactions by the very dance of his mind." The relation of the intellect to perception is paralleled by that of the artist to experience, the artist being one, according to *Stephen Hero,* "who could disentangle the subtle soul of the image from its mesh of defining circumstances." Moreover, McLuhan continues, "the drama of cognition" is "the key archetype of all human ritual myth and legend," enabling Joyce to introduce the whole of human tradition in relation to the immediate stuff of narrative. Perfecting the insights he derived from Mallarmé by means of his application of Aquinas, "Joyce was at home in all labyrinths," those of cognition, of creation, of the human body (*Ulysses*), "of the river of human blood and immemorial racial consciousness" (*Finnegans Wake*). Cubist landscape and mental labyrinth provide the poles of Joyce's art.[55]

Joyce deviates from Aquinas mainly in his erection of the artist as detached, isolated, indifferent observer, an adaptation of the art-for-art's-sake aesthetics of the time, "a rationalization of contemporary literary tenets on scholastic principles," as Haskell Block has pointed out.[56] For St. Thomas, far from asserting the independence of art, held it to be "subordinate to prudence in the effecting of human ends, and all temporal activity as subject to divine sanction." An article in *The Thomist* points the objection to Joyce's isolation of the aesthetic experience; Stephen's superiors, we recall from *Stephen Hero,* sensed a dangerous tendency toward art for art's sake in his theories.[57]

The well-known distinction among the forms of lyric, epic, and dramatic on the basis of increasing impersonality has been applied by Harry Levin, lyrical in the *Portrait,* epic in *Ulysses,* where, as Joyce has Stephen define it, the entire "centre of emotional gravity is equidistant from the artist himself and from others," and dramatic in *Finnegans Wake.* This attractive thesis has recently been disputed, Ellsworth Mason arguing that Joyce is always dramatic—the highest mode in that it shows the most complete control. Describing Stephen's disquisition as "the attempt of a very cocky young man to establish the extreme limits of his ambition," he argues that the dramatic form, with its emphasis on character rather than plot (epic) or personal emotion (lyric), is what Joyce chose, desiring as he did "to write nothing but the best."[58] One may grant a certain cogency to Mason's argument, especially in view of a reading of the *Portrait* as ironical comedy, and yet feel reluctant to give up the distinctions among the major works.

Joyce, already seeking analogies, indicates the similarity of these forms to the modes of apprehension and the likeness of aesthetic to material creation. McLuhan notes here "a shadow . . . of the procession of Persons in the Trinity" but does not elaborate. Certainly the Trinitarian disputes that occupy Stephen's mind in *Ulysses* are related to the aesthetic process and to the Shakespeare theory in particular. Attacking the impurity of loathing and desire, Stephen sees that the creator attains his highest expression in comedy; it is in presenting his subject "in all its aspects as an image imbued with a kind of serene joy" that A. D. Hope finds Joyce most characteristic and most classical.

In contrast to these thoughtful and provocative discussions of Joyce's aesthetic theory, Stuart Gilbert holds that the theory is but a preliminary clarification of ideas "summarily, almost casually, enounced by St. Thomas," who apparently thought little of art "in any other than a very concrete, obvious way."[59] So too Geddes MacGregor finds much in Joyce's theory to be "extremely superficial" and totally inadequate "to suggest anything so technically clever as *Ulysses*." The much discussed epiphany is little more than "the equivalent of a Crocean 'moment of expression.' " Joyce's love of words, his mania for the cryptic, his richness and versatility are in no way accounted for in his "almost incredibly simple" theory.[60] Haskell Block also concludes that it is "essentially the work of a youth, seeking a liberation that would enable him to create."

More to the point, we feel, is the question of the relevance of extended expositions of aesthetic theories at all in a novel like the *Portrait*. No one would dispute Lynch's complaint that they have "the true scholastic stink." The book certainly could have stood as a finished work of art if the elaborate analyses of the beautiful and the lyrical, say, had not been included. The presence of such passages unquestionably adds to the difficulty of the student's first reading of the story—for the passages demand patience, coming as they do at the end of the final, climactic chapter of the book. All these objections, on the other hand, are grounded in the expectation of literary orthodoxy. Yet the *Portrait*, whatever else it may be, is not orthodox in form. In this impressionistic summing up, the mind of Stephen is the key. To him, his favorite theories are neither embellishment nor anticlimactic asides, nor long-winded mouthings. From the point of view of Stephen, the portrait would be inartistically distorted if the highest point in his intellectual development up to graduation from the university had not been adequately presented. Those who complain that the sermon on Hell could have been conveyed to readers intellectually in a page or so, as well as those who deplore Joyce's "digression" into aesthetics, would do better not to read the novel at all until they are ready for it.

Readers with more orthodox tastes will find readily available a rash of competent novels of adolescence published in the years immediately preceding the appearance of *A Portrait*. We know that Joyce read many of these and found their subject matter applicable to the autobiographical circumstances that he had decided earlier to fictionalize. *The Ordeal of Richard Reverel* and *The Way of All Flesh* meant to his generation what the story of Stephen Dedalus means to ours. But in terms of execution, Joyce saw the need, as Virginia Woolf puts it, of breaking windows.[61] Unwilling to fall in with the discursive trend of later naturalistic novels whose authors spared no words to expatiate on the remotest branches of the hero's family tree, he refused to allot, as Samuel Butler does, a full eighty-six pages of commentary before the main character, Ernest Pontifex, is allowed even to be born. Joyce's Stephen hears about moocows in the very first sentence of *A Portrait*. While it cannot be said that the latter method is, all things being equal, preferable to the former, it must be admitted that Joyce's way offers a more considerable challenge to an author's skill and, at the same time, brings the reader into the picture as an active participant in the experience.

Joyce's method, moreover, by eliminating the omniscient narrator, necessarily eliminates explicit moralizing on man and nature, which Butler and Bennett, for instance, found indispensable:

> Granted that Mr. Pontifex's was not a very exalted character, ordinary men are not required to have very exalted characters. It is enough if we are of the same moral and mental stature as the 'main' or 'mean' part of men—that is to say as the average.
>
> It is involved in the very essence of things that rich men

> who die old shall have been mean. The greatest and wisest of mankind will be almost always found to be the meanest. . . .[62]

One of the climactic scenes in *A Portrait* is Stephen's visit to the Rector of Clongowes to entreat justice after his unfair pandying by Father Dolan. To the little boy the head of the school is an awesome deity whom one approaches with trembling and whose commands bespeak superhuman authority. Stephen receives justice and thereafter enshrines the Rector in his collection of childhood heroes. A short time afterward the boy is present at a dinner table conversation between his father and mother:

> He gave me a great account of the whole affair. . . .
>
> Mr. Dedalus imitated the mincing nasal tone of the provincial.
>
> —Father Dolan and I, when I told them all at dinner about it, Father Dolan and I had a great laugh over it. *You better mind yourself, Father Dolan,* said I, *or young Dedalus will send you up for twice nine.* We had a famous laugh together over it. Ha! Ha! Ha!
>
> Mr. Dedalus turned to his wife and interjected in his natural voice:
>
> —Shows you the spirit in which they take the boys there. O, a jesuit for your life, for diplomacy![63]

And that is all. The irony, the blindness, the understatement are so clear that no subsidiary commentary is called for; its presence could only detract from the power of things left unsaid.

In subject matter, the stories of Ernest and Stephen as boys and young men follow very similar lines of development, not because of conscious borrowing, but merely because the upbringing and school days of middle-class English and Irish boys at the end of the last century evoked kindred memories. Butler recalls the emphasis on prayers—"Before Ernest could well crawl he was taught to kneel; before he could well speak he was taught to lisp the Lord's prayer. . . ." He tells also about the repressions and the whippings and adds: "How was it possible that a lad so trained should grow up in any healthy or vigorous development, even though in her own way his mother was undoubtedly very fond of him, and sometimes told him stories?"[64] It is traditional too that the hero of the novel of adolescence should be sensitive, delicate, different from the other boys. Stephen

> kept on the fringe of his line . . . out of the reach of the rude feet, feigning to run now and then. He felt his body small and weak amid the throng of players and his eyes were weak and watery.[65]

Likewise, Ernest Pontifex

> Was a mere bag of bones . . . his little chest was pigeon-breasted; he appeared to have no strength or stamina whatever, and finding he always went to the wall in physical encounters . . . the timidity natural to childhood increased. . . . After he had had the breath knocked out of him and been well shinned half a dozen times in scrimmages at football—scrimmages in which he had become involved sorely against his will—he ceased to see any further fun in football, and shirked that noble game in a way that got him into trouble with the elder boys. . . .[66]

The schoolboy pattern of Ernest and Stephen is part of a respectable and unremarkable tradition. The shocking difference lies in the way Joyce diverges from the accepted models of style to put his schoolboy in a new frame.

A Portrait is a book that repays frequent rereadings, for its concentration and toughness of texture withhold many rewarding elements from the casual reader. One who wishes to see in Stephen the lineaments of Christlike sufferer will perceive dimly, but not on first reading, that Joyce has arranged the background to support such identification. Cranly, designated almost casually in the diary with which the book ends as John the Baptist ("Then he is the precursor"), has throughout the *Portrait* puzzled the reader by his strange presence. Only Cranly's head seems to impinge upon Stephen's consciousness. "Why was it that when he thought of Cranly he could never raise before his mind the entire image of his body but only the image of the head and face?" He sees his friend as "a severed head or death-mask." In almost every passage in which Cranly is mentioned, only the smile, now guilty, now frank, is described. Again and again he is said to have a "priestlike face, priestlike in its pallor . . . priestlike in the lips . . . the face of a guilty priest who heard confessions of those whom he had no power to absolve. . . ."

Throughout the portion of the book in which Cranly appears, he eats figs as John did. In his wrath, he threatens blasphemers with physical punishment.

> —Give us that stick here—Cranly said.
>
> He snatched the ashplant roughly from Stephen's hand and sprang down the steps: but Temple . . . fled. . . .[67]

He acts as spiritual advisor to Stephen and bears to him roughly the relationship of John to Jesus. All this ground is carefully prepared by Joyce and the announcement of what he is doing is made near the end of the book. Yet even close readers often overlook the whole significant motif. J. F. Byrne, the original of Cranly, himself seems to have missed it. Indeed, forty years have elapsed from the date of publication to the explication of this theme and its relationship to the Betty Byrne of Stephen's babyhood by Julian Kaye.

In a cheap reprint edition, *A Portrait* is now thriving as required reading in basic literature courses at many universities. The initial mystification apparent on the faces of sophomores on their first acquaintance with the book recapitulates the mixed feelings with which the literary public greeted this strange work of art during the First World War. But *A Portrait* has in common with all great novels the quality of giving something of value to all readers, at whatever level. Those who have no patience with mystification can enjoy the naturalistic tenseness of the Christmas dinner episode. Historians find the book, as James T. Farrell has pointed out,[68] a moving, though slanted, sociological document. But the novel offers most to those who, dissatisfied with surface appearances, find rich satisfaction in Joyce's symbolic motifs and see in them the seeds of his later method in *Ulysses* and *Finnegans Wake.*

Chapter 6

Exiles

JOYCE'S SOLE SURVIVING DRAMA, *Exiles,* was composed during the spring of 1914. Gorman considered it the author's "farewell to the past" in that it represents his final allegiance to traditional literary form.[1] As a young man in Dublin at the turn of the century, Joyce naturally evinced great interest in the drama. His "Day of the Rabblement" essay protested the parochial tendencies of the Irish theater, with the directors "shy of presenting Ibsen, Tolstoy or Hauptmann," or even second-raters like Sudermann, Bjornson, and Giacosa.[2] Amateur theatricals enliven the youth of Stephen Dedalus, as did charades for Leopold Bloom and undoubtedly many another late-Victorian Dubliner. The Dubliner has been as much a fancier of the theater and music hall as of the pub or race track. Even late in his career the author was known for his readiness at mimicry or a turn at a *pas seul.* Theatrical attractions—*Leah, The Lily of Killarney,* Marie Kendal, and the comedian Eugene Stratton—occupy the minds of Bloom and his friends in *Ulysses.*[3] The translation of Hauptmann, which Joyce later transferred to Mr. Duffy of the "Painful Case" and the lost play, "A Brilliant Career," are not so important as the author's devotion to Ibsen. This devotion, manifest in his learning Dano-Norwegian in order to read the work in the original, and in the first published essay, a review of *When We Dead Awaken,* is based not so much on literary merits as on Ibsen's value as a symbol of the defiant, misunderstood artist. Thus was Ibsen hailed in the essay in *The Fortnightly Review.* In words that prefigure Joyce's own later reputation he characterized the Norwegian, then seventy-two, as one whose name "has gone abroad through the length and breadth of two continents, and has provoked more discussion and criticism than that of any other living man." There follows a list of the insults hurled at Ibsen—"meddlesome intruder," "defective artist," "incomprehensible mystic"—and, according to an English critic, " 'a muck-ferreting dog' "—

The notes to Chapter 6 begin on page 333.

epithets ready to hand twenty years later when *Ulysses* was published.

But, Joyce continued, Ibsen constantly gains stature, "as a hero comes out amid the earthly trials." Master that he is, he has not been disturbed by the cries of petty detractors but has remained loyal to his vision, heedless of "the storm of fierce debate" raging about him.

Almost a year later Joyce wrote a letter to Ibsen congratulating him on his seventy-third birthday. A tentative apology for the "immature and hasty article" is followed by a more characteristic assertion that the undergraduate has "sounded your name defiantly through the college where it was either unknown or known faintly and darkly." Discounting an impression of sentimental hero worship, Joyce claimed that "when I spoke of you in debating societies and so forth, I enforced attention by no futile ranting."

The most important part of the letter, however, is the conclusion, in which Joyce conceived of an apostolic episcopal succession in art, with himself the chosen successor. To sophisticated minds the words may sound naïve or self-centered or both, but to Joyce now without a church, to have a patron saint in the religion of art was an auspicious sign. In "The Day of the Rabblement" he had notified the public that the torch, passed to Hauptmann, would be taken by younger hands—"the third minister will not be wanting when his hour comes." Now he confesses to Ibsen his readiness:

> As one of the young generation for whom you have spoken I give you greeting—not humbly, because I am obscure and you in the glare, not sadly, because you are an old man and I a young man, not presumptuously nor sentimentally—but joyfull, with hope and with love, I give you greeting.[4]

The young aspirant to the temple of art had found a father.

The influence of Ibsen has been examined by Vivienne Koch Macleod and James T. Farrell. The parallels are numerous: rejection of narrow nationalism, estrangement from family, exile with its nostalgia, the concern with paternity, the dilemma of freedom and responsibility, the problem of the status of the artist. Mrs. Macleod feels that Ibsen provided for Joyce "an almost literal blueprint for his own life and art." Farrell adds that both Norway and Ireland, being outside the major streams of European culture, were dominated by alien civilizations. Both countries disappointed their native authors, Norway in failing to aid Denmark, Ireland in remaining servile. Both were entering into a period of nationalist aspiration, but neither Ibsen nor Joyce accepted the narrow limits of national expression. These are interesting parallels, but Farrell is wise in not assuming that Joyce was aware of them or was motivated by them.[5]

Ibsen provides the topic of conversation in two of the most amusing genre scenes in *Stephen Hero*. The student has been carefully developing his theory of art (first step in the new theology he feels he must create) and is in a state of anxiety to communicate his ideas to someone, even if it be to a no more receptive audience than his mother, quietly ironing while Stephen struggles to explain his theories, "garnished with many crude striking allusions with which he hoped to drive it home the better." His mother is "surprised to see the extraordinary honour" bestowed by her son upon Beauty, which, to her, is at best a drawing-room convention, at worst "a synonym for licentious ways." She is discreet enough, however, to ask about Ibsen and to promise to read his "best" play, not, she adds, to censor his reading but, hesitantly and pathetically,

> —Of course life isn't what I used to think it was when I was a young girl. That's why I would like to read some great writer, to see what ideal of life he has—amn't I right in saying "ideal"?

Her opinion of the plays she read was equally tentative. But her husband, who, expecting from Ibsen's notoriety some "anomalous torridity," found the first half of the *League of Youth* merely tedious. Joyce slyly adds that his relief over his son's respectability was mingled with the disappointment of his expectations.

The interview with the President of the College is equally amusing. He accepts the hearsay about Ibsen unquestioningly, though he knows nothing of his work, and warns Stephen that in Ireland such paradoxical criticism as an essay on art will scarcely gain a following.

The young poet in *Stephen Hero* regards Ibsen as "first among the dramatists of the world," an opinion that precipitates the bitter aftermath of his essay reading. One conservative student, falling back on the obvious, opined that

"*Macbeth* would be famous when the unknown authors of whom Mr. Daedalus was so fond were dead and forgotten." Ibsen's "sincere and boylike bravery," his "disillusioned pride," and his "minute and wilful energy" gave Joyce's concepts of art a militancy and masculinity not found in the typical aesthete.[6]

The spirit of Ibsen, like most of the formative influences of Joyce's youth, remained with him; in 1915 he essayed his own version of Ibsen's "naked drama" in *Exiles*. The memoirs of Stanislaus Joyce, so valuable in detailing the impact of literature on his brother, point out that one of the professors was so much impressed by the championship of Ibsen that he prepared a public lecture on Ibsen, borrowing books and information from the precocious student.

Despite Joyce's enthusiasm, *When We Dead Awaken* is not Ibsen at his best. To M. C. Bradbrook the last plays are, like Shakespeare's tragicomedies, inward visions rather than successful dramas. The "descending order of dramatic greatness" of the last four plays culminates in this bitter testament of futility. The sculptor Rubek has repudiated his high artistic ideals, rejected the love of his model and source of inspiration, and settled into a complacent marriage. On the return of the model, Rubek and she climb the mountain peak in the storm, achieving an ecstasy in death that they feared to attain in life. Miss Bradbrook sees "an apocalyptic symbolism" in the mountain setting, the contrasting characters, and the symmetrical construction. The "lurid glow" of madness anticipates Strindberg. The play seems "a last doom-session" of the playwright on his own career.

Resemblances between *Exiles* and Ibsen's last play are too striking to be accidental. In both cases a figure from the past returns to test the sincerity of an artist. Ibsen's almost symmetrical balance of characters—the worldly wife Maia and her hunter lover contrasted with the artist and the model Irene—is paralleled by Joyce in the contrast of the dedicated Richard and his loyal but less inspired wife with the worldly friends Robert and Beatrice. The motivations in *Exiles* are far more complex and unpredictable, however. The issue is not simply that of artistic integrity but a puzzling series of dilemmas concerning the limits of freedom, the demands of love, and the possessiveness inherent in marriage. It seems almost too much for the plot to carry, especially a situation so trite as that of testing a wife's fidelity.

Autobiographical elements are readily recognized—the self-imposed exile in Italy, the lovematch with a woman of inferior cultural status, the temptation to return to Dublin. Less apparent is the attitude Joyce takes to his fictional double, as shall be noted later. Richard shares with Stephen Dedalus a deep-seated suspiciousness of the motives of all, including himself; a desire to find a heroic model—here both Swift and Jesus; sexual distaste; a faint tinge of social concern; and resistance to alien voices, those of the public, but most emphatically that of the dead mother's spirit.

Though its superficial autobiographical interest has long been noticed, its haunting and evocative beauty has had few advocates, the most eloquent being Francis Fergusson. For most readers it remains less a successful drama than an abstract dialectic, an imperfectly realized debate upon principles not clearly perceptible. Without the temperament of Stephen Dedalus in mind, one may find Richard's scruples as tantalizing and infuriating as they are to his wife and friends. His supposed concern for "virginity of soul" is not clarified by his cryptic reference to it. With characteristic bluntness, George Jean Nathan reviewed a 1925 performance and found it "three hours of talk in a single monotonous key." The words were not live and dramatic but "supine and sleepy" and the whole play seemed to have "the spirit and tempo of a German funeral."[7]

Some failure in communication is noted by most critics. For Levin the theme lacks a proper correlative: "No playwright can afford to be a solipsist." For Macleod the "implications are narrowed by centering them in the fairly negligible matter of a seduction"; for Farrell, the problems do not spring from the characters themselves, but are projected upon them by Richard. The lack of resolution makes it "a problem play that ends in a mood." Williams finds the weakness in Joyce's use of representational speech and the absence of commentary; that is, in the limitations of the naturalistic method itself.

What is the basic theme? One who knows the complexity of Joyce's orientation should not be surprised that many answers have been given. We may distinguish two main types, the naturalistic and the metaphysical, the first centering on psychological problems, the latter dealing with ultimate contradictions in existence, but both giving serious treatment to the dilemmas confronting an idealistic individual in his relations to his social group.

The Little Review's symposium in 1919 represents both

views. John Rodker, Israel Solon, and Dr. Samuel Tannenbaum stressed the psychological, Rodker interpreting the play as a conflict of will and instinct, Solon and Tannenbaum suggesting the theme of homosexuality. Later Dr. Alfred Barnes thought that Richard desired to be betrayed in order to escape guilt over his own infidelity. Jane Heap replied with an interpretation of Richard as "neither loved nor lover" but "an incarnation of love." His effect on others is troubling:

> In other people he breeds a longing akin to the longing for immortality. They do not love him: they become him.

He is wearied of his stigmata, yet in this "Midas tragedy" he finds that "Love strikes back at him from every source." Sex is not a paramount concern to him; he terms it "a law of nature which he did not vote." A man of finer quality than most, he sees at last that the others cannot reach his plane and suffers "because he cannot put upon them his special illumination about life and love."[8]

In view of the play's tenuous nature, it is surprising to note how favorable are the early reviews. Only one, that in *The Catholic World,* was obtuse. Joyce is "so afraid of the obvious that he is timid even of the clear . . . leaving his audience hopelessly uncertain upon a vital fact of his plot." It is a pity, the review continued, "to see such manifest literary talents wasted on so futile a piece of work." Life is "difficult enough," but "not so repulsively, and insolubly involved" as this. *The Times Literary Supplement* sensed "resources of spiritual passion." The ambiguity is "merely distracting," though the reviewer contradicts himself by showing that were Robert and Bertha false, it would "diminish the poignancy of his tragic doubt." To Francis Hackett the play was so good "that the defects seem to be an illusion"; Joyce appears "intuitive and occult," even though actions and words lack reality. Robert is too frivolous and trivial to be taken seriously by Richard, whose speeches on love and freedom "seem so unimaginable." Padraic Colum emphasized the "unspoiled, alluring, unconventional, faithful" Bertha, the first notable woman in Joyce. Among other early reviews one may note that of Ezra Pound. Pound uses Joyce as a stick for beating the modern stage, which has succumbed to "interior decorators," never daring to attack real problems.[9]

"To be made to wonder and to think about characters in

a play is a rare experience," said Desmond MacCarthy, to whom the work was worthy of comparison with Ibsen. Though professing to be unsure of its meaning, he ventured to characterize it as "a study in the emotional life of an artist." The artist's imagination "opens the door to a hundred new subtleties and possibilities of action," but his awareness of the feelings of others keeps him at a distance; hence one "can hardly believe he cares for anything but his own mood." Bertha longs for an elemental simplicity but, having "eaten of the tree of knowledge," realizes its impossibility. Robert and Richard reach mutual understanding: "consciousness that each is still at bottom solitary is, in a strange way, the tenderest bond between them."[10]

On the psychological plane, Golding sees Richard as one "who attempts to execute in the medium of life the aesthetic doctrine which Joyce proceeded to execute in terms of words." This involves his keeping "his soul to himself, with corollary that he shall do nothing at all to prevent his associates keeping their own souls to themselves."[11] James T. Farrell's reading is similar. Richard wishes "to avoid the dangers of sick conscience," but it is impossible, for his goal of freedom is incompatible with his own nature. He can neither possess Bertha as the average man might, nor can he relinquish her, granting the freedom that his theory demands. The dilemma is psychological, resting on Richard's own ambivalent nature. Earlier, Joseph Wood Krutch had found an insuperable psychological dilemma at the heart of the play. Richard is "committed to a new morality and yet not sure where it will lead him." The result is that he appears unnaturally fastidious in his moral judgment.

> We meet our problems as best we may, but we do not even in our plays seek so desperately to create them.

Instead of creating a better adjustment to life, as in Ibsen's plays, the new Joycean morality seems merely an additional means of self-torture.[12]

Gorman describes the characters as "spiritual exiles," "highly intellectualized explorers desirous of passing beyond the good and evil of a mutable world." The play is both psychological ("the physical and mental reactions of these four characters") and metaphysical ("that higher, lonelier drama which is played out in the intricate labyrinths of the brain").[13] To Fergusson the drama is metaphysical. Ibsen's heroes are Prometheans, seeking the good of humanity, but Joyce is a Daedalus, a pure artist, free of such feeling. Richard's tragic flaw "is not in him, but in his metaphysical situation." He demonstrates the romantic motives of the others "like a priest or a physician," the undernourished rebellion of Beatrice, the callow romantic revolt of Robert, both "an evasion of that complete, individual ethical awareness which Richard represents." It is Fergusson who best evokes the austere beauty of the play. Richard's final scenes with Bertha, "in their quietness, their tender refusal of a passion which is always present," are comparable to "the grave farewells of Racine's monarchs." Each person expresses his own "intangible esthetic life which is itself and no other thing," appearing "like one of the images in Dante's Hell: cut off, final, unchanging, and brilliant . . . against the surrounding darkness." Richard is not merely an individual, nor merely the artist type: Joyce's theory that pity and terror attract the beholder by "whatsoever is grave and constant in human suffering" and the pagan sages in Dante's limbo.[14]

Thus far there has been virtual agreement on the play's meaning—the presentation of the ultimate loneliness and doubt that must possess the soul, the inevitable exile of man. A contrary view is first expressed by Bernard Bandler. The exile of the secondary characters is not inherent in their nature, but imposed upon them by the impossible demands made by Richard, who "plays the role of the artist without accepting the responsibilities of being a man . . . the patient perfecting of the body which forms the soul."[15] Richard, then, is a horrible example of heresy, though, if I read Bandler aright, Joyce is unaware of the fact.

According to Hugh Kenner, the refutation of Ibsen is consciously Joyce's. Richard's revolt parodies both Ibsen's and Joyce's; his gift of freedom is meaningless. As an "ape of God" he has dominated everyone, forced them to a recognition of their isolation, and set them in the garden for their temptation. His demands upon himself and upon Bertha are impossible to live up to; rejecting society, and normal human needs, Richard thrusts everyone into "a joyless suburban limbo." Pure ethical freedom and utter honesty belong only to angels; "The determination to behave in this angelic way leads fallen man to behave as a fallen angel: the oldest of theological common-places."[16]

One hesitates to reject out of hand arguments so cogent as these. Bandler's criticism exemplifies the practice of taking a work of art as a text for a message of one's own. If a value judgment be neither consciously nor subconsciously in the author's mind, an interpretation based on such value might be called extraliterary, or perhaps extrapolative; that is, using the art object as the subject for an independent discourse upon morals or metaphysics. Much Marxist and dogmatic religious criticism is of this sort. In the case of Kenner, we meet the assertion that Joyce intends Richard to be, as Mulligan terms Stephen in *Ulysses,* "an impossible person." To interpret Joyce's tone is a tricky business, as has already been suggested. But one cannot help but feel that *Exiles* is a serious work; there is no evidence of parody. To be sure, Richard may occasionally appear ridiculous in his demands, but it is the audience and not the dramatis personae who feel this. As for the shortcomings of Richard's personality, we must recognize Joyce's protective coloration of irony. *Stephen Hero* expresses it very well:

> [As Stephen Hero could not use feudal terminology in love poems] with the same faith . . . he was compelled to express his love a little ironically. This suggestion of relativity . . . mingling itself with so immense a passion is a modern note: we cannot swear or expect fealty because we recognize too accurately the limits of every human energy. It is not possible for the modern lover to think the universe an assistant at his love-affair.[17]

One feels less irony in *Exiles* than in almost any other work of Joyce. A suspicion of narcissism intrudes more than once—see the stage directions describing Richard. Second, the problem seems to be deeply rooted in Joyce's own experience. Though Shaw could claim that he was happily unconcerned about being a parasite for years, one can easily see that Joyce, as a fledgling artist, never really at ease at his break from church and country, might have some misgivings at his unconventional marriage. Third, Joyce seems, despite his irony and cynicism, fundamentally romantic. He might at times see the artist as a posturing egotist, but it is unlikely that he would remain among the scoffers in regard to the major decision in his career. And finally, the recently published notes to *Exiles* confirm that though Richard is termed an "automystic," there is a deep respect for his position. Indeed the notes are more permeated with Shelleyan romanticism than the play.

Padraic Colum sees in the work an echo of Joyce's "lonely and hazardous enterprise" of exile. All the characters are taken "beyond the accepted moralities . . . to where they have to make choices for themselves." Colum stresses the role of Bertha. A fine characterization, with her tenderness, pride, and sorrow, she is also representative of "an immemorial and universal order," the means by which Richard will be healed of his wound. "*Exiles* is a series of confessions; the dialogue has the dryness of recitals in the confessional; its end is an act of contrition."[18]

The author's preliminary notes and plans constitute the most valuable of recent Joyce discoveries. The notes, several of which are dated November 1913, five years before the publication of the play, were found among Joyce's effects in Paris after the liberation. On his departure to the south of France in 1940, Joyce entrusted his books, manuscripts, and personal papers to his close friend and volunteer amanuensis, Paul Léon. Despite the tragic death of M. Léon in a concentration camp, most of the materials were preserved. The personal papers, left at the Irish Embassy in Paris, were placed in sealed deposit at the National Library in Dublin. The books and manuscripts were displayed at the La Hune exhibit in Paris in 1949, and a year later the entire collection was sold to the University of Buffalo Library.

The notebook reveals, as the play intimates, many of Joyce's basic preoccupations. The rejection of social convention, the attainment of pure spirit, is dramatized by Richard's repeated refusal to defend Bertha from Robert's advances: "His defense of her soul and body is an invisible and imponderable sword." Though Robert in his romantic passion is unaware of these spiritual values, the outcome

> should however convince Robert of the existence and reality of Richard's mystical defense of his wife. If this defense be a reality how can those facts on which it is based be then unreal?

But such ideal freedom is physically impossible. Joyce notes that love's necessary tendency is "union in the region of the difficult, the void and the impossible." In the case of Beatrice (note the explicit rejection of Dante's vision) Platonic love ends in timid sterility; her mind, comments Joyce, "is an abandoned cold temple" of Protestantism. Bertha understands love as desire and companionship; before the higher goal she displays "lack of spiritual energy" and "mental paralysis."

Yet Joyce is emphatic that *Exiles* must not be misinterpreted as a problem play: "Richard must not appear as a champion of woman's rights." The metaphysical issues must not be clouded with emotional appeals: Richard "does not use the language of adoration and his character must seem a little unloving," or, again, "The greatest danger in the writing is tenderness of speech or of mood." Nor should the theme be considered a study of sensuality and adultery:

> As a contribution to the study of jealousy Shakespeare's *Othello* is incomplete. It and Spinoza's analysis are made from the sensationalist standpoint . . .

Nothing remains but the static poise of the neoclassical drama. All the characters, the notes reveal, "are suffering during the action," or, in more vernacular vein, "The play is three cat and mouse acts." The mood is that of "a long, hesitating, painful story" similar to the changed point of view in literature from Rabelais and Molière to Paul de Kock, an interesting instance of Joyce's search for a literary tradition, as is his speculation on the affinity of Celtic philosophers such as Hume, Berkeley, and Bergson to "incertitude or scepticism."

Richard comes closest to the ideal. He aims for "the very immolation of the pleasure of possession on the altar of love." Though he too fails, he represents an inevitable advance; Robert both combats and prepares for this advance, as Wotan did Siegfried:

> Every step advanced by humanity through Richard is a step backwards by the type which Robert stands for.

As an albeit imperfect representative of a higher order, he "is indignant when he discovers baseness in men and women," an idea directly echoed in the play as Robert says:

> You have that fierce indignation which lacerated the heart of Swift. You have fallen from a higher world, Richard, and you are filled with fierce indignation, when you find that life is cowardly and ignoble.

Richard's motives are, however, far from pure, and his realization of this fact throws him into the existentialist despair that troubles romantic readers. The first notation, "Richard—an automystic," suggests an irony similar to that which Dedalus is treated. His "baffled lust," the notes tell us, is "converted into an erotic stimulus"; "he wills and knows his own dishonor"; he is a masochist. The play renders it thus:

> . . . in the very core of my ignoble heart I longed to be betrayed by you and by her. . . . I longed for that passionately and ignobly, to be dishonored for ever in love and in lust, to be . . . . for ever a shameful creature and to build up my soul again out of the ruins of its shame.

Caught in the dilemma of his unattainable ideal of purity, he fears that Bertha must lose her innocence in order to understand it; he has a prurient desire "to feel the thrill of adultery vicariously"; in his search for beauty, he is unaware that it rests under his own roof. With such remorseless logic, Joyce, the casuist of sin, unfolds the nature of human depravity.

Another theme emphasized in the notes is the possible union of the two men, the idealist Richard and the sensualist Robert, through their love of Bertha (note the resemblance to the final meetings of Bloom and Stephen in *Ulysses*). Bertha desires it, but there is some question as to whether the men do. At least, Of "Richard's friends Robert is the only one who has entered Richard's mind through the gate of Bertha's affection." In the play Bertha explains: "I wanted to bring you close together—you and him."

The notebook elaborates the suspicions that form so central a part of the play's dialectic tensions. Robert suspects that Richard is using Bertha as bait for his friendship; he is bitter that the rumors of Bertha's falseness are untrue; though he idolizes Richard, he is putting Richard's idealism to a test, realizing Richard's knowledge of his actions. Richard in turn suspects that Robert's friendship is false, that Robert may misunderstand his unpossessive attitude toward Bertha as a lack of love for her. In regard to Bertha, Joyce describes her state of mind when left in the cottage by Richard:

> Bertha's state when abandoned spiritually by Richard must be expressed by the actress by a suggestion of hypnosis. Her state is like that of Jesus in the garden of olives. It is the soul of woman left naked and alone that it may come to an understanding of its own nature.

He also notes her resentment against Richard for not saving her.

One important facet of Joyce's thought is not sufficiently dramatized. He plans that Bertha shall undergo a spiritual awakening, which, were it made clear, would have brought her some conclusion or discovery to balance Richard's final and irremovable state of doubt:

> . . . she will suffuse her own reborn temperament with the wonder of her soul at its own solitude and at her beauty, formed and dissolving itself eternally amid the clouds of mortality.

Such a discovery Leopold Bloom seems to make as he meditates on the stars and the infinite perspectives of time.

It is toward *Ulysses* that the notebook points. The correspondences that form the texture of the Dublin epic are suggested by Bertha's age, twenty-eight, indicating the lunar cycle; the comparison between the female and the fertile earth looks forward, as Padraic Colum notes, to Molly Bloom. Indicative of the mythic awareness already at work are the parallels mentioned—with the New Testament, with Siegfried, and, here anticipating *Finnegans Wake,* with Tristan. Only one such is included in the play: Robert's twice asserted comparison of Richard and Swift.

The sharply defined contrast of Richard and Robert likewise points to the broad symbolic figures in *Ulysses*. Richard is "automystic," Robert "automobile" (even the pun is late Joyce); they are, respectively, masochistic and sadistic, indicating Joyce's early interest in psychological terminology. Bertha's sensuality, classed by symptoms visual, gustatious, and tactual, anticipates the elaborate diagrams that Stuart Gilbert has revealed as underlying *Ulysses*. Joyce conceives of, then abandons, a project of following Bertha as wife of Robert in a series of epiphanies that suggests *Ulysses:*

> For instance . . . ordering carpets in Grafton Street, as Leopardstown races, provided with a seat on the platform at the unveiling of a statue, putting out the lights in the drawing room after a social evening in her husband's house, kneeling outside a confessional in the jesuit church.

In the notes on Bertha we find the greatest amount of "felt

life," which is excluded from the naked drama of *Exiles*. In the play Bertha engages in no reminiscence, nor is her dialogue expanded beyond that necessary for her metaphysical situation. But the notebook gives indication of a character more fully developed than that of any other woman in Joyce, with the sole exception of Molly Bloom. More than a quarter of the notebook is devoted to images and experiences that lie in the background of Bertha's soul. Her mind, we are told, "is a grey seamist amid which common objects—hillsides, the masts of ships, and barren islands—loom with strange and yet recognizable outlines." Five chains of images are listed, sometimes followed with narrative explanations. We read, under date of November 12, 1913:

> Garter: precious, Prezioso, Bodkin, music palegreen, bracelet, cream sweets, lily of the valley, convent garden (Galway), sea
> Rat: Sickness, disgust, poverty, cheese, woman's ear, (child's ear?)
> Dagger: heart, death, soldier, war, band, judgment, king.

Bodkin is a young man buried at Rahoon, near Galway. One immediately recalls Gretta Conroy, in "The Dead," weeping over her boy lover, Michael Furey. He is likened to Shelley, despite his homely name. He is "dark, unrisen, killed by love and life, young." Bertha "weeps over Rahoon," an echo of the lyric in *Pomes Pennyeach:* "Rain on Rahoon falls softly, softly falling." Gretta, Bertha, and Nora Joyce—all from Galway. What personal motivations underlie these revelations?

Bodkin lies buried, Shelley arises in Richard, in "the part of Richard which neither love nor life can do away with; the part for which she loves him: the part she must try to kill, never be able to kill and rejoice at her impotence." This is the movement that *Exiles* imperfectly shadows forth: Richard and Bertha are two unsuccessful Pygmalions, Richard attempting to raise Bertha to a spiritual awakening, Bertha trying to suppress the Shelleyan inspiration of her mate.

Bertha's images—bracelet, cream sweets, and the others—"are the trinkets and toys of girlhood," Bodkin's symbols music and the sea, another anticipation of *Ulysses* motifs. Two other chains of images are given, symbols of girlhood and virginity. Joys and regrets of childhood are mingled with Bertha's awareness of her growing hair, "The softly growing symbol of her girlhood." As she reaches maturity, "A proud and shy instinct turns her mind away from the loosening of her bound-up hair," and in joining Richard she guards her inviolate individuality, embracing "that which is hers alone and not hers and his also—happy distant dancing days, distant, gone forever, dead, or killed?"

Other glimpses of Bertha are narrative in nature, recalling the epiphanies of *Dubliners*—Christmas Eve in Galway as a child, the emigration of her friend Emily Lyons. Bertha is tender, shy, virginal, a sensitive sketch never fully brought to life in *Exiles*. The pathos of her maturity colors the cryptic entry at the beginning of the notes, where we read that

> The soul like the body may have a virginity. For the woman to yield it or for the man to take it is the act of love.

This conception also underlies the dialogue between Richard and Robert, in which the husband voices dark forebodings that he has killed "the virginity of her soul."

John Kelleher, in his excellent review of the Colum edition, likewise attributes the relative failure in communication to the limitation of conventional dramatic form. *Exiles* has usually been regarded as curiously unsatisfactory, despite its being "full of fine things" and obviously from a master's hand." Joyce's characteristic method of procedure, the "interlocking of many epiphanies," is barred by his choice of medium. Richard lacks humor, with "disastrous" results; worse, the undisguised "spiritual identification with Jesus" leaves both reader and characters stunned. To act out the process of confession is to make the story unreal. Nevertheless the notes intensify interest in the play, for they not only "confirm the lasting consistency of Joyce's thought" but indicate the importance of his later rejection of the lesser literary forms:

> Previous to this he had wrought beautifully within a small space. Afterwards he wrought more beautifully and with infinitely greater humanity, and took as much time and space as he needed.[19]

Exiles, we may conclude, is a play with suppressed undertones, romantic, perhaps painfully personal. Joyce's adoption of the bare style of Ibsen prevents him from giving the richly symbolic associations that color his conceptions. The play fails as an adequate correlative for the manifold implications of these notes. Joyce's aesthetic practice fluctuates between the poles of romantic symbolism and Scholastic logic. *Finnegans Wake* is one extreme, *Exiles* the other. Though varying from the cumulative detail of *Stephen Hero* to the austere selectivity of *Exiles,* Joyce's happiest results were attained in the associationism of *Ulysses* and *Finnegans Wake*. The neoclassic beauty of *Exiles* is achieved by severe excision, a repression of the lyricism that perceptive readers find not only in *Dubliners* and the *Portrait* but in the pathetic and ridiculous dreams of Bloom, in the unsatisfied loneliness of Molly, and in the transcendently feminine Anna Livia Plurabelle.

Chapter 7

Ulysses

"I AM GOING TO unveil all the mysteries: mysteries religious or natural, death, truth, the future, the past, cosmogony, nothingness. I am a master of phantasmagoria."[1]

Thus the young Rimbaud voices his hieratic ecstasy. The artist, a mystic seer, will reveal the mysteries of all things. His instrument, the word, is possessed of ineffable power. But the ecstasy here shines forth against the nightmare of his *Season in Hell*. Joyce shared many of the same conceptions of the artist as hermetic priest. He was subject alike to dazzling alternations of mood. Revolt from church and country is countered by family piety and respect for tradition. Ancestral patterns derived from myth provide rigid schematisms upon which are woven a bewildering array of symbolic correspondences. Man is at once classic archetype and psychological chaos the macrocosm reflects the microcosm.

An all but pedantic concern with literary form counteracts the lack of verbal decorum. The question whether Joyce be essentially classical or romantic, medieval or modern, realist or symbolist, has engaged critics in controversy. Even wider is his divergence in mood, from an emotional identification almost sentimental, through corrosive irony, to humorous acceptance. Indeed it is in tone that Joyce is most apt to bewilder critics. He has been interpreted as cynic, blasphemer, and nihilist, as godlike observer and social critic, as impersonal metaphysician and divided soul.

In defining the quintessence of poetry for his University College associates, the young Joyce chose the decadent Mangan as his Irish exemplar, and the songs of Shakespeare and Verlaine as exponents of pure poetry, "so free and living and as remote from any conscious purpose as rain that falls in the garden or the lights of evening." Concept and metaphor alike are *fin de siècle*. Pure poetry is the program of Wilde, *The Yellow Book*, and the young Rhymers Club in London, the rain is that of Verlaine's "Il Pleut Doucement Sur La Ville." Of its epoch too is Joyce's definition of the poet as one

The notes to Chapter 7 begin on page 334.

whose life is intense, "taking into its centre the life that surrounds it and flinging it abroad again amid planetary music." In *Ulysses* Stephen hears A. E. describe Mallarmé as "the finest flower of corruption" and Best praise the essay on *Hamlet,* though from Stephen's appropriation of the phrase *"dio boia,* hangman god" it is apparent that young Dedalus too had read that essay that so closely parallels the Shakespeare discussion the young Dubliners are engaging in at the moment.

When Joyce came up to London in 1902 Yeats introduced him to Symons. Gorman thinks him already past admiration for the art of the nineties, which he describes in a barbarous phrase that Joyce would wince to read, "a weak herd urge." Gorman pictures him wincing rather at the romantic *décor* and the lock of hair on Yeats's forehead, sighing "for a clean whistling wind, biting with salt, from the Norwegian fiords."[2] Yet Symons had been a personal friend of Verlaine, and *The Symbolist Movement in Literature* (1899) was the first, and is still in many ways the finest, English introduction to the school. It was Symons, too, who managed to find a publisher for *Chamber Music* and first reviewed it.

In any case, Symons' essays on the symbolists provide many passages, both from the French writers and from their interpreter, that might seem designed to describe the occult and symbolic aspects of *Ulysses*. There is the rhapsody of Gerard de Nerval (Tindall thinks Stephen learned of the lobster from this book).[3] The hermetic poet exclaimed that "All things live, all things are in motion, all things correspond":

> . . . a transparent network covers the world, whose loose threads communicate more and more closely with the planets and the stars. Now a captive upon the earth, I hold converse with the starry choir, which is feelingly a part of my joys and sorrows.

Is Joyce's "planetary music" derived from this "starry choir"? Symons hails De Nerval as the first symbolist who "realised that central secret of the mystics, from Pythagoras onwards, the secret which the Smaragdine Tablet of Hermes betrays in its 'As things are below, so are they above.' " He refers to Boehme's "signatures," those manifestations of the ineffable that Stephen feels called upon to read as he treads Sandymount Strand. The style of the Goncourts, as described by Symons, resembles Joyce's:

> In order to arrive at their effects, they shrink from . . . no excess; slang, neologism, forced construction, archaism, barbarous epithet, nothing comes amiss to them, so long as it tends to render a sensation.

But Joyce must have derived equally from the artists themselves. Mallarmé's definition of his work as "a labyrinth illuminated by flowers" is an unusually accurate characterization of the art of *Ulysses,* as is Huysmans' concept of *"naturalisme spiritualiste."* Symons interprets symbolism as "an establishing of the links which hold the world together, the affirmation of an eternal, minute, intricate, almost invisible life, which runs through the universe"; Mallarmé anticipates the Joycean epiphany, its insight and radiance, in suggesting that "in the intellectual world at its utmost" it may be that we can find, "drawing to itself all the correspondences of the universe, the supreme Music." In *En Route,* Huysmans made the discovery, according to Symons, that the novel could at last compete "with poetry, with the great 'confessions,' with philosophy," that it could reach its consummation in "the revelation of the sub-conscious self," attaining a form "at once a confession and a decoration, the soul and a pattern." The hermetic vision, decadent style, spiritualized naturalism, verbal alchemy, confessional tenor, and labyrinthine pattern—here is the essence of *Ulysses.* And in his pioneering study Symons conveys much of that enthusiasm of the discoverer that is soon translated into the disciple's devotion. It is no wonder that his peroration is a challenge and a hope, reminiscent of Pater's celebrated conclusion to *The Renaissance.* The image of weaving, so prominent in Stephen's thought, leads to an apostrophe of the mystical way:

> And as we realise the identity of a poem, a prayer, or a kiss, in that spiritual universe which we are weaving for ourselves, each out of a thread of the great fabric; as we realise the infinite insignificance of action, its immense distance from the current of life; as we realise the delight of feeling ourselves carried outward by forces which it is our wisdom to obey; it is at least with a certain relief that we turn to ancient doctrine, so much the more likely to be true because it has so much the air of a dream. On this theory alone does all life become worth living, all art worth making, all worship worth offering.[4]

Though source studies are out of fashion, the question of Joyce's derivations should provide some clues to his intent. With Flaubert, the only novelist for whom he retained a lasting admiration, he shared a sense of the value of tone and cadence, though Edmund Wilson feels that Joyce has gone further than his master, in accuracy, subtlety, and the avoidance of monotony.[5]

In *Ulysses* Stephen recalls reading the "fading prophecies" of Joachim de Flora in "the stagnant bays of Marsh's Library." This theological collection, containing such items as the work of John Chrysostom, Gregory the Great, and Aristotle, as well as *The Jesuites Catechisme, The Catholike Moderator,* or *Catholique Traditions* might have satisfied his youthful taste for the medieval hermetic tradition. Even closer to the spirit of *Ulysses* is the title of Louis Le Roy's volume, *Of the Interchangeable Course, or Variety of Things in the Whole World,* published in translation in 1594. Here too he could have found *Ayres, Madrigalls, Canzonets,* and *Balletts* of Adson, Bennet, Farmer, or John Morley, the music Stephen discusses with Bloom on their early morning walk to Eccles Street.[6] Meetings of the Dublin Theosophical Society, under the aegis of George William Russell, and the popularity of *les symbolistes* undoubtedly confirmed his innate bent toward mystic correspondences. Theosophy provided a doctrine, symbolism an aesthetic, which could be harmonized with the symbolic bent of traditional Catholicism. The artist now becomes priest of a new rite, master of the recondite, pioneer in forbidden areas. One recalls Stephen's temptation to join the priesthood, not out of any sense of vocation, but because of the awful power and the occult knowledge that the occupation would provide. A glance at the two most completely documented studies of Joyce, those of Levin and Tindall, would indicate the wide range of the author's intellectual affinities.

As an example of Joyce's finding a use for remote materials, one can cite the work of the French Homeric scholar, Victor Bérard, who enters frequently into Stuart Gilbert's commentary and whose theory of the Semitic origins of the *Odyssey* may have contributed to the choice of the Jew Leopold Bloom as the modern Odysseus. Bérard's lifetime study of the backgrounds of the Homeric poems fills some twelve volumes. His findings, summarized in the volume, *Did Homer Live?* (1931), whatever their immediate relevance to Joyce, constitute a fascinating record of the mixture of geography, custom, fact, and folklore that underlies the Homeric work.

The Achaeans, first mentioned in inscriptions celebrating the victories of the Pharoah Minephta (1234-1224 B.C.), were merchants and carriers of Egyptian and Phoenician culture. The Phoenicians dominated Mediterranean commerce, and founded the colonies of Utica, the site of Carthage, and Gades or Cadiz. From Egyptian sources may be derived the name of the Greek god Proteus, since one circumlocution for the king was "Gate Sublime," or *Prouti,* the more familiar title being "Twin Palace," or *pharao*. Even more significant are the possible derivations of the *Odyssey* from Phoenician pilots' guides, the place names of which are translated so directly from the Hebrew that immediate identification is possible:

> Kalypso's Isle, *Nesos Kalupsous* is the "isle of the Hiding-Place"; *I-Spania* would be the Hebrew equivalent; and sure enough Kalypso's grotto, her four springs and her trees are to be found in Spanish waters.

And so are the meadows of parsley close to Gibraltar, Greek *Kalpe* or "bowl," Molly Bloom's childhood home. Hence Joyce's apostrophe to the buxom Molly as "Pride of Calpe's rocky mount."

Homer, according to this theory, was apparently a landsman who wove together a series of such tales as might have been suggested by names of coasts or headlands, converting them into goddesses of the wild, sirens' meadows, and lotus lands. The poet of the *Odyssey,* it is especially interesting to note, was like Joyce addicted to puns, jingles, and quibbles. Thus we may trace etymologies of "Lotus" to the semitic *l. ou. t.,* with its suggestion of the Greek *lethe,* and can derive the Cyclops or Round-Eye, in the Hebrew *Oin-otra,* from the place in Italy, Oinotria.

Marsh's Library, and the National Library, which was frequented by the University College students, afforded Joyce ample occasion to indulge his restless curiosity. In addition to his formal reading he was also fascinated by the most banal effusions of popular journalism, in which he was following the speculations of Mallarmé on the popular press as the epic of the present. The unpublished letters to Frank Budgen, written while *Ulysses* was being finished, are filled with requests for documentation from old songs, Masonic handbooks, guides to palmistry, and store catalogues. Even the trivial

THE GROUND PLAN OF *ULYSSES*

I. The Telemachiad (Stephen's Morning)

1. Telemachus Breakfast	A Martello Tower on Dublin Bay	8 A.M.		Theology
2. Nestor Teaching	School in Dalkey, a suburb near the tower	10 A.M.		History
3. Proteus Walking on strand	Sandymount, north of Dalkey	11 A.M.		Philology

II. The Odyssey (Bloom's Wanderings)

4. Calypso Breakfast	7 Eccles Street, north of the River Liffey	8 A.M.	Kidney	Economics
5. Lotus eaters Walk to baths	From river south to baths near Trinity College	10 A.M.	Genitals	Botany, chemistry
6. Hades Funeral	From Sandymount northwest through city to cemetery	11 A.M.	Heart	Religion
7. Aeolus Newspaper office	Nelson's Pillar, north of river	NOON	Lungs	Rhetoric
8. Lestrygonians To lunch	From pillar south, past Trinity, to library	1 P.M.	Esophagus	Architecture
9. Scylla and Charybdis Library	National Library, Kildare Street, south of Trinity	2 P.M.	Brain	Literature
10. Wandering rocks Ensemble	Mostly in the old city, southwest, Castle area	3 P.M.	Blood	Mechanics
11. Sirens Barroom	Ormond Hotel, on quay north of river	4 P.M.	Ear	Music
12. Cyclops Kiernan's pub	North of Ormond Hotel	5 P.M.	Muscle	Politics
13. Nausicaa On beach	Sandymount beach	8 P.M.	Eye, nose	Painting
14. Oxen of sun Hospital	Holles Street, near Merrion Square	10 P.M.	Womb	Medicine
15. Circe Brothel	Slum area near Customs House	12 P.M.	Locomotor apparatus	Magic

III. Nostos (The Return Home)

16. Eumaeus Cab shelter	Near Customs House	1 A.M.	Nerves	Navigation
17. Ithaca Bloom's kitchen	7 Eccles Street	2 A.M.	Skeleton	Science
18. Penelope Bedroom	7 Eccles Street	After 2 A.M.	Flesh	——

details of the famed June 16, 1904, from the Ascot Gold Cup to the disaster of the *General Slocum,* are derived from the newspapers, as my own *Fabulous Voyager* has shown. Not only that: actual Dublin characters walk the streets; shops and proprietors are detailed, thanks to Joyce's accurate memory and the use of Thom's *Directory*. Throughout this day the major characters, Stephen Dedalus and Leopold Bloom, pursue their now familiar way. They meet, casually at first, then share cocoa at Bloom's house in the early morning hours, but the significance of their meeting is still a matter of dispute. Is the outcome to be a source of renewed self-confidence to the lonely cuckold Bloom, and a stimulus to Stephen to write *Ulysses,* as Edmund Wilson interpreted it, or merely an ineffectual coincidence, as it seems to Harry Levin?

As almost every schoolboy now knows, *Ulysses* depicts the commonplace activities of three contrasting figures on one day in Dublin, the young writer Dedalus, the middle-aged advertising solicitor Leopold Bloom, and Bloom's voluptuous wife Molly. On the naturalistic level Joyce attains as vivid and seemingly complete a rendition of the mental and physical life as has ever been achieved in literature. Then there is the lusty animal energy of the presentation, the sense of Dublin not as a city to be described but of one the reader has lived in. The seemingly casual events of the day become representative of the flow of human life; literature is discussed in the library, politics in the pub, and the other arts are represented; there is a funeral and a birth. Technically Joyce exploits words and phrases with what might seem joyous abandon, but what is actually lapidary precision, for the tags of speech and thought provide an intricate network of correspondences to the Homeric epic, to Shakespeare, to Catholic, Jewish, and Masonic ritual, even to the legend of Don Giovanni. Perhaps most impressive of all is the strange indefinable radiance that emanates from the material, shadowed forth with musical felicity of phrase and projecting the imagination into strange paths of thought. Whether considered as a social document, a psychological novel, a giant symbolistic poem, or a manual of the art of modern fiction, *Ulysses* has remained for over thirty years a fecundating influence in literature and criticism.

Leopold Bloom has appeared either a miserable caricature of the man in the street or a tenderly pathetic and ridiculous victim of modern society, depending upon the attitude of the interpreter, as Stephen likewise has seemed a lonely and misunderstood artist or a posturing egotist. The selection of a

Jew as a central figure has been attributed to the important role Jews have played in modern culture, to Bérard's theory of the Semitic origins of the *Odyssey,* to Joyce's own acquaintances, to the parallel of Jew and Irishman as men whose land has been usurped, to Jewish shrewdness as a symbol of modern commerce, or to Joyce's own opposition to anti-Semitism, certainly alive in Central Europe during the author's stay there and apparently even spasmodic in Ireland at the time of Bloomsday. The Bloom-Jesus and the Bloom-exile-Joyce parallels have also been noted. Eileen Ellenbogen has remarked the isolation of the typical Jew in every country, the great significance of family life to Jews, the similarities between the rigorous religious discipline of Jew and Catholic, the analogies between Jewish and Irish cultural history; once again the Jew is rejected. The Zion theme has been studied, and incidents of anti-Semitism in early twentieth-century Ireland reported. Wyndham Lewis records Joyce's surprise at the resentment aroused in some of his Jewish friends at the portrayal of Bloom; Jews, said Joyce, "are better husbands than we are, better fathers, and better sons." Their refusal of Christianity was a "heroic sacrifice."[7]

The feature of the work that aroused the most intense interest of its first readers was the stream-of-consciousness style. This new technique was hailed by some as a method of insight into the depths of human personality, enabling the author, in the enthusiastic words of Valéry Larbaud, "to explore the secret places of the Ego and to capture thoughts at the very moment of their conception."[8] Harry Levin has demurred, reflecting the decline in enthusiasm since the early twenties. No more than of any artist can one claim that Joyce "enlarges the domain of consciousness."[9] His work cannot be considered scientific. Apart from those who were shocked by the "human Abyss" that Joyce revealed, serious readers discussed the artistic validity of the technique. To what extent, it may be asked, are verbal signs appropriate indications of unspoken reactions? What limitations has the linear method of prose for the representation of multilayered consciousness? As Auguste Bailly observed, "The life of the mind is a symphony," and any literary method has the effect of dissecting the chords or rendering the melody alone. Again, it has been argued by Wyndham Lewis that Joyce's characters must think in words, not in images, or, by Leon Edel, that the method involves a solipsism in so far as the author can truly know only his own mind and hence is committed to autobiography, no matter how much disguised. As an artistic method, it can equally be open to question on the basis of its effect, whether it be the inevitable confusion of inner and outer points of view, the obscurity of the fragments, or the lack of proportion in the whole work. Hence George Moore found *Ulysses* absurdly subjective and uncontrolled.[10]

In surveying these objections one may find Levin somewhat peremptory in denying validity to the method, though it is worthy of mention that literature is, after all, an art rather than a science. No author would be foolhardy enough to claim omniscience, though some of the claims of the twenties, in *transition* magazine for example, sound pretentious enough to justify the malicious retorts of Wyndham Lewis. More reasonable are the remarks of the film producer Eisenstein, who held that only the sound picture is "capable of reconstructing all the phases and the specific essence of the process of thought," by means of alternating sounds, images, and words, coherent or incoherent, synchronized or unsynchronized.[11]

Whatever the validity of the method, and whether it be termed interior monologue, internal monologue, or stream of consciousness, it certainly provided a stimulus to the creative writers of the twenties and has become established as a basic technique in fiction. David Daiches pointed out that the effect of the subjective method is to make the reader the novelist by providing him with the materials from which he may deduce the character. Thus, "Joyce lets Bloom project himself on to a screen for our contemplation."[12]

Even Joyce's predecessors have been a matter of debate. Affinities have been found in Elizabethan drama, in the dramatic monologues of Browning and Eliot, in Cooper, Melville, Dostoevski, Tolstoi. Of these, Leon Edel's citation of Lady Macbeth's sleepwalking is one of the most convincing, and Wyndham Lewis' of the maunderings of Mr. Jingle the most malicious. Joyce's own statement of his indebtedness to Edouard Dujardin may be allowed to stand, despite Mary Colum's assertion that Joyce was joking. Dujardin, as an elderly and forgotten man of letters, would have provided such a pathetic dupe that one feels sure such a hoax would have been entirely out of character for a man with so strong a sense of filial piety as Joyce. Dujardin himself took it seriously, feeling like Lazarus in the sudden recognition he began to enjoy for his long forgotten novel of 1887, *Les Lauriers sont coupés*. The tale, in imagistic style, depicts the reactions of a Parisian dandy on one evening, and despite some awkwardness, it remains worth reading for its recreation of the atmosphere of Paris. Dujardin's lectures of 1930 are marred by his concern for recognition but do present a summary of French discussions of the technique, which was compared to the cinema, to telegraphic code, or to the diving bell. Dujardin claims that his inspiration derived from the Wagnerian leitmotiv, and Wagner was, of course, a favorite of the symbolists. It was Schopenhauer who found music the true expression of the will, and from him the tradition runs through Nietzsche to Bergson and Freud. Dujardin recounts the early reception of his work: the letter of Mallarmé and his striking phrase, "the instant taken by the throat," the murmuring admiration of Huysmans', "It is curious."[13]

The Homeric parallels of *Ulysses* were eagerly seized upon by early reviewers as a means of grasping the ground plan of the work, and Stuart Gilbert, in his authorized commentary (1930), gave it what might seem to be undue emphasis. To Budgen, Joyce appears to have been most casual about these parallels, and most readers might agree with Levin, Kain, and Tindall that it is possible to pay too much attention to tracing the details. The major effect is, of course, satiric, the revelation of the unheroic in modern life, though Louis Golding was unusually shrewd in seeing that the parallel also reveals "the continuity of the human heart," the conditioning of man by his roots in the past. If Stuart Gilbert gave, as Tindall has argued, "more than enough weight to the details," it is partly the result of his episode-by-episode method of treatment, partly that of his desire to make Joyce appear a scholarly, classical artist. Richard Aldington seized upon these preoccupations with Homer as "critical red herrings intended to divert attention from the essentially medieval and Catholic substance of the work."[14] Again, fairness to Gilbert demands that these parallels constitute but one thread of his interpretation, the others being the theosophical concepts of the unity of life, the historical relationships between Greek and Viking, and the theme of paternity.

The theme of paternity, or the quest of Stephen for his spiritual father, has been termed by Tindall "a suggestive image, perhaps the most adequate of all, for the central occupation of modern man." Little has been added in recent years to Stuart Gilbert's treatment of the motif, which he finds basic to mythologies of mankind, whether in legends of quests or in the parable of the prodigal son. To Gilbert, however,

Stephen's quest is sterile, whereas to Tindall the meeting is climaxed in the evening repast of cocoa, a sort of lay Mass in which Stephen-Joyce comes to accept man and reality.

To revert to the notion of David Daiches, that *Ulysses* is an art form in which each reader creates his own meaning, the fact that such competent critics as Gilbert and Tindall could see entirely opposite outcomes in the book may testify to the inexhaustibility of *Ulysses*. To some it may seem an attempt to arrest the passage of time by immortalizing one day (Edel); to others it may seem a complex of esoteric themes (Gilbert), an acceptance of the flux of life (Lewis), a depiction of the confrontation of mind, body, and spirit (Wilson), of the infinite perspectives of the universe (Kain), or of the awareness of familial and historical cycles (Tindall). Edmund Wilson thought that Joyce and Proust express the concept of relativity, in which the world changes "as it is perceived by different observers and by them at different times." Whether intended or not, such has been the effect of *Ulysses* upon its readers.

Perhaps the best clue to the working of Joyce's imagination is the remark he made to Frank Budgen confessing his interest in Odysseus, not as a character, but as a man of many relationships—as son, father, husband, lover, companion, pacifist, warrior, inventor of the tank, and even the first gentleman, covering his naked body in Nausicaä's presence.

These modes of status can be extended into an infinite number of modes of being: the perspectives of man as a social, physical, psychological, and historic organism with his corresponding levels of physical acts, biological processes, states of consciousness, and historic and literary parallels. In what is called the stream-of-consciousness style the author need not retrict himself to literal dimensions. Much is included that neither Bloom nor Stephen would be likely to sense or feel. Joyce has hit upon what might be considered an almost infinitely expansible metaphor, for terms and symbols may be inserted regardless of their immediate relevance. What may appear on the surface to be merely an eccentric display of pedantry enables Joyce to reach a metaphysical plane unattainable by a realistic style. Everything becomes relevant: witness his insatiable and detailed curiosity, as seen in his constant demands for information from Frank Budgen, his interest in Dublin, his encyclopedic method of comprehensive accretion.

The book's basic plan permits Joyce to include everything

he knows. His awareness of depth psychology can make the brothel scene a psychoanalysis of Bloom and an encyclopedia sexualis or manual of perversions in the manner of Krafft-Ebing. His familiarity with Catholic liturgy and systematic theology will suggest parallels between Trinitarian concepts, human paternity, and artistic creation. In the manner of Dante, whom he admired as a young man in Dublin, and to whom he was compared by fellow Dubliners even as a college student, he can utilize the trip through Dublin as a starting point for excursions into such topics as burial customs, rhetorical tropes, or theories of Shakespeare. Properly understood, the stream-of-consciousness style now seems less important for its psychological validity than as a technique capable of poetic and encyclopedic elaboration. One of the most prescient of critical remarks twenty-five years ago was that by Joseph Warren Beach, who defined Joyce as a postimpressionist, less concerned with "the representation of nature" than with the creation of "an abstract composition for rendering some truth of his own conceiving."[15]

The metaphor is not only infinitely expansible but reversible as well. A commonplace incident can reflect or distort Homer, Shakespeare, or Dante; that is, the nobility of the past can satirize the present or the crassness of the present may throw doubt upon the ideality of the past. Like the clownish antics of Shaw, Joyce's artistic perspectives rest on a dazzling play of paradoxes. Dedalus reaches his most visionary flights while walking amid the debris of Sandymount Strand. Parody jostles poetry, and the concepts of Aquinas rest uneasily beside gypsy argot, obscene limericks, or tags of sentimental verse. Dublin streets echo the music of the spheres. The artist Stephen confronts the man in the street, and on the most sordid street of Dublin at that.

Whatever inspiration prompted the method, there is no doubt that it best suited his own talents. His static, metaphysical imagination, so well evoked in his concept of the epiphany, has here its natural scope. A framework of daily incident offers little opportunity for drama but endless possibilities of revelation. Analogy, symbol, parody, and phrase can add numerous perspectives to the realistic foreground. His subjective outlook finds its métier in the dramatization of the mind. His love of language can be exploited in harmonies and dissonances, and his cultivation of the mask can be indulged in rapid shifts from mockery to sympathy. He need never leave Dublin, as he often remarked, for Dublin can be the cosmos in which he can count himself king.

Personal as these considerations are, they are typical of Irish literary practice. The same amalgam of the realistic and metaphysical can be seen in Yeats, just as his lyricism and bawdry is paralleled by Gogarty's career as romantic poet and author of unprintable limericks.

Joyce's scholastic mind and musical bent alike can be utilized in the large framework of structure or the delicate nuance of the texture. Hence the inevitability of the diagram of chapters in any handbook—and the discussion of verbal motifs or repeated phrases. The counterpoint method has been widely adopted, notably by Dos Passos, Romains, and other slice-of-life novelists; it may be derived, as Levin suggests, from cinema montage, for Joyce was a film enthusiast. On the verbal level, tags and echoes constitute a loose network, the major threads of which are found indexed in my *Fabulous Voyager,* threads that are, in Gilbert's words, "as manifold and withal symmetrical as the daedal network of nerves and blood-streams which pervade the living organism."

Moving outward once more, the pattern of *Ulysses* extends, by analogies beloved of theosophists, to esoteric doctrines of metempsychosis, the omphalos as symbol of birth, the links of generations, and the lost Paradise. Stuart Gilbert, who with the Blake scholar, S. Foster Damon, was the first to tread these treacherous sands, admits that "the analogy-hunter, like the cryptogrammatist dissecting a Shakespearian text, is liable to cut a somewhat ridiculous figure, if he let his hobby run away with him." Gilbert quotes from Hermes Trismegistus, the "thrice great Hermes" of Milton, to the effect: *"That which is above is as that which is below, and that which is below is as that which is above."* The six-pointed star formed by interlocked triangles, known as Solomon's Seal, represents this concept, for each triangle is a mirror image of the other. So microcosmic man reflects the macrocosmic universe. Granted—but two questions arise, one in regard to the process of reading as analogy-hunting (where are the limits of relevance?) and the other in regard to critical evaluation (to what extent is the method acceptable?). The farfetched reading can be "somewhat ridiculous," as Gilbert admits, and no one can tell how far it is permissible to go in the direction of allegorical readings. So we have a Galileo-Bloom getting into bed with "Venus, both goddess and planet," in one recent reading. But analogy is the method of poetry, and the poetry of *Ulysses* leads to the relationships between the past and present, whether past be Egyptian, Hebrew, Celtic, or Homeric. These larger correspondences seem somewhat more significant than the Freudian Silly Symphony that finds a female symbol in the red triangle on the Bass ale label, or a comet from Vega (falling) in the Lyre ("the lyrical or self-centered") beyond Berenice ("a mother killed by her son") towards Leo, Bloom of course, and then mankind.[16] Of seeing such correspondences there is almost no end, it would seem. We are led to that allegorical type of interpretation ridiculed by Plato, or to Baconian "I, Fr. B wrote this" kind of reading of Shakespeare.

Analysis of one chapter will demonstrate the infinitely receding levels of Joyce's insight. Any imaginative reader will find the discussion of Shakespeare in the National Library scene immediately rewarding. Utilizing the rarely exploited form of the symposium, Joyce conveys a lively sense of the Dublin literary scene. His portraits of the library staff are particularly vivid, if we may trust Padraic Colum's memory. John Eglinton, one of the participants, has likewise experienced "a twinge of recollection of things actually said.[17] The theory of Shakespeare is interesting in itself, and also Irish in tenor; we recall similar biographical excursions by Professor Dowden of Trinity, and by those other Dubliners, Frank Harris, Oscar Wilde, and George Bernard Shaw. Joyce manages to introduce not only most of the plays and the names of many commentators, but such *loci classici* of biographical gossip as the second-best bed, the mulberry tree, the William the Conqueror anecdote. Above all, the imaginative reconstruction of Shakespeare's environment is a tour de force.

Remaining on the realistic level, one can note the local color of literary gossip, the references to theosophy, the Irish revival, and current poetry. But more important is the revelation of Stephen's character—his allusive imagination, his psychological obsessions, his taint of insincerity, and his outlook on life. The next step is to recognize him as a latter-day Hamlet in his remorse, sex, nausea, alienation, and ineffectuality.

The Homeric correspondences, detailed by Stuart Gilbert, involve the basic analogies with the Scylla of dogma (Aristotle, Stratford, Dublin, Bloom, nationalism) and Charybdis, where mysticism, Plato, Paris, and Stephen provide the necessary counterparts. Analogical ingenuity is even more extreme in the provision of an organ of the body (the brain), an art (literature), and a technique (dialectic) for the chapter in relation to others in the work. Not only is literature the art discussed, but literature is manifested in an embryonic state, so to speak, in the introduction of verse forms, drama, and literary echoes and turns of speech.

The ulterior direction of the discussion is not Shakespeare, of course, but the mystery of paternity. Every man plays the role of son and father, and the succession of generations is founded upon an unknowable void. And even as Stephen flounders in this morass of metaphysical doubt his spiritual father, Bloom, enters unnoticed, tiptoeing timidly to consult an old newspaper. Yet, in one sense, Stephen is aware of the analogy without understanding it, as Tindall, following Gilbert, has pointed out. For Bloom as the common man is within Stephen, and Stephen is "the recognition by Joyce of how he differs from the common man." Like the device of the play within a play, we have Stephen both discussing and enacting the drama of parental and filial relationships and hence touching upon the mystery of human identity and individuality.

The analogical level reaches through the problem of paternity to the relationship of the figures of the Trinity. So Shakespeare as father of Hamlet is artistic creator of King and Prince Hamlet. Stephen is spiritual son of the mythical Daedalus, the relation that the Sabellians attributed to Christ; he is the consubstantial son of Simon (orthodox dogma) and is to be adopted son to Bloom, as the Arian heresy held. Further correspondences can be traced between Stephen and the Irish figures of Aengus, Columbanus, and Mangan, and with the primitive Celtic bard watching for auguries, while Bloom and Shakespeare partake of a Don Giovanni manifestation. From Hamlet to Homer to the symbolistic—Hamlet; Scylla and Charybdis; the brain; literature and dialectic; paternity, Shakespeare as man and artist, and the Trinity; the Celtic, Don Giovanni—in ever widening circles meaning and association undulate.

The oft-cited letter of Dante to Can Grande della Scala outlined the four levels of his own work, as literal, allegorical, moral, and anagogical, or mystical. Applied to this chapter, the overlapping and interweaving of such meanings is apparent. Each major level has had its critical exponent. The realistic foreground receives its fullest documentation by Kain, the relation of Joyce to the modern world by Levin, the Homeric parallels and occult themes by Gilbert, the anagogical by Tindall. One may well conclude with Harry Levin that *Ulysses* is "an elusive and eclectic *Summa* of its age," including not merely themes of immediate and eternal interest to the questing mind but reflecting, as Levin continues, the major cultural forces of our time, "the montage of the cinema, impressionism in painting, *leit-motif* in music, the free association of psycho-analysis, and vitalism in philosophy."[18]

Chapter 8

Approaches to *Ulysses*

The Little Review, 1918-1920

"WE ARE ABOUT TO publish a prose masterpiece," Margaret Anderson announced confidently to the readers of *The Little Review*. She remembers reading the first installment and calling to her assistant, Jane Heap, "This is the most beautiful thing we'll ever have to publish."[1] Beginning with its first installment in March 1918, *Ulysses* has had a career of censorship, piracy, and controversy as dramatic as the adventures of the Homeric hero. Like the doughty veteran of the Trojan wars, slaying the suitors with his fabulous bow, the book has taken its toll of critics and readers of every cult and creed. To risk a cliché, one could say that, true to its Irish origin, *Ulysses* has always been in the thick of the fight.

Fantastic blend of poetry, parody, psychology, symbolism, and blasphemy, was this gigantic work a huge hoax, a personal confession, an esoteric revelation, or a modern epic? The comments of its earliest readers have been echoed for thirty-five years. Israel Solon considered Joyce "the most sensitive writer alive" but wished to "advise him to make friends with himself," while another reader expressed her gratitude in the same May issue: "I call you blessed, even as the rest of the country will some fifty years hence." But the voice of bewilderment was soon heard. "Really now," exclaimed S. S. B. in June, "what does he think he is doing?" "Joyce will have to change his style if he wants to get on," the perplexed subscriber continued, "for very few have the time or patience to struggle with his impressionistic stuff."

Jane Heap entered the battle with enthusiasm. For Jane art was real and art was earnest. With the double duty of luring subscribers and turning away creditors from the same door, she never deviated from her role as priestess of art, girt with a scrupulously modern signature of lower-case initials. She disarmed her opponent with the brusqueness of

The notes to Chapter 8 begin on page 335.

an emancipated woman. "Did it ever occur to you to read anything on the nature of writers?" she asked; if so, S. S. B. would learn that artists must express their inner compulsions, having "no concern with audiences and their demands." And that was that.

But not quite. For one reader had the effrontery to follow up with a further query: why publish Joyce at all, then, if he has no concern with audiences? "There is an inconsistency here that my mind—a fairly elastic one—cannot away with." Undaunted j. h. retorted that she was dealing with art, not economics. To R. McM., who in the June 1918 issue attributed to the review a belief in "cerise abnormal art," she replied that Joyce was "too concentrated on his work" and "too religious about life" to be obscene. "How could any one begin to discuss Joyce," she asked, "except with a person who has an intense grip on modern thought?" Whether R. McM. has since gained the necessary grip we have no way of knowing. Without it, we fear he has fallen to mysteries, best sellers, and lay sermons on how to live a happy life without benefit of modern thought.

Fortunately, all early readers were not so perturbed. A young man named Hart Crane, better known now than the other correspondents, noted that the charge of decadence is a convenient weapon against any artistic change. Baudelaire and Joyce share "a penetration into life common to only the greatest." But "the most nauseating complaint against Joyce's work is that of immorality and obscenity." Dedalus is "too good for this world" and undoubtedly would have preferred a hermitage could his experience have been attained there. Apart from Dante, the *Portrait* is "spiritually the most inspiring book I have ever read."

A chorus of approval began to rise. "Always light, witty, and playfully incisive," "beggars appreciation," "beyond doubt the most sensitive stylist writing in English," whose single episodes contain enough "to equip a regiment of novelists"—such comments appear, together with anxious inquiries about whether the public will ever accept his writing. One reader, whose enthusiasm is more apparent than his grip on modern thought, asserted that "I read him each month with eagerness, but I must confess that I am defeated in my intelligence." Pleading with the implacable j. h., he asked, "Now tell the truth—do you yourselves know where the story is at the present moment . . . just where are we?" Miss Heap set him right (though she thought the day was Tuesday), and observed that though Bloom "has had a long day . . . he has lost no time."

Meanwhile, *Ulysses* was being noticed elsewhere. Virginia Woolf had published her essay, "Modern Novels," in which she found Joyce "spiritual" in his concern "to reveal the flickerings of that innermost flame which flashes its myriad messages through the brain."[2] But *Ulysses,* though commendably daring, fails in comparison with *Youth* or *Jude the Obscure* "because of the comparative poverty of the writer's mind." If we are tempted to exclaim here, we must remember that until Stuart Gilbert's commentary (1930) or at least until the Larbaud lecture of 1921 the elaborate correspondences and intricate Scholastic tracery of Joyce were unknown. The usual emphasis is to be seen in Jane Heap's reply to another puzzled reader. To him she explained, "If you have not seen him tight-rope-walking the cobwebs of the human conscience," nor appreciated the "masterfully colored abstract picture of the mind of Dublin," if, finally, you are blind to "the luminosity of his genius," the case is hopeless:

> . . . nothing will help you but a work of equal magnitude which no one could write and which you again would not understand.

Virginia Woolf also complained of feeling "confined" in a narrow room. Burton Rascoe, in the Chicago *Tribune* of July 13, 1918, recognized Joyce's sincerity and "unexampled frankness" but found that regardless of its scientific interest *Ulysses* was "hardly of any appreciable value aesthetically." When he hailed the finished work as unique in its "vast, olympian, sardonic humor, its searching psychological insight, its bitter, racy, earthy comedy," he was taken to task by one who remembered his earlier comment. He answered the apparent inconsistency by claiming that *The Little Review* version was "badly cut . . . incoherent, and often unintelligible."[3] A. R. Orage found himself "growing more and more annoyingly mystified, bewildered and repelled" by Wyndham Lewis and Joyce, wondering whether they were writing "for readers like me?" They are becoming "too clever even for coterie, and will soon be read only by each other." Joyce had "the makings of a great . . . a classic writer," but he has begun to "cultivate his faults" to such an extent as to be "in imminent danger of brilliant provincialism." Yet when *The Little Review* installments were suppressed, he was indignant at "America Regressing." Joyce is "one of the most interesting symptoms in the present-day world"; indeed, "such sincerity, such energy, such fearlessness . . . are rare in any epoch." T. S. Eliot found Joyce's mind "subtle, erudite, even massive" but not like Stendhal's, "an instrument continually tempering and purifying emotion." In Joyce, "The basis is pure feeling."[4]

By 1921 Joyce was an established figure; his "cult . . . may be restricted, but it is intense," one observer remarked, anticipating that the published volume "is going to attract almost sensational attention."[5] He "rouses much curiosity" with his "powerful and original mind";[6] Ford Madox Ford thought he was "riding his method to death" but admired his careful development of Henry James's perceptions and Conrad's "early researches after ramified form," as well as his directness."[7] Richard Aldington published the first English critique in the April 1921 issue of *The English Review*. He found the work "an astonishing psychological document" which "has made realism mystic." Bloom was characterized as a "rags and tatters Hamlet, a proletarian Lear." As a "tremendous libel on humanity," the book's humor is harsh and sneering. Aldington saw no possible conclusion but Bloom's suicide, "though no doubt it will terminate in the pleasant purlieus of a public lavatory." Joyce's influence, he feared, would be bad, for though he justifies his own obscurity and indecency, others "will be disgusting without reason" and "will write mere confusion and think it sublime."[8] In *The Dial* Scofield Thayer characterized the atmosphere as "a world of battered derbies and bleared souls." Joyce is a cynical observer of contemporary society:

> Mr. Joyce exhibits the cynicism of a fine nature habituated but not subdued to the sordidity of our industrial civilization, and his pictures are too acrid not to persuade us of their truth. In the end we come uncomfortably near feeling that human life itself may be insolvent.[9]

Meanwhile four issues had been confiscated by postal authorities, and on October 4, 1920, the final blow fell. The editors came to trial on December 13 for violating the postal regulations governing obscene reading matter. Mr. John Quinn (later the owner of the manuscript) took the case for the defendants. The trial, duly reported in *The Little Review*, was to Margaret Anderson "the only farce I ever participated in with any pleasure." John Cowper Powys and others testified to Joyce's distinction as a man of letters. This was deemed irrelevant! One of the judges, hearing of Joyce's unveiling of the subconscious mind, gasped, "Here, here, you might as well talk Russian." Mr. Quinn, undaunted, summed up in words that even the court could understand, but to no avail. A fine of $100 was levied. Serial publication was discontinued.

The twenty-three installments of *Ulysses* in *The Little Review* comprise almost exactly half of the finished work, printing the text only as far as the first quarter of the hospital scene, to the top of page 388 in the Modern Library Giant edition. A comparison of the texts throws considerable light on Joyce's processes of composition. His revisions are almost always additions. The Stephen Dedalus scenes are least touched, with the important additions of the theme word "Agenbite" and the recollection of Columbanus striding over his mother's prostrate body to fulfill his mission. One of the striking technical devices is an afterthought—the use of headlines in the newspaper scene. More crucial, however, is the addition of the two magnificent descriptions that open the chapter, those of the trolleys before Nelson's Pillar and of the royal mail cars at the post office. The descriptive vigor with which streets, traffic, the sights, sounds, and smells emerge in *Ulysses* is almost entirely missing from the earlier version. The small boy smoking and the girl with eczema, the child playing marbles, the ripped-up roadway before the tenements, the gravedigger "with shouldred weapon, its blade blueglancing"—such are a few of the vignettes of city life not to be found in *The Little Review*. Joyce became more conscious of the narrative value of such specific tradesmen and place names as Hanlon's milkman, Boland's bread van, and the house-by-house description of Sackville Street seen from the funeral carriage. It is Bloom's character that gains most in detail, with his stream of consciousness almost doubled in spots. His ingenuity, curiosity, humor, and sympathy are elaborated and the cliché-laden nature of his mind developed.

The First Edition, 1922

The Autumn 1921 issue of *The Little Review* carried a full-page announcement of the first edition to be published by the Shakespeare Book Shop in Paris. Advance press notices by Ezra Pound ("an impassioned meditation on life"), Richard Aldington ("a most remarkable book"), *The Times* ("of the utmost sincerity . . . complete courage"), Evelyn Scott ("a contemporary of the future . . . recreating a portion of the English language"), *The New Age* ("one of the most interesting symptoms in the whole literary world"), Larbaud ("l'Irlande fait une reentrée sensationnelle . . . dans la haute litterature européenne") were quoted. The issue consisted of 1,000 copies: one hundred autographed at 350 francs, the rest, depending on the quality of paper, at 250 and 150 francs. The large, almost square volume, with ample margins and clear type, covered in pale blue paper, with ULYSSES in bold white letters at the top and BY JAMES JOYCE at the bottom (the colors of the Greek flag, as suggested by Joyce himself), looking like a telephone directory, was formal, massive, and dignified in appearance. Here certainly was no ordinary trade book.

Few books have been so well heralded in advance. In addition to the interest aroused by the magazine installments and the trial, an introductory lecture was given in Paris by Valéry Larbaud on December 7, 1921. Summarizing the fable, the distinguished French critic noted that since "all the elements are constantly melting into each other" and since "the whole is movement," "the ilusion of life . . . is complete." But *Ulysses* is more than an elaborate *Dubliners:* it touches upon philosophy, politics, science, and history, and, beyond that, Joyce has incorporated in Bloom those traits of the universal Ulysses he admired as a schoolboy: his loyalty, benevolence, sensitivity, and his foibles. The book has an intricate groundwork, now revealed for the first time:

> . . . each episode deals with a particular art or science, contains a particular symbol, represents a special organ of the human body, has its particular colour (as in the Catholic liturgy), has its proper technique, and takes place at a particular hour of the day.

Ulysses is thus "a genuine example of the art of mosaic." But the question arises of how such an artfully contrived work can be so effective: "one asks how it can be that out of such a formidable labour of manipulation so living and moving a work could issue." Larbaud answers:

> The manifest reason is that the author has never lost

> sight of the humanity of his characters, of their whole composition of virtues and faults, turpitude, and greatness; man, the creature of flesh, living out his day.

As for the frankness, it is attributable to Joyce's desire "to display moral, intellectual, and physical man entire." Neither "salacious nor lewd" in intention, Joyce "simply describes and represents." The essay concludes with the tantalizingly unanswered question of why Bloom is a Jew, the critic suggesting "symbolical, mystical, and ethnological reasons . . . which should be quite clear to readers of the book." But "if Joyce has made his chosen hero, the spiritual father of this Stephen Dedalus who is his second self, a Jew—it is not because of anti-Semitism."[10]

Had early readers and reviewers availed themselves of this important study, the first significant document in the literature about Joyce, many errors of judgment and interpretation might have been avoided.

The book was an immediate sensation. "Waited for these many years with bated breath," as the Paris edition of the Chicago *Tribune* put it, it was soon selling at a premium. By April we hear of the "scramble for copies" being "bought as an investment," the price in England meanwhile rising from £3/3 to four and a half guineas. The "considerable demand among collectors" makes it "bound to become scarce." "The talk is all of one book"; an American publisher has been told not to return without a copy. By May the price is £11. It is "all the rage"; classic status is predicted, and it is "the fashion of enthusiastic youth to consider Joyce the peer of Swift, Smollett, and Fielding." In June, we are told, "London literary circles are just recovering from the craze," but by the end of the year one learns that "it has aroused enemies to fury and friends to exultant prophecy" and that an initial buyer might realize a 100 per cent profit. Copies are bringing £60 by the next February; rumor has it that "the die-hards in Dublin are offering a £100 prize to anyone who will write a novel showing Dublin in a softer light." In 1924 "everybody in Paris continues to talk about James Joyce," but by the end of 1925 one reviewer fears that experimental art may strike "a false note, certain to end in nothing but an unfortunate memory," like *Ulysses*. Yet Galsworthy reflects bitterly in 1925 on the changing tides of taste, in which Dostoevski replaces Turgenev, Proust is seen to usurp the place of France, "and a Joyce replace the Deity."[11]

Early reviews capitalized on the sensational nature of the book with such lurid captions as "A Monstrous Book" or "Poisonous Literature." Miss Harriet Weaver's valuable file of clippings, now in the Slocum Collection at Yale, includes items from the major journals of Europe and America, as well as pieces from as far as Egypt and New South Wales.

Though Edmund Wilson once spoke of the "disconcerting stupidities which have put so many eminent English critics and novelists under the suspicion of not knowing chalk from cheese,"[12] the first reviews are by no means universally lacking in perception. Shock and bewilderment dominate, but Herbert Gorman gives a false impression in his biography by quoting the most sensational attacks. And even though we may now smile at the consternation aroused in some quarters, it must be remembered that *Ulysses* was the first book of magnitude which was of such limited general appeal—and which flouted conventions of taste so explicitly. But if of limited appeal, it was not nearly so incomprehensible as some excited reviewers claimed. Dr. Joseph Collins exaggerated its unreadability in claiming that "Not ten men or women out of a hundred can read *Ulysses* through, and of the ten who succeed . . . five of them will do it as a tour de force." N. P. Dawson likened Joyce to the cuttlefish, which conceals its shortcoming by emitting an inky fluid. Not more than five or ten will be able to read the novel, whose "proper place will be under glass in a museum." Another reviewer found it nothing more than an "immense mass of clotted nonsense," confessing that "I don't know whether I am standing on my head or my heels." Shane Leslie dismissed it as "impossible to read" and "undesirable to quote" and suggested that "a gigantic effort has been made to fool the world."[13]

No plan of organization was detected by the unsympathetic reviewers, who concluded that the author had merely reproduced the chaos of the world or that of the subconscious mind. Thus the "Affable Hawk" of the *New Statesman* editorialized that Joyce "has sunk a shaft down into the welter of nonsense which lies at the bottom of the mind, pumped up this stuff, and presented it as a criticism of life."[14] Henry Seidel Canby, in the *Literary Review,* recognized Joyce's "distinct though peculiar genius" but thought the work "a dirty masterpiece" of such obscurity as to suggest a collaboration of mad Shaws, Moores, Beerbohms, and Anatole Frances.[15]

It was the alleged obscenity that most enraged these reviewers, together with what they felt to be the nihilistic tendencies of the work. "Affable Hawk" found it "a morose delectation in dirt," with no intellect guiding the writing but "only a mass of nerves and a haunted imagination." He continued the attack three years later in refuting Edwin Muir's sympathetic essay on Joyce. *Ulysses* is "the product of a frightened and enslaved mind," a mind "cold, nasty, small, and over-serious." Joyce's humor cannot be compared to the "coarse but glorious fearlessness" of Rabelais, for "If there ever was a writer who was afraid of the Devil it is Mr. Joyce."[16]

Reviewers for the mass journals were less temperate. "Aramis" of *The Sporting Times* flung one epithet after another: "perverted lunatic . . . . literature of the latrine . . . . a demented George Meredith . . . . devoid of wit . . . . coarse salacity . . . . enough to make a hottentot sick . . . . morbidly pornographic."[17] The "Canis Domini" of *The Dublin Review* equalled "Aramis." "The Irish literary movement," he averred, "is not going to find its stifling climax in a French sink." As "the screed of one possessed," *Ulysses* indicates that "a great Jesuit-trained talent has gone over malignantly and mockingly to the powers of evil." This "rotten caviare" is "a fearful travesty on persons, happenings, and intimate life of the most morbid and sickening description," whose only intent could be "to make angels weep and to amuse fiends." To Shane Leslie it was "an Odyssey of the sewer," an example of "literary Bolshevism" by "a striking literary genius, who has since yoked himself to the steeds of Comedy and Blasphemy and taken headlong flight . . . . like the Gadarene swine, into a choking sea of impropriety." Improprieties have appeared in the world's classics, Leslie admitted, but the skill or humor or reprobation with which they have been treated "condone if not excuse their portrayal." Alfred Noyes, under the title "Rottenness in Literature," though it "the foulest book that has ever found its way into print" and lamented "the appalling fact" that such work should be treated seriously by metropolitan criticism at the very time that some of the noblest pages of English literature, such as Tennyson, are being depreciated. James Douglas, though describing *Ulysses* as "the most infamously obscene book in ancient or modern literature," was more reassuring:

> The England of Milton and Wordsworth at least stands firm in defence of decency, decorum, good manners and good morals.[18]

Dr. Collins regarded it as symptomatic of a devastating nihilism, with "no reverence for organized religion, for conventional morality for literary style or form . . . without a sense of duty, of service, of conformity to the State, to the community, to society." To Canby, on the other hand, it suggested an imbalance in Joyce that approaches madness, in that it is "indecent as the alcoholic is intoxicated, driven by an obsession." One is aroused to pity at the spectacle of "the devastating effect of unrestrained obsession upon skillful genius."

Together with Larbaud, the most influential spokesmen for Joyce were Ezra Pound and T. S. Eliot. Pound considered Joyce unique in carrying further the tradition of Flaubert, particularly of *Bouvard et Pécuchet,* so aptly described by Descharmes as "Encyclopedia put into farce." Joyce "has perfected the great collection of objects for ridicule." The book has the form of a sonata, revealing more architecture than any of Flaubert. But the Homeric parallels constitute a mere scaffold, which does not restrict or inconvenience the action or its contemporaneity. Before Joyce, "Only Rabelais and Flaubert attacked a whole century"; with his work, the encyclopedia of idiocy, the revelation of universal imbecility, is achieved for our day.[19]

If Pound emphasized the satirical aspect, Eliot concerned himself with Joyce's use of myth. *Ulysses* is "the most important expression which the present age has found . . . . a book to which we are all indebted, and from which none of us can escape." And its importance rests in releasing narrators from the impasse that the novel has been in since its death with Flaubert and James. The mythical method is "a way of controlling, of ordering, of giving a shape and significance to the immense panorama of futility and anarchy which is contemporary history." It indicates a return to classicism, "a step toward making the modern world possible for art." These remarks, somewhat cryptic even in their full context, become meaningful as we consider the emphasis upon the mythic approach to literary criticism in the last five years; that is, the awareness of recent readers that the most significant works have an implicit mythic structure or at least mythic overtones suggested by style and symbol.[20]

The more perceptive critics were quick to recognize signs of genius. Sisley Huddleston hailed Joyce as a man of complete sincerity. "No book has ever been more eagerly and curiously awaited" than *Ulysses,* where "erudition [is] transfigured by imagination." As for the frankness, Joyce "would be untrue to himself and to his subject were he to tone down and leave out" any of the details of human existence. The trim, taut phrases, the moments of illumination and of color testify to the author's "sheer power of craftsmanship." In content, the book is startling: "blasphemy and beauty, poetry and piggishness, jostle each other." Molly's soliloquy, according to the usual standards, might be called "the vilest . . . in all literature," yet even its "obscenity is somehow beautiful and wrings the soul to poetry." Joyce is true to his vision, in that he has "exaggerated the vulgarity and magnified the madness of mankind and the mysterious materiality of the universe."[21]

Edmund Wilson thought it a work "of high genius" that "has the effect at once of making everything else look brassy." It is the immense scale of development rather than the theme that is imposing, for even though it be "perhaps the most faithful X-ray ever taken of the ordinary human consciousness," it is fundamentally nothing more than "an amusing anecdote without philosophic moral." Yet Joyce shows in his characters "the throes of the human mind straining always to perpetuate and perfect itself and of the body always laboring and throbbing to throw up some beauty."[22]

In view of the official disapproval of Joyce in Ireland, it may come as something of a surprise that two of the fine early reviews were Irish. "Lawrence K. Emery," actually A. J. Leventhal, who later wrote an appreciation for the *Dublin Magazine,* predicted that the book would "carry away young writers on its irrepressible tide." In it are to be found "all the strivings of the modern world." As a humorist he is companion of Boccaccio and Petronius but differentiated from Rabelais by "his canny aloofness." In his detachment he is a scientist, but *Ulysses* is "a human book, filled with pity." Like the Dadaists and Picasso in "expressing life from a new angle with a changed vision," Joyce cannot be denied genius "of a very high order." Style alone "will keep *Ulysses* alive for posterity." Leventhal was one of the first to remark the quality of particular episodes, noting the Shakespeare discussion in the National Library, the supreme buffoonery in Kiernan's bar the "wild, senseless frenzy" of the brothel scene, and Molly's soliloquy.[23]

P. S. O'Hegarty, well-known Dublin bibliophile, contributed a frank defense to *The Separatist*. His first reaction was delight at "the whole panorama of Dublin and of Dublin people," his second nausea, but finally a realization that "here is a big book, perhaps the biggest book that has ever been done in English in the form of fiction." Joyce has used the language "as it never before was used, and used it triumphantly," achieving something Continental rather than English. The book includes "not a story merely, but an epoch." Above all, Joyce is Irish:

> Ireland is all through him, and in him, and of him; and Dublin, its streets and its buildings and its people, he loves with the wholehearted affection of the artist. . . . He may live out of Dublin, but he will never get away from it.

—a remark surprisingly similar to that made by Joyce himself many times in his later life. The frankness is justified, and as for Molly's soliloquy, "there is nothing like it in literature." Though "Ireland at present will probably not love Mr. Joyce," he "has done her honour" and stands with Wilde, Shaw, Moore, and Synge in representing the Irish spirit.[24]

Eimar O'Duffy, in *The Irish Review,* also found that Joyce loves Ireland irrationally, as a faithful lover: "Ireland is his Beatrice, whom he loves without hope and without return." But the reviewer felt indignation at his country's neglect of "a great artist—perhaps the greatest artist in English prose now living." *Ulysses* is monumental in scope and execution, an epic that contains "as much thought and beauty" on a single page as is to be found in entire volumes of well-regarded poetasters. The preliminary chapters dealing with Stephen may destroy the book's unity, and one might desire as hero "one less sexually obsessed," yet the spirit of a bygone age is revealed in the chatter and gossip of the day, and the author's evocative power covers a wide range:

> Figures that Hogarth might have painted . . . ; keen encounters of wits; subtle searching into human souls; passages of description that catch the heart; grim pictures of the foulness of man—such are the memories one retains of this vast prose-poem.

Far from being immoral, it should be a deterrent to vice, yet one may still raise a question about why we should "gratuitously defile our literature." The pages of nonsense and the morbid obsession with sex are "stigmata of degeneracy." One can but conclude that "It is a pity that so great an artist should give his malady full play."[25]

Arnold Bennett's review provides an interesting reflection of the reaction to be expected from the middle-class British intellectual. He is skeptical about the virtue of basing the book on the events of one day; it could be done by anyone, "given sufficient time, paper, childish caprice, and obstinacy." Joyce's "sardonic temper" is apparent in his choice of "nearly the dailiest day possible" (Bennett did not know that on this day Joyce met his future wife). In his obscurity, Joyce has failed to extend to the public "the common courtesies of literature." Bennett's exasperation is amusing, and even pardonable, when he asserts that "After all, to comprehend *Ulysses* is not among the recognized learned professions." Novel reading becomes "a fair imitation of penal servitude"; Bennett finished it with "the sensation of a general who has just put down an insurrection." He then blindly charged Joyce with having "little sense of environment" nor "much poetical sense"—two of the features most frequently remarked by later readers. Nonetheless, he is "a very astonishing phenomenon in letters":

> He is sometimes dazzlingly original. If he does not see life whole he sees it piercingly. His ingenuity is marvellous. He has wit. He has a prodigious humour. He is afraid of naught.

The "staggering indency" is not, on the whole, justified by the results, but in the finest passages (such as Molly's soliloquy) it is.[26]

Virginia Woolf was alternately attracted by Joyce's skill and repelled by his pretentiousness and vulgarity. Her diary reports the early reactions of "Tom Eliot, which are less favorable than one might expect: *Ulysses* succeeds technically, and destroys the novel, but it lacks a central theme and affords no new insights.

The remarks of other contemporary authors are equally interesting. Katharine Mansfield tired to be "doubly fair" because of her dislike, but she could not overcome "the feeling of wet linoleum and unemptied pails." For her it was not art but "a kind of stage on the way" because "the act of projection has not been made." Her first complete reading was more enthusiastic, finding the Blooms "superbly done," though the book was "fearfully difficult and obscure." Three months later her ardor had cooled: "The further I am away from it, the less I think of it." Yet "its appearance sometime was inevitable."[27] A. E. hoped that the Inferno of *Ulysses* might be followed by a Purgatorio and a Paradiso, "to make it unquestionably the greatest fiction of the twentieth century."[28]

To Yeats it displayed "a cruel playful mind like a great, soft tiger cat," yet it was "our Irish cruelty" and "our kind of strength." Later he thought, strangely enough, that Joyce and Lawrence had almost restored "Eastern simplicity" but that their obsessions with sex and sin prevented it. *Ulysses* became for him "more undoubtedly a work of genius than any prose written since the death of Synge." Reverting to the oriental concept, he linked Joyce with Ezra Pound and Virginia Woolf in suggesting the Samhain philosophy:

> a deluge of experience breaking over us and within us, melting limits . . . . man no hard bright mirror . . . . but a swimmer, or rather the waves themselves.[29]

An acquaintance of Joyce in Paris during the early twenties has recalled to the author of the present study an unpublished anecdote, in which Joyce used a similar figure to describe his view of religion. Men, he said to Al Laney, then a correspondent for the Paris *Herald,* are like deep-sea fish, swimming in water that is mysteriously irradiated with light from above the surface but unable to rise to the surface to see—a characteristic figure in its grotesquerie and its relevance to Joyce's own limited sight.

George Bernard Shaw relieved himself of a witticism. To him the book "only proved that Dublin men and boys are as incorrigibly filthy-minded now as they were in my youth." It is an honest document, but once the conditions of Dublin were changed, the ribaldry would "have no more interest than a twelfth-century map of the world has to-day."[30] A. E. Housman "scrambled and waded through" the work, finding only "one or two half-pages amusing" and thinking Lawrence "much more wholesome."[31] Lawrence felt that in Joyce and Richardson "you are sewed inside a wool mattress that is being slowly shaken up, and you are turning to wool along with the rest of the woolliness." Such self-consciousness is "awful" and "childish":

> One has to be self-conscious at seventeen: still a little self-conscious at twenty-seven then it is a sign of arrested development, nothing else. And if it is still continuing at forty-seven, it is obvious senile precocity.[32]

To Aldous Huxley he wrote in exasperation about the "clumsy olla putrida" which is "Nothing but old fags and cabbage-stumps of quotations. . . . stewed in the juice of deliberate, journalistic dirty-mindedness."[33] The reading of *Ulysses* gave F. Scott Fitzgerald "a sort of hollow, cheerless pain," making him "feel appallingly naked." But seven weeks later he was still undecided about "*Ullyses* [*sic*] application to me" (his spelling was always atrocious).[34]

Joyce's scientific impersonality was frequently emphasized. Like an alchemist he places human mechanisms in his crucible, looking "for the philosopher's stone," but "the whitewashed walls of his cell" stand between him and the world. He has "the cold curiosity of a kinematographer"; he is possessed with "amazing precocity, untrammelled license, prodigious patience."[35]

A directly opposing view is forwarded by those who saw a man tormented by deep personal obsessions. Indeed, as one reviews the varying attitudes toward author and work he is reminded of the mutually contradictory theories of Hamlet's motivation. Perhaps this is not merely coincidental, for we recall Stephen's highly personal interpretation of Shakespeare in the library chapter of *Ulysses*. Mary Colum's excellent review in the *Freeman,* entitled "The Confessions of James Joyce," is one of the classic early interpretations. *Ulysses* "belongs to the Confession class of literature," Mrs. Colum averred.

> Like Rousseau, Joyce derived everything from his own ego. . . . like Rousseau, he has a passion not only for revealing himself, but for betraying himself; like him also, he deforms everything he touches.

His method of deforming is that of "a sexual smear." Bloom is "the one character whom Joyce really loves." On the other hand, the revelation of Molly's mind, though it "would doubtless interest the laboratory," would seem to normal people "an exhibition of the mind of a female gorilla." The alarming feature of the work is that it suggests "a real and not fantastic fear that science will oust literature altogether as a part of human expression." Though the work is "a kind of epic of Dublin," which conveys "the psychology of that battered, beautiful eighteenth-century city in its last days of servitude," it seems impossible that it could be fully comprehended "by anybody not brought up in the half-secret tradition of Irish nationalism, or unfamiliar with the philosophy, history, and rubrics of the Roman Catholic Church."[36]

John Middleton Murry likewise found it "an immense, a prodigious self-laceration, the tearing away from himself, by a half-demented man of genius, of inhibitions and limitations." But readers "will profit by the vicarious sacrifice." *Ulysses* was called a "great epic of hell" and a revelation by one "peculiarly sensitive to the brutal and sordid." The reviewer of the Glasgow *Herald,* upon finishing the book, "felt like ringing up a monastery and inquiring about a cell and a hair shirt." The author's obscenity arises from his never finding weapons enough "to destroy the deep roots of his Roman Catholic prejudices," or, in the words of Gilbert Seldes, "marks the defeat of the poet. . . . overcome by the reality of experience," which eventuates in an unequaled "galvanic fury." Stephen's turning to Bloom represents "the broken poet turning to sympathy with the outward going scientific mind," yet Joyce's "immense relish" for actuality lends "humor and kindness and irony" to Bloom's portrait and turns "this epic of defeat" into "a victory of the creative intelligence over the chaos of uncreated things." As "an image of contemporary life," *Ulysses* is "one of the most significant and beautiful" of modern works.[37]

Cecil Maitland bearded the lion in suggesting that Joyce's obsessions were attributable, not to his own personality, but to the Roman Catholic tradition—and this in the Catholic journal, *The New Witness,* edited by that most militant of apologists, G. K. Chesterton! The result was a lively controversy. Joyce's power of eliciting "the subtlest processes of the mind" is recognized by Maitland, yet the "frontiers of the imagination are very rigid," there being "no hint of a conception of the human body as anything but dirty," no "nobility but that of pride of intellect." This narrow vision with its emphasis on "the excremental and sexual mechanism" seems "inexplicable in so profoundly imaginative and observant a student of humanity" but it is to be blamed on the Catholic tradition. Aquinas "would probably be more at home with Freud" than such naïve devotees as Chesterton, who conceive of the Catholic life as "one of simple devoutness, tempered by beer, carols and jollity in public-houses, with perhaps an occasional good fat sin to be expiated by a thumping penance." Joyce's humor is "the cloacal humour of the refectory" and "his view of sex has the obscenity of a confessor's manual." The failure is that "of the Catholic system, which has not had the strength to hold him to its transcendentalism, and from whose errors he has not been able to set himself free."

Chesterton rushed to the counterattack. Maitland's is "An Extraordinary Argument," for, apart from the tiresome instance of the textbooks of the confessional, as threadbare as the tales of Maria Monk or Guy Fawkes, "he denounces the clerical books for immorality: admires the secular story for the same immorality: and is much gratified because the immorality he admires is copied from the immorality he denounces." Chesterton has subtly distorted Maitland's thesis, for the original review lamented what it held to be perverted views in both Joyce and the Catholic tradition. *Ulysses* was admired on other grounds. Chesterton is safer in distinguishing between Aquinas and Freud, who bases his philosophy on the subconscious. For, Chesterton continues, if Aquinas was poisoned by the Catholic tradition, what poisoned Freud? Even Maitland cannot hear the "catlike tread" of the Jesuits "behind the curtains." The most "brazenly irrational" of his theories is that of blaming the church because the individual has not followed its doctrines of purity—like a disobedient son who first despises his mother's advice, "then despises her for giving advice that can be despised." One can find sin in oneself, or "in the ordinary modern materialistic city." The suggestion that one "had to go to the confessional-box" to find it is absurd; the argument "is simply not worth talking about."

A lengthy correspondence ensued. Joyce was charged with utilizing the data of "underground lavatories," and his "inherent vulgarity," "cold venom," and "indecent spiritual pride" were attacked. In vain did Maitland attempt in two letters to clarify his point of view, or one reader defend him. Of all Irish writers, how does it happen that Joyce is "the only one to cabin his soul in a latrine"? And how could a church that celebrates the body and blood of Christ, "which strenuously preaches the sanctity of marriage, forbids all tampering with natural bodily processes. . . . and has always supplied the world's best nurses" be accused of producing "any contempt for the body"?[38]

The astounding psychological insight of *Ulysses* attracted the attention of most early reviewers. Edmund Wilson considered the stream-of-consciousness technique to be Joyce's fundamental contribution to the art of fiction:

> In "Ulysses" we have the record . . . of the mind of man in all its apparent inconsequence and confusion, its mixture of memory of the past and attention to the present, of things thought, things imagined, things felt and things experienced in the subconscious, of practical, gustatory, religious, political and sexual preoccupations, as it shifts and shivers and weaves behind the front we present to the world.

Molly's soliloquy is "the finest thing in the book":

> it is surely one of the most movingly beautiful things in modern fiction. Here one sees the gross, ill-drained body of humanity itself touched divinely by cloudly visions of its creative splendors yet profoundly sunken and bound by its laboring flesh.

Comparable to the passage describing the calling of the artist in the *Portrait,* it stands as one of "the superb twin peaks" of Joyce, "the creative ecstasies of the human mind and of the human body—the supreme justifications, respectively, of the man and of the woman."[39] From the book "there leap out at us all our most secret and most unsavoury thoughts," exclaimed S. P. B. Mais. His "explorations of the mind compel us to regard all other realists as rather timid"; *Ulysses* is "a book that is a man's life . . . the life of Everyman." Yet the amazing thing about Joyce's treatment is that he has saved "the novel of the mind" from "its worst fate," that of "becoming a mere amateur contribution to medical textbooks."[40]

This leads to the final observations, those of structure and style. Nothing material was added to the early remarks by Eliot and Larbaud on the mythic framework, except such qualifications as those of D. M. Curtnesse in *The New Age* that the structure is "broken and swamped by unnecessary detail," since Joyce's "passion for mosaic work . . . covers up his outlines." And comment on style is surprisingly sparse. Ernest Boyd was one of the first to show Joyce's unusual combination of material detail and poetic fantasy. The "bewildering juxtaposition of the real and the imaginary" suggests the German expressionists Hasenclever and Kaiser; this expressionism is Joyce's means of escape from sordid reality, as romanticism was Flaubert's. Matthew Josephson analyzed the remarkable command of language: Joyce's rhetoric is "as bold as that of John Donne." The author has "a madness . . . *for the word;* the play of it, the color, the tempo." Josephson listed and illustrated some of the devices—modulation, reconstruction, neologism, inversion, imagery—but feared the influence *Ulysses* might have on formlessness and vagueness; the "waste stretches of dreary gabble" in the saloons bored him. He wondered how such a talent as Joyce's could be "buried in this trivial vulgarity":

> What kind of mind must he have . . . to continue indefatigably the precious relation of this saloon talk. . . . One grows tired and beer-logged. Someone take him home, sometime! . . . I am the little ragged boy sent by your grandma to pluck you by the sleeve to beg you to come home Mr. Joyce.

Joyce's "new and lovely groupings of words" attracted one reviewer, and the Paris *Herald* exclaimed over "a witchery of words that woos." Ford Madox Ford noted the "immense pleasure" to be derived from Joyce's cadences, as well as the inevitability of the work as a whole:

> the greatest literary influence of the day . . . for good or ill introduced at last into literature the note of complexity that is the note of the life we live. You may not like *Ulysses,* but you cannot get away from it.

Ford deserves recognition for his generous support of Joyce, especially inasmuch as he was probing the same areas of psychological complexities. Free of envy, he defended Joyce's handling of indecency as necessary for the complete portrayal of man and predicted that "gradually across our literature there will spread the Ulyssean complexion." As a member of the "haughty and proud" younger generation, Joyce is its supreme artist, and *Ulysses* resembles "a new continent"; the mind is "analyzed as it has never before been analyzed." Joyce uses language "rather like an orchestra than an instrument," Stephen Gwynn remarked, and *Ulysses* recalls the celebrated Book of Kells in its "almost incredible skill in the manipulation of detail, spiral within spiral"—perhaps the first time this comparison was made. But the book's true value is its passion, "the cry of a tortured soul." The faith that Stephen rejects "clings to his flesh like the poisoned shirt of Hercules."[41]

The Reputation Established, 1924-1934

The first excitement about the monstrous book had died down. The self-appointed guardians of morality had had their way; it was necessary to read *Ulysses* in smuggled copies, and the pornographic reputation was circulated by word of mouth. A Helen Hokinson cartoon of 1931 in *The New Yorker* depicted a middle-aged clubwoman in Paris inquiring in her American French of the bookseller, "Avez-vous *Ulysses?*" More knowledge about the book was clearly needed. Valéry Larbaud, Ezra Pound, and T. S. Eliot had led the way, to be sure, but their work, though still central to discussion of the book, was to prove mere program notes in comparison to the rising bulk of Joyce exegesis. That some of this exposition should be more devout than inspired is to be expected; nevertheless, work of solid merit was achieved, and the result was a more widespread respect for Joyce as an artist and the gradual development of a more intelligent audience.

Herbert Gorman's *James Joyce: The First Forty Years* (1924) was the first study, providing a useful handbook of information, though scarcely breaking new critical ground. Gorman and his early successors Paul Jordan Smith (*A Key to the "Ulysses" of James Joyce,* 1927), Charles Duff (*James Joyce and the Plain Reader,* 1932), and Louis Golding (*James Joyce,* 1933) are frankly introductory. They cover much material that is by now commonplace—Joyce's amoral approach, his treatment of manifold aspects of life, the Homeric parallels, the stream-of-consciousness style, the linguistic, the portrait of a city and a civilization, the theme of paternity. What Herbert Marshall McLuhan says rather severely of practically all the Joyce critics except Pound, Eliot, and Wyndham Lewis does apply to these pioneer popularizers: that they "approach their subject in an awkward and diffident spirit," since they "bitterly resent the strain to which he subjects their powers of attention." Lacking as they do any sense of vital artistic issues, they present Joyce "not as an immediate and relevant source of artistic nutriment but as a monster exhibit to awe the dim of mind."[42]

But they did have the notion, almost lost by the new and "higher" criticism, that a literate public could read Joyce with profit and that perhaps an intelligent reader could discover something for himself. Nor are these books entirely commonplace, despite the necessity of spending many pages summarizing the action. Gorman noted Joyce's thinly concealed patriotism and religious feeling, Duff the paradoxes of the Irish mentality; Golding, the most independent of all, finds Joyce a poor poet, a man frustrated by his terror of religion, and hence lonely, isolated from contemporary affairs, unable to portray women as living creatures. He is blunt in asserting the practical disadvantage of Joyce's frankness, yet subtle enough to see irony in the sermons on Hell in the *Portrait* and in the necessary but unflattering role played by the British private in humiliating Stephen in *Ulysses*. Yet in all these introductions, much of Joyce's magic escapes. Padraic Colum's review of Duff indicates one lack, the failure to note Joyce's ability to reveal " 'essences'—the timeless aspect of the things we can distinguish." Colum attributes Joyce's emphasis upon the eternal to his lack of interest in history, a shortcoming easily understandable in "a proud spirit in a defeated and frustrated country."[43]

The complicated publishing history of *Ulysses* has been recounted in considerable detail by Gorman, and with bibliographical data by Slocum and Cahoon. It constitutes an important chapter in the history of the author's reputation. From January 1924 to May 1920 Shakespeare and Company published eight editions, which, with the first editions, sold 28,000 copies. Doubt has been thrown on reports that United States customs officials destroyed 500 of the 2,000 Egoist Press edition and that all but one of the copies issued to replace these were, in turn, confiscated by English officials. Nevertheless the tale is dramatic and becomes more so with the intervention of none less than the Lord himself. For the Lord appeared unto one Samuel Roth, a New York publisher, saying that "you are today, as Noah was before you, a good man in your generation." Such supernatural intervention must have comforted Mr. Roth, busy defending himself on charges of unauthorized publication of Joyce's work. His pirated *Ulysses* contained some fourteen episodes and appeared from

July 1926 to October 1927 in the magazine *Two World's Monthly*. The blatant theft of literary material led to a protest signed by many writers. Despite the ensuing injunction, Roth, who was also reprinting portions of the unnamed later work in another magazine, remained undeterred. He issued a bound volume of the *Ulysses* portion, with the Preface which described the Lord's visit, and he seems to have sponsored a forged "1927 Shakespeare Press" edition of 1929, the edition which, it has been shown, was used by Random House in setting up the incorrect American editions after 1933.

The years between 1926 and 1931 represent a watershed of English opinion. Arthur Symons and Cyril Connolly on the one hand, and Aldous Huxley and "John Carruthers" on the other, show the perplexed imbalance of valuation. Symons, Joyce's first champion, confirmed in 1926 his opinion of the young poet of *Chamber Music,* seeing in him a "curious mixture of sinister genius and uncertain talent," deriving from an almost morbid awareness of human ills. He is, like St. John of the Cross, one to whom, "if God is a deep but dazzling darkness, He is also the supreme love." Symons prophetically predicted that he would become "the most complex literary problem of this generation." Huxley, though admitting his talent, considered that "his researches are barren —they end in a cul-de-sac." It must be noted, however, that Huxley was undoubtedly thinking as much about *Work in Progress* as *Ulysses*. In 1928 "John Carruthers" found Joyce temporarily the most influential of interior novelists, though a year later Cyril Connolly, surveying "The Position of Joyce," concluded that he was admired only in Paris and America. "Carruthers" saw him as a "complete subjectivist" who in his skepticism was led "to surrender himself utterly to the stream of consciousness" as "the only trustworthy source of truth." The result, despite Aristophanic comedy and linguistic skill, was chaos. Connolly was nearer the fact in asserting that Joyce, as a rebel against his own limitations of Catholicism and Celtic romanticism, spoke of his entire generation, dramatizing "their own forebodings."[44]

The inclusion of Joyce in a series of B.B.C. talks on modern literature in 1931 provoked a protest to the London *Times* by Alfred Noyes. The archconservtive who found Edmund Gosse the most adequate critic of *Ulysses* argued that it would be inadvisable "to entrust the great machine" of the radio to mere "talkers." The public can be better guided than by "any wireless 'educator,' no matter how rosy or supposedly unsafe his opinions, or how conventionally unconventional the pattern of his discreetly disguised herdsman's crook." Douglas Jerrold seconded, claiming that the staff seemed prejudiced in favor of "advanced" critics.

Answers appeared immediately, one noting that hitherto the public has been treated "as if it had grown out of the 'Sanford and Merton' stage of literary appreciation." Most effective of all was a manifesto signed by such publishers as Blackwell, Cape and Longman and a host of writers, including Eliot, Forster, Huxley, Shaw, and Woolf. The threatened prohibition against discussion of living authors was withdrawn, and Alfred Noyes retired to nurse his grievance in his autobiography.[45]

Elsewhere appreciation was growing, and a mounting tempo of important criticism prepared the way for the authorized American edition of 1934. Through the sensitive writing of Edmund Wilson, the charming reminiscences of Frank Budgen, the authoritative exegesis of Stuart Gilbert, the valuable yeoman service of countless reviewers and critics, and, above all, the creative work of John Dos Passos, Thomas Wolfe, and William Faulkner, America was ready for *Ulysses*. Then, in December 1933, Judge Woolsey rendered his famed decision in the United States District Court that the book was not pornographic but "a serious experiment. . . . an amazing *tour de force*." America could now read *Ulysses*.

The Random House edition of 1934 brought forth several perceptive reviews. Robert Cantwell remarked that it "towers so high it has already cast its shadow on the important writing done since"; Padraic Colum re-created the social setting of early nineteenth-century Dublin and remarked on Joyce's amazing reality of character; Horace Gregory emphasized its value as a picture of cultural dissolution. Lewis Gannett regarded it as "an almost undisputed classic" that has influenced all but "a few old fogies like Sir Edmund Gosse." Yet Gannett complained of "a curious poseurishness" which seems to have grown throughout Joyce's career, and he wondered whether the world would not slide past Joyce, leaving him only to be read by students. Gilbert Seldes reiterated his praise of the work as "a great affirmation of everything in life—the good and the evil"; Lloyd Morris saw in it "the tragic career of intelligence in the modern world"; William Troy warned against a too facile identification of the mature artist Joyce with "the morbid-minded aesthete and embryo philosopher" Stephen. Joyce's world is one "of brighter and more tangible human substance, in which the tired ghosts of Aristotle and Aquinas will have to make room for Leopold and Molly Bloom." Cantwell likewise argued that an undue preoccupation with Dedalus has led to the neglect of other aspects of Joyce such as that of the artist's role in society. Stephen's aesthetic theory is "a protection against the horrors of the modern world"; we have lost much by this retreat:

> How much have we lost because Stephen drew back from the revolution that attracted him, rebuffed by the first bluntness of intelligence he found or by an occasional stare of terror . . . in the eyes of those with whom he would have had to throw his lot?[46]

Overwhelmed with contradictory interpretations, readers may find in John Riddell's remarks welcome comic relief. All agree, said he, that the work is "a vast symbol of something," but there seems to be no unanimity of opinion as to "what that *something* is," whether it be a modern *Odyssey,* "a parody of the Catholic Church," a travelogue of Dublin, an autobiography, "a story of wit vs. obstacles," or, finally, "a symbol of the human digestive organs." Facetiously, "In order to clear up the matter once and for all," Riddell reveals the true import of the book to be that of *"a vast allegory showing the progress of a thought through James Joyce's mind."* Thus, whatever happens to Stephen "is really only what Joyce *thinks* happens to Stephen," who is actually somewhere else all the time and "is pretty firmly convinced for his own part that James Joyce is only a thought that is passing through *his* mind." The point of the tale, then, is "to see which of them can stop thinking about the other one without his knowing it." Riddell also proffers advice to the novice, warning him that "several sentences are so long that their source has never been discovered by a white man." He suggests warm clothing, emergency rations, and equipment. One might blaze occasional words with an ax or sight some distant object like a chapter heading. If lost for the night, one must make a fire, and for shelter "the nearest innuendo" must be sought, where one can "crawl deep down into its inner meaning, where he will be comfortable and, according to Judge Woolsey, safe from harm."[47]

Continuing Attacks

Just as early enthusiasm was followed by philosophical contemplation, the heated vituperation of the first unfavorable reviews gave way to a group of reasoned attacks, some of which command respect.

Wyndham Lewis, the notable graphic artist and polemicist (Gertrude Stein is "a Monument sitting upon patience"), hurled an oddly romantic protest against the romantic tendencies of modern thought. In various diatribes, notably in *Time and Western Man* (1928), he slashed at the "time cult" of sensation, personal individuality, and the relativity of values. Bergson is the archvillain of this rebellion against intellect, seeking to return to the life of flux "all that the mind had taken from her to build forms and concepts."[48] The result is everything that Lewis disliked, and he disliked many things—the absurdities of advertising, psychology, the puerilities of Stein, the fashionable daring of Russian ballet. Proust, Pound, and Joyce are the most distinguished victims of this denial of absolutes and the consequent cultivation of novelty for its own sake. Professor Levin has characterized the attack as "well timed and badly aimed"; Kenner describes the method as that of seizing upon a few salient facts and creating "a plausible parchment mask" of an artist susceptible to the very things he is satirizing.[49] McLuhan claims that Joyce had enough respect for his antagonist to answer him in the *Wake*.[50]

For Lewis, Joyce is a mere craftsman, whose "sad, insipid, local colour" creates "the very nightmare of the naturalistic method." Stripped of technical complexities, the book reveals clichés of style and character. The much-vaunted psychological veracity is merely a "gushing of undisciplined life." Yet its "powerful impressionism" makes it, Lewis had to admit, "a masterpiece of romantic art."[51]

Despite the extravagance of his manner, Lewis allies himself with the classical, Humanist position. Some of the conservatives were less balanced. Edmund Gosse warned his friend Louis Gillet of Joyce's "worthlessness and impudence." *Ulysses* is "an anarchical production, infamous in taste, in style, in everything," Joyce "a literary charlatan," an inferior Marquis de Sade, an Irish "hater of England," perhaps pro-German:

There are no English critics of weight or judgment who

> consider Mr. Joyce an author of any importance. . . . He is not without talent, but he has prostituted it to the most vulgar uses.

Though Edmund Gosse had by this time lost all claims of being a representative or responsible critic of modern literature, he scarcely exaggerated English antagonism, and his remarks apply almost as fully to American academic criticism. Readers of such standard texts as the following could hardly be expected to appreciate Joyce: in England, Gerald Gould (1925): "most sinister influence. . . . a waste-paper basket. . . . denial of the human soul. . . . pointless harping upon inessentials"; Gerald Bullett (1926): "heroic pedantry. . . . *reductio ad absurdum* of the extreme subjective method"; E. M. Forster (1927): "a dogged attempt to cover the universe with mud"; A. C. Ward (1928): "wild phantasmagoria. . . . choked with sewage"; A. C. Ward (1930): "time for the James Joyce myth to be dispelled"; Frank Swinnerton (1935): "quite empty of idea . . . a hotchpotch." Even as late as 1941 the modern supplement to the *Cambridge History* warned that "we must not mistake the fervid claims of coteries for the calm voice of general judgment." *Ulysses* is unreadable, continued Mr. Samson, and "The wild enthusiasm of its immature readers can therefore be dismissed as a pretence." Or in America: Weygandt (1925): "a pitiable waste of potential genius"; Myers (1927): "degenerate silliness, foaming fury, and macabre poetry," which contrasts with the work of Dorothy Richardson, who is "safer for study, and really more ingenious"; Cross (1928): Stein and Joyce "the bores of contemporary fiction"; Grabo (1928): "a hoax . . . unbearably monotonous"; Knight (1931): "derides every thought, every aspiration"; Cunliffe (1933): "elaborate but depressing lucubrations." In this wilderness of exaggeration and misunderstanding the one comic note is that of Philo Buck, who omits Joyce from his treatment of *Directions in Contemporary Literature* (1942) because he sees no concern with "the large issues of the meaning of life" in his "undistinguished work."[52]

To claim that Harvey Wickham attained the summit of absurdity is perhaps extreme, yet his finding *Ulysses* easier to write that the *Idylls of the King* and his claiming that "Joyce never did much conscious thinking" places him close to that dubious eminence. Joyce is an animalist who merely let himself sink, becoming a "bad boy staggering beneath the blows of an unholy, illtaught adolescence." *Ulysses* provided the opportunity for him to demonstrate public gullibility, to indulge in "the instinct to soil clean paper," and to express "the rage of the self-condemned."[53] Reading his work gives the same titillation as that of illegal drinking.[54]

Needless to say, the balance is now being righted. The recent studies by B. Ifor Evans, George Fraser, and, most extensive and sympathetic of all, S. Diana Neill, indicate changing English opinion, as does E. M. Forster's recent retraction:

> The more I read Joyce the more I am compelled to recognize his genius. I never can appreciate him; I suppose I should never try. But reading him, I become more humble.[55]

A responsible Humanist attack is that of Paul Elmer More, who questions T. S. Eliot's oft-quoted aside to the effect that in sensibility and sense of tradition, if not in belief, Joyce is "the most ethically orthodox of the more eminent writers of my time." More respects Eliot and admires Stuart Gilbert, but, most important of all, he pays Joyce the honor of taking him seriously, not with scurrilous innuendo. In the conclusion of *Dubliners* and in much of the *Portrait* Joyce is seen to be "a moralist with that penetration into the secret issues of life which can scarcely exist without a keen sense of religious values." The *Portrait* reveals the rejection of the medieval and nationalist aspects of religion and an escape into the liberty of art, with the high purpose of creating the conscience of the race. How, then, can one account for the "weary and ugly" art of *Ulysses?* The answer is that Joyce, in his rejection of reason and spiritual authority, is forced back upon the undifferentiated flux of things. His popularity arises from the intellectual and linguistic mastery he displays. But the "detective pursuit of difficulties" plays a small role in great art, where the grasp of ideas "involves an elevation of the will and the emotions." Actually Joyce's erudition is one of scrappy tags, showing no comprehension of any system of philosophy or of the philosophical tradition. Joyce's aesthetic errs in its insistence that art is not kinetic, for all art arouses lust and loathing or desire or joy. As a matter of fact, Joyce's blasphemy and obscenity promote just these feelings, a loathing for nature and for spiritual authority, a joy in the vain sense of human superiority. One wonders where More could have found this vanity and exultation.[56]

It is surprising that such a bitter attack as that of the Dubliner Michael Lennon should have disturbed Joyce. For the biography is absurdly biased and false, with its account of abnormal childhood and futile academic career. This is followed by such staggering propositions as that the author lacks even "the typically Irish capacity for clever phrase-making" and that *Ulysses* was the work of a frustrated poseur. Nevertheless, he might have some future as a Catholic essayist! Perhaps like Michael Lennon, may we ask?[57]

Rebecca West's criticism reveals the constant attraction and repulsion that Joyce exercises on an intelligent mind. She triumphantly decides to dismiss Joyce as sentimental, narcissistic, and adolescent. She has discovered an inferior poem and exclaims that "Joyce is a great man who is entirely without taste." And yet his works are products of genius. But he is pedantic, though a stylist, incoherent, yet forceful. And yet, and yet. . . . So it goes on, for almost two hundred pages. Why should she waste the last lovely day in Paris worrying about Joyce, when she has to shop for hats? What is the "urgent necessity" that continued to worry her, intruding on her pleasure in the Parisian scene? Regardless of attempts to dismiss the subject, "nothing seemed so real as this persistent, nagging preoccupation with *Ulysses.*" Joyce judged this attack more slyly than the Lennon attack, which hurt him so deeply. He added, inconsequentially, "and forty hats" to a passage in *Finnegans Wake.*[58]

The socially oriented criticism of the thirties confronted Joyce, sometimes emerging with insights of value, sometimes merely showing the inadequacies of a mechanical Marxism. Among the more intelligent critics was R. D. Charques, who observed that though *Ulysses* contains "no revolutionary message," it "seems to portend fundamental change . . . in thought, in religion, in philosophy, in art—not in the organization of society." Such a "divorce between cultural and social development only evidences the malady of the bourgeois mind." Philip Henderson questioned whether the static emotion of Joyce's aesthetic is not a contradiction in terms. To him Joyce was "a great artist infected by the decay and disintegration of the society in which he lives." A Soviet appraisal traced Joyce's social indifference from its roots in "political, religious, national, and racial hatred." His "anarchical proclivities" thwarted his revolutionary tendencies, and the result is "social pessimism, misanthropy, barrenness and doom."[59]

Alick West produced the most careful social reading of *Ulysses in Crisis and Criticism* (1937). The center of interest is Stephen's defiance of church and state; but Stephen is an "individualistic idealist" interested in observing but not in changing the world. His meeting with Bloom indicates the parallel between idealistic ambition and materialistic practice. Joyce's leaning toward Bloom is an indication of intellectual fatigue and the loss of social aspiration, for Bloom "has no strenuous ideals" and "the intellectual quality of his life is infinitely lower." And the last symbol, the feminine spirit, becomes "a kind of mother goddess." Joyce, weary as Bloom, sleeps. Yet the reading of the book is "a profound social experience," with its constant "expectancy of some impending change." The intricate ornamentation of the style contradicts the dynamic energy of the social flux; its "static formal decoration" may be a defense against change. The book is thus at once a reaction against and an exemplification of the social forces that Joyce resented but never escaped. Instead of progressing toward a solution, the author "only shifts from one foot to the other, while he sinks deeper into the sandflats."

Contrast this sensitive and alert analysis with the complacency of mocking Joyce's labors on his "epic-epitaph" in Zurich, where at the same time Lenin was waiting silently for the locked train and the task of "bringing a new world to birth." One wonders what the handsome tenor, with his gift of languages and his failing eyesight, could contribute to the revolution. And, as Joyce well knew, there was no Finland Station in Dublin. Likewise, comments on the "ultrasubjectivism of the parasitic, rentier bourgeoisie," on "internal painting," and warnings against invoking "the aid of the irrational, of the unconscious," show the limitations of party-line criticism.[60]

James T. Farrell provided a sensible antidote. As one indebted to Joyce, an author of some of the highly regarded proletarian novels of the Depression, he argued that instead of condemning Joyce, it would be wise to understand him. Certainly he needs no apologies as an artist:

> future proletarian literature will not *per se* prove the failure of Joyce. . . . a proletarian classic in the future will not

necessarily give rise to dispraise of *Ulysses,* any more than *Macbeth* can . . . in dispraise of Dante's *Divine Comedy.*[61]

The crisis of 1939 brought further charges. The gentility of Oliver Allston, Van Wyck Brooks's *alter ego,* did not guarantee good manners in dealing with the "sick Irish Jesuit" who interpreted life "as a bad joke," ridiculed the past, and was possessed by a death drive. Even so intelligent a critic as Max Lerner editorialized that "The Joyce We Need" is one with the same talent who could articulate "the collective affirmations out of which we should create the future."[62]

A few independent attacks may conclude the survey of opposition. Jack Lindsay traced the author's failure to deepen "our psychological or spiritual perception" to "a division at the root of his poetic energies," to an excessive awareness of his audience—"the vanity of one-man-against-the-world"—and to his subjection to hatred. Ingenious and interesting as he may be, he fails to attain serenity. Desmond MacCarthy's diagnosis is similar. *Ulysses* is an extraordinary accomplishment, despite its pedantry, disgust, and "psychological blind alleys." Joyce is the victim of the French theory of "the mysticism of the word"; that is, "the belief that it is through acquaintance with words and knowledge of how to arrange them that we reach comprehension of life." Nevertheless, "in *Ulysses* now and then a vague majestic beauty glides ghostlike through the bewildering darkness." Joyce's method was one of "closing the petals of his mind tighter and tighter over the seed-bearing center of his being." Hence he became convinced "that he contained the world in himself, and that therefore by sinking an ever-deepening shaft into his own consciousness he would reach the all-embracing." MacCarthy's awareness of Joyce's mysterious power marks him as one of the most effective and revealing opponents. F. R. Leavis finds "no organic principle" controlling the variety of technical devices and concludes that *Ulysses* is "a dead end" in fiction. George Every agrees with Eliot that Joyce's mind remained essentially Catholic in its "pity for human weakness and frailty, and terror of a judgment to come" but that neither hope, nor love, nor faith "could fill the void in his heart."[63]

Three Decades of Interpretation, 1925-1955

The enigma of *Ulysses* continues to invite and repel, to tantalize by suggesting one interpretation only to ridicule it.

If we regard the work as a giant impersonal artifact we must overlook the intense personal anxieties that seem to underlie it; if we follow the symbolic interpreters and read it as a rejection of naturalism we must discount Joyce's delight in detailed documentation (witness his study of Thom's *Directory,* his pride in his knowledge of Dublin, or his letter to his Aunt Josephine, printed by Hutchins, inquiring about how many trees there are at the Star of the Sea Church). If we reject symbolism to the extent of holding with Goodwin that such a careful artist would not allow something "to serve as two or three symbols which . . . serve as an anomalous and distracting confusion," we are confronted with the multi-layered significances of *Finnegans Wake.* It was not Gilbert, we recall, but Joyce who nosed out these correspondences. Yet if the meeting of Stephen and Bloom is to be fraught with such meaning as the exponents of the paternity theme insist, why is it so inconclusive and ineffective? The nihilistic and relativistic aspects seem to be contradicted by the implicit moral criteria, just as the seemingly irresponsible laughter is countered by the pain of conscience. However much faith the critic may have in his own interpretation, an opposite reading has equally valid support.

The method is dialectic and may represent the divided sensibility of the modern mind, so effectively noted by T. S. Eliot. Bloom is both comic and tragic, Stephen both noble and posturing; each counters the other, and both are countered by the Dubliners and by Molly. Joyce's love of Dublin is as apparent as his rejection of it; his allegiance to Catholicism remains despite his grand refusal. His humor is tinged with bitterness, his cynicism with ribaldry. His conception of art as static contradicts his hope of creating the conscience of the race; his pose of indifference is belied by unconcealed loathing of the vulgar. The absence of a single, well-defined tone may pose problems of evaluation, but it also accounts for the work's immense power on the imaginations of his contemporaries. In this mélange of symbolism and realism, of personal pain and aloofness, of poetry and parody, there is evidence for almost any emphasis one might make. Each aspect has had staunch and able advocates.

Apart from Larbaud's initial lecture, the first readings of *Ulysses* had been made on the naturalistic level. Joyce as psychologist, as historian of society, as satirist and parodist, commanded attention. Thus Edwin Muir, in his perceptive essays on the contemporary literary scene, emphasized Joyce's humor, a phase so obvious as to be often overlooked by commentators. The Muir studies, appearing first in *The Nation, The Nation and Athenaeum,* and the *New Republic,* were collected in the volume entitled *Transition* (1926). The list of authors treated, even the order in which they appear, testifies to Muir's sound taste. The *Zeitgeist* is first characterized as a force to which the mediocre succumb and the weak try to escape, but on which provides the resistance that a great artist needs in order to clarify his vision and that of his age. Both Joyce and Huxley express the disillusionment that is typically modern, but Huxley's is merely fashionable while Joyce's is so completely probed and so profoundly expressed as to become much more than an attitude or a mood of the day. Joyce's humor and his psychology are liberating. In bringing literature back to its primeval sources, Joyce has created an atmosphere of black magic. *Ulysses* has "the authority of a scripture." It expresses both its author and our age. Containing within itself sources of energy for others, "it may well become the central point of a literature."

Muir analyzed Joyce's humor as one not of fashion, nor of character, but one that springs from the discrepancies between the ideals of a sensitive artist and the sordid realities of the world. It is universal, profound. It must perforce include blasphemy and obscenity, mocking as it does the pretenses of soul and body:

> It sets the dream of religion, the magic of language, the splendours of the intellect, the revolutions of history, over against the simple facts: the naiveté of physical desire, the functions of the body, the triviality of the floating thoughts the body sends up into our minds.

Like the most profound humor it is most reckless and uproarious "where the suffering of the artist has been most intense." Joyce has mastered language and psychological insight, the skills of art and life. He has inoculated himself against facile sensibility and so achieved an "emancipating comic vision." *Ulysses* destroys falsity in order to create; its vitality derives from the popular imagination, too long excluded from literature. Parody destroys the superficial, while the psychological insights reveal "an overpowering sense of the inexhaustibility of human life."[64] Yet a man of such shrewd insight could still miss Joyce's architectural power. In *The Structure of the Novel* he called the plan "purely contingent and theoretical . . . hardly to be taken seriously."[65] But it was soon to be taken seriously, sometimes too seriously, by others. Meanwhile Ivan Goll continued the interpretation of *Ulysses* as "the most formidable parody . . . ever written on the universe of God and man," owing its force to "deep ethical conviction" and "a sense of cosmic despair."[66]

Not indignation but a sense of remorse gives dynamic tension to *Ulysses,* according to Cyril Connolly in his estimate of 1929. Joyce and Proust share "the tragic intelligence" of knowing that all beauty exists "in ironic contrast to the unrelieved gloom of squalor . . . disease and death." Though remorse is frequently a "second-rate" emotion in life, with its weakness and sentimentality, "its very tranquillity and remoteness from action lend it a glossy literary beauty." Other achievements include Joyce's creation of beauty in an urban atmosphere, his adaptation of language to character, and, above all, his *"pietas"* for Dublin, comparable to "the pagan sentiment of birthplace" rather than to the usual provinciality of the Irish.[67]

Connolly's elegiac Joyce—a Connolly in fact—gives way to the more vital Joyce of Edmund Wilson, whose work is for the most part on the naturalistic level, emphasizing the author's value as psychologist, historian of a disintegrating society, and exploiter of the concepts of relativity. Wilson brought together the insights of several years in his essays on symbolism, *Axel's Castle* (1931). The Joyce study remains the best brief introduction to *Ulysses.* It restates the author's earlier characterization of Joyce's style, though it confesses impatience with the mechanical and boring elaboration of concealed correspondences.

Frank Budgen, Joyce's associate in Zurich during the writing of *Ulysses,* made the Homeric correspondences seem more a matter of the studio than the laboratory and humanized the author by vivid reminiscences and Boswellian quotations. As a painter, he responded to Joyce's tonal patterns with a fresh artistic insight, free of cant or prejudice, and as a man of practical experience on the sea he sensed the earthiness of the author. It is for these reasons that McLuhan exclaims, "Fortunate is the reader who first aproaches Joyce through this book." *The Times Literary Supplement* felt that Budgen's "good sense and sensibility" made it "probably the best running commentary" to date, but *The New Statesman and Nation* thought that, though intelligent and readable, it "faintly disappoints." Joyce's sayings are "rather drearily typical," and so close an associate as Budgen should have been able to throw more light on the inspiration of Bloom.[68] A painter himself, Budgen was well aware that the artist's fundamental concern is with his medium, and that "Religion and politics are the most frequent rivals of words, paint and stone." Joyce is an artist who regards the destinies of his characters "gravely and gently," with an absence of "irony, condemnation or any tendentious contrast." The world is affirmed with humane skepticism and humor:

> It is not to him a brave new world, about to set forth upon some hitherto unattempted enterprise. Rather it is a brave old world, forever flowing like a river, ever seeming to change yet changing never.

Among later naturalistic interpretations, that of G. W. Stonier followed Ezra Pound's thesis that *Ulysses* was an encyclopedic satire. Stonier showed how Joyce's effects rest upon distortions of size that echo the findings of modern physics and psychology:

> To a modern physicist man is an atom in a universe of stars; to the psycho-analyst he is a boundless consciousness containing universes of his own; and between these two conceptions—the outer pygmy and the inner giant—it is possible for the mind to invent the most distorted visions.

Greatness is gone from humanity; the ordinariness of the man in the street "has become monstrous . . . like the giant masks of carnival." Bloom is Joyce's artistic triumph; never has "the final solitude of the individual been more poignantly and forcefully expressed."[69] To Henry Miller, Joyce's *Ulysses* is "a thanatopsis inspired by the ugly tomb in which the soul of the civilized man lies embalmed." In this "Universe of Death" Joyce reveals his desperation by "his chaos and obscenity, his obsessions and complexes, his perpetual, frantic search for God." There is no way out:

> Man returns to the primordial elements; he is washed away in a cosmological flux.

We possess Dublin "as a shade wandering through an excavated Troy."[70] E. B. Burgum finds the book symptomatic of the "Impasse of Individualism," in the fact that the quests of Bloom and Stephen end in failure. Only an illusion of companionship, prompted by drink and sentimental song, makes life tolerable. For David Daiches, the mystical theory of identity reduces the various perspectives of the story—theological, historical, literary, and actual—to mere "differences in method of observation." There remains only the gray monotony of a world without values, in which everything becomes comic. Joyce exemplifies the artist as an impartial recording lens; though "curious and impressive," *Ulysses* is not a masterpiece.[71]

Harry Levin's study achieved a triumph of comprehensiveness, insight, and accuracy, which is even more remarkable when it is realized that the work appeared just one year after Joyce's death. The critic has read everything and forgotten nothing. The result might have been maddeningly pedantic, as Joyce himself can be at times, were it not for a Joycean irony manifested in a constant play of paradox. Levin's learning, never obsessive, enables him to relate Joyce to the main currents of European literature, thus making him academically respectable, much to the amusement of the Irish.[72] The Joyce that emerges is a formal technician who took "all knowledge for his playground." Perhaps reacting from the extreme claims of Joyce devotees, Levin denies any precise message: "The student who demands a philosophy from Joyce will be put off with an inarticulate noise and a skeptical shrug." The author's exile is symbolic of the plight of modern culture, yet Joyce attempts to escape his dispossession "by playing god"; there is neither solution nor escape, only the artist's creative intensity, beating down, "like an aroused volcano upon an ancient city, overtaking the doomed inhabitants in forum and temple, at home or at brothel, and petrifying them in the insensate agonies of paralysis."

Only a monument of artifice, *Ulysses* is devoid of "the epic virtues of love, friendship, and magnanimity," an opinion that brought forth the mocking comment by one reviewer who recalled that these were precisely the virtues of the Horatio Alger series. The book was almost universally praised and immediately accepted as the basic introduction to Joyce, which position it still holds. It was noted, however, that the intellectual approach tended to obscure the terrifying sense of guilt that underlies Joyce's art. Levin does neglect the question of Joyce's Catholic education and his apostasy. As yet, no qualified critic has undertaken the task of relating Joyce to his Catholic background. Barry Byrne, a reviewer whose opinion is always to be respected, felt that Joyce's use of the esoteric reveals the decadence of the modern "materialistic and dehumanized culture" which he substituted for his native Catholicism. Others complained that, like all intellectuals, Levin missed Joyce's feeling for character, "his Swiftian moral grandeur, and . . . almost Shakespearean humaneness." And what shall we make of Molly Bloom, Den Haan reminds us, with the staggering, almost compulsive frankness of her reflections? But it is Joyce the artist who is the hero of Levin's book, and, barring the neglect of the Catholic tradition, and the important contributions of the French symbolists, a lack recently remedied by William York Tindall, Harry Levin's *James Joyce* constitutes a major achievement in modern literary history.[73]

My own *Fabulous Voyager: James Joyce's "Ulysses"* was motivated by a desire to bring out Joyce's feeling for humanity and is thus, in some sense, a supplement to Levin, who generously characterized the author as one whose "great virtue is that he treats *Ulysses* not as a controversy to be fought or a mystery to be expounded, but as a human experience which he has found both exciting and rewarding." In this reading, the symbolic correspondences are neglected and attention is turned to Joyce's awareness of the Dublin scene, his Chaucerian sense of character, and his mastery, through stylistic variation, of poetic tone. Of the four levels that are outlined—classic, with Homeric echoes; medieval, or symbolic; naturalistic, with details of time and place; and poetic, or tonal—my study deliberately concentrates on the latter two, as relatively neglected.

The work has performed the function of introducing many readers to the earthy *Ulysses,* so often lost in the clouds of metaphysical speculation; yet some misunderstanding might have been avoided had I clarified my approach and had I pointed out that while humor, characterization, and surface detail give the narrative its gusto and vitality, symbolic referents extend the depth, richness, and universality of Joyce's reading of life. The book attempts to relate *Ulysses* to its social and personal roots, showing the author's humanity and humor. A true compatriot of Swift, Joyce is a clear-eyed observer and satirist, who presents the keylessness of modern man in his depiction of the incurably lonely Bloom and Stephen. The final perspective places Dublin and the earth itself against the illimitable, ever-moving cosmos.

The study was praised for its rigorous concentration on the text, apart from marginal considerations, and for bringing the epic back into the everyday world of its origin without making it banal. Others attacked the detailed documentation and the neglect of symbolic exegesis, but Henry Rago rightly noted that this focus was intentional and that the extensive examination of contemporary directories and newspapers did demonstrate the underlying data "from which almost every passage in this novel draws its juices." H. V. Routh also considered Joyce's microscope detail an important element in his presentation of civilization's shortcomings and "the pitiful crumbs of interest and consolation to which the human soul, in this atmosphere, languidly inclines."[74] A recent reading of *Ulysses,* an English review of the Slocum-Cahoon *Bibliography,* likewise interprets Joyce as one "impelled . . . by an affection for his material so intense that he could not bear to be thought of as tampering with it." The result, Donald Davie argues, is that trivial facts are rendered poetic "merely by being remembered with affection."[75]

The Hollander Den Haan good-naturedly mocks me for the loving kindness that impelled me to go forth on a crusade and to return with an apostle. If Joyce had wanted to be an apostle, he would have proclaimed it; in any case, the *Portrait* does nothing to mitigate the human stench. One may question both positions—that of assuming that Joyce would be explicit and that of judging the spirit of *Ulysses* from an impression of an earlier work. Another reviewer felt that the book "rightly stresses Joyce's humanity and the vein of genuine idealism in his implicit protest." Even Den Haan admits that "many do not love Joyce because they fail to make out how much Joyce loved them."[76]

Other social readings have emphasized the lack of integration in the spoiled priest Stephen and the shopworn prophet Bloom, each at once a victim and a potential savior of society.[77] And Dublin is merely representative of Western civilization. Its ties to Greece and its availability as a vantage point for a counterepic have been traced—Greece once a rising land in the East, Dublin a declining city in the West.[78] Even the myth of Sherlock Holmes becomes relevant. Holmes is the proudly indifferent artist, his art-form detection, his epiphanies clues, his erudition trivial, his attitude amoral. And the fuddled Watson parallels Bloom. But the Holmes saga, like all inferior art, is rooted in the acceptance of these sentimentalities. Though Joyce is a moralist, utilizing the medieval metaphor of the body politic, the work mirrors society so accurately that a public of Blooms and Stephens that idolizes Watson and Holmes could not understand the cultural sterility it presents.[79]

The aesthetic implications of the social and realistic approach of Levin and myself are further developed by Rudolph Von Abele in his caveat against mythic interpretation. The usual symbolic exegesis of *Ulysses* provides an example of the contemporary tendency to hitch literary works "onto mythopoeic horses" in order to confer upon them democratic respectability as repositories of folk wisdom. The myth hunters fail to give "coherent, complete, and documentable" readings; most amazing is "their contempt for the thick and solid sensuous world" in which the novel is embedded. The allusions to Ulysses, Christ, Hamlet, and so forth are without exception ironic. The famed meeting of Stephen and Bloom is ineffectual, permeated with mockery and misunderstanding. Molly's affirmation is that of a barren, vulgar woman; indeed, "All the so-called 'parallels' or 'identifications' in the book are rinsed in the same water of comic irony." The irony is twofold—ridicule of Bloom and Dedalus as "counterparts" of Shakespeare, Ulysses, or Moses on the one hand and, conversely, the Joycean characters stand as implicit instances of "the commonplace reality to which all the mythopoeic extravagances dwindle." Whether or not Joyce meant his mythic references to be taken seriously, their triviality makes them comic. The book is "triumphant comedy," and it achieves its "most amusing paradox" in that "though saturated with death and *Kitsch,* it yet gives off an authentic and inexhaustible aura of life."[80]

The German scholars Bernhard Fehr and Ernest Curtius were pioneers in the metaphysical interpretation of Joyce. For them the author explored a new dimension of awareness, cutting through planes of reality like a non-Euclidian geometer. The technical devices are not merely verbal and rhetorical innovations but projective points of reference, locating man in the perspectives of history, of human culture, and of the universe. Thus Fehr examined the new world view common to Joyce and Proust, the interactions of time, memory, and space, and the consequent breakdown of the surface school of realism, with its uniform concepts of time and space, character and action. Four technical devices are cited from *Ulysses:* the interjection of alien scenes in the manner of cinema cuttings, which flash from one place to another without transition; the "geometerization of space," or the location of two individuals by relation to a fixed point outside (as in astronomical parallax); the crosscutting at a single time as in the midafternoon chapter giving a survey of Dublin life; and the contrast of the perspectives created by the personality of each individual, found in the meeting of Bloom and Stephen. The geometrical conception is likened to that of Bertrand Russell, the personality perspectives to Bergson. Joyce's originality consists in combining the concepts, in making clear the fundamental nature of spatial transference that is mathematical time, and in extracting from conflicting perspectives a droll humor, the world picture broken up "into grotesque rows which run side by side."

Curtius, with Teutonic thoroughness, unraveled the chains of images, themes, and motifs, happily termed "the stenography of conscious association," that point to the basic concepts of the work—remorse, utopian dreams, the mysteries of birth, and the relativity of law. Despite his spiritual energy and elasticity, "of which one can speak with the highest awe," and which rank him with the masters, Joyce seems to reduce civilization to "the odor of ashes, the fear of death, the pain of conscience." But *Ulysses* is not really nihilistic; it is a purgatory, demolishing the pretenses of the world to prepare the ground for spirituality.

In similar vein the German scholar Hentze has portrayed the work as an expression of relativity and protean change. The themes of transmigration, paternity, and the cycle of life reinforce the perspectivism of symbolic and motion picture techniques. The inner monologue represents a depthwise cutting, while the parodies and changes of style suggest oblique viewpoints. Joyce thus represents the revolt against fixed values, even those of language, and attempts "an all-embracing feeling of unity with men and things"; though he fails, his solution tends toward "loss of self and disintegration of the world."

Carl Jung's study of 1932 brought the resources of a world-famous psychiatrist and a man of wide learning to the interpretation of the problem child of modern literature. To him, the tumultuous energy of the book was like a force in nature. It has no beginning and no end—"what richness and what boredom!" The nervous intensity and the seeming lack of direction suggest the schizophrenic mind, yet the supremely rational control contradicts the evidence. *Ulysses* is cubistic, a characteristic product of an age of cultural incubation. Its destruction of medievalism and of sentimentality is creative, preparing a new world-consciousness of detachment, "the epitome of being and not-being . . . the priceless jewel of the wisdom of India and China."[81]

S. Foster Damon, fresh from the study of Blake, applied mystical insights ingeniously, reaching a similar conclusion. With its satanic Stephen and Christlike Bloom, *Ulysses* is "the affirmation of the eternal paradise of Dream against the 'No' of the temporary Hell which is this world." Homer furnishes only the narrative base; the spiritual planes derive from Dante, the psychological motivation (father-son relationship) from Hamlet, the analogical method from Blake. A vast network of mystical correspondences is elaborated and still further complicated by the postscript of 1947 printed in Givens. The surface realism parallels the Body, Homer the Mind, and references to sacred history the Spirit. The three parts comprise a trinity: I, the wrath of God upon Satan; II, alienation from Christ in history; III, the inspiration of the Holy Ghost and the millennium. And finally the three characters represent Mind, Body, and Spirit. If this may seem to make the head swirl, it must be remembered that by the time Damon wrote, the first parts of *Finnegans Wake* had appeared, an ample testimony to Joyce's love of analogy. And by pun, portmanteau, and parody he was able to encompass practically everything in the universe. Professor Levin remarks wittily that the verbal coincidences of the Irish locale "almost seem to exist for his convenience."[82]

The critical conflict between realist and mystagogue emerges in the reception accorded Stuart Gilbert's analysis (1930), where an imense array of correspondences, mainly with Homer, were nosed out, as Newton Arvin put it, "with the ruthlessness of a slightly mad mineralogist." Gilbert worked in close co-operation with Joyce and may be said to have enjoyed an official imprimatur. Yet Austin Clarke, the Dublin poet, echoed Ernest Boyd's objection to Larbaud by complaining that "much nonsense has been written by admirers" in that "what appears to be unintelligible or profoundly mysterious turns out to be a minute localism."[83] The fallacy here is that a minute localism is often an associational symbol; place names are redolent of national history, churches can provide the saints. And if the author be an inveterate punster, the possibilities are endless: witness *Finnegans Wake*. In Dublin one can find an Eden Quay and an Adam and Eve's Church, a Waterloo Monument, a Swift's Alley, an Arran (to the punster Errin) Quay. One could go on forever, if he would abandon his mind to it, to paraphrase Samuel Johnson's remark on the Ossianic poems. The fact is that Joyce did abandon his mind to such analogies; this, and not Gilbert's faithful documentation, is the point at issue. Hence, much of the adverse criticism that the volume has received is really a questioning of Joyce's method. So the *New Republic* found the mystic correspondences "of rather an infantile character"; *The Nation and Athenaeum* feared that "one is apt to lose one's enjoyment of the aesthetic in the thrill of detection," and *The Times Literary Supplement* questioned the validity of the method:

> What purpose . . . is served by correspondences so involute that they must be referred to a tabulated formula to be recognized at all, and even then recognized with difficulty?

But Gerald Sykes was entirely out in assuming that Joyce was too profound a man to depend upon symbols.[84] The *Exiles* notes provide testimony, not to speak of Joyce's chart for *Ulysses* and any page of *Finnegans Wake,* or the extensive notebooks for the latter work, now in the British Museum and the University of Buffalo. The crucial question in elucidating such an associational art is where, if anywhere, the critic or reader is to stop. How can he tell whether his interpretation be intended, or a flight of his own imagination, irrelevant to the text? In the case of Gilbert, we may assume the commentator's opportunity to check with Joyce himself; later divagations may be more open to question.

Gilbert's avowed purpose in his pioneering commentary was to defend *Ulysses* as "essentially classical in spirit," written "according to rules of design and discipline of almost scientific precision." In rescuing Joyce from those who read him as an apostle of subconscious disorder, Gilbert emphasized the rigorous pattern of Homeric and symbolic correspondences with which all students of modern literature are now acquainted. Edmund Wilson admitted that the Homeric parallels suggest universal significances and that the cultural and biological themes may make the book "comprehensive, if a little laboriously systematic." Nevertheless he concluded that it was these very references which discouraged the reader's interest. Both Professor Levin and I have concurred with Wilson's conclusion that "Joyce elaborated 'Ulysses' too much—that he tried to put too many things into it."

The only review of Gilbert to appear in an academic journal was that of B. J. Morse, a fortunate choice, for he had been a pioneer scholar, having written a study of Shakespearean themes and echoes several years before.[85] Morse hailed the study for its value in elucidating an art form "new and daring" to the English speaking world, though not so unfamiliar to the European tradition. He found it "remarkable and astonishing," though Gilbert is "sometimes too intent on discovering parallels" and hence underestimates the influence of Joyce's Jesuit upbringing and of "the hair-splitting dialectic of the Patristic writers."

Though Gilbert makes no claims as a critic, and hazards few evaluations, he does characterize Joyce as a cunning artificer, to whose Godlike indifference the world's only value is that of a still life posing problems of rendition:

> *Ulysses* is neither pessimist nor optimist in outlook, neither moral nor immoral in the ordinary sense of these words; its affinity is, rather, with an Einstein formula, a Greek temple, an art that lives the more intensely for its repose.

Joyce's "serene detachment," "as absolute as the indifference of Nature," accounts for the striking illusion of reality. Yet Mr. Gilbert does not find the perfect stasis, the freedom from desire and loathing that Stephen postulated in the *Portrait.* Swiftian loathing is approached, especially in the sensual passages, with the result that "The conflict of deliberate indifference (*stasis*) with the loathing of disgust (*kinesis*) is apparent throughout *Ulysses.*" Thus there is "an undertone of despair" beneath "the perpetual deflation of sentiment and the negation of values"; indeed, "the seething vitality" of *Ulysses* may be dependent on this conflict—"the stream of life is fed by the waters of bitterness."[86]

Among the valid limitations of this basic study may be noted the omission of any sense of pathos,[87] the lack of historical background on the development of symbolist art,[88] and, most important of all, omission of the religious tension in Joyce, best expressed in the review by Hamish Miles:

> . . . the Christian and Catholic battle of faith and nihilism which surges through great parts of the book . . . essential to an understanding of Mr. Joyce's mind . . . . the fact of the overwhelming sense of frustration and sterility.

Of later comments, McLuhan charges that Gilbert failed to utilize the pattern of organs of the body, arts, colors, and symbols, consideration of which would have resulted in the elucidation of "a profound symbolist structure" instead of promoting "acrostic and naturalistic fallacies." But he succeeded in his major task, which William Troy described as that of demonstrating that Joyce was a careful artist, not an irresponsible purveyor of "a chaotic and disagreeable mass of uncorrelated material, a betrayal of the intellect."[89]

Elucidation of specific symbols has been carried on with undiminished energy, despite the earlier feeling that Stuart Gilbert had exhausted the subject. Most indefatigable of these researchers is the Canadian lawyer and poet A. M. Klein, who reads the first episode as a Black Mass, appropriately celebrated on the Thursday closest to the Feast of Corpus Christi, the second chapter a paraphrase of the historical cycles of Vico, and the hospital chapter a paradigm of evolution and embryology.[90]

Perhaps it is William York Tindall's flippancy that makes it easy for readers and reviewers to misjudge him. I, myself, in reviewing *James Joyce* in 1950, may have conveyed the wrong impression by characterizing Tindall as a disciple who often outdoes his master, plunging into *Ulysses* in search of sexual symbols and retrieving "such assorted paraphernalia as would delight the most fanatic Freudian."[91] And James Johnson Sweeney was reminded of the antics of "a goodnatured, somewhat roly-poly puppy rushing now here for a sniff, now there," with little plan but with evident enjoyment. But the fault, if fault it be, is as much Joyce's as his critics'. For a basic problem in exegesis is where to stop in tracing analogies, and a related problem of critical judgment is that of separating the essential from the trivial. Tindall evidently believes in pursuing every association to its ultimate conclusion, and it is undoubtedly true, as I noted, that "If the initiate suffer at times a certain headiness from finding symbol within symbol and cycle within cycle, he cannot deny that such correspondences were among Joyce's constant preoccupations." Tindall's wide knowledge of the symbolist tradition enables him to supplement previous studies in an important fashion. Rimbaud's and Mallarmé's names, for example, are not found in Harry Levin's study. His major contribution was well described by James Johnson Sweeney as that of seeing the entire canon as "one large integral spiritual autobiography."[92] Throughout the entire work certain themes recur with the insistence Stephen found in Shakespeare's concern with banishment. So with Joyce the note of exile and alienation, the ironic self-portraiture, the discovery of the father, and the recognition of humanity are never far from the surface.

More remote are the chains of analogy that Tindall pursues with evident relish. The Pyrrhic victory in the history lesson, through "pier" leads to exile, unity of being, art; the fox (Stephen) buries his grandmother (his mother, church, nation, home) under the tree (of life or resurrection). The chandelier (of the old dispensation) is broken (as at Tenebrae) at the brothel, and later Bloom carries a candle (paschal, of Holy Saturday). Outside Bloom's house, the host (a comet) and guest (a meteor) see Vega (falling) in Lyra (the self-centered) near Leo (Bloom) and the Hair of Berenice (a mother killed by her son). They have shared cocoa (mass produced, produced for the masses, hence the Mass—and Joyce drank cocoa in his student days in Paris) and make water (of life; for Stephen who has refused to bathe, is learning the ways of water, coming so far as to have chanted *Vidi aquam,* and soon to write Ana Livia Plurabelle).

Bloom is man, Moses, Christ, the sacrificial lamb, and Elijah as well as Ulysses, Sinbad, and the Wandering Jew. His potato protects his manhood, his soap washes away sin—but since it was cosmetic soap for Molly, we may expect much washing! The advertisement for potted meat suggests Molly, death, Boylan's affair, the parable of the plums, and the Tree of Life; his bee sting is a sin against fertility, as is hoof (male) and mouth (female) disease in cattle. The unknown man in the macintosh represents death, the unknown, and contraception. Freud is everywhere — in tower, sea, bowl, Nelson's Pillar, in the triangular label on Bass's Ale—while the Ascot Gold Cup is portentous, for "Sceptre, the phallic favorite, loses to Throwaway, the outsider, who represents infertility." And tomb rhymes with womb.[93]

Even letters are significant. The three sections begin with S (Stephen), M (Molly), and P (Poldy), respectively, and the final "s" of Molly's "Yes" carries on to the initial "S" of the book (which might mean Symbol or Search, a connotation Tindall does not mention). No one, to this reader's knowledge, has noted that the penultimate chapter begins with "What" and ends with "Where," nor that the last chapter *begins* as well as ends with "Yes." Overextended analysis may produce strange results; yet it should be said that such activity is preferable to superficial treatment.

And now comes an expert in oneirics—that is, psychoanalysis by another name—one Rolf Loehrich, who also carries on into "metaoneirics," and who finds *The Secret of "Ulysses"* to lie in Bloom-Stephen-Man solving conflicts, atoning for sins, escaping impotence by facing "Contending Power Groups," east, west, south, and north, but all in the brothel scene, where KING, QUEEN, MAGICIAN, REDEEMER, and ETERNAL PARENTS lurk in disguise, though always in capital letters.[94]

It is undoubtedly true that Joyce intended the name of Dedalus to suggest both the artist, and, through Icarus, the fall of man; the flight of Icarus resembles that of the birds watched by Stephen as auguries, and the theme of flight is linked with that of exile in his words, "I will fiy by those nets." Since the legendary Daedalus built the labyrinth—and what is *Ulysses* but a vast one—the Minotaur comes into Stephen's nicknames (in the *Portrait* the Greek phrase, "Bull crowned with garlands," in *Ulysses,* "bullockbefriending bard"). The fall of Lucifer is here too, and of the lapwing, which is "seabedabbled" (compare Stephen's phrase on the beach in the *Portrait,* "dappled seaborne clouds"). But this Stephen (protoMartyr-Telemachus-Christ-Shakespeare-Hamlet-the-Ghost-Joyce-Lucifer-Icarus) Dedalus sometimes finds it difficult to live up to his name. And when another commentator expects us to see Bloom picking up matches as Christ (a Jew) dying (stooping) to bring salvation (to pick up), one is reminded of readings of *Revelation* and of Baconian cryptograms.[95]

Among the most extreme is William Empson's interpretation, which even he terms odd and somewhat improper. Is he to be taken seriously, when, disregarding the canon of the new criticism, which excludes biographical data as irrevelant, he proceeds to see the book as an autobiography of Joyce's hypothetical affair with a married woman? Of course we have no evidence of any such liaison, but it is presumed to have freed the author from some complex, thus providing him with the release through which he was enabled to win his wife, escape Dublin, and write *Ulysses!* No wonder he referred in conclusion to some words of Jane Austen regarding a wild imagination. Empson does provide catchword labels for other theories, all of which he rejects—the deer, the remorse, the pure invention, and the acceptance interpretations. Joyce is too earthy to reflect disgust with the world, too sensible to adopt an attitude of sentimental acceptance. As for the much discussed topic of spiritual paternity, it is too close to the creed he rejected.[96]

One may reasonably ask with Philip Toynbee, the English experimental novelist, and a man who defers to none in his respect for Joyce, whether many of the "hard nuts" of meaning are "not only superfluous but positively injurious." Does not Joyce demand too much of the reader, with all his local history and geography, his mythology, theology, and "any number of straws and geegaws of information"? Are we not driven away from the fictional illusion into "alien worlds of scholarship"? This complaint reminds one of Edward Fitzgerald's annoyance at Milton's pedantry forcing the reader from Heaven and Hell into the schoolroom, which was worse than either. Joyce's task, that of rendering the universal in the particular, of reconciling naturalism and symbolism, accounts for the use of Homer, but even here "superabundance clogs *Ulysses*" with many pedantic details. The rendition of stereoscopic vision through the outlooks of the three major characters is brilliant in conception, though in execution it puts impossible demands upon author and reader alike, for "No writer in the world has ever achieved even two distinct styles of equal excellence." Toynbee finds the last half of the book ridden by stylistic theory: the unrelieved parodies of the hospital scene, the monotony of the hallucinations, the superfluous dullness of the final scenes. Yet it "is almost unique in the retrospective satisfaction which it gives in spite of the frequent irritation and weariness which one has felt while reading it."[97]

McLuhan has related symbolism to the medieval tradition, citing St. Augustine's theory of music, in which the chord links "stages of human apprehension, the growth of the soul, the movement of the sun . . . the Incarnation and the Ascension, the mental labyrinth of art and the cloacal labyrinth of commerce." Joyce uses the ancient arts of grammar (the word), rhetoric (figures), and a dialectic of the Eastern, "earthy and cloacal" labyrinth (Bloom), and the Western, "cognitive . . . of the word and of analogy" (Stephen). The first is represented by the Wandering Rocks, "children of the sun, denizens of space," the second by "children of the moon . . . moving in the aquacities of time, memory, and sentiment." The progress from the first to the second is the change from *Ulysses* to *Finnegans Wake,* though the dualism is inherent in all Joyce's work.[98]

The Irish invariably find esoteric interpretations absurd. They prefer to regard their Jimmy as a somewhat annoying variant of the local bad boy, disrespectful, mocking, and yet withal sentimental. Thus *The Dublin Magazine* regarded Gilbert's book as helpful to those who wish to approach *Ulysses* "in an academic and serious fashion," despite the fact that "one can hardly hope to grasp its essence by this method." For though Joyce is often "maddeningly pedantic" in his "hair-splitting ecstasy," *Ulysses* is basically an expression of life in "its majesty and meanness, its sensuality and spirituality." One cannot be sure of its intent, and so Gilbert's esoteric and mystical notions are "largely a matter of faith," not shared by Dubliners.[99] Ernest Boyd has said that the Irish "must always see him as a realist, rather than a portentous symbolist," and J. A. Meagher, finding Joyce "one of the great mocking birds of literature," has the effrontery to suggest that among his parodies "not the least is the travesty of symbolism."[100]

If the symbolism be a leg pull, then the entire Joyce industry is threatened. He cannot be a hoax, Denis Johnston argues, for "Too much depends on him." The industry is the author's final, perhaps finest joke. Johnston paints a hilarious picture of American college students, having been told that Bloom is a sacrificial scapegoat, clinging to "a limb of the Golden Bough," searching for creatures "with whiskers and horns," other escaped goats. It would be impossible for them to read Joyce for amusement, so busy are they "writing papers on Bruno's idea that all created things are the offspring of a Demiurge of Intellect and a Matrix of Necessity" or "shaking their heads over Vico's picture of History as a sort of organ-grinder with only a limited number of tunes."[101] It is most amusing—and Joycean, even to the pun on "Matrix." And so is Niall Montgomery's reference to "subtle overseas doctors in whom, under martial aid, are vested the exegetic rights."[102]

Though the unsympathetic may laugh at symbolic interpretation, we must remember "The Limits of Joyce's Naturalism," as expounded by Richard Ellmann at the Modern Language Association annual meeting of 1954. Ellmann has contributed further documentation to mine in tracing the characters of *Ulysses*. But Dublin is not so much described as taken for granted, he reminds us, and Bloom becomes a community of nature and myth, thus typical of Joyce's mediation between the real and the ideal, for which the images are fall and flight. His works are not mere books but acts of prophecy. Joyce's order is not one of love or providence; it is that of coincidence. If Ellmann's insights be carried a step further we may see that Joyce moves from naturalism through symbolism, not to a transcendental ideal but to a philosophic naturalism in which the accidents of fate result in the repetition and variation of basic situations and themes.

Examinations of particular themes have been made. The underlying current of Freemasonry has been traced and considered not merely accidental, but an important symbol of love.[103] There are echoes of Irish myth that, according to H. E. Rogers, define the conflict between idealist and citizen and parallel Stephen's search for integration.[104] Even *Don Giovanni,* airs from which Molly Bloom is to sing, is not introduced in vain, for Bloom's life parallels aspects of its plot.[105] The most ambitious editorial work of a traditional sort, the identification of allusions, has been carried out by Joseph Prescott, whose diligence has revealed many evidences of Joyce's wide-ranging curiosity and his effort to make *Ulysses* an encyclopedia of popular culture.[106]

More central to an understanding of *Ulysses* are the many references to Shakespeare and Dante. Joyce seems to have invited both comparisons, the first by the important role played by the discussion of Hamlet, the second more remotely by indirect reference to Dante's famed letter of Can Grande, in which the four levels of interpretation are defined. Joyce was early compared by his Irish friends to Dante, and the comparison has been continued by Richard Watts, Jr., and Tindall, and myself among others. The basic scheme of *Ulysses*—the observant traveler as moralist—is that of the *Divine Comedy*. Tindall sees *Ulysses* as a comedy in the Dantean sense of a work that culminates in a positive resolution, for in it Stephen reaches an aesthetic awareness of his subject, a moral and social compassion, and, on the religious level, "finds in mankind a substitute for God."[107]

Cataloguing of the many Shakespearean tags and echoes is less important than consideration of Stephen's resemblance to Hamlet and its effect on the theme. The serious aspect of his Hamlet mask may be taken from the aloof Hamlet of Mallarmé, as Kenner has argued, and the comic aesthetic derived from Laforgue. *Hamlet,* the *Odyssey,* and the Dedalus myth intertwine, Kenner continues, pointing out that even the

Odyssey has its Hamlet, Telemachus being charged by Nestor with a Orestean revenge.[108] Bloom also has his resemblances to Shakespeare, or to the ghost of Hamlet's father.[109] Echoes of *Hamlet* contribute to the atmosphere of *Ulysses* but play an even more important role in uniting the paternity theme with the Christian doctrine of the consubstantiality of God the Father and Christ the Son—Dedalus is the spiritual father of Stephen, as Sabellius held God to be of Christ, Simon is the consubstantial father, as in orthodox theology, and Bloom the adopted father, the Arian concept of God and Christ as being of like but not identical substance.[110] Basically, of course, the echoes of Hamlet lead to a consideration of the modern temper, "the dilemma," in Moody Prior's words, "of a characteristic type of modern man, conscious that the foundations . . . which preserved his ethical values" have been disintegrated.[111]

Joyce's keen ear for the Anglo-Irish idiom was demonstrated by G. J. Visser, who found him "a master of racy Anglo-Irish" with an "amused superiority" to Gaelic. Many of the Anglo-Irish forms are, as might be expected, direct and literal translations of Gaelic idiom: the free "and" construction ("I met him . . . *and he coming out* of that Irish farm dairy"), omission of the relative pronoun ("who is the gentleman *does be* visiting there?"), the "after" wording of the perfect tense ("I'm *after* seeing him not five minutes ago"), the "do be" habitual present ("What *do* they *be* thinking about?"), the uninverted dependent question ("Wonder *how is she* feeling?"), and the loose "on" idiom ("pawning the furniture *on* him") are among the most common Irish expressions in *Ulysses*.[112]

Homeric parallels have been more carefully evaluated since Stuart Gilbert's methodical exegesis. Vivienne Koch has urged critics to consider the essential purpose of these echoes rather than to continue to trace the obvious or to invent absurd correspondences. Any blockhead can trace them, Pound once said. But instead of regarding them as a mere scaffolding for a realistic novel, Vivienne Koch prefers to have them constantly weighted against "the enormous shift in philosophical and physical concepts" since Homer and against the equally great shift in society. In such case, the parallel reveals the twin failures in personal and social relationships, in love and in the city, and provides "the margin for bitter and humorous comment" on modern life. The paternity theme, too, has been oversimplified; Stephen, as an artist, cannot be a son, and he must cling to his dispossession in order to dramatize the plight of modern man.[113]

A new reading of the Homeric element is possible, in which Joyce is not parodying Homer, but rather the namby-pamby version of Butcher and Lang, the "Idyllized" Victorian Homer. Joyce and Pound may be closer to the colloquial, often comic tone of Homer than we had thought. If so, Joyce is neither a simple debunker of the *Odyssey* nor of the modern world, but provides "a succession of rapidly changing perspectives on permanent human relationships." The parallels (to continue with Kenner's insights), sometimes comic, are often cognitive in a symbolic fashion. As Odysseus was sea-tossed by Poseidon because of his treatment of the Cyclops, so Bloom, because of the Jews' treatment of Christ, is thwarted by the hangman god who presides over "the sea of matter" in which man is almost engulfed.

A classicist of University College, Dublin, W. B. Stanford, has examined the *Ulysses* tradition throughout western European literature. He argues cogently that Leopold Bloom, as a lover of home and a dreamer of imaginary adventures, echoes Homer, Dante, and Faust; that his eroticism reminds one of Don Juan, his citizenship of Odysseus, but that, above all, his curiosity has essentially Greek qualities: "a childlike sense of wonder, an omnivorous curiosity, a gift for seizing on the essential point, a freedom from dogmatism."[114]

Joyce remarked to Eugene Jolas, apropos of *Ulysses,* "I am trying to build up many planes of narrative with a single esthetic purpose," and in one of his revealing asides, "Did you ever read Laurence Sterne?" Louis D. Rubin, Jr., has traced affinities between the two writers in their sense of the stream of thought, their flexible concepts of the passing of time, even in their style.[115] Most important of all, however, is their sharing "the same basic view of life as a tragic-comic situation," in which, as I had earlier observed, "the most unpredictable, and hence the most comic, thing in creation is the human mind."[116] Rubin finds that both Joyce and Sterne regard life as a "pathetic, bumbling, ludicrous and enormously tragic attempt" to reconcile the animal and the spiritual aspects of man. Among other predecessors have been Goethe, Pepys, Rabelais, Melville, Spenser, and Blake. If one adds the eccentric works listed by Levin as companions of *Finnegans Wake,* Alexandrian coterie poets such as Lycophron, or the Irish Book of Kells, he may conclude with Joyce's most successful Irish disciple, Myles na gCopaleen, that the author "shared with jackdaws the talent of picking such bright things as suited his purpose." The less sympathetic may agree with Francis Russell that, like Lycophron's *Alexandra,* Joyce's work may survive only "as a sterile freak of literature, accidentally immortal through its monumental emptiness." Such elucidations indicate Joyce's ties with tradition. Even the novel, which he is presumed to have destroyed, had in its beginning a spirit of experiment—parody in Fielding, digressive play in Sterne, subliterary language in Smollett. As the experimental novel was renewed by Henry James, so Joyce may merely have extended the practice of James to an extreme demanded by his concern with the inner life of his characters and their "relation to eternity."[117]

Joyce's similarity to his contemporaries also becomes clearer. With W. B. Yeats, Joyce has been found to manifest a "habit of cranky speculation" and a curious blend of intense localism, mysticism, and dogma, according to Louis MacNeice. F. O. Matthiessen saw in Eliot a similar interest in technique and an "extraordinary historical consciousness."[118]

In Claude Edmonde Magny's incisive analysis of Eliot and Joyce, the two writers are found akin in their attempts to escape the tyranny of time and the modern consciousness. The temporal becomes transmuted into the eternal; the parallels indicate "the profound identity . . . of the Father and the Son" as well as that of Shakespeare, his own father and son, and both Hamlet and the Ghost. In both *The Waste Land* and *Ulysses* a static world is depicted, with no future and no hope of redemption. Eliot moved beyond this impasse, but Joyce remained there, with the result that *Finnegans Wake* is not so much obscure "as boring, because it indefatigably repeats one thing." The Italian critic Giorgio Melchiori has shown that while writing *The Waste Land* Eliot may have had in mind several aspects of Joyce's "Proteus" episode—the barren scene littered with debris, the dog as symbol of evil, the drowning man, as well as references to Ophelia, to thunder, and to the cataclysm of civilization.[119]

Joyce shares with Proust the subjective outlook and the concept of the artist's mission, with Freud and Jung the insights of depth psychology, with Kafka, Malraux, Silone, and Mann the use of myth as "a celebration of the community," to quote Harry Levin, who has done most to relate Joyce to his peers. To know Joyce, it is clear, one must understand the entire range of modern culture as well as the main traditions of the past. Looking back to the nineteenth century, Levin related the work to the vast symbolic efforts of Wagner, Melville, and Zola. Far from being a private eccentricity, the symbol can invest the ephemeral with "ceremonial dignity." The almost contemporaneous deaths of Yeats, Freud, Trotsky, Bergson, Woolf, Frazer, and Joyce seemed to Levin to mark the end of an age. But Herbert Muller felt that such comparisons only emphasized Joyce's failure to give meaningful insights.[120] Despite such doubts, lessening as the years go by, Joyce remains a central figure in modern literature. The variety of technical and literary impulses that he embodies is indicated by his ubiquity in Tindall's *Forces in Modern British Literature,* the most considerable effort to delineate these complex currents. There he appears in almost every chapter—"Exile," "The Left," "The Hunt for a Father," "The Forest of Symbols," "The Stream of Consciousness," and "Myth." He might also be placed in the additional chapters on naturalism and fantasy.

If the position of *Ulysses* in modern letters be entrenched, as it now seems to be, the basic problem remains that of interpreting the narrative's resolution. How seriously must the meeting of Stephen and Bloom be considered in theory, when it remains so ineffectual in fact? Is the end result merely that of ineradicable loneliness, or does Molly's final "Yes" indicate acceptance of the life force? To Tindall, Stephen's quest concludes with his discovery of reality, his personal salvation from pride and egocentricity, and his artistic dedication to the theme of humanity. To D. S. Savage, on the other hand, the only outcome is the pagan acceptance of nature, and the basic themes of the work or "Unbelief, Nature and Necessity, Physicality, Promiscuity." The mystical strands indicate no religious feeling but show that in rejecting Catholicism Joyce felt compelled to embrace pantheism. Everything merges into something else, in the world of flux, hence the denotation of Sabellius as the archheretic, for he conceived of the identity of Father and Son. The only atonement reached by the two major characters is that of universal sexuality, Bloom in the role of Don Juan, famed for promiscuity, and Stephen the pure solipsist.[121]

It is this unresolved resolution that R. P. Blackmur discusses as the "gap between *Ulysses* and its author, between the author and us and between the book and us." In a brilliant essay, marred by such circumlocution as the above, or the characterization of Stephen as "the self struggling with the self to find out the self devours the self," Blackmur argues that the gap is that between idea and reality, Stephen and Bloom. The "omnivorous detail" and the "damnation of imposed orders" such as the Homeric, Shakespearean, and other external forms are to be attributed to the breakdown of authority in our age, "the loss of authority in the forms of the ideal." This moral, cultural, and religious breakdown is not only Joyce's theme but that of Eliot, Mann, Proust, and Yeats as well.

Stephen hopes "to make an epiphany of the darkness shining brightness," a "third testament" such as that of his admired Joachim de Flora, but his pride, aloofness, and sentimentality prevent him from seeing the living Bloom, who represents "what has actually happened to Christianity." We must understand the gap between Bloom and Stephen, conceptually, aesthetically, and on the actual level before we can resolve it—the discrepancy between modern life and our now outmoded conceptual ideals.[122]

Chapter 9

Finnegans Wake

THE READER WHO, like Dorian Gray with Lord Henry's "yellow book," begins "to turn over the leaves" of *Finnegans Wake,* will undoubtedly find it, as Wilde's hero does, "the strangest book that he had ever read. It seemed to him that in exquisite raiment, and to the delicate sounds of flutes, the sins of the world were passing in dumb show before him." The reader of the *Wake* will discover too "Things that he had dimly dreamed of . . . suddenly made real to him . . . . It was a novel without a plot. . . . The style in which it was written was that curious jeweled style, vivid and obscure at once, full of argot and of archaisms, of technical expressions and of elaborate paraphrases, that characterizes the work of some of the finest artists of the French school of *Symbolistes. . . .*"[1] The analogy is not so contrived as might at first appear, for, though the two books—Huysmans's *Against the Grain* and Joyce's *Wake*—are far apart in years and in method both have the faults and virtues of the decadent romanticism that they reflect and exemplify.

With less imagination than Joyce—and not heir to the additional fifty years of stylistic development that the Irishman inherited—Huysmans was content to elaborate merely on the details of subject matter, though with great skill and ingenuity:

> The viands were served on black-bordered plates,—turtle soup, Russian black bread, ripe olives from Turkey, caviar, mule steaks, Frankfurt smoked sausages, game dished up in sauces coloured to resemble liquorice water and boot-blacking, truffles in jelly . . . . The wines were drunk from dark-tinted glasses,—wines of the Limagne and Rousillon vintages, wines of Tenedos, the Val de Penas and Oporto. After the coffee and walnuts came other unusual beverages, kwas, porter and stout.[2]

Joyce also fills *Finnegans Wake* with these bizarrely decadent catalogues, lacking which the book would, with its thin story

The notes to Chapter 9 begin on page 344.

line, be relatively short. But Joyce goes further. Huysmans had carried his bizarre spinning of a web of details as far as it could be carried within the confines of conventional language. His Irish successor carried decadent concern for intricate detail and design, for arrangement and rearrangement of mosaic patterns, into the words themselves. Thus, as William York Tindall has shown, the startlingly new and revolutionary iconoclasm of the *Wake* is merely the ultimate step in the development of creative language, begun officially in 1798 by Wordsworth's *Preface to the Lyrical Ballads*. Knowing this, however, does not make reading Joyce's book any easier for readers who have not reached, in their own evolution, the *ultima Thule* of decadence.

Little wonder that brave men have quailed before the apparent impossibility of making "sense" of *Finnegans Wake*.[3] Since Joyce is unfolding "all marryvoising moodmoulded cyclewheeling history" (186) * it is necessary to "anthrapologise" (151) to the extent that the characters "reamalgamerge" (49) until it is difficult to "idendifine the individuone" (51). Thus, even the rain that falls during this troubled sleep becomes one of Ireland's legendary lovers. "Pouringrainia" (31), and the central character, H. C. Earwicker, becomes Adam, Tristan, Swift, or simply Here Comes Everybody. The language, as can be seen by these examples, is an "alphybettyformed verbage" of "once current puns, quashed quotatoes, messes of mottage" (183). Sometimes it reduces words and things to their "comedy nominator" (283), but one can make a "freudful mistake" (411) in missing its frequent innuendo. Joyce is playing with the mythologies of mankind, but he leans also on the *"Easyathic Phallusaphist"* (72) with his "Lotus spray" (598) of the Cosmic Serpent Ananta, which Joseph Campbell describes as the "sleeping, blissful, macrocosmic giant." And he shows concern with the concept of relativity, the "theorics of Winestain" (149). The fact that the locale is once more Dublin, often invaded by Danes, enables Joyce to enter the "Scandiknavery" (47) of the dark ages; the range is from "pharaoph times" to those of the "alcohoran" (20) and the present age of "pulpic dictators" (185) and such a "payrodicule" (70) as the "Scatterbrains' Aftening Posht" (99). But he always returns to "Errorland,"

* Numbers in parantheses in this chapter refer to pages of the Viking Press edition of *Finnegans Wake*.

the "peasant pastured" (62), with its "romekeepers, homesweepers, domecreepers" (6).

Owing to its obvious difficulties, the book was the subject of numerous explications even before it appeared as a finished product in 1939. As sections of this *Work in Progress* were published, frequent "exagminations" of its meaning were undertaken, especially by admirers of *Ulysses* and of the author himself. These culminated in the voluminous *Skeleton Key,* which attempted a fragmentary paraphrase of the entire *Wake.* There is no need here to attempt a summary of the extended exegesis that has appeared, but an outline of the major facets of the book may be useful. Harry Levin has applied the four-level interpretation in Dante's Epistle to Can Grande della Scala: literal, the household of the Chapelizod pubkeeper Earwicker, comprising his wife, twin sons, daughter, and two servants; anagogical, the development of human history according to Giambattista Vico; allegorical, the environs of Dublin; and moral, the problem of evil, which arises from a vague sexual indiscretion in the park.[4] These fuse under the influence of the sleeping subconscious mind, where Freudian slips of the tongue are numerous. To these basic levels might be added the pantheistic poetry of river and hill, elm and stone, masculine and feminine principles in nature. There are other philosophical dualities of Bruno and Hegel, space and time introvert artist (Shem) and extrovert man of affairs (Shaun). There is the immense and embracing concept of the universe as a dream, the legacy of Hindu philosophy that recurs in Carl Jung, and, finally, the resurrection theme of Fraser's dying god and the Egyptian *Book of the Dead.*

The clearest, most cogent attempt to place before bewildered readers the realistic core of the *Wake* is Edmund Wilson's "The Dream of H. C. Earwicker."[5] In the opening pages, we learn the HCE is Scandinavian in his middle fifties, that he keeps a pub in Chapelizod. Like Billy Budd, perhaps also to indicate his imperfection as a man, he stutters. Being foreign by blood and Protestant by religion, he has the same feeling of isolation as Joyce's other protagonists. Wilson describes Earwicker's three children, his wife, and the circumstances that prevail in the pub on this summer night before Earwicker retires to dream the dream of Everyman. The hero on this night will realize that his love for his wife is cold and that he now has centered his interest on his daughter and at least one of his sons. But, as Wilson points out, this skeleton summary of events and background is pitifully inadequate, just as the prose meaning of a poem is less than the poem itself. It may help the reader to know that on the geographical level, HCE stands for Howth Castle and Environs, and that his wife is the River Liffey, Anna Livia Plurabelle; but the artistic and emotional significance of such a level of action can be conveyed only within the framework of the story—and sometimes it breaks down even there. The plot of *Finnegans Wake* can hardly be talked about; it must be read.

With full knowledge of the impossibility of plumbing the depths of the mystery, we may, for practical convenience, chart the main levels, modifying the diagram of Leslie Lewis in Moholy-Nagy's *Vision in Motion* (1947):

1. Familial	Household	Pub, Phoenix Park, rain, Guinness, stutter
2. Civic	Dublin	Park, Monument, Liffey, Tristan, Swift
3. Historical	Philosophy of Vico	Thunder, cycles, conflicts: Danish-Irish, Waterloo, Crimea
4. Legendary	Irish saga	Finn, Kathleen
5. Mythological	Cosmic dream—Jung, Oriental philosophy	All history, myth
6. Moral	Problem of evil	Guilt of HCE, Adam, *felix culpa,* Humpty Dumpty
7. Poetic	Pantheism	Hill-river, stone-elm
8. Philosophical	Dualities of Giordano Bruno	Shem-Shaun, Mookse-Gripes, Ondt-Gracehoper
9. Religious	Fraser; Egyptian *Book of the Dead*	Dawn, new generations

Lewis adds Cabalist (Adam, Eve, Lilith), Biblical (St. Patrick, St. Bridget), Linguistic, Narrative (Finnegan-Kate), metaphysical, Allegorical, Literary, Anagogical, Psychological (introvert-extravert), Numerological, and, most interesting of all, an autobiographical level.[6] But there is no end of levels in this book that flows as the Liffey.

As Tindall has stated, *Ulysses* and *Finnegans Wake* are two "great epiphanies" that not only disclose "their whatness" but "the whatness of reality." Joyce's purpose was "neither the naturalistic presentation of a night's sleep nor the recommendation of a philosophy" but the representation of "the nature and condition of man." William Troy concluded that, like Mann and Yeats, Joyce seeks salvation "not in any escape from the present but in a transcendence of the present through the past," a thesis which suggests a more positive pressure of moral effort than is usually found by commentators. More akin to the presentational concept is Louis Gillet's exposition of the sleeper as "everything that he thinks," or the "central energy" of the universe, a God, of which "all phenomena and creatures" are but incarnations. Pantheistic as this concept is, it can be suggested only by a verbal "multivalence or polyvalence" which can extend and deepen meanings, relations, and implications.[7]

Perhaps the most rewarding approach to *Finnegans Wake* is to consider it as the myth of its author and of modern man. Few men of letters have had greater need than Joyce, certainly, to construct a framework of belief that would offer some degree of stability in a disintegrating world. Earlier, in *Ulysses,* and some think even in *Dubliners* and *A Portrait,* the author had depended for his effects on the superimposition of myth on the everyday, mundane affairs of his characters. T. S. Eliot puts it this way:

> In using the myth, in manipulating a continuous parallel between contemporaneity and antiquity, Mr. Joyce is pursuing a method which others must pursue after him . . . . It is simply a way of controlling, of ordering, of giving a shape and a significance to the immense panorama of futility and anarchy which is contemporary history. . . . It is . . . a step toward making the modern world possible for art . . . .[8]

But Joyce's use of myth in the books before the *Wake* is generally of the literary, impersonal sort—to prove a point, to illustrate a contrast, to evoke pathos, to provide episodic structure for a long narrative. It would be stretching a point to say that the author really identifies himself emotionally with the wily Greek or that Penelope is anything but a mythical symbol to him. *Ulysses* may contain fragmentary evidence of Joyce's "belief," but the work of art as a whole is hardly a personal myth. *Finnegans Wake,* his final summing up—more mellow, more personal, more human—is different.

Although worked out in intricate and complicated detail in the *Wake,* the framework of his "monomyth" (581) is plain, simple, and sturdy. A disintegrating civilization, one in which, as Yeats says, "Things fall apart," because "the centre cannot hold . . . ," implies eventual destruction and complete oblivion, the negation of human progress. Joyce's means of escape from so negative a view of life lay in his skill in adapting to his peculiar needs the idea of cyclical history. If the final blotting out of our contemporary world be but the prelude to the flowering of a new civilization arising out of the ashes of the old, then despair may give way to the hope of affirmation, and the nervous sense of impending doom may be replaced by the resigned acceptance of the idea that from death will come renewed life. Or, as Joyce put it, "all that has been done has yet to be done and done again, when's day's woe, and lo, you're doomed, joyday dawns and, la, you dominate" (194).

No credit, of course, can be given to Joyce as the discoverer of the cyclical idea. It is at least as ancient as early Hindu culture, and its use in the construction of a pseudo-myth is as recent as Yeats's *A Vision,* which went even further than Joyce's plan in predicting the end of the present cycle of the world's development at the end of the twentieth century. But the explanation of cyclical history upon which Joyce drew most heavily for *Finnegans Wake* is that of the eighteenth-century Italian philosopher, Giambattista Vico.

Vico's conception of universal history, enunciated in his work, *La scienza nuova* (1725), would divide history into three great ever-recurring stages or cycles: the divine, the heroic, and the human, with a smaller, chaotic interlude during which forces are set into motion that result in the establishment of a new series of cycles. These three major cyclical types Vico finds in nature both human and nonhuman; in the customs of people; in natural law; in government; in the characters that form written language; and in many other manifestations of human existence. He had arrived at this rather arbitrary set of divisions as a result of his ambitious attempt to devise scientifically a system that would be able to account for apparently inexplicable similarities in language, custom, and even personal traits among peoples widely separated in space or time. Vico's purpose, in the words of Jules Michelet:

> . . . tracer l'histoire universelle, éternelle qui se produit dans le temps sous la forme des histoires particulieres, décrire le cercle idéal dans lequel tourne le monde réel: voilà l'objet de la nouvelle science. Elle est tout à la fois la philosophie et l'histoire de l'humanité.[9]

The wholeness of Vico's philosophy, its universal scope, appealed strongly to Joyce, at first for its own sake and then for the ease with which its principles could be modified and adapted to his own plan of history. He saw that he could account for the shape of things to come by proving that history had followed a clearly discernible and consistent pattern in the past. History no longer had to be a "nightmare" from which he was trying to escape; it might now become a firm base for prediction.

Educated in the rigorous discipline of Jesuit Scholastic exercises, Joyce naturally would find congenial to his temperament a view of history that, although all-embracing, was nevertheless capable of "exagmination" (497) in orderly, logical sections. He saw clearly the advantage of having ready-to-hand an established, public framework on which to build his private myth. He saw the pragmatic value for himself in the numerous parallels that Vico had drawn: the correspondence, for instance, between the ages, divine, heroic, human, and the prehistoric, fabulous (or mythological), and historical periods; or the parallel between Vico's ages and the development of language from hieroglyphic or sacred symbols of communication, through metaphorical or poetic expression, to the abstract language of our present "human" period. Specifically, he was attracted to the idea of social and political development from the age of blundering giants, propelled forward and upward by their animistic fear of, and reverence for, the thunder, to the age of patriarchs, with its heroic aristocracies (ancient Greece is a good example), and finally to the age of reasonable humanity living under monarchies and democracies until decay sets in and the resulting chaos and turbulence plant the seeds that will reproduce the threefold cycle. To orient his own position, and the plight of contemporary men in general, with respect to Vico's *cercle idéal* of human progress, but in terms of modern narrative projection, became Joyce's major job.

He did not try to obscure his purpose, and *Finnegans Wake* abounds in concrete statements of the theory, in the light of world history. "Gricks may rise and Troysirs fall . . . for in the byways of high improvidence that's what makes lifework leaving and the world's a cell for citters to cit in" (11) contains essential statement of the proposition on which the book is based. Joyce hammered home his point again and again through the six-hundred-odd pages of his "cyclological" (220) novel. "The house of Atreox is fallen indeedust (Ilyam, Ilyum! Maeromor Mournomates!) . . . but deeds bounds going arise again" (55). Although outward forms of things may change, governments may rise, decline, and be replaced by others, actually nothing is permanently lost in the history of the race: "Yet is no body present here which was not there before. Only is order othered. Nought is nulled" (613). In this view, history is the tale of "one world burrowing on another" (275) and deriving from its predecessor primal changeless qualities that it, in turn, passes on intact to the next stage. The institutions of an age, its law courts and churches and literary criticism, may decay and disappear, but religion, married love, bodily disintegration, and hope of rebirth are deathless attributes of any and all ages.

Briefly and inadequately stated—for *Finnegans Wake* defies paraphrase—the narrative projection of cyclical history begins in the *Wake* with the giant Tim Finnegan, bricklayer, whose fall from a ladder and subsequent death bring the prehistoric age to an end. To supplant him, the heroic patriarch, father of us all, Humphrey Chimpden Earwicker (better known as HCE), arises from the debris of the earlier period. Even as the reader is introduced to Earwicker, however, the process of decay is already well advanced, and it is only a matter of time until HCE's twin sons, Shem and Shaun, will eclipse the father, rise in the human age to the ascendant position, to be overwhelmed in turn by the chaos that is inevitable as a prelude to the recommencement of the three cycles.

Although constantly berated, by those who do not take the time to read him, for his "private" frames of reference, actually Joyce appears to be straining to give his admittedly elaborate myth the support of as many established, traditional, publicly recognized writings as he can muster. Side by side, and often intertwining, the Christian story of Paradise lost and regained, the Irish myth of Finn MacCool and Diarmuid and Grania, the Celtic tale of the prankquean, the French romance of Tristan and Iseult, La Fontaine's fable of the Ondt and the Gracehoper—all have the function of helping the reader to get his bearings in unfamiliar territory by serving as guideposts along the "Vico road" (452). Their use in this novel is not unlike the use that T. S. Eliot makes of well-known snatches of verse. They put the reader in the proper mood, help to give him the mental set with which to approach the larger, more significant whole—Joyce's myth of man in history.

Traditional myths in *Finnegans Wake* serve another purpose, too. To prove that through all ages "the same roturns" (18), Joyce needed more elemental, more vibrant evidence than the cold patterns of objectively recorded history. He needed heroes and heroines whose pattern of behavior was drawn from the well of the popular imagination. Here again Vico came to the rescue with his euhemeristic theory of the origin of mythical heroes. The hero, said Vico, is merely the projection of the ideal character of a people. A national or racial group has a tendency to place ideal types under proper names and then to endow those proper names with personal attributes. This may be illustrated by reference to Hercules. A man named Hercules once performed a brave deed. Primitive mentality, not able to grasp the abstraction of "*a* Hercules," simply called any brave man who in later years seemed to fit the pattern, "Hercules." In short, to consider Hermes, Romulus, Athena as names for the expression of the national character of this or that country is to get close to the truth. This was Joyce's cue. If the mythical heroes of a culture can come alive again in the shape of those who resemble the originals, then, in Joyce's myth, the Finn MacCool of heroic Ireland may return, and there is hope of Finn-again: "(Lost leaders live! the heroes return!)" (74). If the patterns of mythical behavior are constant and may recur in modern dress, the way lies open for elaborate identification of the Earwicker household in contemporary Chapelizod with the deathless characters of medieval chivalry in the story of Tristan.

HCE is identified now with Tristan, the passionate lover, now with King Mark, the aging ruler with a fondess for a young, beautiful bride, Iseult. The latter is sometimes the wife of HCE, Anna Livia Plurabelle (ALP), and sometimes, in the incestuous byways of dream, their young daughter, Isobel. In general, there is very little equating of the original mythical characters to those of Joyce's myth. Much more subtly the contrast is drawn by hundreds of allusions to the Tristan story woven into the fabric of the *Wake*. Their appearance throughout the Earwicker saga, in ordered profusion, points up the similarity implicitly. But the cumulative effect of the mighty torrent, continually impinging upon the reader's consciousness, makes the desired conclusions inescapable—and much more effective than the mere telling.

The myth of Tristan and Iseult in *Finnegans Wake* acts as narrative expression for the idea that, in every age, the love of one human being for another forms a predictable and unchanging pattern. With us always we have the gallant hero-lover type—whether Tristan or HCE. The promiscuous, flirtatious Iseult remains constantly inconstant from cycle to cycle. Nor is the third member of the triangle lacking in any age. The lustful King Mark of medieval legend, Earwicker, the middle-aged seducer of Irish womanhood, the "sugar daddy" of Peaches Browning fame—all are manifestations to Joyce of the pattern of history in one of its numerous facets. His overwhelming insistence on telling and retelling in countless guises the plot of the Tristan story is simply his way of projecting into vivid narrative his belief that

> those sort of things which has been going on onceaday in and twiceaday out every other nachtistag among all kinds of promiscious individuals at all ages in private homes and reeboos publikiss and allover all and elsewhere throughout secular sequence the country over and overabroad has been particularly stupendous (66).

Probably to reinforce his argument that the outlines of the Tristan formula are not confined to national boundaries or particular periods, he introduced an analogue, the Celtic myth of Diarmuid and Grania. At times, one myth fades into the other, only to reappear on later pages distinct once more. In the Diarmuid-Grania myth, Finn MacCool is the equivalent of King Mark of the Tristan story. He wishes to marry Grania but she places a spell on Diarmuid, the man of her choice, compelling him to elope with her. Iseult, in the French version, attains the same end by tricking Mark's faithful retainer, Tristan, into drinking a love potion that binds him forever to her in unreasoning passion. In both myths there is wild pursuit of the offending lovers by the aging monarchs and eventual capture in the woods. In both, the hero refrains, through a sense of loyalty, from consummating a marriage undertaken under shady pretensions; Tristan shuns the second Iseult, his legal wife, while Diarmuid refuses Grania the attentions of a husband out of respect for Finn. Joyce's ability to merge the one mythical story with the other succeeds in giving a much tighter texture to his narrative than handling one thread of the old story could have accomplished.

If any one mythical character may be said to dominate the *Wake,* and Joyce's thinking, then purely on the number of times he is invoked, the nod goes to Finn MacCumhal

—pronounced Finn MacCool. A careful comparison of *Finnegans Wake* with John A. Macculloch's *Celtic Mythology*[10] is enough to convince the reader that Joyce was more than superficially interested in the warrior-giant of that period of Irish history which is shrouded in hazy speculation. In Finn, Joyce undoubtedly saw a legitimate ancestor for his modern hero, Humphrey Chimpden Earwicker—as well as for people like Parnell and himself. The title that Joyce gave to his book, arrived at very deliberately and only after years of rumination, is an indication of the importance that the author placed upon the Finn-Earwicker parallel. Like Finn, Earwicker is half Norse, an invader from the mainland who becomes a staunch defender of the soil of Ireland against foreign attack. Finn means "white" or "fair," and Earwicker's son, the embodiment of his father, is given the name of Kevin, which means "Fairborn" in the Irish tongue. Both Finn and HCE live close to Dublin and are connected with activities on the River Liffey. Both are involved in adventures in *Tir fo Thiunn,* Land under Waves, Finn when he enters the heavenly region as a god, Earwicker when he finds himself imprisoned beneath Lough Neagh at the conclusion of his trial. These are significant differences when one considers that Finn loved in the happy days of an earlier, heroic cycle, while the humpbacked bartender of Chapelizod is the representative of our present dying age. "One tradition," says Macculloch, "alleged that, like Arthur, Fionn [Finn] was still living secretly somewhere, within a hill or on an island, ready to come . . . in the hour of his country's need. . . ." It is easy to see why Joyce, "self exiled in upon his ego" (184), "Irish emigrant the wrong way out" (190), should have used Finn as the symbol of a happier Ireland. He had used the memory of the dead Parnell in the same way in "Ivy Day in the Committee Room." "Once it happened, so it may again" (625).

From his storehouse of obscurities, Joyce selected the Irish legend of Jarl van Hoother and the "prankquean" (21) to enrich his myth. Apparently the narrative of Grace O'Malley's three-time kidnaping of the sons of the earl as repayment for a supposed snub by that lord of the castle, and the subsequent wild but fruitless pursuits of the mischievous kidnaper, was carefully chosen for its associative values. The incident, first of all, stresses the ritual aspect of myth, especially important in the cyclical context of *Finnegans Wake.* Three times the prankquean appears at the gate of the castle;

three times she propounds her riddle and is rebuffed. Each time, until the last one, she snatches up one of the earl's children in her anger and leads the anguished earl a merry chase, eludes him, only to reappear after forty years to repeat the ritual. The legend, in other words, rehearses on a small scale the cyclical movement of Joyce's myth. Even the thunder, coming at the end of the third cycle to usher in a new round, is present in the sound of the slamming door.[11]

Going one step further, the prankquean episode contains in microcosm numerous mythical forces that receive their full development later on in the *Wake*. In the two pages that Joyce allots to the incident, most of the major characters of his "Pageant of Past History" (221) pass in review. Adam and Eve set the time of the occurrence. The gay young prankquean who seized the child and "started to rain and to rain" (21) is Anna Livia Plurabelle, riverwife of HCE. Hilary and Christopher, the "jiminy" whom she abducts at regular intervals, are Kevin and Jerry, the twin sons of ALP and Earwicker, another incarnation of Jarl van Hoother. But this is just the beginning. In an attempt to introduce the analogy of Tristan and Iseult, Joyce's ingenuity works overtime. After kidnaping Hilary, "she provorted him to the onecertain allsecure and he became a tristian" (22). Following the episode through on this level, we find that other obscurities become clear. The prankquean prefaces each statement of her riddle with "Mark the Wans," "Mark the Twy," "Mark the Tris." Van Hoother-Earwicker-Mark is undoubtedly King Mark, whose close relative, Hilary-Jerry-Tristan, has been seduced by the woman in the case. Prankquean-Anna Livia-Iseult. The reader is not allowed to forget the Diarmuid-Grania parallel either, for the narrator's favorite oath resolves itself every time into a distorted anagram of the name Diarmuid ("be dermot," "be redtom," "be dom ter"). It would be hard to imagine another passage of comparable length that compressed as many relevant associative variations on a theme as does the episode of the prankquean. Nor has this brief examination exhausted the possibilities of the legend. For if we look at *Finnegans Wake* as the great, sprawling dream of everybody, each of its episodes acquires deeper, fresher meaning.

Though some have held the dreamer to be Joyce or the guide or Shem, the most plausible suggestion, made by Joseph Campbell in his essay in the Seon Givens anthology, is that, though attention is centered mainly on the subconscious of

HCE, the actual point of view is omniscient, moving freely from husband to wife to son and to external points of observation.

Finnegans Wake is, then, probably the dream of H. C. Earwicker, tavern keeper, on a warm evening. After carrying to artistic completion in *Ulysses* a description of an ordinary day in the life of ordinary Mr. Leopold Bloom, Joyce decided to turn his talents to the much more difficult job of depicting just as completely the mind of an average citizen of modern Ireland in sleep. His close friend, Eugene Jolas, tells us that Joyce was "an intensely conscious observer of the unconscious drama" and eager to discuss dreams "because they interested him as images of the nocturnal universe."[12] Living much of his adult life in Zurich and other European capitals, he was close to the excitement surrounding discoveries relating to dreams and the unconscious mind. Freud and Jung were more than names to him. And while Freud and Jung may have disagreed in matters of detail concerning the relation of dream to myth, Joyce's genius for extracting from any system what suited his special needs allowed him to build his "Eyrawyggla saga" (48) on elements from both analysts that, to the mind of the lay reader, would not appear to conflict.[13]

In explaining his race psychology in *Totem and Taboo,* Freud declares that "we base everything upon the assumption of a psyche of the mass . . ." and later that " a continuity in the emotional life of mankind" is necessary to the holding of his theory. As an example of what he means by these abstractions, he cites the "sense of guilt" which may survive for many generations after the act which gave rise to the original emotion in the ancestors of the race.[14] No layman would find difficulty in reconciling these statements with those of Freud's disciple, Jung, who broke with the master over the interpretation of the unconscious. Jung denies that the unconscious is personal in its deeper levels. At least one layer of it is not derived from personal experience. This part, universal in its manifestations, is called the collective unconscious. The contents of this collective unconscious he calls archetypes, ancient and primordial images impressed upon the minds of early men. When these archetypes become conscious and are converted into traditional formulae, the result is myth, a conscious form, handed on relatively unchanged over long centuries.[15] What interested Joyce in all this was the fact that dreams were a primary means of bringing to the surface mythical archetypes or patterns. Keeping in mind the Viconian idea of the recurrence of the hero type, and the concept of cyclical history, Joyce saw with what ease the psychoanalytical idea of myth could be accommodated to the larger myth of man. He saw how smoothly the definition of Karl Abraham would fit his own pattern: ". . . myth is a fragment of the infantile soul life of the race and the dream is the myth of the individual."

Freud contends that "dreams are (disguised) fulfilments of a (suppressed, repressed) wish." In *The Interpretation of Dreams,* he points out that the distortion which often accompanies dreams is simply an act of censorship performed by the mind to protect the dreamer from the shock of the naked wish. Applying this formula to the sleeping Earwicker, Joyce managed to solve it through recourse to myth. Earwicker recognizes the coming of middle age. He feels that he is no longer the dashing lover he once was. Things have not been going well for him: he has lost a local election campaign and gossip accuses him of unspecified, scandalous conduct. Worst of all, his fair young bride, Anna Livia, has grown ugly and old at his side until he has reached the point at which his feeling for her is about to become one of cold neutrality. The waning passion for his wife is gradually being replaced by a socially unsanctioned incestuous interest in their daughter, Isobel. Thoroughly conventional in his waking conduct, quick to feel hurt by the opprobrium of his peers, Earwicker has been able to repress his dangerous wish. But sleep and dream are no respecters of convention. The "dislocated reason" (189) of night-logic will out. Yet the mental censor of Earwicker's dream will not allow a shocking, straightforward presentation of the wish, lest the sleeper awake. So from that part of the collective unconscious that resides in the innkeeper's mind, Joyce drew upon the archetypal pattern of the Tristan myth, the ever-present human situation of eternal triangle. The dream distorts the relationship out of focus, but, at the same time, it allows the psychic energy of the unconscious wish to be dissipated. Earwicker becomes—what he secretly longs to be—the very model of an amorous knight wooing and winning the fair lady Iseult, in real life his own daughter. It is even possible to imagine old Anna Livia, without her once-powerful sex appeal, as the King Mark of the myth, impotent and deserted.

In the "no placelike no timelike" (609) atmosphere of dream, which seems to put "Allspace in a Notshall" (455), there is no need to observe the unities of logical behavior. Therefore the reader is not surprised to find the Tristan pattern fading into the analogical archetype of Diarmuid and Grania. Here, Earwicker is reborn as the blue-eyed, fair-haired youth, Diarmuid, who is in a position to find himself sought after by the Grania-daughter figure of the Irish myth. The scene may shift again to reveal the lovely prankquean-daughter image hotly pursued by Earwicker in his role of Earl van Hoother. Over all the book flows what to Jung is the commonest and perhaps the most powerful symbol of the unconscious: water. For the leading female character of the *Wake,* the symbolic mother of us all, is the River Liffey, Anna Livia Plurabelle, a figure that represents to Jung "an experience of woman far older than that of the individual," an embodiment of the eternal feminine.[16]

An even more obvious case may be made for the presence of the Oedipus archetypal myth in *Finnegans Wake.* If we accept Freud's supposition that the beginnings of society are rooted in the Oedipal situation, the killing of the hated, arrogant father by the band of rebel sons, then his conclusions certainly become meaningful for Joyce. In *Totem and Taboo,* Freud points out that this "removal of the primal father by the band of brothers must have left ineradicable traces in the history of mankind . . . in mythology." He continues with the comment that when this basic situation is portrayed in literature, the hero must suffer.

> He had taken upon himself the so-called "tragic guilt," which is not always easy to explain; it is often not a guilt in the ordinary sense. Almost always it consisted of a rebellion against divine or human authority . . . .[17]

Even a casual reader of the *Wake*—if such there be—might well feel that Freud had aided Joyce directly in the writing of the book, so closely is the substance of his statement followed in the projection of Joyce's myth. The hero of the *Wake,* Here Comes Everybody, is at bottom just such a tragic figure, the All-Father of the race. For a hazy, indefinable indiscretion, he is the butt of his immediate society, the patrons of the tavern and the gossips of the town, who "want to hear all/about" (196) his sin. What the guilt is is never discovered although a profusion of rumors keeps the issue alive. It is not even certain that the crime is HCE's, and thus the prosecutors often blend with the defendant, the accusers change places with the accused, in bewildering confusion. Perhaps this is further explained by Freud's remark that

> He had to suffer because he was the primal father, the hero of that primordial tragedy the repetition of which here serves a certain tendency, and the tragic guilt is the guilt which he had to take upon himself in order to free the . . . [accusers] of theirs . . . .

In much the same way as Christ suffered the jeers of the populace, Earwicker in his tavern submits to the insults of the tipsy customers. Actually it was not he, the hero, who was any more guilty than his tormentors. But in the tragic figure is concentrated the feeling of sin that the rest are able to transfer from themselves. "Thus the tragic hero, though still against his will, is made the redeemer . . . ."[18]

In projecting his narrative, Joyce was faced with problems of linguistic expression which, after a lifetime of concern with words—their sound and their meaning—he was particularly well equipped to handle. In a penetrating essay on *A Portrait of the Artist,* Dorothy Van Ghent, having shown that "language is a creator of reality," demonstrates that the shape of reality that Stephen-Joyce finds is one "determined primarily by the association of words."[19] When, one by one, all the elements that have given stability to his life fail him—father, Parnell, religion, teachers—he still retains, for whatever coherence they can afford him, his word associations. From the first page of *Dubliners,* where the word "paralysis" fascinates the boy narrator as "the word gnomen in the Euclid and the word simony in the Catechism" have done earlier, Joyce's more sensitive characters play with words consciously, as children play with toys. The boy in "Araby" is thrilled by the sound of the syllables of that word, which "called to me through the silence in which my soul luxuriated and cast an Eastern enchantment over me." Stephen Dedalus, in *Stephen Hero,* collected eccentric words, "read Skeat's *Etymological Dictionary* by the hour and his mind . . . was often hypnotized by the most commonplace conversation. People seemed to him strangely ignorant of the value of the words they used so glibly." He would even wander the streets, finding unusual words "in the shops, on advertisements, in the mouths of the plodding public. He kept repeating them to himself . . . ."[20] This tendency is intensified in *A Portrait,* as young Stephen ponders the various uses of the word "belt" or listens with "an avid ear" to the words of his granduncle "which he did not understand" and which "he said over and over to himself till he had learnt them by heart." As a young man, he cannot himself understand the fascination that words have for him:

> Words. Was it their colours? He allowed them to glow and fade, hue after hue: sunrise gold, the russet and green of apple orchards . . . . No, it was not their colours: it was the poise and balance of the period itself . . . .[21]

It is this acute preoccupation that allows the young undergraduate to give the dean of his college an informal briefing on the meanings of the word "detain" and to astonish his fellow students by his fluency in speech and essay writing. Both Stephen and Mr. Bloom, partial surrogates for Joyce, show a propensity for word analysis in *Ulysses,* and even Molly, with her "met him pike hoses," is not immune to curiosity.

Finnegans Wake, the lexicographer's paradise, is abundant testimony to the lifelong hold that words had for the English teacher of the Berlitz schools, who "ran away with hunself and became a farsoonerite, saying he would far sooner muddle through the hash of lentils in Europe than meddle with Irrland's split little pea" (171). By his own admission, he became a "seeker of the nest of evil in the bosom of a good word . . ." (189). To his friend Jolas, he confided, "I have discovered that I can do anything with language I want. . . ."[22] What he wanted was to get away from bare, bald, denotative words of conventional, logical, expository prose—a deadening medium of a modern artist who had become as sensitive to sound as the almost blind Joyce. But there was more to the change than that.

For "this nonday diary, this allnights newseryreel" (489) of the *Wake,* the language of day was particularly inappropriate. A dream is not logical by waking standards, nor can the effect of dream be communicated effectively by the worn-out words of day logic, the language of this chapter. To express his dream-myth, he had to invent a language. The words had to be mixed up, both in their order and in their organic structure, so that they would convey, when unscrambled consciously or unconsciously, not only their "logical" day meaning but, much more important, the wealth of associative values which resulted from their very ambiguity. In this respect, the language resembled in function the language of poetry, offering to the careful reader layer upon layer of rich associative meaning. The rejuvenated words, unbelievably enriched, must bear the responsibility in the *Wake* that the vivid images, flashing in illogical order before the eye of the dreamer, bear in the dream. Moreover, since Joyce in *Finnegans Wake* is concerned with the mythical element of the collective unconscious in dream, his word coinages serve the additional purpose of infusing fresh vitality into the traditional myths. His treatment of myth in the language of dream is best illustrated by reference to the Tristan theme.

Hundreds—perhaps thousands—of puns on the names of characters in the Tristan story are sprinkled through the pages of the *Wake* to keep the motif constantly alive. Where the motif dominates, the page bristles with veiled and obvious references. Here is a case in point:

> . . . The new world presses. Where the old conk cruised now croons the yunk. Exeunc throw a darras Kram of Llawnroc, ye gink guy, kirked into yord. Enterest attawonder Wehpen, luftcat revol, fairescapading in his natsirt. Tuesy tumbles. And mild aunt Liza is as loose as her neese. Fulfest withim inbrace behent. As gent would deem oncontinent. So mulct per wenche is Elsker woed. Ne hath his thrysting. Fin. (387-388)

Obviously, to those who have been conditioned to Joycean verbal fireworks, the excerpt is simply one more link in the chain of evidence that world history is cyclical. In this instance the Tristan theme is the concrete example chosen. The clues to the passage are the inverted names: "Kram of Llawnroc" is Mark of Cornwall, the cuckolded husband of "Tuesy," or Yseut (Iseult). The key words of the phrase "Wehpen . . . in his natsirt," when inverted, yield "Nephew . . . tristan." The actors of the myth are now revealed. But why the hocus-pocus of inversion in the first place? Is Joyce seeking merely to fascinate puzzle addicts or to flaunt his disdain of direct communication in the language of men? A reading of the Tristan-Iseult myth provides a likely answer. In the original narrative, Tristan is forced by the dangerous circumstances of his activities to conceal his true identity behind an alias. He invariably adopts an anagram of his own name, calling himself most often Tantris (or Tremtriss). Evidently Joyce has seen here a natural opportunity to alter the organic constitution of the words, not arbitrarily, but within the framework of the public and almost universal myth.

But the twisting of key words here serves also the purpose of associative enrichment. Thus Mark is a "gink," the four letters carrying the double meaning of king and, in modern slang, fool. Perhaps there is implicit here a contrast between the nobility of the past and the tawdriness of the present cycle, which we have come to expect from modern artists. Similarly, "Wehpen, luftcat revol" means "Nephew, tactful lover," since Tristan was Mark's nephew as well as being the cagey lover of Mark's bride. On another level, however, the words in the context of the passage quoted here may stand for "weapon, lifted revolver," a phrase which would have a surface, as well as a phallic, significance. Again "revol" may have here the additional connotative force of "rebel" or "revolt," since Tristan is bucking royal authority by "fairscapading in his natsirt" with the queen. "Fairscapading" too has its associations. From the French *"faire,"* "to make," the word takes on the meaning of "to make an escape." Since Tristan's meetings with Iseult in the present cycle of the world's development take place in one-night cheap hotels, the word has the additional meaning of "fire-escape" escapades, in which the hero makes a sudden, "tactful" withdrawal through the window.

Inasmuch as the episode from which this extract is taken describes the honeymoon voyage of Tristan and Iseult aboard the dream ship, it is natural that the new world, Tristan, should press, having supplanted the old, King Mark—as Earwicker's sons are supplanting him. Mark and his alter ego, Kram, have been gotten rid of, so the Shakespearean stage directions proclaim their departure: "Exeunc throw a darras" the king. It will be noted that "Exeunt," the stage direction indicating the exit of characters from the scene, has been distorted in Earwicker's dream to "Exeunc," which conveys the same meaning but has the additional force of its comic connotation, "Exit-unc(les)" Mark and/or Kram. The ejection is forcible, "throw a darras" (through an arras), reminiscent of the exit of the old Polonius from the world through the swift action of young Hamlet. At any rate, Mark is "kirked into yord," kicked into the yard. But "kirk" is the Scotch word for church, so that the latter phrase may also be translated by "churchyard." The incident occurs on a ship, however, and Joyce must provide a reasonable means for disposing of the unwanted Mark. Again word distortion plays its part, for "yord" may be anagrammatized as "dory," the small boat often tied to the stern of a ship for the use of the crew in an emergency. A possible inference would be that the king was kicked into the dory, symbolically of course, while the unsanctioned love affair was taking place on the honeymoon ship. With the king out of the way, the passage continues, "Tuesy tumbles," passion is unabated, "Ne hath his thrysting. Fin." The last line is richly ambiguous, for "thrysting" may mean in this context "thirsting" or "trysting," and, at the same time, it obviously stands for "Tristan." The line may therefore be read: "Nor had Tristan's thirsting and/or trysting an end."

When one considers that this brief and incomplete analysis has attempted merely to mention several of the high lights of fewer than seven lines of *Finnegans Wake,* leaving numerous associations and motifs in them untouched for fear of overwhelming the reader in details, the complexity and profuse richness of Joyce's dream-myth language become apparent. When one further remembers that to each reader additional associations may present themselves in the distortion of conventional words and phrases, some idea of the advantage of using such a linguistic system in assembling a myth of Everyman is inescapable. Purely from a practical standpoint, such a system had to be worked out if Joyce was to satisfy the scientific description of the collective unconscious and the Freudian representation of dream. Frederick J. Hoffman, in *Freudianism and the Literary Mind,* points out clearly that the condensation, displacement, and distortion of dream images, required by Freud's interpretation, had somehow to be approximated in language if they were to be recorded faithfully. In the telescoping of words ("Exeunc" for "exit, uncles"), in his distortion of language ("Enterest" or "entereth" or "interest"), in his puns all through the *Wake,* Joyce makes an admirable leap from image to word.

"Was it worth doing?" is the question most frequently asked. Were the seventeen years that Joyce spent building up his system worth the effort? It is by now one of the trite ironies of our world that, in proportion as Joyce succeeded in the task of reducing his myth to the only expression capable of exposing it fully, the number of readers who were prepared to puzzle out the result diminished. His difficulties with a conventional and mentally slothful public had prepared him for this reaction. "Please stop if you're a B. C. minding missy, please do. But should you prefer A. D. stepplease" (272). He realized that his apparent obscurity would alienate a public suspicious of what it did not understand; he expected to be scorned for "his root language" (424). "The whacker his word the weaker our ears for auracles who parles parses arileys" (467). It is to Joyce's credit that he chose to abjure popularity if it had to be bought at the expense of weakening the all-embracing dream of the race. Perhaps a sensible approach to a satisfactory answer is to decide just what he accomplished in those seventeen years.

First, he continued his career as poet, begun in *Chamber Music* and evident through many sections of *Ulysses*, especially in the musical Sirens episode. But the beauty of the new poetry in *Finnegans Wake* is of another sort. The lines have a thick texture—a fundamental sediment of English overlaid with traces of the beauty of foreign tongues somehow not foreign in the *Wake*. It is beauty whose depth is extended through the wealth of meaning implicit in the thousands of expressive puns. As anyone who has heard Joyce reading a section of the Anna Livia Plurabelle episode is aware, it is a beauty of sound especially compelling when uttered in a musical tenor voice with an Irish lilt. Those who complain that the language of the book conveys no meaning at all must surely have had the experience of enjoying a melodious selection in a language unknown to them—an Italian aria, perhaps, or a skillful reading of Dante's *Divine Comedy* in the original. Surely, then, many parts of Earwicker's story are aesthetically satisfying for the sound alone:

> Can't hear with the waters of. The chittering waters of. Flittering bats, fieldmice bawk talk. Ho! Are you not gone ahome? What Thom Malone? Can't hear with bawk of bats, all them liffeying waters of. Ho, talk save us! My foos won't moos. I feel as old as yonder elm. A tale told of Shaun or Shem? All Livia's daughtersons. Dark hawks hear us. Night! Night! My ho head halls. I feel as heavy as yonder stone. Tell me of John or Shaun? Who were Shem and Shaun the living sons or daughters of? Night now! Tell me, tell me, tell me, elm! Night night! Telmetale of stem or stone. Beside the rivering waters of, hitherandthithering waters of. Night! (215-216)

He succeeded in verbalizing in literature levels of consciousness and unconsciousness which had hitherto appeared inexpressible. Susanne K. Langer, in *Philosophy in a New Key,* defines the relation of dream to myth:

> Myth begins in fantasy, which may remain tacit for a long time; for the primary form of fantasy is the entirely subjective and private phenomenon of *dream.*
>
> The lowest form of story is not much more than a dream-narrative.[23]

The plan of writing this "dream-narrative" in order to get below the surface emptiness of ordinary prose and ordinary, trite audience appeal was daringly conceived and executed. To have novelized the Viconian idea of history alone would not have been enough; to have written a dream-narrative on a trivial theme would have indicated a degree of virtuosity. But to do what Joyce did, to treat an epic theme in a technique designed to pierce the shabby cloak of channelized language and feeling through recourse to the "private phenomenon" of dream made public—that is enough to demand of one man in one lifetime.

He was able, in addition, to reconcile, and often to fuse, numerous conceptions of myth into a greater whole, his own myth of man. Freud and Jung, irreconcilable in their personal careers, are tapped for their contributions to the study of myth, and, under Joyce's skilled hand, both yield fruitful material. HCE suffers dismemberment in his dream, reliving the ordeal of Osiris in the Egyptian myth and acknowledging the influence of Frazer. The obscure Viconian stab at defining the origin of myth in language takes its place beside the traditional, archetypal myths. Yet the reader does not feel that he is being asked to endure layer upon layer of unrelated mythical writings stuffed between the covers of a book. Perhaps it is the atmosphere of dream—or that created by the language of the dream-narrative—that accounts for the reader's willingness to suspend his disbelief in the presence of such an unlikely blend. Whatever the reason, the juxtaposition of a great mass of logically incongruous mythical material seems just as natural to the reader as do disconnected images in a dream to the dreamer. That, in itself, is no mean literary accomplishment.

There is a chorus of agreement concerning *Finnegans Wake* as a "Comic Synthesis" in which past and present are united and accepted in Joyce's "characteristic boundlessly bitter, boundlessly sad, and still humorous" spirit. Stuart Gilbert characterized it as "A carnival of the Comic Spirit" somewhat akin to the animated cartoons of the cinema, but to E. B. Burgum this humor arises from "the dialectic absurdities of the particular" and is an inevitable product of skepticism: "When one value is as good as another . . . living has become a hoax and the pun the appropriate verbal reaction to it." Thus, though we may enjoy a taste of what the author gives us, our innate belief in a world "capable of order and harmony" is revolted by his rejection of whatever we have come to love in the world. "The laughter cannot erase the bitter cynicism from which it is distilled."[24] In his study of comedy, *The Dark Voyage and the Golden Mean* (1949), Albert Cook places *Finnegans Wake* with "the boisterous mechanical comedy" of Rabelais, Aristophanes, and Shakespeare's early plays in contrast with the poetic comedy of *The Odyssey* or *The Tempest*. Its themes—sex, law, politics, war—are those of rationalistic comedy; the "orgy of language" common to this form resembles the saturnalia of "sex and feasting" in "the primitive comic ritual." To merit comparison with such comic masters is hardly to have wasted the seventeen years of creation.

Joyce's comedy, moreover, is not only in his subject matter but in his words. Like Lewis Caroll, whose creations could "gyre and gimble in the wabe," Joyce gave to words a humor of their own over and above their function as conveyors of a basic meaning. And the constant temptation, in speaking of *Finnegans Wake,* is to recall dozens of puerile but profound phrases which in their incongruous congruity arouse the laughter of escape, superiority, and mockery. To take only one instance, the phrase "funnominal world" indicates that the world is one of ridiculous phenomena, that philosophically we see only the phenomenon and not the thing-in-itself, the noumen, and that the world of *Finnegans Wake* is one of fun with names. For "The real romance is between Joyce and the language," as Professor Levin puts it. He notes "the gay garrulity. . . . persuasive blather. . . . mellow lyricism," the breath-taking but heartwarming experience of hearing "the seraphim and cherubim speak with an Irish accent."[25] Richness and vitality have been restored to the language with what is usually described by critics as a "strange and unusual beauty" and "haunting music."

In terms of cyclical history, he was able to explain the wasteland atmosphere of his time. The present cycle of the world is fast decaying; it is almost ready to give way to the new era. Its inhabitants are sterile:

> Who are the component partners of our societate, the doorboy, the cleaner, the sojer, the crook, the squeezer, the lounger . . . the bleakablue tramp . . . who are late-comers all the year's round by anticipation, are the porters of the passions in virtue of retroratiocination . . . who crunch the crusts of comfort due to depredation, drain the mead for misery to incur intoxication, condone every evil by practical justification and condam any good to its own gratification, who are ruled, roped, duped and driven . . . ?
>
> Answer: The Morphios! (142)

But the new cycle, Joyce felt, would bring good. He waited for this good with patience and resignation born of long disappointment and disillusion: "Such is manowife's lot of lose and win again. . . . So what are you going to do about it? O dear!" (117)

The critics have been doing plenty about *Finnegans Wake* in the past score of years. Enemies of Joyce's earlier works have found in its murky alleys all the justification they need to question the sense, and even the sanity, of its author. Joyce's friends, after a time of stunned silence, have found much to praise in the brave and heroic attempt to blaze new literary trails, even if they have reservations about the final judgment. Both the matter and the manner of Joyce's ambitious myth have been under severe critical scrutiny.

The philosophical implications of the giant myth have been questioned. Rather than suggesting the triumph and transcendence of man, Louis Gillet found "nowhere a more desolate view of our world and of the sheer emptiness of ourselves and things." Life is "only a dream and this dream is always the same—always as absurd, incoherent and futile as a useless and wearying delirium." The book is one "of derision, nihilism and modesty, and, basically, of despair." To Louise Bogan "it has nothing to do with man's future, which, we can only hope, will lie in the direction of more humanity." "There are better gods," she complains, "than Proteus." Joyce's use of myth and legend confirmed Margaret Schlauch's view of his reactionary pessimism; to Ernest Bernbaum the crucial question is that, far from being a treasury of the great traditions of man, as Campbell and Robinson assert, it is rather an "embittered hostile protest against those very traditions." Joyce's outlook is "essentially secular, without Christian hope, faith, and charity" and hence, like Oswald Spengler's, "deeply pessimistic," "a product of a concluded past, not an inspiring force to shape our future." A sensitive Catholic attack on Joyce's perversion of Vico's spirit is that of T. J. Fitzmorris, who protested that Joyce was "incapable of accepting more than Vico's externals." The result is that the Italian's faith is replaced by a "diatribe of disgust at a world in decay." The artistic effect is a discord, "a deaf man's orchestration of the single, clear, sweet note of Vico's tribute to the Providence of God."[26]

Richard V. Chase summarized the adverse opinions:

> 1) that the book is irreverent, anti-intellectual, and tries to destroy the past; 2) that it is coterie literature. . . . 3) that it is not a novel. . . . 4) that it is simply a book of pedantic and irresponsible word-play; 5) that it is a parochial curiosity because it is based on the questionable technicalities of Vico, Freud, and Jung; 6) that the rewards are not worth the effort of reading Joyce's language.

He countered by arguing that the book is an important landmark in the Indian summer of our civilization, Alexandrian in its "erudite synthesis" and "mystic cultism," attaining universality, like the work of Toynbee, Frazer, and Eliot's *Waste Land,* by its "religious panprimitivism."[27] L. A. G. Strong concurs that the role of the book is religious: "His attempt was no less than to integrate and redeem the deepest levels of the human psyche." Traditional Christianity had erred, so the argument goes, in sealing off rather than in redeeming these impulses. The concept of the *Wake* as a mythico-religious work, the principle behind this chapter, was brilliantly suggested as early as 1930 by Michael Stuart in a pioneering article in *This Quarter.* The plan of the entire work, Stuart thought, might become "a geometrical representation" of the ideas of Nicolas of Cusa in regard to the limitations of human reason:

> . . . reason approximates ever more and more to the Divine Mind, as a polygon approaches more and more to the form of a circle when the number of its sides is increased.

Though of course the limits of man are recognized by the

philosopher, "the Divine reason may be known ever and more truly through human reason, but never quite truly." Stuart sees as a framework not only the historical cycles of Vico but the concepts of Bruno "that the universe is everywhere the same" and "that its center is everywhere . . . and nowhere." Undismayed by the impenetrability of the early installments, Stuart compared the symbols to stars "which are invisible to the eye, because their light has not yet reached the earth."[28] This mythic significance of *Finnegans Wake* has been urged also by such critics as Mary Colum: "A step further in the revelation . . . of Man the Unknown"; by Padraic Colum: "History made present through these vasty figures who sum up the race, who are also the mountain and the river of the land"; and by John Peale Bishop, who found Anna Livia "such a mythological creature as, were she not there, I should have said the modern mind could not make."[29]

The language of the *Wake* has come in for the greatest share of critical attention. Needless to say, critics have pointed out the difficulties of penetrating his jungle of words and have suggested once more that Joyce is a godsend to Ph.D. candidates. G. W. Stonier feared that the book would demand of him an exploring expedition:

> The reviewer foresees a day when he, too, will be expected to go out with a search party, ice-axe and Vico in hand, to examine the new landmark and scratch his initials in the ice.[30]

So far, only initials have been scratched, though some interesting special studies have appeared. References to Boucicault, to Rowntree's *Poverty,* and to the game of cricket have been studied by J. S. Atherton, who has said that "Joyce tried to put everything into *Finnegans Wake.*" Echoes of Shakespeare, Sterne, Swift, and Blake have been ferreted out.[31]

The staggering size of a complete exegesis is suggested by the fact that the *Skeleton Key* devotes thirteen pages to the opening page of Joyce's book—and misses much in the process! The reviewer of the *Key,* in *The Irish Times,* claimed that such an ideal exegesis would have to come from (1) an Irishman, (2) one suffering, in Joyce's words, from "an ideal insomnia," (3) one afflicted with Joyce's malady, "the dread cacoethes scribendi."

> It is a nice speculation to consider what type of man,

competent to undertake the labour of such an opus, would at the same time be satisfied with the limited and austere form of self-expression available from trailing the steps of the master with foot-notes.[32]

Some readers were not so patient. Richard Aldington, "having spent several hours a day for more than a fortnight in wretched toil," declared that he had "no intention of wasting one more minute of precious life over Mr. Joyce's futile inventions, tedious ingenuities, and verbal freaks." If the *Wake* is a hoax, Joyce is "impudent"; if not, he is "insolent" in expecting the world to spend the necessary time to read it.[33] Even more sympathetic reviewers had their reservations. To Paul Rosenfeld, the language was "cold and cerebral" and the work gave one "the sense of repletion and a mark overshot." John Crowe Ransom felt that Joyce was constantly "obfuscating discourse" with his allusiveness and that the critical problem of the limits of relevance must be raised. Joseph Prescott found that understanding and enjoyment "do not coincide often enough to make the *Wake,* as a whole work of art, successful."[34] Undaunted by the work's obscurity, J. S. Atherton has recently suggested that "human nature being what it is, it is probable that the task of unlocking the multitudinous boxes which contain and conceal Joyce's message will be continued for many years." Even if the final box turn out to be empty, the commentator claims that he would be satisfied to "have played a small part in unwrapping the richly varied foliations in which it is ensheathed."[35]

E. E. Stoll bought an armory of citation to demolish what he felt to be the pretensions of the style, concluding that the world's masterpieces have never seemed nonsensical at first reading, and that the portmanteau word is "a cheap and simple . . . way of being funny." He is amazed at "such patient and humble industry" on the part of scholars, "weighing and considering—racking and cudgelling their brains over—ingenuities both so pedantic and so puerile."[36] If this seem but the peevish diatribe of a traditionalist, more respect might be accorded to Louis Gillet, who had been one of Joyce's longstanding and intelligent admirers. Despite his sympathetic understanding of the philosophical implications and his admission that "Language has been bathed in a fountain of youth," he admitted to a "mixture of admiration and irritation." The "gratuitous clowning," the frequent "happiness of expression," the "verbal drollery," and the "unerring music" do not prevent one from being "seized with impatience against this rattling of words, this logomachy."[37]

Quite possibly the chorus of irritated critical disapproval of the language of the *Wake* was primarily a reaction against the extravagant claims of his literary friends that in this new book the lingustic millennium had arrived. The gentlemen of the *Exagmination* of *Work in Progress,* and especially the members of the *transition* group, in their desire to be helpful to Joyce and faithful to the Revolution of the Word, succeeded only in alienating most of the "respectable" academic and journalistic critics, who were unwilling to be identified with their wild manifestoes. Of the sincerity of people like Eugene and Maria Jolas there is no question. Friends of Joyce and enthusiastic admirers of his techniques, they did what they could to place before the public fragmentary portions of what later became *Finnegans Wake.* Not content with this very worth-while service to Joyce and to modern letters, they secured the critical aid of writers sympathetic to verbal experimentation and filled the pages of their avant-garde magazine with explications, imitations, and exhortations. Seeking to pay "Homage to James Joyce," they succeeded mainly in perpetuating a series of clichés: that "from the moment he first tried to get a public hearing, there developed a sullen resistance against Joyce . . . ," that he "would never compromise," and that, though perhaps true, certainly old hat in 1932, "ecclesiastical cliques" were responsible for some of the damage. Now, however, Joyce has friends and, in *transition,* a "mouthpiece."

With Joyce as its apparently willing captive and star, *transition,* emanating from Paris, embarked upon as ambitious a campaign as any magazine had ever undertaken. Jolas, in the tenth-anniversary issue, reminisces upon the accomplishments of a decade: the magazine created "a new narrative in a magic realism (paramyth) and a new form of dream-poetry (Hypnologue)"; it attempted a "de-banalization of creative language"; it advanced James Joyce in this regard and issued the "Revolution of the Word," to the effect that "the writer should have more liberty . . . in subjugating syntax and vocabulary to his individual ends." It went even further along constructive lines, says Jolas, "by associating the mutation of language with the new discoveries related to the expansion of consciousness (night-mind) and the inter-continental, social amalgamations occurring today. It was the first to relate this problem to the reconstruction of the myth. It asked for a linguistic reformation because such a reformation was really taking place in real life." If these sound like reasonable enough objectives for a Parisian little magazine, Jolas, even ten years later, must conclude with an extravagant, cosmic summary, so destructive to the dignity of the foremost Continental author of the time:

> *transition* sought a welding together of all the lingustic elements that are about to make the new English language.
> *transition* will continue to seek a pan-symbolic, pan-linguistic synthesis in the conception of a four-dimensional universe.[38]

Or, writing in *Our Exagmination,* the mouthpiece must again resort to exaggeration. Different concepts of beauty in the modern world, he says, require new words. "James Joyce, in his new work . . . has given a body blow to the traditionalists. As he subverts the orthodox meaning of words, the upholders of the norm are seized by panic, and all those who regard the English language as a static thing . . . are afraid." "In spite of the jeers of the professors," Jolas concludes, Joyce will preside at the "rebirth" of the English language.[39]

These hopes and intentions are praiseworthy, but, as time has proved, wild. *Finnegans Wake,* like the *Anatomy of Melancholy,* appears to be slated, at least in our time, for existence in a class by itself. Only a very few—and these the best—of contemporary writers have seen fit or been able to carry forward the violent revolution announced in *transition* in the way he expected. Young writers have learned much about linguistic virtuosity from the *Wake,* but in their own work they seem wisely unwilling to forsake orthodox means of expression for "the ultimate note of a word multilated in the night mind." The consideration that Joyce's genius does not occur in many writers of an era inhibits Joyce's literary successors as it never did the members of the *transition* group.

Joyce, extremely conscious of public relations, must have seen all this too. Why then, the question is often asked, did he not dissociate himself from the more blatant extravagances of this admittedly plucky magazine? Surely the author of *Ulysses,* the star product of orthodox Jesuit education, did not take literally the exhortations of the group. Surely he recognized, and is supposed to have said publicly, that the fate of his literary reputation lay in hands of the very professors and traditional universities that *transition* sought to provoke and denigrate. Perhaps, though unlikely, he was not consulted before his "mouthpiece" spoke for him. Perhaps it was a matter of friendship. Regardless of his defects as editor and publicizer of Joyce, Eugene Jolas and his wife were unsparingly kind and helpful to Joyce and his family—almost their only active support when the World War II upset the normal life of the author's menage. Joyce was always fanatically loyal to his friends, giving them his valuable papers, helping them write their books about him, while refusing to criticise the bad ones. It is quite conceivable that he remained silent before the distorted adulation of *transition* just to do a favor for a friend. A final possibility is that Joyce weighed the practical advantages of silence and disavowal and decided on the former course. After all, many of the writers for *transition* were also friends of the author. They helped him with sources that his impossibly poor eyes could not read; they acted as copyists; they were the right arm of the invalid writer. Maybe the fear of alienating such a group kept him silent. The possibility that he concurred entirely in the adulation of himself as the savior of language, and thus encouraged the worship of the faithful, is unlikely. Yet the Joyce of numerous grinning masks may have fancied himself in the role of hero to this literary clique.

Both Joyce and the *transition* group have suffered because of their alliance. The members of the group have been ridiculed as sentimental subjectivists. Louise Bogan has described them as the "rolling-along-in-great-delight-with-a-great-work-of-art" school, and Hugh Kenner has spoken of its "voodoo rites" that elevated the Dedalus pose into "a major literary racket," complete with cult, bookstore, and magazine. Kenner's picture of Joyce "sardonically" presiding over his own legend a-building is not so obvious as its dogmatic assertion may make it seem. Kenner would also have Joyce engaging in "the most elaborate legpull of his career" in leading Stuart Gilbert "to believe that he was writing the authorized exposition of *Ulysses*." These words remind one of the early attacks on *transition*—read backward as "no it isn art"—which appeared in the Paris review *This Quarter,* where Joyce's role in the Jolas circle was likened to "another Assumption." Joyce has been "appropriated for their very own . . . by the Illuminati" and elevated by them to the role of a fountain of wisdom. On more serious grounds, F. R. Leavis also attacked the *transition* group. Denying the parallels indicating that Shakespeare too experimented with language, Leavis argued that Shakespeare's language results from "the pressure of something to be conveyed," while Joyce's "develops continually at the suggestion of the words." If this language be "the esperanto of the subconscious" as it has been claimed, then "the subconscious is sadly boring." It is even "offensively spurious" in that it is prey to "an inveterate solemn ingenuity" and too often "the very willing pimp to a poor wit."[40]

From the *transition* atmosphere and circle came the strange cultist appreciation, respectfully helpful, which has come to be known simply as the *Exagmination.*[41] Kenner glosses the title as "Our sightseer's stroll round the fortifications behind which he maintains the meaning of his Work in Progress *in camera.*" Most of the *Exagmination* centered about Joyce's linguistic innovations, with parallels traced in the neologisms of Lewis Carroll and Edward Lear, Fargue, and other moderns, as well as Shakespeare and Rabelais. Elliot Paul identified certain of the themes, Robert Sage noted Joyce's progressive widening of the boundaries of language and his continued universalization of character throughout his career, until here we see "such a picture of the entire universe as might be registered in the slumbering mind of a capricious god." The text has "developed like a living organism," as Sage shows in his comparison of successive versions of a passage from Anna Livia Plurabelle, until it becomes "writing of almost unparalleled beauty, rhythmic and mellowly colored, endlessly suggestive in its ideological content, frequently humorous, stimulating in its resourcefulness, and, above all, unmistakably branded with the unique genius of Joyce."

"Here," Samuel Beckett enthusiastically asserted, "form *is* content, content *is* form," and if the reader cannot understand it, it is because he is too decadent, that is, too habituated to the "intellectual salivation" of rapid reading. Joyce has created "a quintessential extraction of language and painting and gesture," restoring to the word its immediacy, "the savage economy of hieroglyphics." In this he is following the doctrine of Vico and the practice of Dante. Robert McAlmon, who also deals with Joyce's language, writes the most penetrating of the individual essays in the *Exagmination,* though in his readable (and perhaps fictitious) autobiography he disclaimed the essay as a legpull. He points out that prose that is evocative rather than explicit should inevitably appear in an age of awareness of relativity and the subconscious.

Joyce, he adds, has freed himself from "metaphysical pompositie" and has created "An Irish Word Ballet," which might give to any receptive reader an unverbalized meaning similar to that of music.

The *Exagmination* was supplemented by four outstanding reviews of the finished work in 1939—those of John Peale Bishop, Harry Levin, William Troy, and Edmund Wilson. These reviews remain a basic introduction to *Finnegans Wake,* differing only in emphasis. Edmund Wilson stressed the realistic and psychoanalytic aspects and, in accepting Earwicker as an almost traditional character, was led to the conclusion that he "seems swamped in the myths." Harry Levin found the real theme to be original sin, and responded more fully than Wilson to "the gay garrulity" and mellow lyricism of the style. Bishop and Troy establish the direction of much later interpretation in their readings of the work as a giant dream-myth of mankind.[42]

The caliber of these reviews is the best answer to other critics who feel that Joyce had nothing to say in the *Wake.* It is unlikely that people like Wilson, Bishop, and Troy would be inveigled into wasting their time on a book without substance. Yet Brinsley MacNamara, for instance, came to the conclusion that the work represents "complete fatigue in creativeness," in that "although after *Ulysses* he had no more to say, in *Finnegans Wake* he went on saying it." One may compare Alfred Kazin's feeling that Joyce "has lost his hold on human life" and has become "obsessed by a spaceless and timeless world" or Louise Bogan's sense of the "vicious atmosphere of a closed world" that is not only "stifling" but gives rise to the frightening suggestion "the Joyce himself does not know what he is doing." To G. W. Stonier the book seemed "the superb verbiage of a man exiled, disillusioned and without a theme; and what a great pity that is."[43] It is curious that Levin did not include in his book on Joyce the telling characterization of the author as "one with so much to express and so little to say," which appeared in a *New Directions* essay. Eugene Jolas told a story, now discredited, of Joyce's remarks to Harriet Weaver about his lack of a theme:

> Miss Harriet Weaver . . . had asked him what book he was planning to write after *Ulysses.* He replied that now *Ulysses* was done he considered himself as a man without a job, "I am like a tailor who would like to try his hand at mak-

ing a new-style suit," he continued. "Will you order one?" Miss Weaver handed him a pamphlet . . . giving a description of a giant's grave found in the parish lot. "Why not try the story of this giant?" she asked jokingly. The giant's narrative became the story of Finn McCool [*sic*], or *Finnegans Wake.*[44]

The giant's narrative, it appears, was not sent to Joyce until 1926, three years after the tale was begun. Even had the remark been authentic, one might reply that the sense of joblessness is merely a sign of nervous fatigue and the acceptance of the giant story a mere excuse for continuing his verbal and metaphysical quest—of what importance is the story anyway? But the unsympathetic reader could reasonably have found the tale damaging, and it is surprising that it was never cited by Joyce's critical foes.[45]

Joyce's *Wake* has few stauncher friends than Joseph Campbell and Henry Morton Robinson. Their *Skeleton Key to Finnegans Wake,* a page-by-page fragmentary paraphrase of the entire book in the language of waking logic, must have been at best a difficult and frustrating task. It must have been selfless too, for such a project could have looked forward to small critical approval from those who question the value of extended redactions of a work of art. But the beginner in Joyce studies welcomes even a slender thread to guide him through the labyrinth of the *Wake,* and, as such, the *Key* has beeen in continuous honorable use since its publication. Of course it is not a substitute for the *Wake* itself, nor does anyone who seriously entertains ideas of reading Joyce's book so consider it. Yet, if the *Wake* is "a kind of terminal moraine in which lie buried all the myths, programs, slogans, hopes, prayers, tools, educational theories, and theological bric-a-brac of the past millennium,"[46] even the determined adventurer may feel more at ease if he carries a map of the junk yard.

The flaw of the *Key* lies not in the inadequacy of the paraphrase—the authors are the first to admit that the *Key* is not the *Wake*—but in the unlimited hyperbole of the editorial comments. No epithets are too extreme—"a mighty allegory of the fall and resurrection of mankind," "a gigantic wheeling rebus," "Treasury of Myth," "saga of man's tragicomic destiny." The volume is "a powerful act of reintegration" that the commentators find "yielding more for the present, and promising more for the future, than any work of our time." So extravagant are these claims that even confirmed Joyceans lift their eyebrows. Professor Levin considered that with their "turgid and strident" style the collaborators "render him no service" in making "assertions which cannot withstand scrutiny." "Joyce's exponents," he continues, "are still suffering from an excess of hierophantic zeal, a belief that what must be so laboriously decoded must somehow contain a message of mystical profundity." Other reviewers of the *Key* were, for the most part, awed by the homework displayed by Campbell and Robinson, though few went so far as Max Lerner in finding them "ideal readers" in their "piety, passion and intelligence." Edmund Wilson pointed out that the abridgement "strips away most of the master's poetry" and hence conveys "no idea at all of the *emotional* power of the original." More drastic is the limitation of meaning implicit in the method of condensation. The problem is attacked on the wrong level. The story thread is the least important aspect of a linguistic poem of multilayered ambiguities. "Even a *Reader's Digest* editor ought to know, or be able at least to learn," John Kelleher asserted, "that Joyce is no nickel-a-word magazine stuffer." While such objections have a point, their tone is unfortunate, for they imply that the makers of the *Key* are not aware of the pitfalls implicit in their method.[47]

In salutary contrast to the hierophantic zeal of Campbell and Robinson is the careful, if cautious, appraisal of Benedict Kiely, who found the *Key* rewarding, despite moments when it fails to fit all locks and the door slams on the faces or fingers of the commentators. Their "new world reverence" for Joyce is their major error; lacking the detachment of Andrew Cass, they also emphasize the universal aspects to the exclusion of the central portait of the artist as unhappy exile. After analyzing Joyce's complex personality, Kiely further urges us to remember that Vico's theory of history is dubious, that Joyce's preoccupation with the mystical significance of numbers is questionable, that the stylistic monotone may be "a retrogression after the always appropriate uniting of language and event that gave such definite variety to *Ulysses,*" and that, most important of all, "Joyce was a pedant and a punster and, at some awful moments, both together." A final assessment will probably conclude that as a universal history *Finnegans Wake* is a failure, based on a faulty theory, marred by pedantry, and colored more by comic than philosophic insight. Yet its achievement is undoubted:

> With all its oddities, obscure symbolism, associative words, melting of character into character and all characters into mist and nothingness, with its misplaced devotion to doubtful philosophical and historical theories, *Finnegans Wake* remains one of the most remarkable works of genius produced in western Europe.[48]

Neither the praise of the *Skeleton Key* nor the puffing of *transition* gave *Finnegans Wake* as much publicity among masses of readers as the stage presentation in 1942 of Thornton Wilder's play, *The Skin of Our Teeth.* Campbell and Robinson, writing in *The Saturday Review of Literature,* directed a two-page blast at the playwright for giving to the public a "thinly disguised" re-creation of the *Wake.* Deploring the many unacknowledged borrowings from Joyce, they proceed to list the numerous specific ways in which the two works are similar: the circular form, the river-stream, the periodic catastrophes, and even the backgrounds of the main characters. Yet the authors of the article—in the face of overwhelming evidence of conscious borrowing—are uneasy in their position. Apparently they cannot believe that a writer of Wilder's character and ingenuity would so clumsily steal from a fellow genius that the clues to his crime would scream for recognition. They offer the possibility that he has been "hoaxing" the playgoing public.[49]

Reaction to this exposé was quick and virulent. Many letters came to the magazine, most of those published taking the side of Wilder in the argument, though the playwright maintained a wise and dignified silence. A Carl Baillett, Jr., pointed out that most modern writers borrow to achieve their effects, Joyce's debt to the *Odyssey* being a glaring case. Other correspondents offered comments in the language of the *Wake* to absolve Wilder of his alleged crime. Melville Cane commented:

> The right-and-wrong of "Finn" and "Skin"
> Has raised a din of angry voices,
> While, blissfully exempt of sin,
> Wilder, withal, re-Joyce's.

The "Trade Winds" column of the review editorialized that a writer who could extract a hit play from a work like the *Wake* deserved all glory.[50] Joyce's book, little commented on in popular journals when it appeared in 1939, was becoming a *cause célèbre*.

Time certainly seems to be on the side of Wilder and also of those correspondents in *The Saturday Review* who supported his right to unabashed borrowing. The irrepressible playwright has done more good than harm to the *Wake* by his use of whatever in it lends itself to dramatic presentation. By his enthusiasm for the book, moreover, Wilder has helped to spread its valuable attributes over a wider area of public awareness. Joyce, we may be sure, would have advised Wilder to do just what he did: neither to advertise the resemblance nor to deny it, neither to bask in Joyce's reflected glory nor to reject, as Joyce refused to reject Vico and Homer and Dante, the springboard of an already available modern myth.

The best work on *Finnegans Wake* is probably yet to be published. Though many critics have written general appreciations and criticisms of the book, relatively few have thus far had the time or the inclination to spend years explicating the text. Lately, detailed analyses have appeared that, if elaborated and augmented, should result in important books. The articles of Nathan Halper, in the *Partisan Review* and elsewhere, on the architecture and motifs of the *Wake*, show promise of a book of remarkable value.[51] Moreover, the intensive communal reading of *Finnegans Wake* in graduate seminars by students of widely varied linguistic backgrounds, under the direction of Professors Tindall, Levin, and Kelleher should be highly productive of future scholarship.

In England, important studies of the *Wake* by J. S. Atherton are now appearing with regularity. The work of a careful and intelligent scholar, they begin by tracing sources and influences, but the author's purpose usually goes beyond the pointing out of incidental similarity to arrive finally at some principle behind Joyce's work or to suggest Joyce's view of the world. In "Lewis Carroll and 'Finnegans Wake,'" Atherton shows the indebtedness of the author of the *Wake* to Carroll for his Jabberwocky language, his conception of the dream state, and even for specific scenes in the book. Atherton's passing reference to Parnell's escape from the boudoir of Kitty O'Shea down a fire escape adds still another level to our analysis of the Tristan passage earlier in the chapter, in which the mythical lover is shown "fairescapading in his natsirt." The triangle of the medieval Viconian cycle has given way to the Parnell affair of modern Ireland. Though Atherton does not connect the one theme with the other, it is provocative work such as his that future scholars will build on to make Joyce's book easier. An article of his in *Accent* compares the *Wake* to a pantomime, which sums up Joyce's final word on creation. After demonstrating that a pantomime may be an entertainment in dumb show, with one character playing the parts, as well as a Christmas performance stressing an absurd breakdown of something organized, Atherton establishes Joyce's probable familarity with the art of pantomime and shows specifically the elements of the art that the Irishman needed in order to construct his own version: the transformation scene, the idea of cyclical return, the clowning. Atherton concludes that, to Joyce, life is a pantomime. It is "meaningless, repetitive, traditional, and yet entertaining."* In this same tradition of purposeful tracing of sources is another Englishman, M. J. C. Hodgart, whose explications of the *Wake* in the *Cambridge Journal* make the reader hope for further articles.[52]

A thoroughly sound and remarkably helpful unpublished work† on Joyce is the Oxford University doctoral dissertation "The Evolution of James Joyce's Style and Technique from 1918 to 1932." Written by Arthur Walton Litz, it is obtainable in typescript on microfilm from the Wayne University Library in Detroit. The work is mainly concerned with Joyce's method of composition. Litz approaches the problem through the chronology of the episodes of *Ulysses,* showing that they were not composed in the order in which they appear in the book. Yet, as in all of Joyce's works, the total plan of the book was before its author in such vivid detail that he was able, working from the end, or the beginning, or the middle, to contribute the fragments for his elaborate mosaic.

Litz demonstrates further that *Finnegans Wake* underwent this same piecemeal, though far from haphazard, creation. As in *Ulysses,* first would come a skeleton summary of the episode under construction, to be filled in and embellished right up to the moment of final printing through the inclusion of hundreds of words and phrases, culled from multi-

* Atherton's work is now gathered together in a Viking Press volume called *The Books at the Wake.*

† Recently published in altered form by Oxford University Press as *The Art of James Joyce.*

colored note sheets, and used to strengthen bare statements of motifs. This dissertation would deserve publication simply on the basis of its appendices, covering the dating of the various parts of Joyce's later works. His publication in parallel columns of items in Joyce's notebooks and these same jottings as they were finally incorporated into his books is an important aid to understanding Joyce's methods.

Professor Tindall begins his book on Joyce with the remark that the works of this Irishman "compose an elaborate design."[53] The distinctive contribution of this critic to the understanding of Joyce is his ability to point out insistently this pattern of development from work to work. There is no trick to identifying the obvious extension of plot from *A Portrait* to *Ulysses,* but to show where in *Chamber Music,* let us say, and *Finnegans Wake* are complimentary jewels in the same general setting advances considerably the student's appreciation of Joyce's literary labyrinth. Tindall is able to demonstrate consistent strands of plot and imagery from Joyce's early to his later writings—love tinged with shame, illusion blasted by reality, or recurring symbols of decay. He analyzes also the tone of Joyce's works, which ends in the lofty indirection of the *Wake*—indicating that the last of Joyce's books, far from being a freak, stands as the culminating point of the Joyce canon and the personal myth. Rescuing this design from the critical chaos that threatened permanently to engulf it has been this critic's valuable and practical gift to readers of Joyce. Without it, *Finnegans Wake* would elude classification even more than it does now.

Finnegans Wake is an end—but not a dead end. It carries the development of language as far as it can profitably go in the framework of our present alphabet. It paints the ultimate picture of the struggle of the exiled artist with his less sensitive, more ordinary fellow creatures. The tragicomic view of Shem the Penman (a surrogate of Joyce the artist), whose ugly "bodily getup," including an "artificial tongue with a natural curl" (169), alienates all respectable burghers, is the logical finish to the autobiography of Stephen-Joyce as a young man. Having attained his goal of artist, Shem "scrabbled and scratched and scriobbled and skrevened nameless shamelessness about everybody ever he met" (182) and thus lost personal friends and impersonal public. According to his brother Stanislaus, Joyce once thought of giving up the project; he confessed doubts to Louis Gillet. "Perhaps it is craziness," he is reported to have said. "One will be able to judge in a century."[54] In any case, a note of anxiety lurks behind the grimaces of laughter. With his poor eyesight in mind, we see him as "a poor achesyeld from Ailing" or, in more humorous mood, as Shem the sham penman. He is scolded for his proud indifference:

> . . . condemned fool, anarch, egoarch, hiresiarch, you have reared your disunited kingdom on the vacuum of your own most intensely doubtful soul.

Note the questions, "Was liffe worth leaving?" (230) and "Was Parish worth thette mess?" (199). But the fact that Joyce went ahead for almost two decades with the completion of this book, his personal myth, indicates that he gave at least poetic assent to the questions.

This wake, like all wakes, is both an end and a beginning. Its accomplishment must have meant for Joyce bringing to full circle the symbolic design that, as Professor Tindall shows, *Chamber Music* had begun. It meant that he had freed himself from the necessity to assume always the role of his own hero. A new cycle, to use Vico's terminology, was about to offer him impersonality of subject matter as well as of execution. His death places undue emphasis on the position of *Finnegans Wake* at the end of the Joyce canon, where it might not properly have belonged. But the point is that the book *is* there and that, in a manner of speaking, it can be read. One of its curious effects has been noted by G. W. Stonier, that "For an unreadable book *Finnegans Wake* turns out to be remarkably quotable."[55] The final impression is best stated by Leon Edel, who characterizes this book and *Ulysses* as works

> which will haunt us and to which we shall return, baffled, sometimes puzzled, and yet finding there great power and suggestiveness and inventiveness—and impression as of the complexity of the whole of life poured into a book's mould, which neither music, nor language, nor any artifice of man has yet captured.[56]

PART III

The Reputation

Chapter 10

The Position of Joyce

THROUGHOUT THE JAZZ AGE all the sad young men took Stephen Dedalus to their hearts. Sherwood Anderson (alias the Bruce Dudley of *Dark Laughter*) recalled literary evenings in Chicago where Joyce, Pound, and Lawrence were discussed. The frankness of *Ulysses* irritated "a raw sore." His employer had been introduced to the *Portrait* in college. In 1924 Thomas Wolfe (alias Eugene Gant) noted in his diary that the best contemporary writing had been done by Joyce, and Wolfe, under the second alias of George Webber, modeled his first book on *Ulysses,* so much so, wrote Wolfe, that the hero became a prig like Dedalus. The publisher Stoat reveals his literary naïveté by inveighing against Joyce, to the amusement and disgust of Webber. Like his creator, the Cardinal of Wilder's *Cabala* (1929) has *Ulysses* on his table.

Flappers and philosophers alike turned to the banned blue book, though many of the former undoubtedly were most interested in the last chapter. The *cognoscenti* numbered such groups as Lionel Kein's salon in Wyndham Lewis's *Apes of God* (1931). The international set at Cannes included McKisco, who had done the first American criticism of Joyce who dreamed of using the scheme of *Ulysses* for a historical novel. If he failed to accomplish this, the activities of his associates in Fitzgerald's *Tender Is the Night* (1934) must have proven too distracting. In the neighboring artist colony at Antibes, Cyril Connolly's young author, Edgar Naylor, of *The Rock Pool* (1936) proposed Joyce, with Eliot and Norman Douglas, as the greatest moderns, his friend claiming Firbank and Hemingway. On the Orient Express the insipid pulp writer Savory took his stand in favor of sanity rather than Joyce's "morbid introspection," as Graham Greene recounted in the first of his popular thrillers. Back in Dublin Jimmy's departure was recalled by the crowd at the Ormond, if we can credit Norah Hoult. Tommy Langdale thought him "a gorgeous blasphemer" with "the biggest headpiece I ever

The notes to Chapter 10 begin on page 347.

knew," more clever than most in the art of touching friends for loans.

Arthur Koestler, languishing in a Seville prison during the Spanish Revolution, was pleased that the librarian gave him Mill's *Autobiography,* for Hemingway, Huxley, or Joyce would have been too disturbing. Huxley's novelist, Anthony Beavis, considered Joyce's *personalité de bain* inferior to Proust. Meanwhile, Charles Norman's young hero, David Gerald, witnessed Anthiel's *Ballet Mécanique* at the Théâtre des Champs Elysées, where "Calm, dignified, aloof, James Joyce sat in a box, a black patch over one eye; the lean, immortal figure of James Joyce looked out aloof . . . and even the black patch was scornful of the mob."

As the Depression deepened, Joyce was heavily subjected to the rigors of party-line criticism, though he still enjoyed a measure of respect. The conflict is epitomized in Charles Lane Harrison's delightful and little-known book, *Meet Me on the Barricades* (1938). In a discussion at a bar a leftist writer exclaims at the filth, smut, and depravity of *Ulysses,* a product of bourgeois decadence. He opines that "communist art now needs a Tolstoi more than it does a James Joyce." His opponent, a sophisticated newspaperman, replies that it is a work of monumental value as a "portrait in acid of the lower middle class." A cliché of Marxist criticism is voiced by the radical Spike, one of Edmund Wilson's Hecate County crowd, who rages at Joyce's spending years on *Finnegans Wake* when he could "so easily" have helped prevent Pearl Harbor!

Elliot Paul's American tycoon, K. Parker Seldon, is alarmed at the big blue book his daughter had him buy for her in Paris and decides that on returning to America he will put her in "a Baptist finishing school and have a heart to heart talk with the mistress about reading lists." He soon becomes absorbed in the book, and despite the robberies and sudden deaths of *Hugger-Mugger in the Louvre* (1940) continues to read it. With Joyce reaching the dubious eminence of reading lists, it is natural that Mary McCarthy's young instructor in *The Groves of Academe* (1952) should give the Proust-Joyce-Mann course and identify himself with "the sacred untouchables of the modern martyrology" to the extent of carrying an ashplant, not to speak of the trouble he causes the administration. Inevitably Dublin became the mecca of such researchers as the co-authors of this book; the heroine of Ann Willets's *Never Give the Heart* (1951) recalls "the man who collected James Joyce papers and had just returned from a pilgrimage to Dublin." No better final glimpse could be given than that of the latter-day Noah in T. H. White's *The Elephant and the Kangaroo* (1947), who passed through Dublin on his ark and glimpsed on the quays "the barmaids copper and gold," "O'Madden Burke leaning upon his umbrella," and "Fr. Conmee in tolerance of invincible ignorance," as well as the "gentle Leopold."

Some writers may have suffered as did Dodie Smith's fictional Mr. Mortmain, whose creative work was paralyzed by the master's brilliance. But probably many more, like Thomas Wolfe and James T. Farrell, discovered that Stephen Dedalus reflected their own struggles with their environment, and that Joyce gave them models of style and structure. Sherwood Anderson was perhaps the first to be influenced, using *Ulysses* as a model for the prose rhythms of *Dark Laughter*. Dos Passos and Faulkner were to follow, not to speak of the many described by Sinclair Lewis in his Nobel Prize acceptance speech as "a little insane in the tradition of James Joyce," yet courageous enough to refuse to be "genteel and traditional and dull."

It is obviously impossible to trace all the references to Joyce in fiction or to list the many poetic tributes. Even more difficult is the problem of his influence on creative writing, so widespread it is, and so thoroughly permeated with kindred elements in the modern consciousness. Without getting involved in the tangle of establishing priorities or direct indebtedness, one may say that he seems to have given impetus to several distinguishable avenues of approach, which, though perhaps not entirely original with him, were so successfully exploited in his work as to be termed Joycean.

The stream-of-consciousness style or, more correctly speaking, the style that develops motif and symbol in musical fashion, was most effectively adopted by Virginia Woolf, Thomas Wolfe, and William Faulkner, for in their hands it became the vehicle for a highly individual outlook. Others who adopted the syntactical fragmentation for the purpose of psychological studies are too numerous to identify.

His structural experimentation, particularly in *Ulysses*, seems to have provided the model for such slice-of-life novels as those of the early Aldous Huxley, John Dos Passos, James T. Farrell, and numerous European social novelists like Jules Romains, Hermann Broch, and Alfred Doeblin. Joyce is reported, however, to have been more interested in the similarity of the latter's name to that of Dublin than in the German writer's work.

The use of alien materials from such documentary sources as the daily press, the encyclopedia, or the scientific report is common to the slice-of-life writers already mentioned.

Often these alien materials may give a Dadaist or Shandean humor to a work, particularly through parodying the art form or the art illusion itself. The most successful of these Joyceans have been the author's compatriots Samuel Beckett and Flann O'Brien. Since O'Brien's *At-Swim-Two-Birds* (1939) was loved by Joyce, and since the author is such a stern Joycean (pun intended), examination of the work may be permitted. In this rollicking novel or series of novels-within-a-novel the reader is interrupted with intermittent catechisms, definitions, extracts from books, and even summaries of the book itself. The synopses are certainly needed, for O'Brien, who has two other names himself—his given name, Brian Nolan, and another pseudonym, Myles na gCopaleen—O'Brien has at least three stories to tell. There is the autobiography of the lazy narrator, whose furnishings, duly catalogued, include the works of Joyce. He is writing a story of a novelist whose characters, taken from real life, rebel at the actions devised for them by their creator. Intermingled with these escapades that turn the looking glass of fiction into a hall of comic mirrors are parody renditions of Irish folklore and legend. The whole work thus constitutes a preposterous pastiche of the major literary traditions of Ireland, from the exploits of Finn to those of *Finnegans Wake*.

Parallels to Joyce's linguistic experiment may be seen in the exuberance of Joyce Cary, Henry Green, and Christopher Fry, to name three prominent British writers.

Finally, the use of myth has been found in so many forebears, such as Melville, Rimbaud, even in Shaw, and so many contemporaries that one cannot assert any direct influence.

Each of these streams has had its manifestation in the best seller, or "massproduct," to use Joyce's own word. One recalls Hersey's *Hiroshima,* Thornton Wilder's plays, and the word distortions of popular journalism and advertising.[1]

Inevitably Joyce has attracted the composer. Music, language, and theology seem to have been his major areas of ability and interest, and each tempted him as a vocation. His musical feeling for the phrase as well as the word has been demonstrated, the most extensive treatment being that of

Fabulous Voyager, which devotes a chapter to the "Sirens" scene, the cadenza of *Ulysses.* In addition to thirty-one settings of various poems, the Slocum-Cahoon *Bibliography* lists a David Diamond work derived from the *Portrait,* compositions by George Anthiel, Matyas Seiber, and Thomas de Hartmann inspired by *Ulysses,* and settings by Hazel Felman and Samuel Barber of parts of the *Wake.*

Seiber's program notes tell of his enthusiasm for Joyce's handling of tempo and development of motif, with their "exciting parallels to musical construction." The astronomical chapter, which inspired the cantata, seemed to express his own emotions, "that indescribable 'cosmic awe' which overcomes me (and probably most people) at the sight of the starlit sky." Never had he experienced such a strong desire to set something to music. Though the critic Mosco Carner was unable to find Joyce's words anything but arid and prosaic, he praised the composer for distilling from them a poetic sense of the "utter loneliness which human beings experience when confronted with the vastness of the cosmos and its inscrutable mysteries." It is suprising, as a correspondent pointed out, that so sensitive an analyst could have missed the imaginative power of Joyce's words.[2]

G. W. Stonier, reviewing *Stephen Hero* in 1944, sighed, "In the end, I suppose, you either give up Joyce or devote your eight hours a day to him." Noting that he was an author, like Dickens, "who encourages manias," he speculated on the formation of a club of disciples:

> . . . a Joyce Fellowship—Sodality, perhaps, would be the word—which would meet regularly to weigh ash-plants, feast off kidneys, exchange puns and generally celebrate in the steps of the master. The unravelling, sentence by sentence, of *Finnegans Wake,* should provide members with a programme Dickensians and Janeites lack.

In 1947 Stonier's predictions were fulfilled by the formation in New York of the James Joyce Society, encouraged by Miss Frances Steloff of The Gotham Book Mart. The Society has been amusingly described by Gilbert Millstein:

> The society has sponsored publication of three slender volumes on Joyce and a recording of a broadcast made over the British Broadcasting Company system by his family and friends. Meetings, at which Joyce and his works are

naturally discussed, are apt to be what is known as ding dong.

The society was founded and most of the meetings have been held in what Millstein describes as "the impossibly book-cluttered back room" of the shop, "with a terra cotta bust of Joyce, by the late Jo Davidson, looking on," his expression "quizzical, but on the whole approving." One of the members, Patric Farrell, is quoted as saying, " 'Everything about the society is about. . . . We have about 350 members from about fifteen countries.' "[3] John J. Slocum, noted collector and bibliographer of Joyce, was first president, followed by the incumbent, Padraic Colum.

It is hard to know which of two recent news items might have amused the author most. The very Reuben J. Dodd of *Ulysses,* now a Dublin solicitor, having heard tell of a reading of the funeral scene on the B.B.C.'s program marking the fiftieth anniversary of Bloomsday, entered suit and won a settlement.[4] This, like the revolt of Flann O'Brien's novelist's characters against their creator, is an instance of the revenge of life upon art. Perhaps the revenge of art upon business is illustrated in the use of *Ulysses* as part of a post-graduate program of study for telephone executives. The picture of American business administrators, in seminar, bending their heads over "the extensive 'pony' literature . . . dictionaries of mythology, encyclopedias," and other apparatus might have delighted the author as much as Dodd's indignation.[5] May we say of Joyce, as did young Cato of Julius Caesar at the battle of Philippi:

> . . . thou are mighty yet!
> Thy spirit walks abroad, and turns our swords
> In our own proper entrails.

Meanwhile radio forums have been devoted to Joyce in the American "Invitation to Learning" series, the *Portrait* has been presented as a radio drama, and the B.B.C. has given numerous programs, nineteen of which, from May 1946 to June 1950, are listed by Slocum and Cahoon. A letter to me adds talks on the Homeric aspect by the one Joyce scholar of his own college, W. B. Stanford, discussion of Ibsen by Vivienne Koch, talks by unidentified speakers on Svevo, the Paris Exhibition, and James Joyce. Stanislaus Joyce's recollections of the background of *Dubliners* brings the tale to June

16, 1954, when, in addition to readings from *Ulysses,* an interpretation by William Empson and a presentation by Sean O'Faolain on Joyce's interest in music comprised a three-hour program.[6]

Of the numerous poetic tributes,[7] the most ambitious and most fitting, certainly, is Hugh MacDiarmid's long poem, *In Memoriam James Joyce* (1955), which is well described by its subtitle, *A Vision of World Language.* The vigorous and free poetic lines encompass the philosophy of symbolic form, as well as comparative linguistics, semantics, and poetic ontology. The volume is tastefully decorated by John Duncan Fergusson with initials in the Ogam alphabet and "symbols that convey Joyce's concern with music, creation, feeling and his native Ireland." Language rather than Joyce is the true hero. The reader cannot help being puzzled but exhilarated at the multilingual phenomena of human expression.

The poet's concept of Joyce is similar to that of Jung, but the new world consciousness is both discovered and expressed through language. He quotes Compton Mackenzie's praise of Joyce as the only writer aware of the transition of man into "a way of thought a thousand times more different from our present ways of thought" than our present ways differ from those of neolithic man. MacDiarmid hails the evolution of a language metaphysical and empirical, in keeping both with quantum mechanics and with the human nervous system:

> Language,
> Accomplishing what it pleases, traversing all things,
> By subtlety of nature; rising to colossal dimensions.

Such an art form breaks the bonds of traditional logic, as befits a generation "'More and more self-, sex-, race-, and world-conscious.'" In this creative task Joyce is the master

> Of the seen merging with the unseen,
> Of the beautiful sacrificed to the ugly,
> Of the ugly transformed to the beautiful,
> Of this intricate yet always lucid and clear-sighted
> Agglomeration of passions, manias, occult influences,
> Historical and classical references
> —Sombre, insane, brilliant and sane,
> Timeless, a symbol of the reality
> That lies beyond and through the apparent. . .

This new awareness brings with it an epistemological emancipation from the unenlightened or the mediocre

> . . . who mistake blind eyes for balanced minds,
> Who practise, in Disraeli's words,
> 'The blunders of their predecessors.'

It leads the initiate beyond the dimensions of space and time into a universe of organic and elastic fluidity. As for art,

> . . . Schoenberg was right. The problem involved
> In mental vocalisation
> Is not that the evolution of music
> Must wait on the human ear
> But that the human ear must catch up
> With the evolution of music.[8]

Man and Artist

The Gorman biography (1940) and Joyce's death early in 1941 brought forth a multitude of personal interpretations and reminiscences. The story of the author's perseverance under chronic eye troubles did much to win sympathy, while his flight from the chaos that he had seemed to have envisaged, the brief haven in Zurich, and his sudden death suggested to *Time* magazine "the great bishop of Hippo, St. Augustine, dying at the close of the Roman world to the echo of the Vandal swords against the city gates."[9]

Among the finest personal tributes are those of Frank Budgen and Eugene Jolas and of three lifelong Irish friends, Padraic Colum, Constantine Curran and Arthur Power. All spoke of his gentleness, his genial humor, his affection for family and friends. Mr. Curran, whose charming recollections lead one to hope that he will draw further on his memories to furnish an Irish portrait, was the most eloquent on Joyce's artistic integrity:

> The fierce intensity of his will made his life a struggle with circumstances. He followed his inflexible purpose in poverty, in exile, in physical suffering, in good and evil, and even in the manner of his literary expression, with a sort of heroism not easy to understand and certainly not common.[10]

Despite complaints of his indifference to current political and social concerns, his admirers thought that this artistic dedication made the world itself seem vulgar. Joyce remained immune to the temptations and distractions of society, even to the blandishments of literary coteries. Though we may not understand him, wrote J. P. Hogan, we must respect his achievement:

> We have to pay the price of our consciousness, or supraconsciousness. . . . We may regret the passing of our innocency; we may deplore Joyce's complexity and obscurity; but we are bound to respect the singleness and integrity of his vision.[11]

Alfred Kazin characterized him as a perennial outlaw whose Byronic display of his own soul might seem ridiculous were it not redeemed by seriousness and significance, thus becoming invested with "an almost classic sense of tragedy." Though his pride and egotism led him to the absurdity of equating himself with Parnell as one of the foremost men of modern Ireland, he does remain, in Kazin's opinion, among the last great European men of letters.[12]

Stephen Spender agreed, finding his major contribution to be that of the subjective outlook, a revolutionary vision that reveals the connections of the individual with the entirety of human culture, past as well as present. Thornton Wilder, one of the most devoted of disciples, found in *Ulysses* "the climate of the great books." This classic stamp appears not only in the vividness of the setting and the humanity of the characters but also "in the resources of the style, equal to every mood and to every game" and in the urgency and earnestness of the confessional tone.[13]

Joyce's role in modern culture becomes clearer with the years, but the insights of such readers as Eliot or Wilder still suggest paths for investigation. At the time, few seemed to understand Eliot's early comment on the use of myth in *Ulysses* as "a step toward making the modern world possible for art," yet as critics concern themselves with the interrelations of myth, ritual, and art, Joyce seems more traditional than esoteric. Artistic innovations thus are acclimated; as our knowledge of Joyce increases he becomes not merely characteristic of modern tendencies in art but a master, as Niall Montgomery characterized him, "of the line and stature of Dante." Such a provocative study as Northrop Frye's analysis of the types of fiction, a fourfold division into novel, romance, confession, and anatomy, inevitably brings forth illustrations from Joyce. For each is exemplified in his career—the novel in the Dublin background, the romance in the use of heroic archetypes, the confession in the stream-of-consciousness approach, and the anatomy in the encyclopedic coverage.[14]

Joyce's relationship to currents of contemporary art is also becoming clearer. Joseph Frank's study of "spatial form" in literature reveals a common artistic purpose in Eliot, Pound, Proust, and Joyce. For each in his individual manner is experimenting in a medium that will annihilate the dependence of literature upon logical and temporal sequence. Phrases do not proceed consecutively, nor do words convey their full meaning immediately. The result is that meaning is suspended in the entire complex; space logic has replaced time logic. In *Ulysses* Joyce seemed to be composing by means of incremental addition of fragments, assuming the ultimate possibility of "a unified spatial apprehension of his work." Through this agglomerative technique he conveys a sense of the totality of Dublin life. One could extend Frank's concept even better to *Finnegans Wake,* seeing as its informing principle an immediate, timeless awareness of the totality of human experience.

Frank's consciousness of the mutual interrelations of the arts makes him a valuable interpreter. He knows the rich and relatively untapped fields of stylistics and cultural history, developed by such European scholars as Worringer, Dagobert Frey, Wölfflin, and Spengler. Just as the work of Arnold Toynbee has made a wider public aware of the concepts of universal historiography, so the recently translated *Voices of Silence,* by André Malraux, may serve to acquaint the English-speaking world with the principles of stylistic analysis. The theory that style is a form of seeing and hence an index to the spirit of a culture is still relatively unknown, though it links the arts to each other and to society in a much more profound sense than does the rather shallow parallel between economics and culture exploited by the Marxists. Without undertaking any literary analysis, Louis Danz has used the provocative term "dynamic dissonance" to describe the quality Joyce's art shares with that of Picasso, Schönberg, Henry Moore, and Frank Lloyd Wright, men who constitute "a veritable new constellation" in the emancipation of art from tradition. So too has the artist Moholy-Nagy found *Ulysses* analogous to a cubistic collage in its fusion of fragments and blending of external reality with the subjective response. The result is new richness and precision, particularly in the expression of the author's gay acceptance of "the grand spectacle of life." By montage Joyce has extended the boundaries of "space-time thinking," a concept that returns us to that of Joseph Frank. Stuart Gilbert has likewise recently pointed out Joyce's distance from the traditional writer, for instead of seeking *le mot juste,* he invests the text with overtones of meaning.[15]

As early as 1934, in his *Music Ho!,* the music critic Constant Lambert had shown an almost perfect parallel in the development of Joyce's writings and Schönberg's compositions. Both share an unusual outlook, "half-mathematical, half-sentimental." The work of both evolved from an academically romantic realism to a personal style, thence developing into the revolutionary *Ulysses* and *Pierrot Lunaire* and culminating in the cerebral puzzles of the postwar creations. Both reveal a disgust with life that is not to be put off by escape into romantic dream.

Such perceptive analyses should do much to dispel notions that Joyce represents the utmost in decadence, that, as Ivor Winters has insisted, the succession from James through Proust to Joyce represents "a progressive decay" in style, little better than the illusions of trick photography.[16] In answer one might ask what subject could be more important than the exploration of perspectives opened by modern science and psychology. Thus as we become more aware of the forces acting upon our outlook we may hope to understand better those artists who first exploited the modern vision of the world.

An important field for investigation is that of Joyce's style. On the technical side, Gilbert's illustrations of the use of rhetorical figures could be extended and multiplied; tonally, Joyce progressed from the obviously aesthetic *fin de siècle* style to subtle and varied rhythms, as Edmund Wilson has noted. One of the most unusual of Joyce's feats is the creation of a style, rhythmically and tonally appropriate to each character, a form of nonsatiric imitation for which we have no rhetorical term. Parody has been further analyzed, Harry Levin arguing that many passages are less strictly parodies than we might think, in that Joyce does not subdue himself to his material. Tindall has held that parody is itself a method of characterization by distortion.[17] It is Joyce's almost unerring command of sense, sound, and rhythm that led Eliot to consider him the greatest master of the English language since Milton. With Milton he shares innate talents in music, scholarship, and language, also "remarkable powers of memory," which may have been strengthened by defective vision. But he is more visual, and always maintains a conversational tone. One is reminded of the words Dorothy Richardson used in her 1938 Preface to *Pilgrimage,* describing her distinguished colleague in fiction as "a man walking, weaving as he went a rich garment of new words wherewith to clothe the antique dark material of his engrossment."

Ezra Pound had first likened the structure of *Ulysses* to the sonata form, and Tindall, following Pound and Levin, finds the works "more like poems or symphonies or statues" than novels.[18] Such perceptions as Pound's and Eliot's can stimulate the curious reader or serious student to forage more thoroughly in the Joycean pasture.[19] Both Synge and Joyce, V. S. Pritchett has noted, are "sedulous linguists" who, in a happy metaphor, "sport like dolphins in the riotous oceans of an English language which has something of the fabulous air of a foreign tongue for them." One recalls the age-old statement that the best spoken English is that of Dublin, and the remark—was it Shaw's?—that in revenge for their subjugation by the English the Irish have given their masters models of how to write and how to speak.

In answer to this claim we may note the assertion of Harold Laski that one can hear more nonsense as well as sense in an hour's conversation with an Irishman than one could hear anywhere else. The Irish gift of tongues is more than a legend—and more than blarney. Gaelic is apparently a naturally eloquent, poetic, and witty language. Padraic Colum characterizes Irish expression as having an unusual blend of the imaginative and the realistic. Poetry is discussed in pubs, and there is always a plow amid the stars. I was told by Jack Yeats that Sir Robert Ball, the astronomer who wrote one of Bloom's favorite books, "brought the stars down to sit in the children's laps." At Joyce's grave, the English representative, Lord Derwent, said that whatever injustice Ireland had suffered in the past, she would continue to enjoy the revenge of producing masterpieces of English literature.[20]

John Crowe Ransom sensed something frightening in Joyce's sense of language.[21] If sometimes the talent is displayed for its own sake, must we hold with those Puritans who maintain that linguistic play is a wicked and irresponsible activity? And if Joyce sometimes falls into the snares of imitative form—exemplified in the spellings of the cat's cry in *Ulysses*—even imitative form is capable of hauntingly romantic effects, as is shown in my analysis of the "Sirens" scene. In addition to specific investigations of the language, or textual exegesis, more speculative studies of the nature of style may be undertaken. One of the few such attempts is that of Jackson I. Cope, who defines the essence of Joyce's style as an effort to achieve "simultaneity of movement encased in stability." This is effected by a stability of the image's referents contrasting with their active role in forming new combinations "in a dialectic of situation."[22]

The Humorist

Too few have noticed Joyce's humor, felicitously described by John Crowe Ransom as his "genius for bright disorder." Eugene Jolas reported the author's astonishment at the neglect of his comic powers, but, unless Nora Joyce was engaging in a family joke, she too failed to understand. For, as Joyce recounted to Budgen, she once asked her husband to recommend a book that would teach her about Irish humor. Almost alone among the obituaries in emphasizing Joyce the humorist was the *Saturday Night* magazine. The solemnity with which critics treated him, the writer said, must have amused the author greatly. The result is disastrous, however, for his "wild delight in the vagaries of human nature" is almost rendered inaudible by the clamor of admirers, "many of whom are humorless persons," and of his detractors, "all of whom are humorless persons." Had this editor remarked the equally wild delight in the vagaries of language he would have done still more injustice to the author. Even in what may seem the most irresponsible punning there is more than mere verbal fun; as W. R. Rodgers has observed, "Truth lies in the cracks—and in the wisecracks of speech."

A rather heavy-handed Germanic approach to the humor of *Ulysses* was undertaken by Josef Baake in his monograph of 1937 on the "Giant Joke-Book," as the title may be translated. The novel is a series of grotesque caricatures, "a fool's mirror," an appalling Hall of Horrors, devoid of love or sympathy, reflecting the author's indifference and loss of convictions. Perhaps only a German scholar would find such a work humorous. Of the earlier commentators, Frank Budgen best understands Joyce's geniality, finding humor the prevailing note, but a humor of great variety: "Laughter in all tones and keys, now with the world and now at it, is heard continually." It ranges, Budgen notes, from the gentle mockery of Sterne to the caricature of Dickens or the grim irony of Swift. Harry Levin, in keeping with his thesis of the divided soul, attributes the indignation—*saeva indignatio*—to his reaction against the age, but considers the "*vis comica*" his natural bent. Joyce once admitted to Miss Harriet Weaver that his last work was "no more than a game" but it was nevertheless "a game that I have learned to play in my own way." Confirming the kinship of tears and laughter, he concludes that "Children may just as well play as not," for "The ogre will come in any case."

I have asserted that "*Ulysses* is fun to read." Joyce has the "joyicity" of the transmogrified grasshopper in *Finnegans Wake*. This leads him into Rabelaisian gusto, Chaucerian awareness of human foibles, a mockery of the mind that resembles Sterne's, and a final cosmic humor that embraces and rejects the world and humanity. The Irish find the funniest thing about Joyce the seriousness with which he is taken by Americans. Niall Montgomery remarks that "Academic machinery . . . cannot handle fun: that is one reason why the college dispatches on Joyce have not been too gay." Mocking Levin's separation of indignation and the comic, Montgomery asks whether if an author operates with both, would "Equity" call "the whole shop out"? On the contrary, this constitutes "the perfect manner in art, with *s. indignatio* and *v.c.*—illegally?—in combined operation."

Lawrance Thompson has recently argued that the comic mode is used by Joyce as a means of bringing under artistic control his moral indignation, the protest apparent in his letter concerning the "scrupulous meanness" and "paralysis" as style and theme of *Dubliners*. The method is that of reversal—love reduced to coarseness, friendship to selfish loneliness. Yet Vivian Mercier reminds us that parody has a long and—shall we say reputable or disreputable?—history in Ireland from the days of the bards and the goliard scholars to the nineteenth-century figures Mangan, Maginn, Mahony, or "Father Prout," and Percy French, whose "Phil the Fluter's Ball" lurks in *Finnegans Wake*. Joyce's mockery is part of a long tradition, exemplifying the revolt of the scholar against the clergy, as well as that of the humanities against science and pseudo science. His position may not be consistent, but, in Mercier's words, "it's a grand place to start a fight from." Mercier neglects to notice that this sophomoric humor may be one more manifestation of Joyce's arrested concern with the time of his own school days.[23]

The Indifferent Observer

With such meager understanding of Joyce's humanity and humor, it is not surprising to find him generally characterized as an impersonal artist, removed from the concerns of mankind, or, in more extreme fashion, often decried as one who had retreated from the world entirely. Thus the *New Republic* editorialized on the passing of a nonpolitical "research scientist of letters" and Stephen Spender worried about whether it was possible for an artist to remain outside political and social issues. Such were the tensions of the early forties, or, rather, such were the romantic hopes still surrounding the role of the artist. It may seem easy to mock such statements as those of W. H. Auden, who defined the current problem as that of not being a Joyce character, or of Max Lerner, who called on writers to weld Joyce's artistry "to the collective affirmations" upon which the world of the future will be founded.[24] Is it a measure of our sophistication that such expectations seem naïve today? Less defensible, certainly, are such attitudes as those of journalists who compared him unfavorably to Lenin or who pointed a moral at the expense of Irish neutrality, finding the author as aloof from "the great passage of events" as were his own countrymen.[25]

It is true that by the time of World War I Joyce had disavowed all political concern. To Georges Borach he confessed to being "against every state," for the state must inevitably oppose the interests of the individual: "The state is concentric, man is eccentric." Of course he admitted the need to recognize existing institutions.[26] But, as he said to Padraic Colum, "It would be a great impertinence for me to think that I could tell the world what to believe."[27] Maria Jolas was forced, by the tone of some of the obituaries, to defend him against charges of indifference. She wished to suggest that all who are to dismiss him as unimportant should look again at his work. If they do, she predicted that they would find one who is "indignant at the hyprocrisy, stupidity and injustice he saw about him." So too did Padraic Colum protest that Gogarty never sensed "the tragedy and compassion" which is in *Ulysses,* and that Van Wyck Brooks had missed what should be apparent to any careful reader, namely, the honesty, compassion, and discipline of Joyce.[28]

Certainly if *Ulysses* were nothing but the immense artifact it has often been assumed to be, it would long since have been dismissed as a monumental curiosity. How can one explain the mingled terror and rage with which it was first read? It seems to derive force from some "deep ethical conviction" or "strong purposiveness."[29] Does the whole of Joyce's work stem from an agonizing examination of conscience, in the Jesuit sense of the word, or is it an attempt to create an art form that is beyond good and evil? Whatever the answer, there is no doubt that the work has puzzled, excited, and disturbed two generations of readers.

The predictable and almost automatic response of party-line criticism is found in the *New Masses* obituary, which characterized the author as a brilliant exponent of an art devoid of vitality or hope. His gestures of revolt remained futile, and his presumed rejections of logic, language, and man were found to be merely an artistic reflection of capitalism's "anarchic and destructive impulses."[30]

Thomas Mann's obituary in *The New York Times* attributes to him the remark that "politics is neither my passion nor my strength." Yet no reader of *Buddenbrooks* or of the Joseph story can fail to note the firm sense of history, of time as a sweeping force, that these works display. Perhaps it is too much to expect that in a single individual who combines superior intellect and surpassing creative power there should be found also a flair for everyday politics. In the emotional swirls of market-place opinion seldom is found the serenity that analyzes long-term curves of the graph of history. To condemn a novelist like Mann or Joyce for refusal to propagandize is like taking the historian Toynbee to task for not campaigning actively for a local Member of Parliament. Very likely, the measure of their success as novelists is their ability to keep aloof from national and international events.

Some of Joyce's friends, anxious to absolve him of the charge of political indifference, have sought to identify him with one class or another, one party or another, in a petty struggle. Maria Jolas, for instance, answering Max Lerner's charge that Joyce does not say much in the *Wake*, finds in the missing apostrophe of the title a cautionary admonition to the powers that be. Finnegans (the small men of our world) do eventually Wake—and Joyce is here warning of the coming day of judgment. These friends have additional support for their view in the lectures on Parnell that Joyce gave on the Continent not long after leaving Ireland. Certainly these youthful outbursts were vitriolic and bitterly personal. Attempts to satisfy Joyce's critics by making him an active revolutionary, however, merely serve to confuse the issue.

Joyce, like Mann, was interested in effecting broad changes in the basic attitudes of men. One who presents a manuscript of short stories to a prospective publisher as "the first step in the spiritual liberation of my country" is either a charlatan or a dedicated reformer, however overoptimistic. That this liberation is to be accomplished by allowing the Irish to see themselves in his "nicely polished looking glass" gives more than a hint of Joyce's method. What may seem, in his works, simply detached reporting is actually the presentation by an intensely concerned countryman of the existing state of affairs—political, religious, aesthetic, social. By letting them see themselves as others see them, Joyce evidently hopes to effect a slow and unspectacular movement toward improvement in their lot. But is this not the avowed purpose of the serious artists of any age—of Fielding in *Tom Jones,* Milton in *Samson Agonistes,* Mann in *The Magic Mountain?* Can we ask more from Joyce?

Joyce's interest in the broad sweep of history is plain. The very pervasiveness of its presence makes it in *Ulysses* the "nightmare" from which escape seems unlikely. In *Finnegans Wake* he envelops himself in history, and, by those cycles of man's past that he accepts or rejects, he establishes values for himself and his readers. That he looks ahead to Finn again, rather than to Sinn Fein or Arthur Griffith, places him beyond indifference. It is not necessary to go, as Zola does, from the fine naturalistic implicitness of *Germinal* to the cloudy, nebulous novels of political and social utopia that characterize the Frenchman's declining years. Both Joyce and Zola are better at painting history as it was and is than seeking to rise to the heady atmosphere of prophecy. Mr. Deasy is a more pungent comment on the state of Joyce's world than are the prophetic utterances of J. Alexander Dowie.

The Nihilist

Lower middle-class Dublin was scarcely more enlightened in 1941 than it was in Joyce's youth, when Ibsen constituted the notorious but unread menace to complacency. It is an irony, certainly not lost upon the author, that he came to occupy in the eyes of his countrymen the same role that had been held by his literary idol. Though the ungrudging tributes of Curran and Power testify to the respect he enjoyed among the discerning, one should not be surprised that the semi-educated Dubliners who knew the work only by hearsay should echo the common prejudices of a provincial society. The types are in *Ulysses,* for those who can understand—not only Deasy, but a host of the sanctimonious and the superficial. Was Joyce only a name, as the *Irish Independent* was happy to report, or was he the recipient of such "foolish and false —and even fiendish—praise" as to force *The Irish Rosary* to attack him at his death? These journals did agree that his country could scarcely be proud of him. Had he not reviled his own religion and "fouled the nest which was his native city" by his blasphemy and obscenity? In his apostasy he illustrated what the *Rosary* deemed a usual combination of moral and mental incapacity. Such attacks are understandable, considering the source.[31]

It is also understandable that Joyce should be compared to Stalin or Hitler, though it is scarcely compatible with views of his social ineffectiveness.[32] But to call *Ulysses* one of the world's worst books on the basis of its being merely "a ponderous, fakedly insane combination of dictionary cross-word puzzles . . . and backhouse jokes" is to outdo the Irish themselves in ignorant vituperation.[33] More reasonable attacks centered on Joyce's presumed limitations of arrogance, resentment, egocentricity, and sentimental self-pity. Admitting that the true person was as much of a mystery as his fellow Dubliner, Jonathan Swift, Donagh MacDonagh could still oversimplify the case by finding half his troubles springing from an absurd refusal "to bow to an authority which was principally inside his own head."[34] When we read that the other half were prompted by the author's own artistic integrity we are in the presence of as neat a case of critical schizophrenia as one might ever hope to find. What method can one use to sift the real from the imagined grievances? We seem here to see Shem the notorious or any of the other rebels in the *Wake.*

T. S. Eliot was moved by the incompetence of the London *Times* obituary to write two protests, the more forceful of which he did not send.[35] The news release went to the extreme of once more quoting Gosse on the "worthlessness and impudence" of *Ulysses,* even though Gosse had long since lost all claims to being an adequate critic. The *Literary Supplement* admitted occasional brilliance but felt it more than offset by "acres of boredom and brain-sick words." Joyce's intensity and acumen were heightened by his revulsion, but the vision is partial and distorted, almost overwhelming the reader; "only his feeling for the comic and the almost magical music . . . give relief to the prevailing bleakness." While *The Times* found him the victim of a persecution mania, intensified by the fact that Dublin "gave the lie to his phantoms" and that the rest of the world was like Dublin, *The Irish Press* thought him a proud egotist who considered himself "the chosen one of modern literature." In his disappointment he nursed his wounded vanity, with the result that "The artist in him devoured the man and the Catholic, and he became his own *lex eterna*."[36]

It has been difficult for Dr. Oliver St. John Gogarty, poet, wit, scholar, raconteur, and successful physician, as well as senator, to become eclipsed by his acquaintance of medical-school days and to be threatened with the prospect of being known primarily as the original of Buck Mulligan. A Gogarty letter, printed in 1932, characterized Joyce as "a joke" who recites and drivels and whose literary pretensions are ridiculous.

> He has no *Saeva Indignatio*. He lies down with the abandoned and howls *Holy Murder*. . . . He is not a mocking Dante but a mockery of him.[37]

Joyce replied to these charges in a letter, admitting to Miss Harriet Weaver that "I cut a poor figure, eyeless, etc." in comparison to this "swimmer, boxer, cyclist, aviator, motorist." Yet one can never tell:

> . . . still the world begins from an egg. Enough of them and all alien annoyances. I have a job on hand.[38]

Vivian Mercier has suggested that "It is easy to see what Joyce grew to hate in Gogarty—his constant good health and high spirits, the absence of a sense of sin."[39] Niall Sheridan, acquainted with both men, corroborates this opinion in a letter to me:

> They were mutually antagonistic early on. G. was fairly wealthy by Joyce's standards, physically, athletic, etc. Gogarty had *wit*, whereas Joyce's strong suit was humour. Gogarty was a man of affairs, Joyce a mental recluse.

Sheridan also suggests personal insults though of course such will never be known. As Den Haan has remarked: "Who can tell what is the truth when these Irishmen start telling lies about each other?"

Gogarty reviewed the *Wake* as "the most colossal leg pull in literature since MacPherson's *Ossian,*" attributing to Joyce little more than incurable resentment:

> This arch-mocker in his rage would extract the Logos, the Divine Word or Reason from its tabernacle, and turn it muttering and maudlin into the street.

As "a dishevelled harbinger of the Bolshevic revolution" he rejected beauty "to howl outcast for the rest of his life through the dark recesses of his soul." Later diagnoses elaborate the theme. His resentment is attributed to a "raw deal" from his father, though two of Joyce's sisters recall Jimmy as his father's favorite. From Rimbaud he turned to the "garbage pail" or "ash can" school of literature, whose representatives, for lack of an audience, must "talk to themselves," but even here Joyce went one better, "and talked to himself in his sleep." He sacrificed everything, even his humanity, to art; "He never escaped the prison he had built around him: the Church." Resentment, a persecution complex, dehumanization, the force of the church on the one hand, and, on the other (never mind an inconsistency here or there) "an artist" in the Dublin sense of "a merry droll, a player of hoaxes." But the crowning absurdity is the seriousness with which *Ulysses* is read. Only in America could he have been taken seriously, America "the country *par excellence* of the detective story, the crossword puzzle, and the smoke signal."[40] Gogarty's diagnosis of Joyce's schizophrenia is only part of a general picture of Ireland as an ideal outdoor asylum, in which Einstein, Freud, and Field Marshal Montgomery could be confined. The King and Queen of England would thrive there, for boredom is to them so much a matter of course as to become first rather than second nature. There might even be some ground for doubting whether they would realize that they were confined. As William York Tindall remarked in a review of Gogarty's last book, the irrepressible Irishman palliates some of the sting by cheerfully regarding himself as insane too, though safe enough to be allowed to roam abroad.[41]

Mary Colum has attempted to correct some of Gogarty's

errors, though the task of making him understand his former friend is probably impossible. She does, however, protest his judgments. For though a sincere critic might have numerous reservations about *Ulysses,* he could not write it off in Gogarty's cavalier manner. Joyce's brother Stanislaus found it difficult to separate error from deliberate misrepresentation. Anyone could see from the author's career that the works are not a deliberate hoax. Most amazing of all, however, is it for one who knew the Gogarty of fifty years ago, the medical pal with his "vast repertory of bawdry," to find him now standing as a champion of decency.[42]

In general the Irish rather resent the notion that their most recent wild goose should be taken seriously as a thinker. Happily enough, they usually present their view in a much more casual and humorous spirit than Gogarty's. So has Niall Montgomery commented genially on Joyce's presumed lack of a positive outlook. Philosophy is "the Monte Carlo of the spirit," where, regardless of the systems conceived by players, "the bank is never broken." Joyce's method is merely to accept the insolubility of the problem. It is art, not the game, that is threatened with bankruptcy.[43]

A more carefully documented Gogarty, Robert Glynn Kelly finds the basic conditioning force in "a fearful insecurity" and "a self-mistrust begotten of family failures" that gave rise to such defensive measures as arrogance, self-discipline, "an evasive esotericism, and numerous iron-clad literary theories." Ashamed of his father, physically inferior to his classmates, he began by "making intellectuality a virtue in its own pedantic right." To excel his rivals he delved into esoteric bypaths; his aesthetic theories "are his treasures and his weapons." Failing to attract sufficient attention to himself, he became a clown, just as the fear of others gave him the role of captious critic. For all the sedulous restraint and protective irony of the major works, the childhood grudges remain and the author of *Ulysses* is still "the pompous young exhibitionist reciting theories for admiring friends."[44]

That artistic creativity may be a form of personal sublimation is too well established to deny, but the desire of young poets to voyage into strange seas of thought is too universal to be described adequately merely as a defense reaction to an inferiority complex. Blake had sought an antidote to what he felt to be the death chill of Newtonian physics and current rationalism; in Mark Schorer's words, "he had to oppose the visionary to the physicist."[45] Yeats considered himself to be the voice of a renaissance, "the revolt of the soul against the intellect"; in what others called the decadence he saw "the autumn of the body," "the trembling of the veil," "the crowning crisis of the world," in which man would again ascend toward spirituality.[46] Admittedly a "Partial Explanation," Kelly's is a slanted thesis. The posturings of the young Joyce were not in vain.

The Divided Soul

Crude as these attacks may be, there is a danger of rejecting them as Philistine, and of turning from their often irrational bitterness to an equally irrational sentimentality. One can sense deep-seated conflicts underlying the art, from the violence of the sermons on Hell in the *Portrait* to the never fully repressed tensions of the later works. In *Ulysses* Stephen projects his own despair upon Shakespeare. To what extent does this arrogant loneliness reflect the author's scorn and despondency? We catch glimpses of a confession that is always denied by a sneer or a shrug of the shoulder. Someone asks Stephen whether he believes his own theories of Shakespeare. He will not serve, not even his own imaginative creations, nor is he interested in publishing his interpretation unless he is paid for it. In his life too, Joyce presented to his friends the appearance of an aloof gentleman, gracious but retiring, with a family loyalty that one could almost term piety. No wonder that to Cyril Connolly there seemed to be two Joyces:

> . . . the legendary Joyce, blind but patient, pompous, cold, easily offended, unapproachable . . . . and underneath the warm sympathetic bawdy Irish character.[47]

Morton Zabel also noted the "complex and multiplied consciousness" that was apparent in the combination of proud intransigence and the humor and compassion "for the meanest pathos of obscure and blundering lives." The mercurial changes in his temperament were rigidly controlled and disciplined by aesthetic theory and personal loyalty. Zabel was perhaps the first to enumerate the basic elements in his character: "its Catholic conscience, its racial and aesthetic sentimentality, its formal discipline, its expressive faculty, and the continuous sublimation of its fancies."[48]

One may be reminded, on a deeper level, of Hans Castorp in *The Magic Mountain,* mockingly characterized as the petty bourgeois with the moist spot on the lung. But Mann makes clear that there is an element of ineradicable mediocrity about his hero and thus protects both author and reader from taking too seriously what is being said. In contrast, the violence of Joyce's inner conflicts imparts an energy almost volcanic to his work. The critical reader is constantly tempted to speculate on the secret sources. The appalling indecencies and blasphemies have been generally attributed to two main factors, alone or in combination, those of religion and sexual experience. Blasphemy may be the literature of Catholic countries, as George Moore is credited wth saying, but Joyce seems to push beyond such lighthearted definition. The repressive aspects of Irish prudery may be responsible, or the author himself may manifest an inherent puritanism in defacing the lovely if false images of tradition. Gorman considered him "a religiast without a religion," with his heart "crying for that very thing which the brain persuades him does not exist." Did he remain a Catholic to the end, his outbursts constituting, in the words of Patrick Kavanagh, "the horrible howl of the believer," or was his mingled mockery and rage the effect of trying to suppress the pain of his apostasy?[49]

Joyce's disturbed awareness of the body has been attributed to the Jesuits and, conversely, has been interpreted as a reaction against a sentimentalized religious training. One is reminded of the controversy that attended the review of *Ulysses* in Chesterton's *New Witness*. To Jack Common it seemed that the work "trembles with the primal shock of discovering the horrible empire of the corporeal." Having been "sold a pup on the soul-stuff," Joyce discovered reality, and, being true to his artistic conscience, he could never eradicate his physical disgust:

> Body was real; so let it be. And, by god, body has been real enough ever since.[50]

Floyd Dell likewise attributes the sex obsession to some personal experience, wisely avoiding the dangerous grounds of blaming the disillusionment on religious education:

> Joyce was horrified by what seemed to him the nastiness of life; he felt a morbid guilt over his own adolescent participation in its vileness, and he went to great lengths to pass on his disgust to his readers.

In Dell's reading, Joyce's world is one of meaningless and ugly sexual drives.[51]

Sean O'Faolain makes a penetrating comparison between Joyce and Dante. Of all the similarities—their Catholicism, their learning, their love and hatred of their native cities, their exile—the most prominent is the "struggle between lyricism and brutality," which arises from the fact that both were "disdainful, secretive, inturned, lonely." Though the difference in their achievement is, in O'Faolain's opinion, "immense," the result of this obsessive, passionate inner vision is that their work is personal rather than universal. But if their works lack the serenity of the classics, "they have an intimacy which the classical can never achieve, being not only works of art, but human testaments."[52] To Andrew Cass it seems that *Ulysses* afforded its author an opportunity "to get off his chest a great deal of juvenile resentments and self-pity" but that the urge toward autobiography was checked by "mental paralysis inhibiting direct self-expression." Perhaps Kavanagh is right in finding art to be "life squeezed through a repression," though one may doubt his diagnosis of Joyce as a man, lacking inspiration, who found an "introvert formula," "an unmannerly child enjoying destruction."[53]

The many instances of Joyce's concern with excretory and reproductive functions lead one to agree with H. G. Wells that the author had a cloacal obsession. The eructation, evacuation, and micturition that shocked readers of the *Portrait* and *Ulysses* may perhaps be excused on realistic grounds, but if the poems, so serene and classical on the surface, are as full of innuendo as Professor Tindall finds them to be, the case is not closed. When *Finnegans Wake* appeared, the reviewer for *Time* anticipated that the notoriety of *Ulysses* would give rise to the question about the new book, "Is it dirty?" He concluded that the book was so obscure that no one would know. The answer is yes. Nora Joyce put it bluntly to Robert McAlmon: "I guess the man's a genius, but what a dirty mind he has, hasn't he?" The psychologist would no doubt call it infantilism, but judging from past experiences with psychological criticism, we appreciate the wisdom of Joyce's refusal to accept Mrs. Edith Rockefeller McCormick's suggestion that he be psychoanalyzed.

As has been shown, the Gorman biography throws little light on the subject. Autobiographical fiction will also conceal almost as much as it will reveal, for the dramatized self is somewhat removed from the inarticulate cry of the heart and hence more effectively presented in an art form. Of all the masks Joyce adopted in fiction or in life, none is more impenetrable than that of the bourgeois paterfamilias. Hence his casual opinions were found by Malcolm Cowley to be "those of a fourth or fifth-rate mind," and Alfred Kazin also felt it easy to quarrel with his "lean and narrow greatness." *The Irish Times* thought that Gorman presented "a remote colourless creature" who moved almost invisibly "behind his vast undertakings."[54] The result is that, interesting as it is to speculate on the precise nature of Joyce's attitude, it is highly improbable that any single explanation will suffice.

A divided soul can attempt sublimation through what Kristian Smidt terms "cultic fiction," meaning work that has the effect of exorcism. For though Joyce rejects Dublin, parents, and God, he never throws off their power, particularly the last, remaining "Dublin-haunted," "parent-haunted," and "God-haunted." Smidt notes the frequency of the "usurper complex"—with Boylan, Mulligan, Robert Hand, and Shaun as examples. Are these usurpers merely projections of the one powerful force Stephen-Joyce never succeeded in forgetting, that of God? Nostalgia and rebellion or exhibitionism and concealment may be the double-faced masks of an unsuccessfully repressed tension. The novels might be read as rituals of parricide, attempts to destroy the power of God and to substitute the deities of ego and art, completing the trinity with the artist as demiurge of his creations, combining nature and spirit, creative mana and created matter.

The division may be necessary for Joyce the artist, Richard Ellmann suggests, since the author, whose exile was voluntary, needed a series of incidents and misunderstandings in order to renew and to intensify his quarrel. Ellmann also notes the "usurper" theme, the false friend who dominates, imitates, or betrays. And in his career Joyce found a succession of betrayers—Ireland, publishers, the English officials in Zurich, as well as his former friends. Joyce thus projects himself as Christ the betrayed, but also as Faust, who arranges his own betrayal. The thesis is challenging, though it relies considerably upon biographical detail for which we lack adequate data—the break with Gogarty, for instance. Also, may not these constant soul-searchings in the work echo Joyce's own loss of a father-confessor and the consequent necessity for a Puritan examination of conscience, his own as well as those of his friends and his fictitious characters?

Early reviewers of the *Wake* suspected it to be an obscure

confession. Edmund Wilson noted a "curious shrinking solicitude to conceal," and Louise Bogan sensed "a masked attempt" at an apologia. A strong case can be made for the interpretation of Derek Vershoyle, that the sexual allusions evidence "a mind trying to free itself from obsessions." Surely the mockery with which the writer Shem is treated indicates deep bitterness. The "low sham" (170), "national apostate" (171), "hiresiarch" (188) or "poor acheseyeld from Ailing" (148) images the immemorial guilt of Cain as he trails his "pillgrimace of Childe Horrid" (423) to the accompaniment of distorted echoes of "Come Back to Erin" (428), while the ever-forwarded letter carries in disguise Joyce's early Dublin addresses, scribbled over with such comments as "Gone . . . Tried Apposite House . . . Noon sick parson" (420). Certainly homelessness and hurt pride are important ingredients of the work, and there is even a possibility that Joyce, unhappy and disappointed at his lack of Irish recognition, contrasts himself with the Shaun of Irish politics, Eamon de Valera, as "Andrew Cass" argued in the *Irish Times* of April 26, 1947.

Uneasiness about his exile, some degree of obsession with sex, an ineradicable fear of the Four Last Things (Death, Judgment, Heaven, and Hell, as every Catholic knows), mingled pride and shame, possibly even some degree of pose, seem apparent. The precise nature of Joyce's motivation should interest us less than the effects it had upon his art. The role of genius is that, in presenting its own problems, it reflects those of its age and of humanity. These factors, together with others yet undetected, enabled Joyce to penetrate the modern consciousness. From them derive the passion, the awareness, the dramatic tension of *Ulysses.* Joyce's pride may be less a matter of arrogance than "the necessary self-confidence of genius, the vital egoism of a pioneer," as L. A. G. Strong pointed out, infusing *Ulysses* with its undoubted power:

> It raises and faces issues of the first importance. Its subject is the human spirit. It is profoundly, shockingly moral. It is brutal, tender, lyrical, delicate, heavy-footed, coarse, religious.[55]

The tensions of Joyce's character are likewise related by Zabel to the triumphs of his art:

The daemon that possessed it made virtues of its defects, and so gave Joyce's books the tragic insight, the long persistence, the comprehensive humor, and the isolated courage that form their claim to distinction among the discoveries of the spirit.[56]

Anima naturaliter catholica

A strong case can be made for Joyce's essentially Catholic frame of mind, but one must not canonize him to the extent of blinding oneself to his bitterness against the church. Padraic Colum early remarked Joyce's "intellectual interests that go with Catholic philosophy," and Damon found the characters in *Ulysses* "observed through the eyes of St. Thomas Aquinas," while the framework is "mediaeval, Dantesque."[57] Colum's argument that Joyce "could be an infidel, even a blasphemer, but never a heretic" is borne out not only by Stephen's refusal to accept the "illogical and incoherent" absurdity of Protestantism but by his admission of respect and fear for the church. The intellectual structure of his major work, the subtle psychological analysis of human motives, the moral judgment (most apparent in *Exiles*), are Catholic.

Eliot's observation of Joyce's orthodoxy as revealed by his awareness of sin, seems more questionable from a doctrinaire point of view.[58] Could not the same sense be possessed by an unbeliever? It may well be that a realization of man's fallen nature is the first step toward faith, but atheistic existentialism also recognizes the prevalence of evil. The nameless guilt of the Kafka hero, neurotic disgust with the body, or despair are only preliminary; the doctrines of prevenient Grace, of the atonement and redemption through the blood and body of Christ must follow, as well as acceptance of the church visible and invisible. In any case, emphasis on original sin, though an aspect of Augustinian and Jansenist Catholicism, is more characteristic of Lutheranism and the austerities of Calvinist predestination.

Perhaps L. A. G. Strong is on safer ground in not only finding the moral judgments of *Ulysses* colored by the sense of sin, "that terrific spiritual legacy which the Catholic Church irrevocably leaves her children," but, more significantly, the blasphemies as "the deeper gestures of a man doomed to accept certain Last Things."[59] So, too, feels W. J. Igoe, who found Joyce's Catholicism providing him with an immunity "to private metaphysics and theosophic visions."

His religious foundation makes him at once a difficult artist and a profound moralist, "fascinated by the blundering pilgrimage of the human soul."[60] Padraic Colum, in reviewing Ussher, notes the author's argument that an age that has rediscovered Aquinas should inevitably call forth "like a derisive echo" such a "jesting, wordmincing scholastic" as Joyce. Yet Joyce remains to Colum "the last great Christian," who calls us to a "farcical" rather than "a corrupt or Satanic communion."[61]

Joyce once confessed to Georges Borach that both Protestantism and Catholicism were "false" but that he preferred Catholicism to its "cold and colorless" opposite. His native church "is constantly associated with art; it is a beautiful lie —something at least."[62] Niall Montgomery thinks Joyce not a heretic: "His theological differences were really social; he felt it was not the thing to be a Dublin Catholic."[63] Joyce's widow told me that at her husband's request he was buried without any of the rites of the church.

Some Catholic observers feel that Joyce's attitude travestied the true church, that the damnation sermon in the *Portrait* is an exaggeration, and that, in any case, he never shared the joy in Christ crucified, the *felix culpa* of Augustine, and the love that "Our Lady" and the Communion of Saints manifest for fallen man. From his conflict arises a spiritual tension that imparts energy to his work. Thus, according to George Barker, Joyce suffered "the same sense of guilt that devastates the Dostoevskian," and his work is permeated by the "hysterical and desperately heretical gestures" which prove that "he fought on the end of an orthodox religious tether." His books were "written in spiritual circumstances that only a Dante, Aquinas, or a Julian the Apostate could perfectly visualize."[64] A contributor to *Commonweal* read *Ulysses* as "the image of a divided soul," but he was taken to task by another who found Stephen merely "a relict" and Mulligan "a parody" of Catholicism, Bloom being the only character who shows "awareness of that charity . . . which can redeem the individual."[65] To Dorothy Sayers, Joyce seems to exemplify a precarious imbalance of great energy and insufficient thought, "son-ridden" or Sabellian—we recall that Sabellius is denominated in *Ulysses* as the "subtlest heresiarch" of all, to whom "the Father was Himself His Own Son."[66]

Often the distinction between the local and the universal church is made, as by Robert R. Hull, who argues that Joyce was consciously an unbeliever but basically not a rebel against the church universal. His sin is pride, leading him to scorn the shortcomings of the visible church; "he did not forget nor did age mellow him." The result is complete egocentricity, his characters becoming projections of himself, his attitude "the Godlike detachment of the rebel egoist." Hull finds that Irish Catholicism, in its fear of being outdone by nonconformist Protestant morality, turned to puritan repression. The British kept the Irish poor, the church kept them moral, and, in the Parnell case, the church forced the Irish to remain British, thus compounding the subjection. Joyce's fault is one of "a too vivid imagination joined to a weak will," with the consequence that *Ulysses* illustrates an attempt to find adventure in a dull society through vice. Nonetheless, Hull confidently predicted in 1930, Joyce will return to the Communion.[67] A recent analysis shows the conflict basic to Ireland. For the Irish intellectual, Catholicism is "a web" that can "either support or enmesh" and that "sometimes seems to do both alternately." Hence arises, in particular, the Irish ambivalence toward Joyce, who represents what the intellectual hopes and yet fears to be. The big question is, "can Joyce be truly Irish, and truly Catholic, and a writer of Dirty Books?"[68]

It is the impression of Ramon Sender that Joyce, as Catholic and Latinist, is "the devil" of the northern European imagination, "elusive and yet omnipresent," who though "condemned to darkness," is "the prince of light in his wisdom, lucidity, and beauty." In Joyce's work we sense "something tremendous," the "death-agony" of an era. But unlike the Mediterranean thinker, who would be affirmative in accepting the devil and the identity of reality and perfection, Joyce shows an English "inability to assimilate the Devil."[69] In contrast, Arland Ussher reads Joyce's attitude as a "deadly clear-sighted, yet almost too-complacent, acceptance of human imperfection." Like Eliot's footman, he "holds our coat —and snickers." His concern for sin seems belied by "the happy shamelessness of Molly Bloom" and to him sin appears to be "nothing but a jest."[70] A positive identification of Joyce with Cain is seen by J. Mitchell Morse in *Finnegans Wake,* where the author "has mastered the pain of apostasy enough to make use of it through pity and laughter alike." A romantic rebel, whose heresy consisted in maintaining an open mind, he could sympathize as well with the conventional Shauns or Abels who condemned him. Yet the mockery remains. "There can be no doubt that in *Finnegans Wake* Joyce is on the side of the devils."[71] He did not wish "to be saved by default," in Vivian Mercier's phrase, though one suspects that this very process is being carried on today by well-intentioned interpreters.[72]

The Yale doctoral thesis of William T. Noon, S.J., published in the "Yale English Series," is a long-needed study of Joyce and Aquinas. Father Noon demonstrates that Joyce's Thomism was largely self-taught, as St. Thomas was not given the usual emphasis at University College during his time. The theory of art provided a personal weapon, though Joyce interpreted Scholastic notions freely in the light of the art-for-art's-sake spirit of the nineties. But Joyce did apparently derive from Aquinas several basic concepts—the epiphany, the analogy between poetry and divine creation, and the role of the verbal symbol, the word as mediating between its lower level of being a hieroglyph of sound and sense and its higher reach of becoming an instrument that shadows forth a transcendent reality. In the realm of value judgment, Joyce seems to have remained a good enough Thomist to conceive of *Ulysses* as "a criticism of modern society in the light of the 'natural law' of Aquinas." In the *Wake*, Father Noon concludes, "the whole mythic material revolves around a center of theological acceptance."

A brief consideration of the church's attitude toward apostasy may clarify Joyce's position. Karl Adam defines the legitimate limits of inquiry by believers, distinguishing between genuine doubt and that which is "merely subjective," the latter being marked by "proudly and arrogantly" excluding the "light of grace." Yet faith "should be in accordance with reason," so the questioning student may be led to a "profound conflict of soul." There is no easy solution: "He must wrestle with God until He bless him, and there is no help for him save in grace alone." Should he find himself "compelled in moral sincerity" to leave the Communion, his conscience is left to God's mercy, "for the Church cannot and may not endure that there should be some among her members who are Catholics only in name." Such reasoning may lie behind Joyce's alleged remark to Morris Ernst:

> I paused to ask Joyce just when he had left the Catholic Church. He said, "That's for the Church to say." Which to me meant that inside himself he had never left the Church, try as he might have.

The church can also look dispassionately on personalities too strong to bow to authority, for "the richer a personality is, the more does it suffer from the community, especially from that average level of life and its requirements which go necessarily with a common organisation." Nevertheless, common life implies "a definite norm for the community, a creed and a law," and, regardless of the cost, "the individual must willingly accept this norm, in dogma, morals, law, and worship." Joyce could hardly assent to Adam's assumptions that "the community richly repays whatever the personality sacrifices" and that in Catholic communities "the poisonous plant of materialism cannot grow."[73] If Joyce's work is even a partially sound picture of the author's religious enviroment, the reader may also doubt that Irish Catholicism had the vitality to command his allegiance.

An orthodox interpretation of Joyce as a "dark angel," a tragic failure, appeared in the July-August 1953 issue of the *Redemptorist Record,* a publication of the Clonard Monastery at Belfast. It is the opinion of H. A. McHugh, C.SS.R., D.C.L., that Joyce had accomplished "a debatable little" in contrast to the "unquestioned lot" he had lost; his willful farewell to the church was unsuccessful, for "it was his torment that he never got beyond being a bad Catholic." The "miasma" of *Ulysses* led only to the "bewildering darkness" of *Finnegans Wake*. He was "so drunk with the music of words" that final incoherence followed inevitably. Only a few have noted the suppressed orthodoxy in Joyce—Gogarty, Strong, Wells, Eliot, and Woolf: "It is curious that only those who love or hate the Church have noticed this dark sorrow." He is a spiritual writer only in the negative sense, railing against his conscience "like a lost soul railing against existence." Throughout his work "the pain of loss rages in wild blasphemy, in frenzied obscenity and a chaos of speech." Such is the anguish of "the mystic who failed."

Yet we recall Thomas Merton's claim of being converted through his reading of Joyce, much as it surprised some of his spiritual advisers. McLuhan and Kenner have recently attempted to show that *Ulysses* is based on an orthodox scheme of values, though one may still doubt the validity of relying on Joyce's use of the medieval metaphor of the body. In the Catholic magazine *Thought* Francis X. Connolly scolded an unnamed "liberal Catholic critic" for considering *Ulysses* "a Catholic masterpiece" on the grounds of its "many ecclesiastical references." He warns Catholic novelists against trying to adopt Joyce's techniques, for "Literary styles are modes of thought not modes of dress."[74] And more recently in the same magazine William F. Lynch, S.J., questioned whether analogy in itself is significant of belief. If any symbol, "even the elements of dialectical conclusion and theological belief," become no more than "usable material" for the artist, the result is a "symbolistic degradation" of doctrine. Analogy itself is neutral:

> There is no more blessed gift given to men than a proper theory of analogy, but it can also become the great corruptor of history and belief.

The question is whether the essential elements of belief are "allowed to stand in their own hard, committed purity" or whether they become mere symbols. In Joyce's case the question remains unsettled:

> Mr. McLuhan . . . has, better than anybody else, revealed the remarkable analogical resources of the Irish writer, but it still remains an unsettled question in the minds of some people whether or no Joyce was not to be numbered among the corrupters of some important aspects of analogical workmanship.[75]

Nevertheless it is difficult not to find some implicit moral criterion in *Ulysses*. The blasphemies of the Black Mass provide a basis for judging the behavior of the thralls of Circe, as the vespers service suggests a moral counterpart of Gertie MacDowell's sensuous reveries. Stephen Dedalus is a horrible example of unbelief; his conception of history as nightmare is an explicit rejection of orthodox teleological historiography, and, as Mulligan notes, he is a sentimentalist in parading his own remorse and indulging in self-pity, thus blinding himself to the good in Bloom, in Dublin, and in the Dubliners about him. He enjoys the luxury of unbelief. Bloom is a secularist, a man with charity, to be sure, but few would be happy in his pragmatic Bloomusalem. Stephen's symbolist doctrine is a kind of manifestation as well as a parody of the epiphany. In one sense all things show the glory of God, but the epiphanies of the sordid and trivial imply Stephen's hatred for the world and the works of man, which, through Grace, may be perfected.

What is needed to supplement the already copious material concerning Joyce as a Catholic and an apostate is analysis of the religious (or irreligious) element in his work by critics whose knowledge of their ground is intimate while their view is detached. Thus far it has been difficult to find critics who possessed boh of these attributes. Catholics in good standing must have certain inhibitions about approaching a discussion of apostasy without preconceived and understandable reservations. Apostate Catholics, usually sympathetic to Joyce's position, have tended to use his defection as an emotional bulwark for their own decision. On the other hand, those critics with no Catholic background, though they have brought to their work the requisite disinterested attitude, have often been handicapped by a mere schematic acquaintance with the practices and philosophy of a religion with which they had no personal connection. Much can be hoped for from work now in progress by practicing Catholics.

Dubliner

Pedant and moralist alike overlook one important fact—that Joyce was a Dubliner, "the complete Dubliner," who "hardly ever wrote a line that was not steeped in the atmosphere of his native city." "If Dublin were destroyed," wrote his university classmate Constantine Curran, "his words could rebuild the houses; if its population were wiped out, his books could repeople it."[76] Joyce confessed to Cyril Connolly, "I am afraid I am more interested, Mr. Connolly, in the Dublin street names than in the riddle of the universe."[77] My own *Fabulous Voyager* (1947) is the first attempt to trace the wanderings of the modern Ulysses by means of Thom's *Directory*. Curran had said, "Joyce was many things, but he was certainly the last forty volumes of Thom's *Directory* thinking aloud." In this "fictional Baedeker of Dublin" I found several hundred Dublin personages and business establishments that give the narrative not only "an astounding degree of concreteness" but a constant sense of movement:

> Bakeries, schools, auction-rooms, antique shops, confectioners, hotels, public buildings . . . above all, pubs—here is the confusion of a modern city. Nearly two hundred establishments are mentioned. And in describing them, Joyce almost always creates a sense of movement. Trams pass, pigeons fly, smoke drifts upward, sounds are con-

stantly heard, the reek of lunch pervades the air, the sunlight brings out the glossy sheen of silk in a show window.[78]

Remembering that the author was removed some ten to fifteen years in time as well as in space from his subject, I suggested that Joyce undoubtedly felt as though he were "viewing the world from a distant perspective" and that the medieval poetic question, *"Ubi sunt?"* must have come to his mind:

"Where bronze from anear? Where gold from afar?" Where, now, Thomas Johnson and his neighbor, the retired registrar?[79]

Padraic Colum and Vivian Mercier have re-created the Dublin of the turn of the century, as has Gogarty, albeit with a bias.[80] There emerges a composite picture of a city, home of the phrase bitter or witty (better both), of cheap liquor and light opera. Devoted to gossip, idle yet seedily respectable, it was an ideal setting for the cultivation of personality —after all, there was not much else to cultivate. Yet even I, though not a Dubliner and still less a Joyce, can understand something of his lifelong yearning for his native city. George Bernard Shaw attacked the futility of Victorian Dublin with more earnestness than Joyce, but then Shaw was a puritan. He, like Joyce, had had all he could stand of it by the age of twenty; he found the sordid environment described in *Ulysses* "with a fidelity so ruthless that the book is hardly bearable." According to him, Dublin is unique among cities in its spirit of "flippant futile derision."[81] The remark is surely pertinent to Joyce's outlook, with this difference. The resentment of the young Joyce gradually mellowed, and Father Conmee, Simon Dedalus, and the barmaids at the Ormond add charm and humor to *Ulysses,* while in *Finnegans Wake* the entire area is bathed in a dream atmosphere not unlike that created by the changing half-lights and shadows that play over Dublin in sunshine and shower.

Horace Reynolds considered *Ulysses* a faithful picture of the world's "most brilliantly and completely thwarted city," whose residents, finding no occupations worthy of their talents, can escape their frustration and envy only through drink and talk, the latter being "the national pastime, glory, and disease." Such is the charm of this lotus land that men, though they flee it—"fearful of its seduction, ashamed of its sordidness, weary of its envy, disgusted with its futility"—never escape its influence. Yet Dublin remains the perfect city for a modern epic, large enough to provide variety, small enough to be comprehended, a city of legend and life. Haunted by dreams yet teeming with the excitement of a cultural renaissance, Dublin is, as Reynolds has so well said, most distinguished for its citizens, "an unconventional people, witty, gossipy, satirical, fond of a song and a story, the most volatile talkers since the Greeks."[82] The Irish climate, with mist, cloud, and diffused sunlight, lends to landscape and street the tone of an oil painting. Its tradition and legend have given it an atmosphere of nostaglic charm that even Joyce was unable to escape. So the young Stephen, standing on an island by the bay, looked back upon the city wistfully, "Like a scene on some vague arras, old as man's weariness." That Joyce could deface this episode in *Finnegans Wake* is but one more evidence of the deep division in his nature.[83]

Perhaps Padraic Colum is right in asserting that his writing about Dublin almost "as one might write about a beleaguered city" gives to his characters mythological dimensions.[84] So too Austin Clarke felt that his conversation about Dublin indicated that for him it assumed the quality of "that strange allegorical city from which Christian fled" as well as "that shining one of which the faithful desire to be good citizens."[85] As Stephen said of Shakespeare, the theme of exile remained with him always. Joyce often claimed that he never left Dublin, and indeed he seemed to remain desperately homesick. One suspects that his private dream was that of being recognized by his country, returning in glory to the city he loved and hated. Is not Richard Rowan seriously tempted to accept a language post at the university and eager to read the editorial welcoming him home? And is not the theme "Come Back to Erin" one which has been underestimated in many assessments of *Finnegans Wake*?

Elizabeth Bowen's obituary notice in the Irish *Bell* pleaded for local recognition of a man who, though acclaimed abroad, could only be fully appreciated by his fellow Irishmen. In his buffoonery, scorn and pity, even in that cruelty that expresses a reaction from pity, he "belonged to us, and was of us, wherever he went." The Irish should forget alike "the exaggerations of foolish intellectual worship he got abroad, and the notoriety he got at home." If such were possible Joyce would come to be respected as "a writer out of the Irish people" who derived from and contributed to the national tradition.[86]

Others have argued that the lack of a long-standing native tradition accounts for the violence of Joyce's art, that his is a belated work of a renaissance that never occurred in Ireland. So Arland Ussher finds him "a prodigious birth out of time" who summed up the entire Middle Ages in himself:

> . . . by turns, a St. Augustine crying aloud his sins, a Scholastic glossing on Aquinas, the producer himself of a "Summa" or great synthesis, and finally a Duns Scotus splitting hairs and mangling words.[87]

To G. W. Stonier, on the other hand, the shattering power derives from the fact that nineteenth-century English literature lacked such revolutionaries as Strindberg, Niezsche, or Dostoevski, and hence the long unexpressed currents of modern thought reach flood tide.[88] Such contradictions—Joyce as belated medievalist, as epitome of renaissance individualistic heresies, or finally as the overdue modern revolutionary—such divergences go to show that the analyst can select such aspects of a culture as suit his own purposes. Still another view is that of Hugh Kenner, who finds Dublin representing the last vestiges of an eighteenth-century tradition, where classic values were both maintained and debased side by side with modern vulgarity. So the ironic perspective is at hand, for Joyce need but to look about him, rather look into his memory, in order to see the distortions of something valuable. Dubliners are connoisseurs of language, yet their conversation is trifling. The city itself is a parody of the classical age, the music halls debasing heroic drama as journalism did heroic eloquence. So too is Simon Dedalus a last ridiculous remnant of the ideal gentleman, now a mere garrulous and ineffective lounger. Bloom also could be interpreted as the decayed Ciceronian statesman, his mind vulgarized by bourgeois banality.[89]

The Dublin popular press tended to ignore rather than to attack their notorious wild goose. Occasionally one of the major writers would be quoted, such as Yeat's remark that *Ulysses* was "indubitably a work of genius," or that of A. E. referring to Joyce as "the profound surgeon of the soul." *The Irish Times,* traditionally the organ of the Anglo-Irish ascendancy, remained a champion of Joyce blaming his exile on the narrow attitude of the Free State toward art, reviewing installments of the *Work in Progress,* and defending even these last stages of his career on the basis of the artist's right to express his message regardless of the public. By 1937, Niall Sheridan, himself a promising poet, noted in a little magazine that no predictions in regard to Joyce's influence could have anticipated the reality, for the approach has "become almost a social convention," while Dublin itself was beginning to seem "an inferior plagiarism from *Ulysses.*"[90]

The Irish Times found *Finnegans Wake* "endlessly exciting," though it seemed to lack "the necessary enlargement of a theme" and thus remained "a mere tortured piece of self-analysis." The obituary editorial of the same journal termed Joyce "probably the most important English prose-writer of the present century," whose *Ulysses* is destined to survive as "a magnificent monument to the Dublin of thirty-five years ago." The *Irish Independent* soon remarked the "veritable landslide of reminiscences" that had been appearing in the press.[91]

Yet as late as 1947 John Swift, a Dublin painter who admitted that he was "generally baffled and not infrequently bored" by Joyce, found in Europe, much to his surprise, a Swedish writer who was interested not in Patrick Weston but in "the one and only James Joyce."[92] Swift is far from typical of enlightened Dublin opinion. Vivian Mercier in his cleverly titled "Dublin under the Joyces," adapted from a historical classic, *Dublin under the Georges,* pointed out in 1948 that both Trinity and Universtiy Colleges have had their Joyce cults, that Johnston, Beckett, and O'Nolan have written successfully in the Joyce tradition, and that though not completely accepted, Joyce has been honored to the extent of having the Blanche portrait hung in the National Portrait Gallery. The president of University College could in 1950 refer to his institution as "the college of Gerard Manley Hopkins and James Joyce," and a literary critic of his staff could shortly thereafter write that the achievement of Yeats and Joyce "looms like a cliff," though she shied away from any detailed analysis.[93]

Patrick Kavanagh, one of the leaders among the younger Dublin poets, remarked in a review of Thomas Merton's autobiography that the Trappist's conversion through his reading of Joyce should not seem strange to those perceptive enough to see that Joyce was "one of the best interpreters of Thomism," whose work is "steeped in the blood of tortured

Catholicism." And Austin Clarke, dean of Dublin poets, protested the insensitivity of Swinnerton's diatribe in *The Georgian Literary Scene* against Joyce as a cynical purveyor of sensationalism: "nothing could be less true of the morbid introspective writer." This morbid introspection has been the burden of Andrew Cass's several brilliant essays and reviews. In addition to the already noted analyses of *Finnegans Wake,* he criticized L. A. G. Strong's study for its tendency to show Joyce as "a literary magpie" rather than a man with deep preoccupations. Tindall, though a keen and perceptive critic, misses the "pain of self-pity" of the personal references, "a cover-up for a sense of guilt" and a justification for being absent from Ireland in the days of the struggle for independence. As for the third book of Joyceana to be reviewed in 1950, Patricia Hutchins' *James Joyce's Dublin,* it must be admitted that "research of his environment does not go far to explain his art, the mind that made it or the heart that fed," for "His mind was its own place and of itself it made a hell of it."[94]

A note of weariness begins to appear in recent Irish comment. Francis McManus observes that Joyce has been "continually and tiresomely celebrated."[95] Thomas Hogan sensed a tone of disillusionment in the Joyce number of *Envoy* and shared A. E.'s doubt whether the author had enough chaos in him:

> The cold, hard, rigid mind had to erect its chaos in a calculating, pedantic, painstaking manner.

Hogan has recently suggested that a point of diminishing returns may have been reached in Joyce studies and that, barring the discovery of new source material, we can expect that "solemn and reverential" searches through the Joycean "rubble" will lead only to the discovery of "a particularly mangled piece of old hat."[96] Yet even "old hat" can be appealing to the nostalgic Dubliner. Witness Denis Johnston, who has asserted that to Dubliners of his generation *Ulysses* remains a sort of store room "in which one can spend a delightful hour taking objects of no great significance out of trunks, and putting them back again." Such a view leads to two conclusions that seem heretical to the Joycean: that Dubliners alone can enjoy the work and that "It is only a coincidence when those who have the supreme gift of self expression . . . have got anything startling to express' and that Joyce may be like his fellow Dubliners Swift and that "very readable Smart Alec" Shaw in having "a good line." Andrew Cass also finds Joyce incapable of adding anything to his favorite fields of history and religion, incapable even of commenting on them without personal allusions. Hence the *Wake* form enabled him to "give vent to his Irish memories" and also to "epiphanise himself as an all-wisest Stagirite who could express all knowledge in the most intricate symbolic terms." It can only be called art if it is regarded as "the moonshine of art, the reflection of the art of others"; it is "the literary and historical requiem of Western Europe."[97] Needless to say, such a view ignores the very life conveyed by the poetic word, not to speak of the humor, insight, and sympathy that are seldom hidden from the perceptive reader.

Yet the fiftieth anniversary of Bloomsday did not pass unnoticed in Dublin. Donagh MacDonagh followed "In the Steps of Leopold Bloom" in two essays in *The Irish Times*. Though Mabbot Street, the ship, the drays and the trams are gone, "The Joyce Country is all about us." Of the literary figures mentioned in *Ulysses,* only Starkey (Seumas O'Sullivan), Colum, Gogarty, Best, Curran, and Magee survive. But Joyce's Dublin has a larger population than its half million, "since he has given its freedom to all nations." And on the sixteenth of June 1954 a group started from the Martello Tower on the excursion known to thousands. A cynic remarked that the procession of cars and horse-drawn cabs resembled a funeral without a body; but a true-blooded Irishman noted that there were plenty of spirits. With stops at pubs in Monkstown, Williamstown, and Ringsend, it has not yet been determined where the procession ended. Adcadger that he was, Bloom himself would have been delighted at the advertisement of Prescott's dye works—a pencil portrait of Joyce followed by the text:

Prescotts . . . Bloomsday

. . . Dubliners . . . To-day is the fiftieth anniversary of Bloomsday. June 16th, 1904, was the day which James Joyce immortalised in Ulysses, in which the central character is Leopold Bloom. . . . And when I sent her for Molly's

Paisley shawl to Prescott's. . . . Trams: a car of Prescott's dyeworks. . . . Even then Prescotts had given decades of dependable cleaning to Dubliners.[98]

Joyce's intense concern with the physical details of his native city should not be allowed to overshadow the fact that he writes novels—not street directories. Irish critics who insist that no reader can appreciate Joyce without a personal and intimate knowledge of the city of Dublin need to keep in mind Joyce's conversation with Heinrich Straumann:

> In answer to my question, as to whether a knowledge of local conditions in Dublin would make the reading of *Finnegans Wake* any easier, he replied firmly in the negative. One shoud not pay any particular attention to the allusions to place-names, historical events, literary happenings and personalities, but let the linguistic phenomenon affect one as such.[99]

Finally, the impartial reader should bear in mind that while Joyce may have told the truth about Dublin, he did not tell the whole truth. A Joycean of our acquaintance, seeing Dublin for the first time, expressed his shock at finding so much beauty in the city. Joyce had given him no idea that here in this capital he would find handsome examples of eighteenth-century public buildings in the massive façades of the Four Courts, Customs House, Parliament, and Trinity College. Nor had the author prepared him for the dignity of St. Stephen's Green, the Shelbourne Hotel, nor the handsome suburban estates. To the disillusioned sightseer, it was as though Joyce had deliberately suppressed mention of mankind's best efforts and concentrated exclusively on his worst in accompanying Ulysses through Dublin. In a purely naturalistic work, with avowed propagandistic purposes, this might have been justifiable. But in an epic of the contemporary world, which attempts to put "Allspace in a Notshall," is this oversight or suppression not a weakness?

The Classic

Joyce's appeal to his sensitive contemporaries resembled that of Byron a century before; Cyril Connolly has likened his first reading of *Ulysses* to "Narcissus with his pool before him." A generation found its aspiration and melancholy reflected in Stephen Dedalus. William Troy, looking back with the nostalgia of those who associate their first experience of Joyce with the Sylvia Beach edition, or even with issues of *The Little Review,* recalls that for them Joyce was "the grand archetype of literary genius" and not merely an author subject to annotation and evaluation.[100] The passage of time, and Joyce's gaining of status, have undoubtedly lessened the immediacy of his work. So too, as the depression deepened, the appeal of Stephen became replaced by that of Bloom's more mellow frustration and vague idealism. With the contemporary interest in myth, philology, and aesthetics, Joyce, the fabulous artificer himself, comes to the forefront.

But now, *eheu fugaces,* Joyce has reached "the embalming chambers of the graduate schools," to the regret of William Troy. One is not certain of the qualifications of a *Reader's Digest* editor, Henry Morton Robinson, for charter membership in the circle, but he, like Troy, recalls the day when *Ulysses* was "a sacred grove for disciples only" and laments the fact that "all the bright young men" seem to him to be "turning to Joyce for promotion and pay."[101] The entertaining irony that a writer of best sellers and an inveterate digester should complain of the obviousness of Joyce studies was not missed by one reader.[102] And Troy himself broke off his nostalgic reverie with an admission of its setimentality. Yes, the tall figure with the thick lenses and hands on his cane is no longer to be seen at the Coupole, Dome, or Select. Joyce has reached the graduate schools. If this be inevitable, it is by no means inevitable that his appeal will become limited to the bureaucratized Bohemian or complacent card indexer who fails to sense the impact of his moral imagination. The academic approach, so easy to ridicule, may in the end be as rewarding as the attitude of the boulevardier. After all, there's another crowd now at the Deux Magots.

Courses dealing in whole or in large part with his work are offered by Buffalo, Columbia, Harvard, Louisville, and Wayne. Doctoral theses have been written: Joseph Prescott's "Joyce's Revisions of *Ulysses,*" Harvard, 1944; Ellsworth Mason's "Vico's Cycles," Yale, 1948; Hugh Kenner's "A Critique," Yale, 1950; Marvin Magalaner's *"Dubliners,"* Columbia, 1951; and "Joyce and Aquinas," Yale, 1954, by William T. Noon, S.J.; Fred Hall Higginson's "The Revisions of *Finnegans Wake,"* Minnesota, 1953; William Schutte's "Joyce's Use of Shakespeare in *Ulysses,"* Yale, 1954; Patrick E. Kilburn's *"Ulysses* in Catawba: A Study of the Influence of James Joyce on Thomas Wolfe," New York

University, 1954; Stanley Sultan's "The Argument of *Ulysses*," Yale, 1955. Studies of psychological, poetic, musical, or symbolic style, or of the relationship of the modern novel or novelist to social, political, or philosophical currents must include Joyce. Americans abroad have added to the literature. At the University of Paris Haskell M. Block wrote on the theory of the novel in Joyce and Flaubert (1948), and at Oxford A. W. Litz treated of *Finnegans Wake* in 1954. Many theses are now in progress. The Modern Language Association has published a large number of items, especially since 1945, and its 1948, 1952 and 1955 annual meetings had programs devoted almost entirely to Joyce, as did the English Institute in 1955. A section of the February 1952 issue of the College English Association *Critic* discussed pedagogical problems of teaching the works of Joyce.

In terms of classroom popularity, limited experience over a decade of teaching leads to interesting though unscientific conclusions. Ten years ago, the instructor was always able to bolster sagging enthusiasm by assigning a lesson in the works of Joyce. In fact, failure to do so usually elicited a request for such study from the members of the group. Today, perhaps surfeited by too much of a good thing, students vote for Kafka or Dylan Thomas as subjects most likely to succeed in touching class needs. Yet, without making comparisons, Joyce seems most vigorous—his future most assured—in the American college. Perhaps the situation is a historical accident: censored in Ireland, generally deplored, in spite of his recognized genius, by English scholars, Joyce and his works got a head start as required study in the United States. Maybe the other English-speaking countries simply have not caught up. Or perhaps it is America's love of analysis, of explication, of puzzles, that has put Joyce, as man and artist, in our scholarly spotlight. How much of our current interest in Joyce may be traceable to American rooting for the underdog is worth considering. Students seem keenly interested in details of the blind Joyce, writing lines of the *Wake* on large white sheets in red crayon. They want to read the works of the man who defied convention, his instructors, his religious advisers, his father, and good taste—to become the brightest literary star of his era.

One problem that arises is that of reconciling the inadequate picture we now have of the man himself with the works he produced. Students now in college do not remember Joyce as a living person. His entire generation is receding into history. Gide is gone, Wallace Stevents too, and, as this is written, newspapers carry the story of Mann's death. Mature critics, Joyce's contemporaries, must remember that to this college generation Joyce is no more a living figure than Proust or perhaps Browning. This necessitates not only the biographical reassessment already mentioned, in a broader, more objective, more intimate perspective than what is now available; it requires also, within the next few years, a biographicocritical re-evaluation such as Henry James and Rudyard Kipling have recently undergone. It means also the recognition by college curriculum makers that increased attention should be given to contemporary Irish history, especially for students majoring in English and Irish literature. There is no way to see Joyce intimately and whole unless we place him within the frame of his Irish background. Granted that colleges cannot alter substantially their offerings in history to afford a glimpse of local color for a study of one writer, nevertheless, the entire Celtic renaissance calls for such increased emphasis. Most of the significant writers of this century in English have Irish backgrounds: Yeats, Shaw, Synge, O'Casey, Joyce, Wilde, Moore—the list is long. American students will be poor relations in Irish literary studies until our conservative Departments of English recognize the need.

It is foolish to try to anticipate Joyce's final standing in literary history, if any position could ever be considered final. In any case, ranking of authors is not only out of fashion but may remain so, with the awareness of diversity in taste and temperament. R. P. Blackmur has asserted that no critic can possibly anticipate an artist's fame, for it is established only after considerable time and then mainly through the sense of "inexhaustibility." To datc Joyce gives this sense, whatever his limitations. Whether or not his provocative power, amply demonstrated by this study, will remain in later generations, his place at the center of modern literature is assured. For, as Stuart Gilbert has argued, if not classics in the universal sense, the major works attain classic status in that they represent "the *Weltanschauung* of a period." T. S. Eliot has denominated *Ulysses* "the most considerable work of imagination in English in our time, comparable in importance (though in little else) with the work of Marcel Proust."[103]

Earlier predictions and assessments of the reputation certainly give little encouragement to the literary prophet. As early as 1925, we recall, *Ulysses* had presumably ceased to interest. Max Lerner in 1942 found Joyce no longer important, but placed, "along with Sanskrit, on a shelf of the things that one doesn't get around to because they take too much effort." In 1944 Stonier sensed a slump in England.[104] Yet recent English histories of literature are devoting an increasing amount of space to Joyce.[105]

J. B. Priestley remains unconverted. He repeats Gogarty's conception of the "character parts" played by Irish writers on the small stage of Dublin. Do not the Irish themselves, "even while boasting of this wealth of genius, twinkle sardonically"? And is it not odd for Joyce to show no interest in the other cities he dwelt in but to continue "to dig deeper and deeper into Dublin"? Priestley believes that too many people have accepted the extravagant claims made by admirers. He did not invent the stream-of-consciousness method; his frankness shows courage rather than psychological insight; and the crucial fact is that he neither wrote like a great novelist nor has he been read as one. He remains "a marvellous lord of language" who can play with styles and ideas, "a comic poet in prose" who "will vanish from the highway of Fiction, but will endure as one of the glorious eccentrics, an enchantment to many others."[106]

Frank O'Connor has recently announced the death of the subjective novel, "at least in Europe," and C. P. Snow now regards the whole movement as "the most hopeless cul-de-sac" in the history of fiction, one which is now "as dead as cold potatoes." Even Leon Edel seems somewhat uneasy in his concession that "The vitality of a Proust and a Joyce will suffice for the second half of this century's fiction," a judgment from which Mark Schorer dissents. But how many times has fiction been declared dead and the future of the novel viewed dismally? One recalls Samuel Johnson's confident assertion: "Nothing odd will do long. *Tristram Shandy* did not last." Like Sterne, Joyce refuses to abide the coroner's verdict.[107]

His influence has been regarded as dangerous. When Ransom found it "notoriously bad," he may have been thinking of inevitable imitations by epigones. In England, however, it has been thought that his achievement might have killed the modern novel just as Latin literature had been killed by the immensity of Virgil.[108] But to blame Joyce for the sedulous apes or the timid talents who follow him is manifestly unfair.

One cannot will a masterpiece. The combination of necessary talent, large informing conception, and strong personal motivation is always rare. Philip Toynbee has recently urged that, far from being the dirge of fiction, *Ulysses* is filled with "rich, almost unexplored innovations." Experiment is necessary to the life of any art form, he continues, and the importance of modern issues demands "a novelist in the grand manner."[109]

Certainly there has been no decline in critical interest. With the publication of the *Wake* in 1939 the flood of books and articles on Joyce began, and almost every year since has seen the publication of a major work. Scholarly interest is still rising, with no end in view.

Interestingly enough, most of the new studies are appearing under the imprint of university presses in this country. Indications are, presumably, that Joyce scholarship has now reached the stage of respectability and may even hold out hope of financial reward to publishers who must be fairly certain of their audience before they can afford to go ahead.

Joyce's position in contemporary criticism is in the process of consolidation. The period of extravagant claims and badly printed manifestoes has given way to the stage of enlightened explication of individual works. Now the trend is toward summary and critical evaluation. At least two anthologies are now contemplated: one, an extension of the Givens book, *Two Decades of Criticism;* the other, a collection given over to a reprinting of the most noteworthy explications of significant passages from the works. There is talk of recording for distribution those songs which Joyce liked and used as background for his novels and poetry.

Finally, the James Joyce Society is planning the obvious step, long contemplated, of publishing a James Joyce *Miscellany*. The desire to retain permanently and in easily available form the best of Joyce and criticism of Joyce is quickly observed in any large bookstore. Stuart Gilbert's *James Joyce's "Ulysses,"* which many college students had not been able to obtain or read in the forties, when it became almost a rare book, is now available to readers both in a hard cover reissue by Knopf (1952) and in a popular reprint edition at less than a dollar. The Signet-Mentor paperback edition of *A Portrait* has recently added an introduction by Sean O'Faolain as a further inducement to uninitiated readers. Now that the Slocum-Cahoon *Bibliography* has said the last word on publication of Joyce's own books, the authors are gathering material for a much vaster bibliography of critical writing on the same author. The published manuscript of *Stephen Hero* is being augmented by a considerable number of additional pages of the manuscript, which recently became available. In addition to all this, the libraries of the University of Buffalo and Yale University offer to the serious student large collections of invaluable letters, manuscripts, and other material relating to the study of Joyce.

In this constantly swelling literature about Joyce there is a real danger of the author's becoming more remote and being replaced, as Robert Gorham Davis fears, "by a textbook ideogram of his works." In order to correct the "Narrow Views of Joyce," of which he writes, the repetitious recital of the aesthetic theory, the symbolic correspondences, and the Homeric parallels, it will be necessary to combine a knowledge of the author's environment with that of his temperament and his work. Such a combination of the inner and outer view will have to reckon with the political position of Ireland, the influence of Catholicism, and, perhaps most important of all, the contemporary flight "from the historic sense to the cosmic sense."[110] It may be impossible for any one commentator to combine the insight and knowledge necessary for a final evaluation, but of the many minds that have turned to Joyce during four decades few have not contributed to our understanding. Hence we must regard as parody the Bloomesque catalogue of the traits that Stonier finds common to Joyce and his devotees: revolt against convention, faith in poetic incantation, delight in obscure analogies and symbols, a Rabelaisian humor of pedantry and smut, an encyclopedic mania for inclusiveness, and, finally, a mind like a camera that reveals the world "with extraordinary clarity, but upside down, in the dark."[111] If he be an author to reread rather than to read, Joyce has been and will continue to be reread. He will invite and repel, reward and frustrate. His place in modern letters is secure.

The Symbolist

A more serious question is that of the validity of Joyce's analogical method. Can he be excused from what seems an inveterate habit of idiosyncratic and irresponsible association? Ezra Pound thought the parallels with the *Odyssey* "mere mechanics" that "any blockhead can go back and trace."[112] *Ulysses* is "a monument of obsessive learning," according to

John Lehmann, but "all this elaboration and erudition . . . is almost totally irrelevant to the value of *Ulysses* as a work of art." In trying to escape from the influences that threatened his freedom, Lehmann continues, the author grew more and more preoccupied with the internal levels of consciousness, and "the vast obscurities, the fantastically perverse ingenuities" of the later works became "a new, perhaps a more terrible prison round his freedom."[113] There may be some validity in the comparison with the late Alexandrian writers, long forgotten, but to assume with Francis Russell a like fate for Joyce is to ignore the vitality, humor, and suppressed poetry that permeate his work.[114] More seriously, it is to read out of court the entire symbolist aesthetic, as yet not fully comprehended by readers nor even fully explored by literary critics, but still a modern aspect of an ancient mode of art, enjoying a recognized position in man's cultural heritage.

Symbolism, when better understood and more widely practiced, may not turn out to be the dead end of romantic decadence that it is often assumed to be. New areas of consciousness are developed by mankind, and the creative writer is the pioneer. The symbolic mode of perception, which has languished since the Renaissance, may enjoy a healthy and widespread revival. If so, it will not be the symbolic interpreters, Gilbert, Kenner, and Tindall, who seem eccentric, but the common-sense and often commonplace naturalists. Levin has placed Joyce in the main current of European literature, relating him to the change from naturalism to symbolism during the last half century, and showing how closely the career parellels that of Thomas Mann, from the city (*Dubliners—Buddenbrooks*) to the artist (*Portrait—Death in Venice*), society (*Ulysses—The Magic Mountain*), and myth (*Finnegans Wake—Joseph in Egypt*). Complementary work on the symbolist tradition, the role of depth psychology, and mythology is being carried on by Tindall, while the medieval heritage of symbolism appears in the essays of McLuhan and Kenner.

Joyce has been termed "the most incarnational of artists." When André de Bouchet reviewed the surviving "epiphanies," some twenty slight episodes of Joyce's college days displayed at the Paris Exhibition of 1949, he remarked their "uncanny intensity":

> . . . words, things and beings, indissolubly intertwined,

> resound as through an endless series of mirrors. . . . The most ordinary episode . . . stirs faint and strange echoes which show that the writer already had *something else in mind.*

His whole work is a development and elaboration of the simple epiphany. His career "reflects his pressing need to find a semantic dimension capable of being substituted for the infinite speechless depth of reality."[115]

Wallace Fowlie's brilliant study of the movement finds in modern symbolism "the secularization of medieval Christian man." Pascal, "the poet of the abyss," has Baudelaire, Kierkegaard, Joyce, Eliot, and Mauriac as disciples. Poet and clown seek the Grail, but in their own hearts. The work of Joyce forms a triptych of artist, common man, and humanity, corresponding to, and continuing the cycle of child, adolescent, and artist in Proust. Proust finds his lost paradise in memory but remains in "the hell of modern subjectivism." Joyce reaches toward humanity and attains the purgatory of constant change. Together they have constructed fiction that is "grandiose, architectonic, and profound." The symbolic novel seems the type "most surely destined to survive," for "a work which is not a symbol is quickly consumed and destroyed," while "a pure work, which is a symbol, is protected by its profundity and forbids its own creator, and other men . . . to rid themselves of its deep layers of universal and personal meanings."[116]

J. F. Hendry similarly concludes that the final impression of Joyce is that "of an independent mind involved in the struggle against chaos." The pattern of *Dubliners,* from childhood to maturity and finally to the mystery of death, becomes, in Irene Hendry's words, "a vast Human Tragedy, an epiphany of all mankind."[117] The minute localism of *Ulysses* is projected against the infinities of cosmic space, and Man is the "Fabulous Voyager" of my study, where Joyce's affinities to Sir Thomas Browne, Montaigne, and Pascal are traced. For Tindall, Joyce "found eternity in the historical pattern, the family, and man"; above all, he found it in art, a symbolic "image of the absolute."

The most valuable of recent insights into the orientation of the symbolist aesthetic are the essays by two distinguished Catholic critics, Herbert Marshall McLuhan and Hugh Kenner. McLuhan notes that Joyce "finally was able to complete the work of the symbolists because he discovered how to perfect their insights by means of Aquinas." Not until the roots of his art are found in medieval thought and French symbolist poetry will he be understood; "the feebleness of grasp among Joyce critics is not so much their ignorance of St. Thomas as their half-awareness of what Joyce found in Flaubert, Rimbaud, and Mallarmé." This complex matrix, involving the procession of the Persons of the Trinity, the nature of the Thomist form of argument, the role of language and metaphor, is only beginning to be analyzed.

This aesthetic also reflects the impact upon literature of the other arts, McLuhan has recently demonstrated, pointing out that "Much of the novelty" of Joyce's work "is an illusion resulting from inattention to technical development in the arts." The popular press, with its "spatial manipulation of mental states," its contemporaneity, and its impersonality, was hailed by Mallarmé "as a guide for the new impersonal poetry of suggestion." While *Finnegans Wake* translates "the auditory into the visual" and "time into space," *Ulysses* remains "relatively static and newspaperish." Like the press, it vibrates with the rhetoric of society; like the art of detection, Joyce reconstructs aspects of culture, *Ulysses* in a limited setting of time and space, the *Wake* throughout human existence.[118]

More than forty years of discussion in many countries have been surveyed. We have seen the man compared to figures as diverse as Lucifer and Augustine or Dante and Sterne. Is it time, now, to hear from Joyce himself? In a letter to Harriet Weaver in 1921 he amusingly recounts rumors of being a spy, a cocaine addict, and a victim of insanity. He suggests that "The truth probably is that I am a quite commonplace person undeserving of so much imaginative painting." He admits some truth in the charge of Ulyssean craftiness and selfish cynicism but insists that "it is by no means all of me (nor was it all of Ulysses) and it has been my habit to apply this alleged quality to safeguard my poor creations."[119]

After the analyses, diatribes, apologies, and panegyrics, are we any nearer to a solution of the enigma? And yet the quest goes on. Each investigator of the labyrinth discovers new passages, each is equipped with his own clues, but none can tell which is Ariadne's thread. Even those who, like Den Haan, eschew a solution, finally turn up with their own portraits of the artist. For the witty and learned Hollander, despite his preference for delineating contradictions rather than attempting answers, ends with accepting the puzzle itself as the solution. Joyce is the grin of the Cheshire cat. Like life itself he flows through our fingers. His aloofness stems from scientific curiosity and a need for secretiveness. Experiments with language, depth psychology, and the epiphany are directed to the investigation of the shadowy boundaries that lie between object and sensation, symbol and word. In his dedication to his art he forgot to live, turning ever inward, existing on the accumulated capital of youthful experience. He thus built his mausoleum from the inside out. A tragic monomania impelled him in this gigantic effort. And, Den Haan concludes, if we did penetrate to the center of the pyramid and through the dark corridors did reach the throne room, there, lying in state, would by an empty sarcophagus.

Yet it seems that we are coming closer to the heart of the mystery. These diverse paths appear to be converging, as Gilbert's scholar-artist tends to coalesce with Levin's inheritor of the European tradition, and the humane author of Budgen or Kain seems to move behind Tindall's drama of acceptance, culminating in the geniality of the *Wake*.

Despite the mystery, confusion, and what often seems irresponsible japing, we sense the presence of themes as old as mankind. Beneath the volcanic despair is the awarness of exile and banishment, detected in Shakespeare by Stephen Dedalus. Though the individual remains alone, he becomes conscious of his paternity. Elaborate analogies orchestrate the inherent unity of existence. From the hill, permanent in space, one hears the hither and thithering waters of the river of time. In man and woman and from parent to child flows life's mysterious current. Structural complexities and linguistic pyrotechnics proclaim a single thought, that of the eloquent poem, "Ecce Puer." Inspired by one of those patterns that fascinated the author by their seeming fatality, the lyric celebrates the coincidental death of his father and birth of his grandson. Biblical and Shakespearean echoes suggest Joyce's dependence upon moral and literary tradition. An immediate occurrence has transcendental implications, for in it are united the darkness of the past, the remorse of the present, and a hope for the future.

James Joyce: A Biographical Sketch

James Joyce: A Biographical Sketch

BORN IN DUBLIN in 1882, James Joyce was raised in a large family whose upper-middle-class financial condition steadily worsened. His father, a convivial wit but an irresponsible spendthrift, was reduced to moving the family from one dwelling to another at night in order to avoid creditors. (Penniless but proud, he would always take charge of removing the family crest.) Joyce's mother, pious, well-meaning, but weak, was powerless to help. Nor was the young man's interest in literature and aesthetics calculated to improve the family's fortunes. Either the priesthood, his mother's fond hope, or a clerkship in the Guinness Brewery, as his father suggested, would have been more lucrative.

Despite family poverty, James and his brothers had good educational opportunities. Joyce attended one of the most fashionable Catholic boarding schools, Clongowes Wood in County Kildare, then returned to Dublin for preparatory work at Belvedere and a degree at University College, the school of Cardinal Newman and Gerard Manley Hopkins. The author's later treatment of school days and family life cannot be taken literally, for though Clongowes in the *Portrait* seems far preferable to George Orwell's school in his essay "Such, such were the joys," we must remember to read as fiction what was written as fiction. Far from the stereotyped romantic rebel, Joyce maintained throughout life a love for his father sufficient to enable him to tolerate the elder's foolish improvidence. As a militant young idealist, he was perhaps less patient of his mother's quiet conformity. Yet he was solicitous of his many sisters and displayed an unusual filial piety to friends as well as members of his family. So too the Catholic church always commanded his respect for its intellectual tradition, even though he early lost his faith. He seems to have cherished particularly his brother Stanislaus (1885-1955), encouraging him to live in Trieste with him. There, as professor of English literature at the university, Stanislaus made his career.

One should note Joyce's unusual tastes and abilities. Possessing a fine tenor voice, fortunately preserved in recorded readings, he once competed in the national music contest, in which the winner was John McCormack. No reader can fail to detect the important role music plays, in fact and in spirit, throughout the works. An even more remarkable gift was that of languages—Latin and French as a matter of course; Dano-Norwegian, self-taught, in order to read Ibsen in the original; Italian, ever his favorite, not to speak of the miscellaneous scraps of others that merge in his creative vocabulary. As a student he read extensively. His idols—Newman, Peter, Dante, and Augustine, to mention a few—left indelible marks on his style. He delved into odd bypaths of learning and seems to have been a curious visitor at theosophical meeting sponsored by George William Russell, the poet A. E. Politically he showed some interest in socialism but remained a Parnellite like his father rather than a follower of more militant groups pressing for Irish independence. He was contemptuous of the sentimentalities of the revival, with its recovery of old legends and its classes in Gaelic. Yet even in lack of sympathy for the Dublin of 1900 cannot fail to disguise the fact that it provided the young man with an atmosphere both intellectual and imaginative.

Joyce's early writings testify that his many interests were subordinated to an intense and sometimes arrogant concern about his own career. At the age of nine he wrote a poetic tribute to Parnell, now lost; his first publication, remarkably appearing in Britain's most respected journal when the author was only nineteen years old, was a review of Ibsen's last play; there were poems and numerous manuscript jottings on aesthetics, a lost play dedicated to his own soul, an essay on the Irish poet Mangan, a polemic against the provinciality of the Irish theatre, and the manuscript "A Portrait of the Artist," to be published by its owner, Miss Sylvia Beach. Never in later life did he escape either the subjects of Dublin, family, and church or these early preoccupations with music, language, and literature.

Driven by a frustration that was fostered by the floundering state of Irish politics after the repudiation of Parnell, goaded by what he considered the repressive and stifling atmosphere of Catholic control, and resentful of the cultural limitations of his environment, Joyce left Ireland for what he hoped would be a more congenial career in Europe. After a few months in Paris he returned to his dying mother in Dublin, remaining from April 1903 to October 1904, during which time transpired the day commemorated in *Ulysses,* June 16, 1904—known as "Bloomsday" from the name of the central character, the advertising solicitor Leopold Bloom.

He returned to Europe with Nora Barnacle, whom he later married. They had two children, Giorgio and Lucia. Before the First World War he lived mainly in Trieste, teaching English, where he became a close friend of the businessman-novelist "Italo Svevo," actually Ettore Schmitz, said to be one of the models for Bloom, as his wife Livia was the partial inspiration for the feminine river symbol, Anna Livia Plurabelle, of Joyce's final work. Even while his eyesight worsened, he wrote the books that made him famous.

The publishing history of these works is a complex of misunderstanding. Nine years of haggling with publishers and the destruction of two sets of page proofs preceded the issuance of the short story collection *Dubliners* two weeks before the assassination at Sarajevo in June 1914, the first note of the four-year conflict. Although the years of the World War were scarcely propitious for the launching of a literary career, Joyce's books aroused immediate attention and precipitated a conflict of opinion that has continued to the present. The disputes over a few stories were only a foretaste of twenty years of annoyance to the author. Suppressions, censorships, and piracies continued. Publicity it was, but often of an undesirable and undeserved sort, for the author's name became almost a byword for obscurity and indecency. Nonetheless, Joyce early received support of the most influential and effective kind. Ezra Pound, then campaigning against literary conventionality and sentimentality, was the first champion. He brought Joyce to the attention of Miss Harriet Weaver, editor of the *Egoist* magazine and an alert and informed sponsor of modern expression. She published installments of Joyce's work and subsequently established a considerable fund for his support. *A Portrait of the Artist as a Young Man* (1916), a fine novel of adolescence, was followed by the enigmatic play *Exiles* (1918). Meanwhile Joyce lived in Zurich and labored over *Ulysses,* which Miss Margaret Anderson serialized in part in her magazine, *The Little Review*. Installments appeared from March 1918 until a court injunction halted continuance in the winter of 1920. After the war, Joyce moved to Paris, where *Ulysses* was published in 1922 by a young American, Miss Sylvia Beach. At once a stylistic tour de force, a monument of seemingly inexcusable obscurity, an astonishingly frank psychological document, and a symbol of the dislocations of modern culture, *Ulysses* established Joyce as a writer of great originality and gave the *avant-garde* a hero and a sacred book. It did bring the author some measure of financial security, supplemented by the income from Miss Weaver's gift, but it also began another long struggle with the forces of censorship that the courts did not end until more than a decade later. Throughout the confusions of piracy, protest, and praise Joyce remained aloof, receiving unstinting support from his Parisian friends, among whom should be mentioned the Americans Eugene and Maria Jolas, editors of the experimental magazine *transition,* which published many portions of Joyce's final work, and Stuart Gilbert, retired judge of the British Civil Service of Burma, whose wide classical learning enabled him to elucidate Joyce's use of Homer in *Ulysses* and to defend the author as a meticulous craftsman. Meanwhile, almost blind, continually worried about the mental instability of his daughter, Joyce lived quietly in Paris, working doggedly at *Finnegans Wake,* an epic in dream language, which was published in 1939. With his wife and son he escaped from Paris at the time of the Nazi invasion, but he had scarcely reached Zurich when he succumbed to postoperative pneumonia in January 1941.

Notes

Notes

AUTHORS' NOTE: For the most part, notes that lack title of article, date, or page references refer to material from the Harriet Weaver file of early press notices, prepublication sheets, and broadsides quoting from periodical reviews without exact citation. Many of these circulars were prepared with the advice of James Joyce himself, as his unpublished letters to Harriet Weaver show. All available information has been given in the notes. This highly valuable file, now in the Slocum Collection of Yale University, is used extensively in this book for the first time.

Occasionally the authors have reduced the size of other notes by eliminating nondescriptive titles of articles and by identifying unimportant references either by volume number or by date rather than by giving both. Otherwise, after the first reference to an article in a periodical, only the author's last name, the periodical title, and serial information are given in subsequent citations.

CHAPTER 1

1. Joseph Prescott, "James Joyce: A Study in Words," *PMLA,* LIV (March 1939), 304-15.
2. Donald Davie, "Books in General," *The New Statesman and Nation,* XLVII (April 10, 1954), 473.
3. Robert G. Kelly, "James Joyce: A Partial Explanation," *PMLA,* LXIV (March 1949), 26-39.
4. Brian Nolan, "A Bash in the Tunnel," *Envoy,* V (April 1951), 11.
5. William Bragg Ewald, Jr., *The Masks of Jonathan Swift* (New York: Oxford University Press, 1954).
6. The essay on Mangan is available in Patricia Hutchins, *James Joyce's Dublin* (London: The Grey Walls Press, Ltd., 1950).
7. Herbert Marshall McLuhan, "James Joyce: Trivial and Quadrivial," *Thought,* XXVIII (Spring, 1953), 75-98.
8. Ned Polsky, letter to the editor, *Partisan Review,* XXI (March-April 1954), 240.
9. Frank O'Connor, "A Matter-of-Fact Problem in the Writing of the Novel," *The New York Times Book Review,* December 12, 1954, p. 31.
10. Rudolph Von Abele, "Symbolism and the Student," *College English,* XVI (1955), 424-29.
11. Robert Lynd, *Books and Writers* (London: J. M. Dent and Sons, Ltd., 1952), 147-51, 207-23.
12. Frank O'Connor, *Leinster, Munster, and Connaught* (London: R. Hale, 1950), pp. 30-31.
13. M. J. C. Hodgart, "Work in Progress," *The Cambridge Journal,* VI (October 1952), 23-39.

CHAPTER 2

1. Allanah Harper, "A Magazine and Some People in Paris," *Partisan Review,* IX (July-August 1942), 315.
2. Aidan Higgins, "Aspects of James Joyce," *The Fortnightly,* MXII (n.s.) (April 1951), 265.
3. Elliot Paul, "Farthest North," *The Bookman,* LXXV (May 1932), 157.
4. George Antheil, *Bad Boy of Music* (Garden City: Doubleday, Doran and Company, 1945), p. 146.
5. Margaret Anderson, *My Thirty Years' War: An Autobiography* (New York: Alfred A. Knopf, 1930), p. 244.
6. Djuna Barnes, "James Joyce," *Vanity Fair,* XVIII (April 1922), 65.
7. Ford Madox Ford, *It Was the Nightingale* (Philadelphia: J. B. Lippincott Company, 1933), p. 203.
8. Malcolm Cowley, "The Religion of Art: Readings from the Lives of the Saints," *New Republic,* LXXVII (January 3, 1934), 218-20.
9. James Joyce, unpublished letter to Frank Budgen, dated 9-10-1932, now in the Yale University Library. This letter and all other unpublished letters of Joyce quoted in whole or part in this book are published here with the generous permission of Miss Harriet Weaver and the Administrators of the Joyce Estate. Faber and Faber, Ltd., and The Viking Press have also approved the publication here of these letters. These publishers plan to bring out in the future a volume of Joyce's letters.
10. Antheil, *Bad Boy of Music,* p. 151.
11. *Ibid.,* p. 155.
12. Robert McAlmon, *Being Geniuses Together: An Autobiography* (London: Secker and Warburg, 1938), pp. 14-15.
13. Antheil, *Bad Boy of Music,* p. 152.
14. James Joyce, typewritten letter, unsigned, to "Mr. Huntington," dated 22-5-1932, now in the Yale University Library.
15. Anderson, *My Thirty Years' War,* p. 248.
16. Maria Jolas, "Joyce in 1939-1940," *Mercure de France,* CCCIX (Mai-Août 1950), 48.
17. Stanislaus Joyce, "Early Memories of James Joyce," *The Listener,* XLI (May 26, 1949), 897.
18. Herbert Gorman, *James Joyce* (New York: Rinchart and Company, 1939).
19. James Joyce, unpublished letter to Grant Richards, dated May 20, 1906, now in the New York Public Library. Acknowledgement is gratefully made to the Henry W. and Albert A. Berg Collection of the library as well as to the Administrators of the Joyce Estate, and to The Viking Press and Faber and Faber, Ltd., for permission to quote from the letter.

20. James Joyce, unpublished letter to Grant Richards, dated 2-2-1915, now in the Yale University Library.
21. James Joyce, unpublished letter to Frank Budgen, dated 24-10-1920, in the Yale University Library.
22. James Joyce, unpublished letter to Grant Richards, dated May 20, 1906, in the Henry W. and Albert A. Berg Collection.
23. Alessandro Francini-Bruni, *Joyce spogliato in piazza* (Trieste: La Editoriale Libraria, 1922), p. 30.
24. Barnes, *Vanity Fair,* XVIII (April 1922), 104.
25. Alfred Kerr, "Joyce en Angleterre," *Les Nouvelles litteraires* (January 11, 1936), p. 6.
26. Stanislaus Joyce, *The Listener,* XLI (May 26, 1949), 896.
27. D. S. Mirsky, "Joyce and Irish Literature," *New Masses,* XI (April 3, 1934), 31-32.
28. "Portrait of James Joyce: The Artist in Maturity," ed. W. R. Rodgers, presented over the B.B.C. Third Programme, February 13, 1950.
29. Gerald Griffin, *The Wild Geese: Pen Portraits of Famous Irish Exiles* (London: Jarrolds Publishers, n.d.), p. 24.
30. See Peter Kavanagh's letter in *The New York Times Magazine,* February 28, 1954, p. 6, and accompanying material. See also *ibid.,* February 14, 1954, p. 53, and March 7, 1954, p. 6.
31. Oliver St. John Gogarty, "They Think They Know Joyce," *The Saturday Review of Literature,* XXXIII (March 18, 1950), 6.
32. Mary Colum, "A Little Knowledge of Joyce," *The Saturday Review of Literature,* XXXIII (April 29, 1950), 8.
33. *Ibid., passim.*
34. Gogarty, *The Saturday Review of Literature,* XXXIII (March 18, 1950), 37.
35. J. F. Byrne, *Silent Years: An Autobiography with Memoirs of James Joyce and Our Ireland,* with a Foreword by Harvey Breit (New York: Farrar, Straus and Young, 1953).
36. In *The Irish Homestead,* 1903-1904.
37. See below, Chapter 5.
38. Marvin Magalaner, "Joyce, Nietzsche, and Hauptmann in James Joyce's 'A Painful Case,'" *PMLA,* LXVIII (March 1953), 95-102.
39. For a more extensive treatment of the Joyce-Mangan relationship, see Marvin Magalaner, "James Mangan and Joyce's Dedalus Family," *Philological Quarterly,* XXXI (October 1952), 363-71.
40. James A. Joyce, "James Clarence Mangan," in *St. Stephen's* (University College, Dublin), May 1902. This essay is reproduced by Patricia Hutchins in *James Joyce's Dublin,* pp. 57-59.

41. James Clarence Mangan, "Fragment of an Unfinished Autobiography," in *The Poets and Poetry of Munster* (5th ed.; Dublin: James Duffy and Company, Ltd., n.d.).
42. *Ibid.*, pp. xxxvii-xl.
43. James Joyce, *Dubliners* (New York: The Modern Library, n.d.), pp. 35, 38.
44. James Joyce, *A Portrait of the Artist as a Young Man* (New York: The Modern Library, 1916), pp. 68, 70-71, 75, 93, 175.
45. *A Page of Irish History,* comp. Fathers of the Society of Jesus (Dublin and Cork, 1930).
46. Gorman, *James Joyce,* chaps. 1 and 2; Kelly, *PMLA,* LXIV (March, 1949), 26-39.
47. For biographical data see Gorman's opening chapters; for the Irish political events of this period, see Dorothy Macardle, *The Irish Republic* (London: Victor Gollancz, 1937), and P. S. O'Hegarty, *A History of Ireland Under the Union, 1801-1922* (London: Methuen and Company, Ltd., 1952).
48. O'Hegarty, *History of Ireland,* p. 519.
49. Joyce, *A Portrait,* chap. 1.
50. Henry Harrison, *Parnell Vindicated: The Lifting of the Veil* (New York: Richard R. Smith, Inc., 1931), p. 68.
51. Joyce, *A Portrait,* p. 36.
52. Donald R. Pearce, " 'My Dead King,' The Dinner Quarrel in Joyce's 'Portrait of the Artist,' " *Modern Language Notes,* LXVI (April 1951), 250-51.
53. John J. Slocum and Herbert Cahoon, *A Bibliography of James Joyce (1882-1941)* (New Haven: Yale University Press, 1953), p. 3. (Hereafter cited as Slocum-Cahoon.)
54. Harrison, *Parnell Vindicated,* pp. 94-95.
55. *Ibid.*
56. Maria Jolas, *Mercure de France,* CCIX (Mai-Août, 1950), 45.
57. Herbert Gorman, *James Joyce: His First Forty Years* (New York: B. W. Huebsch, 1925), p. 75.
58. Thomas Merton, *Elected Silence* (Dublin, 1949), pp. 168-69. This book was published in the United States under the title, *The Seven Storey Mountain.*
59. Lloyd Morris, *A Threshold in the Sun* (New York: Harper and Brothers, 1943), p. 244.
60. Morris L. Ernst, *The Best Is Yet* (New York: Harper and Brothers, 1945), p. 118.
61. Stephen-Joyce's mother is best seen in the portrayal of Mrs. Daedalus in *Stephen Hero,* ed. Theodore Spencer (Norfolk, Conn.: New Directions, 1944).
62. Joyce, *Dubliners,* p. 208.
63. This dialogue begins in *A Portrait* on p. 281.

64. James Joyce, unpublished letter to Frank Budgen, dated March 1, 1932, now at Yale University Library.
65. M. D. Zabel, "Wild Goose," *The Nation,* CL (March 9, 1940), 339.
66. G. W. Stonier, *The New Statesman and Nation,* XXI (March 8, 1941), 256.
67. Donagh MacDonagh, *The Dublin Magazine* (October-December 1941), 71.
68. Conal O'Riordan, *Time and Tide* (March 15, 1941); Louise Bogan, *Partisan Review,* VII (1940), 318-20.
69. J. Den Haan, *Joyce, Mythe van Erin* (Amsterdam: De Bezige Bij, 1948), pp. 16-18 *et passim.*
70. "James Joyce's Rebellion," *The Times Literary Supplement* (London), March 1, 1951; S. MacP., *The Bell,* II (August 1941); Mary Colum, "Portrait of the Artist," *The Saturday Review of Literature,* XXI (March 16, 1940), 10.

CHAPTER 3

1. Arthur Symons, *The Nation* (London), LXXIII (October 15, 1907). Thomas Kettle, *The Freeman's Journal* (Dublin), June 1, 1907. See James Joyce, *Chamber Music,* ed. William York Tindall (New York: Columbia University Press, 1954), pp. 18-20, for other appearances of Symons, though Tindall overlooks *Two Worlds' Monthly,* I (1926), 86-92.
2. Slocum-Cahoon, pp. 163-69.
3. Joyce, *Stephen Hero,* ed. Spencer, p. 174.
4. Joyce, *Chamber Music,* ed. Tindall, p. 85*n.*
5. For occasional verse, see Slocum-Cahoon, A2, A7, B22, B23, B26, B27, C104, C106, E16f, E17b.
6. July 23, 1927.
7. M.A., "Lyrics of James Joyce," *New Republic,* XVIII (1919), 191.
8. John Anderson, *Some Questions in Aesthetics* (Sydney: University of Sydney Literary Society, 1932).
9. *The United States Quarterly Book List,* X (1954), 197; Horace Gregory, *New York Herald Tribune,* April 11, 1954; Anthony Kerrigan, "News of Molly Bloom," *Poetry,* LXXXV (1954-1955), 109-12.
10. M. D. Zabel, "The Treasure of Dedalus," *The Nation,* CXLV (October 9, 1937), 382.
11. L. R. Holmes, "Ecce Puer," *Explicator,* November 1954.

CHAPTER 4

1. "Dubliners . . . J. A. Joyce," reader's report prepared for Grant Richards, publisher, now in Houghton Library, Harvard University.
2. Gorman, *James Joyce,* pp. 145 ff.

3. George Russell (A. E.), letter to James Joyce, undated, written on letterhead stationery of *The Irish Homestead,* probably in 1902 or 1903. The letter is in the Yale University Library. The authors acknowledge with thanks the kindness of Mr. Diarmuid Russell and of the library in allowing the letter to be published here.
4. James Joyce, unpublished letter to Grant Richards, dated June 23, 1906, now in the Berg Collection of the New York Public Library, published with the permission of the Administrators of the Joyce Estate and the approval of the Berg Collection.
5. James Joyce, unpublished letter to Grant Richards, dated May 20, 1906, now in the Berg Collection.
6. Joyce, letter to Grant Richards, dated June 23, 1906, in Berg Collection.
7. Gerald Gould, *New Statesman,* June 27, 1914; *The Saturday Review of Literature,* June 20, 1914; *Everyman,* July 4, 1914; *Daily Courier* (Liverpool), July 3, 1914.
8. *Manchester Guardian,* June 24, 1914.
9. *Ezra Pound, The Egoist,* I (July 15, 1914), 267.
10. Harry Levin, *James Joyce: A Critical Introduction* (Norfolk, Conn.: New Directions, 1941), p. 34.
11. V. S. Pritchett, "Current Literature," *The New Statesman and Nation,* XXI (February 15, 1941), 162.
12. H. E. Bates, *The Modern Short Story: A Critical Survey* (London: Thomas Nelson and Sons, Ltd., 1941), pp. 36-41.
13. Elizabeth Bowen, *The Faber Book of Modern Stories* (London: Faber and Faber, Ltd., 1937), p. 8.
14. Louis Cazamian, *Essais en deux langues* (Paris: Henri Didier, Editeur, 1938), p. 48.
15. Louis Golding, *James Joyce* (London: Thornton Butterworth, Ltd., 1933), p. 28.
16. Allen Tate, "Three Commentaries: Poe, James, and Joyce," *The Sewanee Review,* LVIII (Winter 1950), 10; Mary Colum, *From These Roots* (New York: Charles Scribner's Sons, 1938), p. 350.
17. Stanislaus Joyce, *Recollections of James Joyce by His Brother* (New York: The James Joyce Society, 1950), p. 18.
18. Edmund Wilson, *Axel's Castle: A Study in the Imaginative Literature of 1870-1930* (New York: Charles Scribner's Sons, 1931), p. 191.
19. Gorman, *James Joyce,* p. 181.
20. Avrahm Yarmolinsky, "Foreword," to "Chekhov in English: A List of Works by and about Him," by Anna Heifetz, in *Bulletin of The New York Public Library,* LIII (January 1949), 27-28; see also Vivienne C. Koch, "Anton Chekhov," unpublished Master's thesis, Coumbia University, 1933; and Anton Chekhov, "Two Tales from the Russian of Anton Tschechow [*sic*]," *Temple Bar,* CXI (May 1897), 104-13.

The stories in *Temple Bar* are "The Biter Bit" and "Sorrow."

21. Anton Chekhov, "Darling: A Story by A. Tchekhof [*sic*]," trans. A.B. and E.A., with an Afterword by Leo Tolstoy, *The Fortnightly Review*, CCCCLXXVII (September 1, 1906), 560-71. This periodical had also published Chekhov's "In Exile" in September 1903.
22. Chekhov, *The Black Monk*, ed. R. Long (London: Duckworth and Company, 1903).
23. See William Gerhardi, *Anton Chekhov: A Critical Study* (New York: Duffield and Company, 1923).
24. Matthew Josephson, *The Personal Papers of Anton Chekhov* (New York: Lear Publishers, 1948), p. 10.
25. Chekhov, in a letter to Gorki, quoted in Gerhardi, *Anton Chekhov*, pp. 146, 147.
26. Evelyn May Albright, "Introduction" to Chekhov, *Short Stories*, trans. Constance Garnett (New York: The Macmillan Company, 1932), p. x.
27. Chekhov, *The Black Monk*, pp. 220-21.
28. Ivan Turgenev, *A Sportsman's Sketches*, trans. Constance Garnett (New York: The Macmillan Company, 1917).
29. George Moore, *The Untilled Field* (London: William Heinemann, 1915); the book was first published in 1903.
30. Gustave Flaubert, *Bouvard et Pécuchet* (Paris, 1885).
31. *Ibid.*, p. 2.
32. James Joyce, *Dubliners*, p. 208.
33. Unsigned interview in a Dublin newspaper, discovered by Richard M. Kain in the files of the National Library in Dublin.
34. Vernon Louis Parrington, *Main Currents in American Thought*, "Addenda" to Vol. III (New York: Harcourt, Brace and Company, 1927), 323-27.
35. William York Tindall, *James Joyce: His Way of Interpreting the Modern World* (New York: Charles Scribner's Sons, 1950), p. 108 ff.
36. William Butler Yeats, "The Tables of the Law" and "The Adoration of the Magi," in *The Collected Works in Verse & Prose of William Butler Yeats* (Stratford-on-Avon: Shakespeare Head Press, 1908). These stories first appeared in 1897.
37. *Ibid.*, p. 143.
38. Joyce, *Stephen Hero*, p. 211.
39. *Ibid.*, p. 213; see also Tindall, *James Joyce*, p. 120.
40. James Joyce, "The Sisters," *The Irish Homestead*, X (August 13, 1904), 676-77. The La Hune *Catalogue* (Paris: Librairie La Hune, 1949) lists and describes many epiphanies which Joyce had scribbled down but which he never made into full-length stories.
41. This manuscript draft is now in the James Joyce Collection of the Yale University Library.

42. The historical associations and contemporary description of the Ringsend-Pigeonhouse section of Dublin are adequately presented in Weston St. John Joyce's *The Neighbourhood of Dublin: Its Topography, Antiquities and Historical Associations* (Dublin: M. H. Gill and Son, Ltd., 1939), p. 2 ff.
43. James Joyce, *Ulysses* (New York: The Modern Library, 1934), p. 42.
44. *Ibid.*, p. 20.
45. Cleanth Brooks and Robert Penn Warren, *Understanding Fiction* (New York: F. S. Crofts and Company, 1947), pp. 420-23.
46. James Joyce, *James Clarence Mangan* (London: Ulysses Book Shop, 1930); this essay was published originally in *St. Stephen's* (Dublin), in May 1902.
47. *Ibid.*
48. From Yeats's "September 1913" in *Collected Poems* (New York: The Macmillan Company, 1947).
49. Joyce, *A Portrait*, p. 137.
50. Joyce changed the name of this story from "Hallow Eve" to "Clay." See Gorman, *James Joyce*, p. 145.
51. Robert Chambers, *The Book of Days: A Miscellany of Popular Antiquities, etc.* (Edinburgh, 1864), II, 519.
52. E. H. Sechrist, *Red Letter Days* (Philadelphia: Macrae-Smith Company, 1940), p. 179. I believe that Mr. Leonard Albert of Hunter College first discussed witchcraft in "Clay" with me.
53. Joyce, *Ulysses*, p. 307.
54. Stanislaus Joyce, "The Background to 'Dubliners,'" *The Listener*, LI (March 25, 1954), 526-27.
55. Eugene Jolas, "My Friend James Joyce," in *James Joyce: Two Decades of Criticism*, ed. Sean Givens (New York: The Vanguard Press, 1948), p. 16. (Hereafter cited as *Two Decades.*)
56. David Daiches, *The Novel and the Modern World* (Chicago: The University of Chicago Press, 1939), p. 92.
57. Stanislaus Joyce, *Recollections*, p. 20.
58. Tate, *The Sewanee Review*, LVIII (Winter 1950), 5.
59. John Macy, *The Critical Game* (New York: Boni and Liveright, 1922), p. 322.
60. Golding, *James Joyce*, p. 30.
61. Joyce, *Dubliners*, p. 254.
62. *Ibid.*, pp. 255-56.
63. *Ibid.*, p. 262.
64. *Ibid.*, p. 283.
65. *Ibid.*, p. 284.
66. Joyce, *A Portrait*, p. 104.
67. Joyce, *Ulysses*, p. 109.
68. *Ibid.*, p. 68.
69. Tindall, *James Joyce*, pp. 30-31, 116.

70. Joyce, *Dubliners,* pp. 246, 259.
71. Joyce, *Ulysses,* p. 143; *Finnegans Wake* (New York: The Viking Press, 1939), p. 8.
72. Joyce, *Dubliners,* pp. 287-88.
73. David Daiches, "James Joyce: The Artist as Exile," *College English,* II (December 1940), 202.
74. Tate, *The Sewanee Review,* LVIII (Winter 1950), 15.
75. Richard Levin and Charles Shattuck, "First Flight to Ithaca," in *Two Decades,* ed. Givens, pp. 47-94; the article first appeared in *Accent,* Winter 1944.
76. *Ibid.,* p. 53.
77. *Ibid.,* p. 50.
78. James Joyce, unpublished letter to Grant Richards, dated May 20, 1906, now in the Berg Collection.
79. Levin and Shattuck, in *Two Decades,* ed. Seon Givens, p. 63.
80. Tindall, *James Joyce;* Richard Ellmann, "The Limits of Joyce's Naturalism," *The Sewanee Review,* LXIII (1955), 567-75.

CHAPTER 5

1. Harriet Weaver, *The Egoist,* III (March 1, 1916), 35.
2. *The Athenaeum,* February 1917.
3. *Post* (Birmingham), February 21, 1917; *Everyman,* February 23, 1917; *The Freeman's Journal* (Dublin), April 7, 1917; *The Independent,* May 5, 1917; *Weekly Times* (Manchester), March 3, 1917.
4. *The Irish Booklover,* VIII (1916), 9-10.
5. *The Bellman,* March 3, 1917.
6. *The Sphere,* IV, 74.
7. Diego Angeli, *The Egoist,* February 1918.
8. Clippings from the *Herald* (Boston); *Cambrian News,* August 16, 1918; and *The Cambridge Review.*
9. *Eastern Morning News,* February 28, 1917; *Land and Water; New Age,* July 12, 1917.
10. W. N. P. Barbellion, *A Last Diary* (London: Chatto and Windus, 1920), pp. 35, 92-93, 95; see also *Gazette* (Birmingham), March 29, 1917; *The Nation,* CIV, 403; *The English Review,* XXIV, 478; *The Irish World,* March 15, 1919.
11. J. C. Squire, *The Dublin Review,* CLXVI, 137; *Irish Times,* April 14, 1917.
12. H. G. Wells, *New Republic,* X (March 10, 1917), 158.
13. *The Catholic World,* CV (June 1917), 395-97.
14. *Guardian* (Manchester), March 3, 1917; *The English Review,* XXIV, 278; *The Nation,* CIV, 403; *New Ireland,* March 3, 1917.
15. Francis Hackett, *New Republic,* X (1917), 138; Ernest Boyd, *New Ireland,* March 3, 1917; *Evening Post* (Chicago), March 30, 1917; *Literary Review,* December 17, 1921.

16. *Reedy's Mirror,* February 3, 1917.
17. James G. Huneker, *Unicorns* (New York: Charles Scribner's Sons, 1917), pp. 187-94.
18. Padraic Colum, *Pearson's Magazine,* May 1918.
19. *Evening Post* (Chicago), March 30, 1917; *The Freeman's Journal,* April 7, 1917; *Herald* (Glasgow), March 8, 1917.
20. Ezra Pound, *The Future,* May 1918.
21. Margaret Anderson, ed., *"The Little Review" Anthology* (New York: Hermitage House, 1953), reference to CXXXI, 101.
22. H. L. Mencken, *Smart Set,* LII (August 1917).
23. Joyce, *Stephen Hero,* pp. 59-60.
24. Richard M. Kain, "A Joyce Bibliography," *The Sewanee Review,* XLI (Autumn 1953), 721.
25. *Literary World,* March 1, 1917; *The Catholic World,* CV, 395-97; *The Future,* June 1917; *Herald* (Glasgow), March 8, 1917; *Evening Post* (Chicago), May 3, 1918.
26. Francis Hackett, *New Republic,* X, 138; *Daily Post* (Liverpool), March 7, 1917.
27. *The Times Literary Supplement* (London), March 1, 1917; *Guardian* (Manchester), March 2, 1917.
28. T. Corcoran, *The Clongowes Record: 1814-1932* (Dublin: Browne and Nolan, Ltd., n.d.), p. 163 *et passim.*
29. Joyce, *A Portrait,* pp. 74, 11, 26.
30. In *Two Decades,* ed. Givens, p. 137.
31. Joyce, *A Portrait,* p. 2.
32. *Ibid.,* p. 3.
33. *Ibid.,* pp. 10, 52-54.
34. *Ibid.,* pp. 85-91.
35. This ingenious explanation is offered by Dr. Julian Kaye in an article published in *Modern Language Notes.*
36. Joyce, *A Portrait,* p. 110; Sir Edward Bulwer-Lytton, *The Lady of Lyons: or Love and Pride: A Play in Five Acts* (New York, 1846).
37. Joyce, *A Portrait,* p. 112; I am indebted to Dr. Julian Kaye, who identified Claude Melnotte for me as the hero of the play.
38. Joyce, *Ulysses,* pp. 340-76.
39. Joyce, *Dubliners,* pp. 33-41.
40. *A Portrait,* p. 68.
41. *Ibid.*
42. *Ibid.,* p. 73.
43. *Ibid.,* pp. 111-12.
44. Bulwer-Lytton, *The Lady of Lyons,* p. 16.
45. *Ibid.,* pp. 16-17.
46. *Ibid.,* p. 17.
47. Harry Levin, *James Joyce: A Critical Introduction,* chap. 3.
48. *A Portrait,* pp. 196, 192, 188.
49. *Ibid.,* p. 199.

50. C. G. Anderson, "The Sacrificial Butter," *Accent,* XII (Winter 1952), 3-13.
51. Hugh Kenner, "The Portrait in Perspective," in *Two Decades,* ed. Givens. See especially pp. 142-43 *et passim.*
52. Dorothy Van Ghent, *The English Novel: Form and Function* (New York: Rinehart and Company, 1953), especially pp. 263-76.
53. Irene Hendry, "Joyce's Epiphanies," in *Two Decades,* ed. Givens, p. 38 *et passim.*
54. A. D. Hope, "The Esthetic Theory of James Joyce," *Australasian Journal of Psychology and Philosophy,* XXI (1943), 93-114.
55. Herbert Marshall McLuhan, "Joyce, Aquinas, and the Poetic Process," *Renascence,* IV (Autumn 1951), 3-11.
56. Haskell Block, "The Critical Theory of James Joyce," *The Journal of Aesthetics and Art Criticism,* VIII (March 1950), 172-84.
57. Frank L. Kunkel, "Beauty in Aquinas and Joyce," *The Thomist,* XI (1949), 261-71.
58. Ellsworth Mason, "Joyce's Categories," *The Sewanee Review,* LXI (Summer 1953), 427-32.
59. Stuart Gilbert, "James Joyce," in *Two Decades,* ed. Givens, pp. 459-60.
60. Geddes MacGregor, "Artistic Theory in James Joyce," *Life and Letters,* LIV (1947), 18-27.
61. Virginia Woolf, "Mr. Bennett and Mrs. Brown," a pamphlet published in London, 1924.
62. Samuel Butler, *The Way of All Flesh* (New York: The Modern Library, n.d.), p. 83.
63. *A Portrait,* pp. 79-80.
64. Butler, *Way of All Flesh,* pp. 88 and 107.
65. *A Portrait,* p. 3.
66. Butler, *Way of All Flesh,* p. 128.
67. *A Portrait,* pp. 293, 207, 276, 279.
68. James T. Farrell, "Joyce's *A Portrait of the Artist as a Young Man,*" in *Two Decades,* ed. Givens, pp. 175-97.

CHAPTER 6

1. Gorman, *James Joyce,* p. 227.
2. *Ibid.,* pp. 71-73.
3. Richard M. Kain, *Fabulous Voyager: James Joyce's "Ulysses"* (Chicago: The University of Chicago Press, 1947), pp. 53, 57-58.
4. Gorman, *James Joyce,* p. 70.
5. Vivienne Koch Macleod, "The influence of Ibsen on Joyce," *PMLA,* LX (1945), 879-98, and "The influence of Ibsen on Joyce: Addendum," *ibid.,* LXII (1947), 573-80. James T.

Farrell, " 'Exiles' and Ibsen," in *Two Decades,* ed. Givens, pp. 95-131.
6. Joyce, *Stephen Hero,* ed. Spencer, pp. 83-87, 91-98, 40, 103, 41.
7. George Jean Nathan, "The Theater," *American Mercury,* IV (April 1925), 499-504.
8. Anderson, ed., *"The Little Review" Anthology,* pp. 215-21.
9. *The Catholic World,* CVIII (1918), 404; "The Mind to Suffer," *The Times Literary Supplement* (London), August 25, 1918; Francis Hackett, *New Republic,* XVI (1918), 318; Padraic Colum, "James Joyce as a Dramatist," *The Nation,* CVII (1918), 430; Ezra Pound, "Mr. James Joyce and the Modern Stage . . . ," *The Drama,* VI (February 1916), 122-32.
10. Desmond MacCarthy, "Exiles," *New Statesman,* XI (1918), 492-93; also in his *Humanities* (New York: Oxford University Press, 1954), pp. 88-93.
11. Golding, *James Joyce,* p. 81.
12. Joseph Wood Krutch, "Figures of the Dawn," *The Nation,* CXX (1925), 272.
13. Gorman, *James Joyce: His First Forty Years,* p. 111.
14. Joyce, *Exiles,* ed. Francis Fergusson (New York: New Directions, 1945), pp. v-xviii.
15. Bernard Bandler, "Joyce's 'Exiles,' " *The Hound & Horn,* VI (1933), 266-85.
16. Hugh Kenner, "Joyce's 'Exiles,' " *The Hudson Review,* V (1952), 389-403.
17. Joyce, *Stephen Hero,* ed. Spencer, p. 174.
18. Joyce, *Exiles,* ed. Padraic Colum (New York: The Viking Press, 1951), p. 11.
19. John Kelleher, review of Colum edition, *Furioso,* VII (Spring 1952), 65-67.

CHAPTER 7

1. Arthur Rimbaud, *A Season in Hell,* trans. Louise Varese, in *Baudelaire, Rimbaud, Verlaine . . . ,* ed. Joseph Bernstein (New York: Citadel, 1947), p. 181.
2. Gorman, *James Joyce,* p. 86.
3. Tindall, *James Joyce,* p. 110.
4. Arthur Symons, *The Symbolist Movement in Literature* (New York: E. P. Dutton, 1919), pp. 89, 133, 181, 272, 200, 267-68, 328-29.
5. Wilson, *Axel's Castle,* p. 203.
6. Newport J. D. White, "A Short Catalogue of English Books in Archbishop Marsh's Library, Dublin, Printed before MDCXLI," Bibliographical Society, *Catalogues of English Books, Number 1* (London: Oxford University Press, 1905).

7. Eileen Ellenbogen, "Leopold Bloom—Jew," *The Changing World* (Winter 1947-1948), 79-86; Leo Shapiro, "The Zion Motif in Joyce's 'Ulysses,'" *Jewish Frontier* (September 1946), pp. 14-17; Marvin Magalaner, "The Anti-Semitic Limerick Incidents and Joyce's 'Bloomsday,'" *PMLA*, LXVIII (1953), 1219-23; Wyndham Lewis, *Blasting and Bombardiering* (London: Eyre and Spottiswoode, 1937), p. 246; Frank Budgen, "James Joyce," in *Two Decades*, ed. Givens, p. 23.
8. Larbaud, quoted by Stuart Gilbert, *James Joyce's "Ulysses"* (London: Faber and Faber, Ltd., 1930; New York: Alfred A. Knopf, 1931), pp. 24-25.
9. Levin, *James Joyce: A Critical Introduction,* p. 93.
10. For attacks, see C.C.M., *The Dublin Review,* CLXXI (October-December 1922), 273-76; Alec Brown, "Joyce's 'Ulysses' and the Novel," *The Dublin Magazine,* IX (January-March 1934), 41-50; Auguste Bailly, quoted by Gilbert, *Joyce's "Ulysses,"* p. 27; Wyndham Lewis, *The Art of Being Ruled* (New York: Harper and Brothers, 1926), p. 414; Leon Edel, *The Psychological Novel* (New York: J. B. Lippincott Company, 1955), pp. 157-82; George Moore, quoted in Aristide Marie, *Le Forêt symboliste* (Paris: Firmin-Didot et Cie, 1936), pp. 136-37.
11. Sergei Eisenstein, "An American Tragedy," *Close-Up,* X (June 1933), 121.
12. David Daiches, *New Literary Values* (Edinburgh: Oliver and Boyd, 1936), p. 76.
13. For predecessors, see Levin, *James Joyce: A Critical Introduction,* pp. 91-93, Kain, *Fabulous Voyager,* pp. 18-19; Mary Colum, *Life and the Dream* (Garden City: Doubleday, Doran and Company, 1947), pp. 394-95; see answer in Edel, *Psychological Novel,* p. 44; Édouard Dujardin, *Le Monologue intérieur . . .* (Paris: Messein, 1931).
14. Richard Aldington, "A Forbidden Masterpiece," *Sunday Referee* (London), June 29, 1930.
15. Joseph Warren Beach, "The Novel from James to Joyce," *The Nation,* CXXXII (1931), 634-36.
16. Tindall, *James Joyce,* p. 30.
17. Padraic Colum, "Dublin's Library and Joyce's 'Ulysses,'" *New Republic,* May 16, 1955. John Eglinton, "The Beginnings of Joyce," in *The Portable Irish Reader* (New York: The Viking Press, 1946).
18. Levin, *James Joyce: A Critical Introduction,* p. 89.

CHAPTER 8

1. Margaret Anderson, *The Little Review,* February 1918, in Anderson, ed., *"The Little Review" Anthology,* p. 176.
2. [Virginia Woolf], "Modern Novels," *The Times Literary*

Supplement, April 10, 1919; as "Modern Fiction," in *The Common Reader* (London: L. and V. Woolf, 1925).

3. Burton Rascoe, *News* (Chicago), August 2, 16, 1922.
4. A. R. Orage, "The Too Clever," *The New Age,* June 6, 1918, and "America Regressing," *ibid.,* April 28, 1921; both in *Readers and Writers* (New York: Alfred A. Knopf, 1922), pp. 31-33, 171-73; T. S. E[liot], "A Foreign Mind," *The Athenaeum,* July 4, 1919.
5. "Paris Week by Week," *Observer,* April 17, 1921.
6. *The Outlook,* July 16, 1921.
7. Ford Madox Ford, *Thus to Revisit* (London: Chapman and Hall, 1921), pp. 64-65.
8. Richard Aldington, "The Influence of Mr. James Joyce," *The English Review,* XXXII (April 1921), 333-41; in Aldington, *Literary Studies and Reviews* (New York: Dial Press, 1924), pp. 192-207.
9. Scofield Thayer, "Sketch," *The Dial,* LXV (1918), 201-3.
10. Valéry Larbaud, "James Joyce," *La Nouvelle revue française,* XXIV (April 1922), 386-409; translation in *Criterion,* I (October 1922), 94-103.
11. *Chicago Tribune* (Paris edition), February 13, 1922; *Daily Courier* (Liverpool), April 6, 1922; *Evening News* (London), April 8, 1922; *London Opinion,* April 8, 1922; *Herald* (Glasgow), April 27, 1922; *Scots Pictorial,* May 12, 1922; *Evening Standard* (London), May 26, 1922; *The Bookman,* LV (1922), 505; *New York Herald* (Paris edition), April 24, 1922; *Daily Courier* (Liverpool), June 15, 1922; *Yorkshire Post,* December 6, 1922; *Tatler,* February 7, 1923; *The Dial,* LXXII (1922), 189; *The Bookman,* LIX (1924), 518; *The Daily Express* (London), December 17, 1925.
12. Edmund Wilson, "An Introduction to James Joyce," *The Dial,* LXXVII (November 1924), 430.
13. Joseph Collins, M.D., "James Joyce's Amazing Chronicle," *The New York Times Book Review,* May 28, 1922; reprinted in *The Doctor Looks at Literature* (New York: Harper and Brothers, 1923), pp. 35-60; N. P. Dawson, "The Cuttlefish School of Writers," *Forum,* LXIX (1923), 1174-84; *Teacher's World,* May 10, 1922; Shane Leslie, "Ulysses," *The Quarterly Review,* CCXXXVIII (October 1922), 219-34.
14. "Affable Hawk," *New Statesman,* XX (April 17, 1923), 775.
15. Henry Seidel Canby, "Crazy Literature," *Literary Review,* July 22, 1922.
16. "Affable Hawk," *New Statesman,* XXV (1925), 574.
17. "Aramis," *The Sporting Times,* April 1, 1922.
18. "Canis Domini," *The Dublin Review,* CLXXI (1922), 112-19; Alfred Noyes, *Sunday Chronicle* (Manchester), October 29, 1922; James Douglas, "Beauty—and the Beast," *The Sunday Express* (London), May 28, 1922.
19. Ezra Pound, "James Joyce et Pécuchet," *Mercure de France,*

CLVI (June 1, 1922), 307-20; trans. Fred Bornhauser, *Shenandoah,* III (Autumn 1952), 9-20.

20. T. S. Eliot, "'Ulysses,' Order, and Myth," *The Dial,* LXXV (November 1923), 480-83; in *Two Decades,* ed. Givens.
21. Sisley Huddleston, "James Joyce and 'Ulysses,'" *Observer,* March 5, 1922.
22. Edmund Wilson, "'Ulysses,'" *New Republic,* XXXI (July 1922), 164-66.
23. "Lawrence K. Emery," "The 'Ulysses' of Mr. James Joyce," *The Klaxon,* Winter 1923-1924.
24. P. S. O'Hegarty, "Mr. Joyce's 'Ulysses,'" *The Separatist,* September 2, 1922.
25. Eimar O'Duffy, "'Ulysses,'" *The Irish Review,* December 9, 1922.
26. Arnold Bennett, "Concerning James Joyce's 'Ulysses,'" *The Bookman,* LV (August 1922), 567; also in *Things That Have Interested Me* (New York: Doran and Company, 1936), pp. 185-94.
27. Katherine Mansfield, *Letters* (London: Constable and Company, Ltd., 1932), pp. 434-35, 436, 464.
28. [George William Russell], *The Living Torch* (New York: The Macmillan Company, 1938), pp. 139-40.
29. Yeats, in Joseph Hone, *W. B. Yeats* (New York: The Macmillan Company, 1943), pp. 371, 476; Norman Jeffares, *W. B. Yeats, Man and Poet* (New Haven: Yale University Press, 1949), p. 281; W. B. Yeats, *Wheels and Butterflies* (London: Macmillan and Company, 1934), p. 65.
30. Golding, *James Joyce;* Bernard Shaw and Archibald Henderson, "Literature and Science," *The Fortnightly Review,* CXXII (1933), 504-23.
31. Grant Richards, *A. E. Housman* (London: Oxford University Press, 1941), pp. 197, 251.
32. D. H. Lawrence, *Phoenix* (New York: The Viking Press, 1936), pp. 517, 518.
33. *The Letters of D. H. Lawrence,* ed. Aldous Huxley (New York: The Viking Press, 1932), p. 750.
34. Edmund Wilson, ed., *The Crack-up* (New York: New Directions, 1945), pp. 260, 262.
35. D. M. Curtnesse, "The English Novel Since 1914," *The New Age,* November 29, 1923; "Mr. James Joyce," *Daily Mail* (London), April 17, 1922; George Slocombe, "The Week in Paris," *Daily Herald* (London), March 17, 1922.
36. Mary Colum, "The Confessions of James Joyce," *Freeman,* July 19, 1922; in *The Freeman Book* (New York: B. W. Huebsch, 1925).
37. John Middleton Murry, "Mr. Joyce's 'Ulysses,'" *The Nation* (London), XXXI (1922), 124; H. C. Harwood, "Novels: 1922—Retrospect," *The Outlook,* December 30, 1922; J. M. Hone, "A Letter from Ireland," *The London Mercury,* V

(January 1922), 306-8; *Herald* (Glasgow), September 1, 1923; Curtnesse, *The New Age,* November 29, 1923; Gilbert Seldes, " 'Ulysses,' " *The Nation,* CXV (August 1922), 211-12.

38. Cecil Maitland, "Mr. Joyce and the Catholic Tradition," *The New Witness,* August 4, 1922; G. K. Chesterton, "An Extraordinary Argument," *ibid.,* August 18, 1922; letters, *ibid.,* August 11, 25, September 1, 8, 15, 1922.
39. Edmund Wilson, "An Odyssey in Expressionism," *Evening Sun* (Baltimore), August 5, 1922.
40. S. P. B. Mais, "An Irish Rebel: And Some Flappers," *The Daily Express* (London), March 25, 1922; *Daily Telegraph* (Sheffield), September 12, 1923; Slocombe, "The Week in Paris," *Daily Herald* (London), March 17, 1922; Aleister Crowley, "The Genius of Mr. James Joyce," *The New Pearson's,* July 1923.
41. Curtnesse, *The New Age,* November 29, 1923; Ernest Boyd, "The Expressionism of James Joyce," *The New York Tribune,* May 28, 1922; Matthew Josephson, "One Thousand and One Nights in a Bar-Room," *Broom,* September 1922; *Evening Transcript* (Boston), July 10, 1922; *New York Herald* (Paris edition), April 24, 1922; *Chicago Tribune* (Paris edition), February 17, April 6, 1924; Ford Madox Ford, "*Ulysses* and the Handling of Indecencies," *The English Review,* XXXV (December 1922), 538-48, and "A Haughty and Proud Generation," *Yale Review,* XI (n.s.) (July 1922), 702-17; Stephen Gwynn, "Modern Irish Literature," *Guardian Commercial* (Manchester), March 15, 1923.
42. Herbert Marshall McLuhan, "A Survey of Joyce Criticism," *Renassence,* IV (Autumn 1951), 12-18.
43. Padraic Colum, review of Duff, *The Spectator,* June 18, 1932, and *Contempo,* February 15, 1934.
44. Arthur Symons, *Two Worlds' Monthly,* I, No. 1 (1926), 86-92; Aldous Huxley, quoted by Lefevre in *Stream,* July, 1931, thence by Anderson, *Some Questions in Aesthetics* (1932); "John Carruthers" [John Y. T. Greig], *Scheherazade* (London: K. Paul, Trench, Trubner, 1927), pp. 12-13; Cyril Connolly, "The Position of Joyce," *Life and Letters,* II (April 1929), 273-90, and in *The Condemned Playground* (New York: The Macmillan Company, 1945).
45. *The Times* (London), December 14, 16, 19, 21, 22, 24, 1931; Alfred Noyes, *Two World's for Memory* (Philadelphia: J. B. Lippincott Company, 1953), pp. 218-23.
46. Robert Cantwell, "Books and Reviews," *New Outlook,* CLXIII (March 1934), 57; Padraic Colum, " 'James Joyce's *Ulysses*' by Stuart Gilbert," *The Saturday Review of Literature,* X (January 27, 1934), 433; in Henry Seidel Canby, ed., *Designed for Reading* (New York: The Macmillan Company, 1934); Horace Gregory, "Joyce's *Ulysses* No Longer a

Banned Book," *New York Herald Tribune Books,* January 21, 1934; Lewis Gannett, *New York Herald Tribune,* January 25, 1934; Gilbert Seldes, "True to Type . . . ," *Journal* (New York), January 27, 1934; Lloyd Morris, "James Joyce," *The Sunday Review, Daily Eagle* (Brooklyn), January 21, 1934; William Troy, "Stephen Dedalus and James Joyce," *The Nation,* CXXXVIII (February 14, 1934), 187-88; Robert Cantwell, "The Influence of James Joyce," *New Republic,* LXXVII (December 27, 1933), 200-1.

47. John Riddell, "The People's Joyce," *Vanity Fair,* June 1934.
48. Lewis, *The Art of Being Ruled,* pp. 413-15.
49. Hugh Kenner, "Joyce's Anti-Selves," *Shenandoah,* IV (Spring 1953), 24-41.
50. McLuhan, *Renascence,* IV (Autumn 1951), 14.
51. Wyndham Lewis, *Time and Western Man* (London: Chatto and Windus, 1927).
52. Gerald Gould, *The English Novel of Today* (London: J. Castie, 1924); Gerald Bullett, *Modern English Fiction* (London: H. Jenkins, Ltd., 1926); E. M. Forster, *Aspects of the Novel* (New York: Harcourt, Brace and Company, 1927); A. C. Ward, *Twentieth Century Literature* (London: Methuen, 1928), *The Nineteen Twenties* (London: Methuen, 1930); Frank Swinnerton, *The Georgian Literary Scene* (New York: Farrar and Rinehart, 1935); George Samson, *The Concise Cambridge History of English Literature* (New York: The Macmillan Company, 1941); Cornelius Weygandt, *A Century of the English Novel* (New York: Century, 1925); Walter L. Myers, *The Later Realism* (Chicago: The University of Chicago Press, 1927); Wilbur L. Cross, *The Modern English Novel,* (New Haven: Yale University Press, 1928); Carl Grabo, *The Technique of the Novel* (New York: Charles Scribner's Sons, 1928); Grant Knight, *The Novel in English* (New York: Farrar and Rinehart, 1931); J. W. Cunliffe, *English Literature in the Twentieth Century* (New York: The Macmillan Company, 1933); Philo Buck, *Directions in Contemporary Literature* (New York: Oxford 1942).
53. Harvey Wickham, *The Impuritans* (New York: Lincoln MacVeagh, 1929), pp. 235-90.
54. See also C. D. McCole, *Lucifer at Large* (New York: Longmans, Green and Company, 1937) for a virulent attack.
55. E. M. Forster, *The New York Times,* June 19, 1949.
56. Paul Elmer More, "James Joyce," *American Review,* V (May 1935), 129-57; in *On Being Human* (Princeton: Princeton University, 1936), pp. 69-96.
57. Michael Lennon, "James Joyce," *The Catholic World,* CXXXII (March 1931), 641-52.
58. Rebecca West, "The Strange Case of James Joyce," *The Bookman,* LXVIII (September 1928), 9-23, and *The Strange Necessity* (London: Jonathan Cape, 1928), pp. 13-198;

Nathan Halper, "James Joyce and the Russian General," *Partisan Review,* XVIII (July-August 1951), 424-31.

59. R. Miller-Budnitskaya, "James Joyce's 'Ulysses,'" *Dialectics,* No. 5 (1938), 6-26.
60. *New Republic,* LXXIX (1934), 190; Mirsky, *New Masses,* April 3, 1934, and "A Communist on Joyce," *The Living Age,* CXLVII (1934), 268-70.
61. James T. Farrell, *A Note on Literary Criticism* (New York: Vanguard Press, 1936), p. 86.
62. Van Wyck Brooks, *Opinions of Oliver Allston* (New York: E. P. Dutton and Company, 1941), pp. 225-26; Max Lerner, "The Joyce We Need," *New Republic,* CVII (September 28, 1942), 386.
63. Jack Lindsay, "James Joyce," in *Scrutinies,* ed. Edgell Rickword (London: Wishart, 1931), II, 99-122: Desmond MacCarthy, *Criticism* (London: Putnam and Company, Ltd., 1932), pp. 296-311, and *Memories* (London: Oxford University Press, 1953), pp. 113-20; F. R. Leavis, *The Great Tradition* (New York: George W. Stewart, Publishers, Inc., 1949), pp. 25-26; George Every, in F. W. Martin, ed., *The New Spirit* (London: Dodson, Dennis, Ltd., 1946), pp. 54-57.
64. Edwin Muir, "James Joyce," in *Transition . . .* (New York: The Viking Press, 1926).
65. Edwin Muir, *The Structure of the Novel* (London: L. and V. Woolf, 1928), p. 127.
66. Ivan Goll, "The Homer of Our Time," *Die Literarische Welt,* June 17, 1927, and in *The Living Age,* CCCXXXIII (August 15, 1927), 316-20.
67. Connolly, *The Condemned Playground,* pp. 1-15, reprinted from *Life and Letters,* II (April 1929), 273-90.
68. *The Times Literary Supplement* (London), March 29, 1934; G. W. Stonier, "The Author of 'Ulysses,'" *The New Statesman and Nation,* VII (1934), 156; *The Spectator,* CLII (1934), 418.
69. G. W. Stonier, *Gog, Magog . . .* (London: J. M. Dent and Sons, Ltd., 1933), pp. 1-42.
70. Henry Miller, "The Universe of Death," in *The Cosmological Eye* (Norfolk, Conn.: New Directions, 1939), pp. 107-34; from *The Phoenix,* Spring 1938.
71. Daiches, *The Novel and the Modern World,* pp. 80-157.
72. Levin, *James Joyce: A Critical Introduction;* for Irish reaction, see Montgomery in *Envoy,* V (April 1951).
73. On Alger, N. L. Rothman, "New Appraisals," *The Saturday Review of Literature,* January 24, 1942; on Catholicism, G. Barker, "James Joyce, Heretic," *The Nation,* CLIV (1942), 236-37; W. J. Igoe, *The Catholic World,* March 31, 1944; Barry Byrne, "A Review of *James Joyce* by Harry Levin," *The Commonweal,* XXXVI (1942), 91; *Time,* January 19, 1942.

74. Richard Watts, Jr., "An Irish Dante's Pilgrimage," *The New York Times Book Review,* March 2, 1941; Geddes MacGregor, *Life and Letters,* LVI (February 1948), 165-67; Guilio de Angelis, *Rivista de letterature moderne,* I (1950), 72-73; *Notes & Queries,* CXCIII (1948), 154; Henry Rago, "Books of the Week," *The Commonweal,* May 10, 1947; H. V. Routh, *The Year's Work in English Studies,* XXVIII (1949), 256-57; attacks by William Troy, " 'To So Little Space,' " *Partisan Review,* VI (1947), 424-27; Henry Morton Robinson, "No Joy *re* Joyce," *The Saturday Review of Literature,* June 7, 1947.
75. Davie, "Books in General," *The New Statesman and Nation,* XLVII (April 10, 1954), 473.
76. Den Haan, *Joyce, Mythe van Erin,* p. 44.
77. Douglas Knight, "The Reading of 'Ulysses,' " *E.L.H.—Journal of English Literary History* (hereafter cited as *E.L.H.*), XIX (1952), 64-80.
78. Murray Godwin, "A Rushlight for the Labyrinth," *Pacific Spectator,* VI (1952), 84-96.
79. Hugh Kenner, "Baker Street to Eccles Street," *The Hudson Review,* I (Winter 1949), 481-99.
80. Rudolph Von Abele, "*Ulysses:* the Myth of Myth," *PMLA,* LXIX (1954), 358-64.
81. Bernhard Fehr, "James Joyce's 'Ulysses,' " *Englische Studien,* LX (1925), 180-205; E. R. Curtius, "Technik und Thematik von James Joyce," *Die Neue Schweizer Rundschau,* January 1, 1929; Hentze, *transition,* June 1929, pp. 310-25; C. G. Jung, "Ein Monolog," *Europaische Revue,* VIII (1932), pp. 547-68, later in *Wirklichkeit der Seele . . .* (London, 1933), and translated by W. Stanley Dell, Analytical Psychology Club of New York, 1949.
82. S. Forster Damon, in *Two Decades,* ed. Givens.
83. Newton Arvin, "Interpreting 'Ulysses,' " *New York Herald Tribune Books,* February 1, 1931; Ernest Boyd, "A Propos de 'Ulysses,' " *La Nouvelle revue française,* XXIV (1925), 304-13; Austin Clarke, "James Joyce," *Everyman,* May 15, 1930.
84. "Book Notes," *New Republic,* LXV (January 28, 1931), 306; R. P. F. Strachey, *The Nation and Athenaeum,* XLVII (1930), 597; "A Guide to 'Ulysses,' " *The Times Literary Supplement* (London), XXIX (1930), 510; Gerald Sykes, "The Meaning of 'Ulysses,' " *The Nation,* CXXXII (February 4, 1931), 130.
85. B. J. Morse, " 'James Joyce's *Ulysses*' by Stuart Gilbert," *Englische Studien,* LXIX (1934), 287-91, and "Mr. Joyce and Shakespeare," *ibid.,* LXV (1931), 367-81.
86. Gilbert, *James Joyce's "Ulysses,"* p. 34.
87. Conal O'Riordan, "Guadeamus," *New Statesman,* XXXV (1930), 247.

88. Francis Fergusson, " 'James Joyce's *Ulysses,'* A Study by Stuart Gilbert," *The Hound & Horn,* V (October-December 1931), 135-37.
89. Hamish Miles, "Tales Told of Shem and Shaun,' *Criterion,* X (1930), 188-92; McLuhan, *Renascence,* IV (Autumn 1951), 12-18; William Troy, "James Joyce and His 'Ulysses,' " *The New York Times Book Review,* January 18, 1931.
90. A. M. Klein, "The Black Panther—A Study of Joyce," *Accent,* X (Spring 1950), 139-53; "A Shout in the Street," *New Directions,* XIII (1951), 327-45; "The Oxen of the Sun," *Here and Now,* III (1949), 28-48.
91. Richard M. Kain, "Joyce's Mystic Mazes," *The Saturday Review of Literature,* March 4, 1950.
92. James Johnson Sweeney, "Out of the Joycean Maze," *The New York Times Book Review,* February 19, 1950.
93. William York Tindall, "The Symbolic Novel," *AD 1952,* No. 1, pp. 56-68, and "Dante and Mrs. Bloom," *Accent,* XI (1951), 85-92.
94. Rolf Loehrich, *The Secret of "Ulysses"* (McHenry, Ill.: Compass, 1953).
95. George Basalla, "Joyce's 'Ulysses,' " *The Explicator,* December 1952.
96. June 16, 1954; "The Theme of Ulysses," *Kenyon Review,* XVIII (1956), 26-52.
97. Philip Toynbee, "A Study of James Joyce's 'Ulysses,' " in *Two Decades,* ed. Givens, 243-84.
98. McLuhan, *Thought,* XXVIII (1953), 75-98.
99. *The Dublin Magazine,* VI (April-June 1931), 64-65.
100. Ernest Boyd, "James Joyce: Memories," *Decision,* I (February 1941), 58-60; J. A. Meagher, "A Dubliner Reads 'Ulysses,' " *Australian Quarterly,* XVII (June 1945), 74-86.
101. Denis Johnston, *Envoy,* V (April 1951), 13.
102. Montgomery, *ibid.,* pp. 31-43.
103. Leonard Albert, "James Joyce—Freemasonry in 'Ulysses,' " *AD 1951,* No. 3 (Autumn), 265-83.
104. H. E. Rogers, "Irish Myth and the Plot of 'Ulysses,' " *E.L.H.,* XV (1948), 306-27.
105. Vernon Hall, Jr., "Joyce's Use of Da Ponte and Mozart's *Don Giovanni," PMLA,* LXVI (1951), 78-84.
106. Joseph Prescott, "Leopold Bloom's Memory Concerning Cormac's Death," *Notes & Queries,* CXCVI (September 29, 1951), 434; "A Song in Joyce's 'Ulysses,' " *ibid.,* CXCVII (1952), 15; "Notes on Joyces 'Ulysses,' " *Modern Language Quarterly,* XIII (June 1952), 149-62; "Mosenthal's Deborah and Joyce's 'Ulysses,' " *Modern Language Notes,* LXVII (May 1952), 334-36; "Local Allusions in Joyce's 'Ulysses,' " *PMLA,* LXVIII (1953), 1223-28.
107. Kain, *Fabulous Voyager,* pp. 2, 121, 129-30; Watts, Jr., *The New York Times Book Review,* March 2, 1947; Tindall,

Accent, XI (1951), 85-92; B. J. Morse, "Mr. Joyce and Shakespeare," *Englische Studien,* LXV (1930-1931), 367-81; Hyder Rollins, ed., *Shakespeare's Sonnets,* variorum edition (Philadelphia: J. B. Lippincott Company, 1944), II, 366; Arthur Heine, "Shakespeare in James Joyce," *Shakespeare Association Bulletin,* XXIV (1949), 56-70; William Peery, "The Hamlet of Stephen Dedalus," *Studies in English,* XXXI (1952), 109-19.

108. Kenner, Hugh, "Joyce's 'Ulysses': Homer and Hamlet," *Essays in Criticism,* II (January 1952), 85-104.
109. C. R. Edwards, "The Hamlet Motif in Joyce's 'Ulysses,'" *Western Review,* XV (Autumn 1950), 5-13.
110. Edward Duncan, "Unsubstantial Father: A Study of the Hamlet Symbolism in Joyce's 'Ulysses,'" *University of Toronto Quarterly,* XIX (1950), 126-40.
111. Moody Prior, "Hamlet and the Modern Temper," *E.L.H.,* XV (December 1948), 261-85.
112. G. J. Visser, "James Joyce's 'Ulysses' and Anglo-Irish," *English Studies,* XXIV (1942), 45-56, 79-90.
113. Vivienne Koch, "An Approach to the Homeric Content of Joyce's 'Ulysses,'" *Maryland Quarterly,* I (1944), 119-30.
114. Kenner, *Essays in Criticism,* II (January 1952), 85-104; W. B. Stanford, "Ulyssean Qualities in Joyce's Leopold Bloom," *Comparative Literature,* V (1953), 125-36.
115. Louis D. Rubin, Jr., "Joyce and Sterne: A Study in Affinity," *The Hopkins Review,* III (1950), 14-22.
116. Kain, *Fabulous Voyager,* p. 137.
117. For Goethe and Pepys, see Louis Cazamian, "L'Oeuvre de James Joyce," *Revue anglo-américaine,* II (December 1924), 97-113; for Rabelais and Melville, Hamish Miles, *Criterion,* IX, 372; for Spenser, Edwin Honig, "Hobgoblin or Apollo," *The Kenyon Review,* X (1948), 664-81; for Blake, Damon, in *Two Decades,* ed. Givens; for Book of Kells, Godwin, *Pacific Spectator,* VI (1952), 84-96, and Myles na gCopaleen, *Irish Writing,* No. 10 (1950), 71-72; Francis Russell, *ibid.,* December, 1951, and *Three Studies in Twentieth Century Obscurity* (Aldington: Hand and Flower Press, 1954); Giorgio Melchiori, "James Joyce and the Eighteenth Century Novelists," *English Miscellany,* II (1951), 226-45; L. A. G. Strong, *Personal Remarks* (London: Peter Nevill, Ltd., 1953), 184-89.
118. Louis MacNeice, *The Poetry of W. B. Yeats* (London: Oxford University Press, 1941), pp. 203-5; F. O. Matthiessen, *The Achievement of T. S. Eliot* (New York: Oxford University Press, 1935).
119. C. E. Magny, "A Double Note on T. S. Eliot and James Joyce," *T. S. Eliot: A Symposium,* ed. Richard March and Tambimuttu (Chicago: Henry Regnery Company, 1949),

208-17. Giorgio Melchiori, "*The Waste Land* and *Ulysses*," *English Studies*, XXXV (April 1954), 56-58.
120. Herbert Muller, review of Harry Levin's *James Joyce*, *Accent*, II (Spring 1942), 189-90.
121. D. S. Savage, "James Joyce," in *The Withered Branch* (London: Eyre and Spottiswoode, 1950), 156-99.
122. R. P. Blackmur, "The Jew in Search of a Son," *Virginia Quarterly Review*, XXIV (Winter 1948), 96-116.

CHAPTER 9

1. Oscar Wilde, *The Picture of Dorian Gray* (New York: Illustrated Editions Company, 1931), p. 140.
2. J. K. Huysmans, *Against the Grain* (*A Rebours*) (New York: Hartsdale House, n.d.), p. 92. The book first appeared in 1889. I use the Hartsdale House edition.
3. Joyce, *Finnegans Wake*.
4. Levin, *James Joyce: A Critical Introduction*, p. 156 ff.
5. In *Two Decades*, ed. Givens, pp. 319-42.
6. Leslie L. Lewis diagram, in L. Moholy-Nagy's *Vision in Motion* (Chicago: P. Theobald, 1947), p. 347.
7. Tindall, *James Joyce*, p. 121; William Troy, "Notes on Finnegans Wake," in *Two Decades*, ed. Givens, p. 318; Louis Gillet, "Joyce's Testament: Finnegans Wake," *Quarterly Review of Literature*, I (1944), 87-99.
8. T. S. Eliot, first published in *The Dial*, November 1923. The quotation is published here with the permission of Mr. Eliot. The full essay may be found in Mark Schorer and Others, *Criticism: The Foundations of Modern Literary Judgment* (New York: Harcourt, Brace and Company, 1948), pp. 269-71.
9. Jules Michelet, "Discours sur le system et la vie de Vico," *Histoire et Philosophie* (Paris: Calmann Lévy, Editeur, 1900), p. 275. More recently, Vico has been translated into English: Thomas Goddard Bergin and Max Harold Fisch, *The New Science of Giambattista Vico* (Ithaca: Cornell University Press, 1948).
10. John A. Macculloch, *Celtic Mythology*, Vol. III of *The Mythology of All Races* (Boston: Marshall Jones Company, 1918). This book may also be consulted for information on the Diarmuid and Grania myth.
11. See Joseph Campbell and Henry Morton Robinson, *A Skeleton Key to "Finnegans Wake"* (New York: Harcourt, Brace and Company, 1944), p. 51.
12. Jolas in *Two Decades*, ed. Givens, p. 15.
13. For an interesting account of Joyce's relationship to Freud and his psychology, see Frederick J. Hoffman, "Infroyce," in *Two Decades*, ed. Seon Givens, pp. 390-435.

14. Sigmund Freud, *The Basic Writings of Sigmund Freud* (New York: The Modern Library, 1938), p. 927.
15. Carl G. Jung, *The Integration of the Personality* (New York: Farrar & Rinehart, Inc., 1939), chap. 3.
16. *Ibid.*
17. *Freud, Totem and Taboo,* in *Basic Writings,* pp. 925-26.
18. *Ibid.,* p. 926.
19. Van Ghent, *The English Novel: Form and Function,* p. 264.
20. Joyce, *Stephen Hero,* pp. 26 and 30.
21. Joyce, *A Portrait,* pp. 68, 193.
22. Jolas in *Two Decades,* ed. Givens, p. 13.
23. Susanne K. Langer, *Philosophy in a New Key: A Study in the Symbolism of Reason, Rite, and Art* (New York: Penguin Books, Inc., 1948), p. 139.
24. Stuart Gilbert, "Homage to James Joyce," *transition,* XXI (1932), 249; E. B. Burgum, *The Novel and the World's Dilemma* (New York: Oxford University Press, 1947); A. Glendenning, "Commentary," *Nineteenth Century,* CXXIX, 269-75; Paul Rosenfeld, "James Joyce's Jabberwocky," *The Saturday Review of Literature,* XX (May 6, 1939).
25. Harry Levin, "New Irish Stew," *The Kenyon Review,* I (Autumn 1939), 464-65.
26. Louise Bogan, "Proteus, or Vico's Road," *The Nation,* CXLVIII (1939), 533-35; Margaret Schlauch, "The Language of James Joyce," *Science and Society,* III (1939), 482-97; Bernbaum, *College English,* VII (December 1945), 151-54; T. J. Fitzmorris, "Vico Adamant and Some Pillars of Salt," *The Catholic World,* CLVI (1939), 568-77; Louis Gillet, "Joyce's Testeament: Finnegans Wake," *Quarterly Review of Literature,* I (1944), 87-99.
27. Richard V. Chase, "Finnegans Wake: An Anthropological Study," *The American Scholar,* XIII (Autumn 1944), 418.
28. Michael Stuart, "Joyce After Ulysses," *This Quarter,* II (1930), 242-48.
29. Mary Colum, *Forum and Century,* CII (1939), 158; Padraic Colum, *The New York Times,* May 7, 1939. For John Peale Bishop, see bibliography for this chapter.
30. Stonier, *The New Statesman and Nation,* VIII (1934), 364.
31. See J. S. Atherton, *Notes & Queries,* CXCIV (1949), 430-32; *The Times Literary Supplement* (London), November 23, 1951, and May 9, 1952; *English Studies,* XXXIII (1952), 1-15; *Comparative Literature,* VI, 240-55. See also Joseph Peery, "Shakisbeard at Finnegans Wake," *Studies in English,* XXX (1951), 243-57; Ned Polsky, "Literary Backgrounds of Finnegans Wake," *Chicago Review,* III (1949); and L. A. G. Strong, *The Sacred River: An Approach to James Joyce* (New York: Pellegrini & Cudahy, 1951).
32. Marcus MacEnery, "The Joyce Country," *The Irish Times,* September 13, 1947.

33. Richard Aldington, *The Atlantic Monthly,* June 1939.
34. Rosenfeld, *The Saturday Review of Literature,* XX (May 6, 1939); John Crowe Ransom, "The Aesthetics of Finnegans Wake," *The Kenyon Review,* I (1939), 424-28; Joseph Prescott, *Modern Language Notes,* LX (February 1945), 137-38.
35. J. S. Atherton, "The Koran in Finnegans Wake," *Comparative Literature,* VI (1954), 240-55.
36. Elmer Edgar Stoll, *From Shakespeare to Joyce: Authors and Critics; Literature and Life* (Garden City: Doubleday, Doran and Company, 1944).
37. Gillet, *Quarterly Review of Literature,* I (1944), 87-99.
38. Eugene Jolas, "Frontierless Decade," *transition,* XXVII (April-May, 1938), 8.
39. Eugene Jolas, "The Revolution of Language and James Joyce," in *Our Exagmination* (London: Faber and Faber, Ltd., n.d.), p. 80.
40. Bogan, *The Nation,* CXLVIII (1939), 533-35; Edward Titus, "Sartor Resartus," *This Quarter,* III (1930-1931), 129-41; F. R. Leavis, "Joyce and 'The Revolution of the Word,'" in *The Importance of Scrutiny,* ed. Eric Bentley (New York: G. W. Stewart Company, 1948), pp. 316-23; Kenner, *Shenandoah,* IV (1935), 24-41.
41. Samuel Beckett and Others, *Our Exagmination;* this book was issued in the United States by New Directions as *An Exagmination of James Joyce.*
42. See appropriate items in Bibliography for the chapter on *Finnegans Wake.*
43. Brinsley MacNamara, *The Irish Times,* June 3, 1939; Alfred Kazin, *New York Herald Tribune,* May 21, 1939; Louise Bogan, see above, Note 40; G. W. Stonier, *The New Statesman and Nation,* XVII, 788-90.
44. Jolas in *Two Decades,* ed. Givens, p. 6; the story is challenged by Joseph Prescott, "Concerning the Genesis of 'Finnegans Wake,'" *PMLA,* LXIX (December 1954), 1300-2.
45. See W. Litz, "The Genesis of Finnegans Wake," *Notes & Queries,* CXCVIII, 445-47.
46. Campbell and Robinson, Foreword to *A Skeleton Key to "Finnegans Wake,"* p. x.
47. Harry Levin, "Everybody's Earwicker," *New Republic,* III (1944), 106-7; John Kelleher, "Joyce Digested," *Accent,* V (Spring 1945), 181-86; Edmund Wilson, "A Guide to 'Finnegans Wake,'" *The New Yorker,* XX (August 5, 1944), 54-60.
48. Benedict Kiely, "A Key to James Joyce," *Irish Bookman,* II (December 1947), 9-19.
49. Joseph Campbell and Henry M. Robinson, "The Skin of Whose Teeth–" *The Saturday Review of Literature,* XXV (December 19, 1942), 3-4.

50. *The Saturday Review of Literature,* XXVI (January 2, 1943), 11; and January 9, 1943, 11-13.
51. J. Mitchell Morse, "Jacob and Esau in 'Finnegans Wake,'" *Modern Philology,* LII (November 1954), 123-30, also "Cain, Abel and Joyce," *E.L.H.,* XXII (March 1955), 48-60; Nathan Halper, "James Joyce and Rebecca West," *Partisan Review,* XVI (July 1949), 761-63, and "The 'Most Eyeful Hoyth' of Finnegans Wake," *New Republic,* CXXIV (May 7, 1951), 20-23.
52. J. S. Atherton, "Lewis Carroll and 'Finnegans Wake,'" *English Studies,* XXXIII (February 1952), 1-15, and "Finnegans Wake: 'The Gist of Pantomime,'" *Accent,* XV (Winter 1955), 14-26; see also Atherton's article on the Koran and the *Wake* in *Comparative Literature,* VI (1954), 240-55. Hodgart, *The Cambridge Journal,* VI (October 1952), 23-39.
53. Tindall, *James Joyce,* p. 5.
54. Louis Gillet, *transition,* XXI, 263-72.
55. G. W. Stonier, "Joyce's Airy Plumeflights," *The New Statesman and Nation,* XVII (May 20, 1939), 788-90.
56. Leon Edel, "James Joyce and His New Work," *University of Toronto Quarterly,* IX (1939-1940), 68-81.

CHAPTER 10

1. Sherwood Anderson, *Dark Laughter* (New York: Boni and Liveright, 1925), pp. 39, 120-21, 126, 162; *Letters* (Boston: Little, Brown and Company, 1953), p. 148; for Joyce's influence on Wolfe, see Nathan L. Rothman, "Thomas Wolfe and James Joyce: A Study in Literary Influence," *The Southern Vanguard* (1947), pp. 52-77; Norah Hoult, *Coming from the Fair* (New York: Covici, Friede, 1937), pp. 158-59; Arthur Koestler, *Dialogue with Death* (New York: The Macmillan Company, 1938), p. 125; Aldous Huxley, *Eyeless in Gaza* (New York: Harper and Brothers, 1936), p. 106; Charles Norman, *The Well of the Past* (New York: Doubleday and Company, 1949), p. 219; Dodie Smith, *I Capture the Castle* (Boston: Little, Brown and Company, 1948), pp. 141, 337; Sinclair Lewis, Nobel Prize Address, "The American Fear of Literature" (December 12, 1950), in *The Man from Main Street,* eds. Maule and Crane (New York: Random House, 1953), p. 3; for the La Hune listing of the Joyce tree of influence, see Bernard Gheerbrandt, *James Joyce: Sa vie, son oeuvre, son rayonnement* (Paris: Libarie La Hune, 1949).
2. Matyas Seiber, "A Note on 'Ulysses,'" *Music Survey,* IV (April 1951), 263-70; also on B.B.C. Third Programme concert, Royal Festival Hall, April 19, 1954; Mosco Carner, "Matyas Seiber and His 'Ulysses,'" *Musical Review,* XII (1951), 105-12; cf. *ibid.,* p. 268.

3. G. W. Stonier, "The Young Joyce," *The New Statesman and Nation,* XXVIII (July 29, 1944), 74; Gilbert Millstein, "A Valentine for Joyce," *The New York Times Book Review,* February 14, 1954.
4. *Evening Herald* (Dublin), July 1, 1954, August 10, 1954, November 29, 1955.
5. E. D. Baltzell, "Bell Telephone's Experiment in Education," *Harper's Magazine,* March 1955.
6. Letter to Richard M. Kain. Program dates, February 16 and 21, May 21, June 21, 1950; January 27, 1952; February 21, June 16, 1954.
7. To the tributes listed by Alan Parker, *James Joyce: A Bibliography* (Boston: F. W. Faxon Company, 1948), pp. 255-56, may be added: Ted Borum, "Finnegans Wake," *Poetry,* LII (1943), 250; Patrick Kavanagh, "A Wreath for Tom Moore's Statue," *A Soul For Sale* (London: Macmillan and Company, 1947), and "The Paddiad," *Horizon,* XX (1950), 80-95; Roy Fuller, *Epitaphs and Occasions* (London: John Lehmann, Ltd., 1949), p. 50; Robert Graecen, "James Joyce," *Irish Writing,* No. 10 (1950), 57; Bryan Guinness, *Twenty Three Poems* (London: Gerald Duckworth and Company, 1931); Archibald MacLeish, "Years of the Dog," *Collected Poems, 1917-1952* (New York, 1952), pp. 134-35; Ewart Milne, *Diamond Cut Diamond* (n.p.: The Bodley Head, 1950), 23, 39-45, 54-55; Ezra Pound, *Pisan Cantos* (London: Faber and Faber, Ltd., 1948), pp. 25, 34, 51; Henry Savage, *A Long Spoon and the Devil* (London: Cecil Palmer, Ltd., 1922), p. 12; Karl Shapiro, *Essay on Rime* (New York: Reynal and Hitchcock, 1945).
8. Hugh MacDiarmid, *In Memoriam James Joyce* (Glasgow: William Maclellan, 1955), pp. 59, 60, 87, 89, 142.
9. "Silence, Exile, and Death," *Time,* February 10, 1941, p. 72.
10. Constantine Curran and Arthur Power, *The Irish Times,* January 14, 1941, reprinted in *Envoy,* V (April 1951), 73-78; Budgen and Jolas, reprinted in *Two Decades,* ed. Givens; cf. Curran, "When James Joyce lived in Dublin," *Vogue,* April 1947.
11. J. P. Hogan, *The Adelphi,* XVII (3d ser.) (1940-1941), 298-300, and XIX (1942-1943), 64.
12. Alfred Kazin, "A Man Unafraid to Make Great Mistakes," *New York Herald Tribune Books,* January 26, 1941.
13. Stephen Spender, "James Joyce: 1882-1941," *The Listener,* January 23, 1941; Thornton Wilder, "Essay on Joyce," *Poetry,* LVII (March 1941), 370-74, reprinted as *James Joyce, 1882-1941* (Aurora, N.Y.: Wells College Press, 1944).
14. Northrop Frye, "Four Forms of Prose Fiction," *The Hudson Review,* II (1950), 582-95.
15. Joseph Frank, "Spatial Form in Modern Literature," *The Sewanee Review,* LIII (1945), 221-40, 433-56, 643-53; Mo-

holy-Nagy, *Vision in Motion* (Chicago: Theobald, 1947), pp. 341-352; Gilbert, Introduction to *Joyce the Artificer* (London: Chiswick, 1952).

16. Winters, *In Defense of Reason* (Denver: University of Denver Press, 1947), pp. 56, 341. Cf. V. Weidle, *The Dilemma of the Arts* (London: S C M, 1948), p. 69; W. Shewring, *Dublin Review,* CCXII (1942), 95-96; V. Iremonger, *The Bell,* VIII (1944), 260-63.
17. Levin, *James Joyce,* p. 106; Tindall, *James Joyce,* p. 44.
18. Tindall, *ibid.,* p. 18.
19. T. S. Eliot, "A Note on the Verse of John Milton," *Essays and Studies by Members of the English Association,* XXI (1935), 37-38.
20. V. S. Pritchett, "Synge and Joyce," *The New Statesman and Nation,* XXI (1941), 413; David Dempsey, "Speaking of Books," *The New York Times Book Review,* July 16, 1950; Padraic Colum, *A Treasury of Irish Folklore* (New York: Crown Publishers, Inc., 1954), pp. xiv, 3; Leon Edel, *James Joyce, the Last Journey* (New York: The Gotham Book Mart, 1947), p. 41.
21. John Crowe Ransom, "Bright Disorder," *The Kenyon Review,* IV (Summer 1942), 430-32.
22. Jackson I. Cope, "James Joyce: Test Case for a Theory of Style," *E.L.H.,* XXXV (1954), 221-36.
23. Ransom, *The Kenyon Review,* IV (Summer 1942), 430-32; Jolas, in *Two Decades,* ed. Givens; *Saturday Night,* January 18, 1941; W. R. Rodgers, *The New Statesman and Nation,* September 27, 1952; Josef Baake, *Das Reisenscherzbuch 'Ulysses'* (Bonn: Hanstein, 1937); Budgen, 71-72; Levin, 217; Joyce, Letter to Harriet Weaver, October 16, 1926; Kain, *Fabulous Voyager,* pp. 3, 34, 98, 136, 235; Montgomery, *Envoy,* V (1951), 31; L. Thompson, "A Comic Principle in Sterne—Meredith—Joyce," British Institute, University of Oslo, 1954; Vivian Mercier, "Parody: James Joyce and an Irish Tradition," English Institute Lecture, Columbia University, September 8, 1955.
24. "Scientist of Letters," *New Republic,* CIV (January 20, 1941), 71; Spender, *The Listener,* January 23, 1941; W. H. Auden, "James Joyce and Richard Wagner," *Commonsense,* March 31, 1941; Lerner, *New Republic,* CVII (September 28, 1942), 386.
25. *Manchester Guardian,* January 14, 1941; *Herald* (Glasgow), January 18, 1941.
26. Georges Borach, "Conversations with James Joyce," trans. Joseph Prescott, *College English,* XV (March 1954), 325-27; also in *Meanjin: A Literary Magazine* (Spring [September] 1954), and in *The London Magazine,* I (November 1954).

27. Padraic Colum, "A Portrait of James Joyce," *New Republic,* LXVI (May 13, 1931), 346-48.
28. Maria Jolas, "Joyce as a Revolutionary," *New Republic,* CVII (November 9, 1942), 613; Padraic Colum, letter, *The New York Times,* December 4, 1941; "The Joyce I Knew," *The Saturday Review of Literature,* XXIII (February 22, 1941), 11.
29. Goll, *Die Literarische Welt,* June 17, 1927; reprinted in *The Living Age,* CCCXXXIII (August 15, 1927), 316-20.
30. *New Masses,* January 21, 1941.
31. *Irish Independent,* April 29, 1941; "What of James Joyce," *The Irish Rosary,* March 1941.
32. P. Kelly, "Literary Wake over James Joyce," *America,* May 3, 1941; J. S. Collis, "Conversation Piece on Joyce," *Time and Tide,* March 29, 1941.
33. Clement Wood, "The World's Worst Books," *Books Abroad,* XV (January 1941), 51.
34. Donagh MacDonagh, *The Dublin Magazine,* October-December 1941, p. 71.
35. T. S. Eliot, "A Message to the Fish," *Horizon,* March 1941, in *Two Decades,* ed. Givens, pp. 468-71.
36. "Literary Biography: James Joyce's Rebellion: "Silence, Exile, and Cunning,' " *The Times Literary Supplement* (London), March 1, 1941; F. MacM. "Portrait of an Irish Writer," *Irish Press,* April 15, 1941.
37. [Oliver St. John] Gogarty, "The Veritable James Joyce . . . ," *transition,* No. 21 (1932), 273-82.
38. Harvey Breit, "Speaking of Books," *The New York Times Book Review,* February 21, 1954.
39. Vivian Mercier, "The Cranly of Joyce's Famous Portrait," *The Commonweal,* December 25, 1953, p. 311.
40. Oliver St. John Gogarty, "Roots in Resentment," *Observer,* May 7, 1939; "The Joyce I Knew," *The Saturday Review of Literature,* January 25, 1941; "James Joyce: A Portrait of the Artist," *Tomorrow,* January, 1947; "James Joyce as a Friend of Music," *ibid.,* December, 1949; *The Saturday Review of Literature,* March 18, 1950; *Rolling Down the Lea* (London: Constable and Company, 1950); *It Isn't This Time of Year at All* (New York: Doubleday and Company, 1954).
41. William York Tindall, *New York Herald Tribune,* February 24, 1954.
42. Stanislaus Joyce, "Open Letter to Dr. Oliver Gogarty," *Interim,* IV (1954), 49-56.
43. Niall Montgomery, *Envoy,* V (April 1951), 34.
44. R. G. Kelly, *PMLA,* LXIV (1949), 26-39.
45. Mark Schorer, *William Blake, The Politics of Vision* (New York: Henry Holt and Company, 1946), pp. 110-11.
46. Richard Ellmann, *Yeats, The Man and the Masks* (New York: The Macmillan Company, 1948), pp. 94-95.

47. Cyril Connolly, "A Note on James Joyce," *The New Statesman and Nation,* XXI (January 18, 1941), 59
48. Zabel, *The Nation,* CL (March 9, 1940), 339.
49. Stephen Spender, *Left Review,* December 1936; John Lynd, *John o' London's Weekly,* March 25, 1935; Patrick Kavanagh, *Envoy,* I (1950), 85; Fergusson, *The Hound & Horn,* V (October-December 1931), 135-37.
50. Jack Common, "James Joyce and the Making of 'Ulysses,'" *The Adelphi,* VIII (1934), 68-70.
51. Floyd Dell, "Sex in American Fiction," *The American Mercury,* January 1948.
52. Sean O'Faolain, "Dante and Joyce," in *A Summer in Italy* (New York: The Devin-Adair Company, 1950), pp. 113-18.
53. Andrew Cass, "Childe Horrid's Pilgrimage," *Envoy,* V (April 1951), 19-30; Patrick Kavanagh, "Diary," *ibid.,* pp. 69-72.
54. Cowley, *New Republic,* LXXVII (January 3, 1934), 218-19; Alfred Kazin, "A Portrait of the Artist as a Human Being," *New York Herald Tribune Books,* February 18, 1940; *The Irish Times,* March 22, 1941.
55. Kristian Smidt, *James Joyce and the Cultic Use of Fiction* (Oslo: Academisk Forlag; Oxford: Basil Blackwell, 1955); see also Richard Ellmann, *Kenyon Review,* XVIII (1956), 53-67, for his English Institute lecture, September 9, 1955; L. A. G. Strong, "The Art of James Joyce," *John o' London's Weekly,* January 24, 1941.
56. Zabel, *The Nation,* CL (March 9, 1940), 339.
57. Padraic Colum, "A Portrait of James Joyce," *The Dublin Magazine,* VII (April-June 1932), 40-48; S. Foster Damon, "On Explaining Joyce," *The Adelphi,* I, 3d ser. (1930-1931), 79-82.
58. T. S. Eliot, *After Strange Gods* (New York: Harcourt, Brace and Company, 1934), pp. 40-41.
59. L. A. G. Strong, "James Joyce and the New Fiction," *The American Mercury,* XXXV (August 1935), 433-37.
60. Igoe, *The Catholic World,* March 31, 1944.
61. Padraic Colum, "A Gaelic Thrill," *The Saturday Review,* September 5, 1953.
62. Borach, trans. Prescott, *College English,* CLXV (1954), 325-27.
63. Montgomery, *Envoy,* V (April 1951), 31-43.
64. Barker, *The Nation,* CLIV (1942, 236-37.
65. *The Commonweal,* February 22, May 16, 1952.
66. Dorothy Sayers, *Mind of the Maker* (1941), p. 205.
67. Robert R. Hull, "A Key to the Mystery of James Joyce," *The Fortnightly Review,* XXXVII (St. Louis, 1930), 223-25, 251-53, 274-76.
68. Jack White, "The Bloomsday Book," *The Spectator,* CLIXII (June 11, 1954), 702-4.

69. Ramon Sender, "Speaking of Epitaphs," *Books Abroad,* XIX (July 1945), 222-27.
70. Arland Ussher, *Three Great Irishmen: Shaw, Yeats, Joyce* (New York: The Devin-Adair Company, 1953), p. 130.
71. J. M. Morse, *E.L.H.,* XXII (March 1955), 48-60.
72. *The Commonweal,* LIX (February 12, 1954), 479.
73. Karl Adam, *The Spirit of Catholicism* (London: Sheed and Ward, 1929).
74. Francis X. Connolly, "The Catholic Writer and Contemporary Culture," *Thought,* XIV (1939), 373-83.
75. *Ibid.,* XXVIII, 105-10.
76. *The Irish Times,* January 14, 1941.
77. Connolly, *The New Statesman and Nation,* XXI (January 18, 1941), 59.
78. Kain, *Fabulous Voyager,* p. 121.
79. *Ibid.,* p. 238.
80. Padraic Colum, "With James Joyce in Ireland," *The New York Times,* June 11, 1922; "Dublin in Literature," *The Bookman,* LXIII (July 1926), 559-61; Vivian Mercier, "Dublin Under the Joyces," in *Two Decades,* ed. Givens.
81. George Bernard Shaw, *Immaturity* (London: Constable and Company, 1931).
82. Horace Reynolds, "A Note on 'Ulysses,'" *The Irish Review,* April 1934.
83. Joyce, *A Portrait,* p. 194; *Finnegans Wake,* p. 53.
84. Colum, *The Bookman,* LXIII (July 1926), 559-61.
85. Austin Clarke, "Stephen Dedalus, the Author of 'Ulysses,'" *New Statesman,* XXII (February 23, 1924), 571-72.
86. Elizabeth Bowen, "James Joyce," *The Bell,* I (March 1941), 40-49.
87. Ussher, *Three Great Irishmen,* p. 127.
88. Stonier, *Gog, Magog . . . ,* pp. 9-10.
89. Hugh Kenner, "The Trivium in Dublin," *English Institute Essays* (1952), pp. 202-28.
90. Yeats, quoted in *The Irish Times,* August 11, 1924; A. E., *ibid.,* November 15, 1932; cf. *ibid.,* February 18, 1933, October 27 and December 8, 1934; Niall Sheridan, *Ireland Today,* November 1937.
91. *The Irish Times,* June 3, 1939, January 14, 1941; *Irish Independent,* January 17, 1941.
92. *The Irish Times,* August 2, 1947.
93. Mercier, in *Two Decades,* ed. Givens; *Studies* (University College, Dublin), XXXIX (1950), 369; Lorna Reynolds. "Thirty Years of Irish Letters," *ibid.,* XL (1951), 457-68.
94. *The Irish Times,* September 10, 1949, and July 22, February 18, April 22, October 21, 1950.
95. Francis McManus, *Studies* (University College, Dublin), XLI (March 1932), 121-23.
96. Thomas Hogan, *The Irish Times,* April 21, 1951.

97. Cass, *Envoy,* V (April 1951), 14, 16, 24, 25.
98. Donagh MacDonagh, *The Irish Times,* June 15, 16, 17, 1954; *Irish Press,* June 17, 1954.
99. Heinrich Straumann, "Last Meeting with Joyce," *James Joyce Yearbook* (Paris: Transition Press, 1949), p. 114.
100. Troy, *Partisan Review,* XIV (1947), 424-27.
101. Robinson, *The Saturday Review of Literature,* June 7, 1947.
102. *The Saturday Review of Literature,* July 19, 1947.
103. R. P. Blackmur, "The Enabling Act of Criticism," *American Issues,* II (1941), 876-79; Gilbert, in *Two Decades,* ed. Givens; Eliot, *Horizon* (March 1941), and in *Two Decades,* ed. Givens.
104. Lerner, *New Republic,* CVII (September 28, 1942), 386; Stonier, *The New Statesman and Nation,* XXVIII (July 29, 1944), 74-75.
105. S. Diana Neill, *A Short History of the English Novel* (London: Macmillan and Company, 1952), pp. 312-24; A. S. Collins, *English Literature . . . .* (London: University Tutorial Press, 1951); G. S. Fraser, *The Modern Writer and His World* (London: British Book Centre, 1953).
106. J. B. Priestley, "gems choice in fuchsia yaws," *Sunday Times* (London), January 2, 1955.
107. O'Connor, *The New York Times Book Review,* December 12, 1954; Edel, *Psychological Novel;* Mark Schorer, "Airy Realms of Light," *The New York Times Book Review,* June 19, 1955.
108. Ransom, *The Kenyon Review,* IV (Summer 1942), 430-32; Henry Reed, "James Joyce: The Triple Exile," *The Listener,* XLIII (1950), 437-39.
109. Philip Toynbee, "The Decline and Future of the English Novel," *Penguin New Writing,* No. 23 (New York: Penguin Books, Inc., 1945), 127-39.
110. Robert Gorham Davis, "Narrow Views of Joyce," *Partisan Review,* XV (September 1948), 1015.
111. G. W. Stonier, *"Finnegans Wake," The New Statesman and Nation,* XXXIV (October 25, 1947), 334.
112. Ezra Pound, "Past History," *English Journal,* XXII (May 1933), 349-58.
113. John Lehmann, "Portrait of the Artist as Escaper," *Penguin New Writing,* No. 33 (New York: Penguin Books, Inc., 1948) and *The Open Night* (New York: Harcourt, Brace and Company, 1948).
114. Francis Russell, "Joyce and Alexandria," *Irish Writing,* XVII (December 1951), 33-53, and *Three Studies in Twentieth Century Obscurity,* pp. 7-44.
115. David Jones, *The Dublin Review,* CCXXIV (1950), 118-21; André de Bouchet, "The James Joyce Exhibition," *The Listener,* XLII (1949), 1100.

116. Wallace Fowlie, *The Clown's Grail* (London: Dennis Dobson, Ltd., 1947).
117. J. F. Hendry, "James Joyce," and Irene Hendry, "Joyce's Epiphanies," in *Two Decades,* ed. Givens.
118. McLuhan, *Renascence,* IX (Autumn 1951), 3-11; "Joyce, Mallarmé, and the Press," *The Sewanee Review,* LXII (1954), 38-55.
119. Joyce, letter to Harriet Weaver, June 24, 1921.

Bibliography

Bibliography

The Problem of Biography

Antheil, George. *Bad Boy of Music*. Garden City, N. Y.: Doubleday, Doran and Company, 1945. Anecdotes of Joyce's life in Paris.

Barnes, Djuna. "James Joyce," *Vanity Fair,* XVIII (April 1922), 65, 104. The woman's view of Joyce at the time of the publication of *Ulysses.*

Benco, Silvio. "James Joyce in Trieste," *The Bookman,* LXXII (December 1930), 375-80. Details of Joyce's personal life on the Continent.

Budgen, Frank. *James Joyce and the Making of "Ulysses."* New York: Harrison Smith and Robert Haas, Inc., 1934. Conversations with Joyce, mainly about the meaning of *Ulysses.*

———. "James Joyce,' in *James Joyce: Two Decades of Criticism,* ed. Seon Givens. New York: Vanguard Press, 1948. This article appeared originally in *Horizon* of February, 1941.

Byrne, Barry. "Flight from Eire," *The Commonweal,* XXXIII (April 4, 1941), 597-98.

Byrne, J. F. *Silent Years: An Autobiography with Memoirs of James Joyce and Our Ireland.* New York: Farrar, Straus and Young, 1953.

Clarke, Austin. " 'Stephen Dedalus': The Author of Ulysses," *New Statesman,* XXII (February 23, 1924), 571-72. A short account of his meetings with Joyce in Paris.

Colum, Mary. *Life and the Dream.* Garden City, New York: Doubleday & Company, Inc., 1947. Interesting personal memories of Joyce.

———. "A Little Knowledge of Joyce," *The Saturday Review of Literature,* XXXIII (April 29, 1950), 10-12. A reply to Oliver Gogarty's attack on Joyce and Joyceans in an earlier number of the magazine.

Colum, Padraic. *The Road Round Ireland.* New York: The Macmillan Company, 1926. Anecdotes of Joyce during his student days.

———. "Portrait of James Joyce," *The Dublin Magazine,* VII (April-June 1932), 40-48. A view of Joyce as a family man, etc.

Connolly, Thomas E. *The Personal Library of James Joyce: A Descriptive Bibliography.* Buffalo: University of Buffalo Monographs in English, No. 6 (April), 1955. A valuable detailed list including notation of all entries that Joyce made in each of his books.

Curran, Constantine P. "When James Joyce Lived in Dublin," *Vogue,* CIX (May 1947), 144-49 ff. Interesting photographs of the locale.

Edel, Leon. *James Joyce: The Last Journey.* New York: The Gotham Book Mart, 1947. A sentimental journey to Joyce's grave.

"Eglinton, John" (W. K. Magee). *Irish Literary Portraits.* London: Macmillan and Company, 1935. Joyce as a young author in Dublin.

Ellmann, Richard. "The Backgrounds of 'Ulysses,'" *The Kenyon Review,* XVI (Summer 1954), 337-86. In writing of the autobiographical labyrinth of *Ulysses,* the author provides many fascinating sidelights on Joyce's youth.

———. "The Grasshopper and the Ant: Notes on James Joyce and His Brother Stanislaus," *The Reporter,* XIII (December 1, 1955), 35-38.

———. "Joyce and Yeats," *The Kenyon Review,* XII (Autumn 1950), 618-38. The relationship of the two men is explored from the biographical rather than from the literary point of view.

Ford, Ford Madox. *It Was the Nightingale.* Philadelphia: J. B. Lippincott Company, 1933. Joyce as the literary god of Paris.

Gilbert, Stuart. "Souvenirs de Voyage," *Mercure de France,* CCCIX (Mai-Août 1950), 38-44. On Joyce the middle-class family man and vacationer in France during the thirties.

Gogarty, Oliver St. John. *As I Was Going down Sackville Street: A Phantasy in Fact.* London: Rich and Cowan, Ltd., 1937. The young Joyce seen mainly in an uncomplimentary light.

———. "The Joyce I knew," *The Saturday Review of Literature,* XXIII (January 25, 1941), 3-4, 15-16.

———. "They Think They Know Joyce," *The Saturday Review of Literature,* XXXIII (March 18, 1950), 8-9, 35-37. Attack on Joyce as a person and an author.

Gorman, Herbert. *James Joyce.* New York: Rinehart and Company, 1939. The authorized biography containing many letters and documents nowhere else obtainable.

Griffin, Gerald. *The Wild Geese: Pen Portraits of Famous Irish Exiles.* London: Jarrolds Publishers, n.d.

Hutchins, Patricia. *James Joyce's Dublin.* London: The Grey Walls Press, Ltd., 1950. Fine photographs of Joyce's Irish background.

"Interview with Mr. John Stanislaus Joyce: (1849-1931)," in *A James Joyce Yearbook,* ed. Maria Jolas. Paris: Transition Press, 1949. Comment on Joyce and other related matters by his father.

John, Augustus. "Fragment of an Autobiography, XV," *Horizon,* XIII (January 1946), 49-61. Short reminiscence of days with Joyce, while the artist painted his portrait.

Jolas, Eugene. "My Friend James Joyce," in *James Joyce: Two Decades of Criticism,* ed. Seon Givens. New York: Vanguard Press, 1948. This piece appeared originally in the *Partisan Review,* March-April 1941.

Jolas, Maria. "Joyce in 1939-1940," *Mercure de France,* CCCIC (Mai-Août 1950), 45-58. The effect of the Second World War on the Joyce family.

Joyce, James. *Stephen Hero,* ed. Theodore Spencer. Norfolk, Conn.: New Directions, 1944. Though this must be read with care to separate Stephen from Joyce, it is essentially an autobiographical document.

Joyce, Stanislaus. *Recollections of James Joyce by His Brother.* New York: The James Joyce Society, 1950. A good account of Joyce's reading and other youthful interests.

———. "Early Memories of James Joyce," *The Listener,* XLI (May 26, 1949), 896-97.

———. "Joyce's Dublin," *Partisan Review,* XIX (January-February 1952), 103-9. Tries to set straight distortions concerning Joyce's life in Dublin, relationships with Jesuits, with relatives, etc. The article is a long review of Patricia Hutchins's *James Joyce's Dublin.*

Joyce, Stanislaus, and Ellsworth Mason. *The Early Joyce: The Book Reviews, 1902-1903.* Colorado Springs: The Mamalujo Press, 1955. An edition of reviews in Irish newspapers, written by young Joyce.

"The Joyces," *The New Yorker,* X (January 12, 1935), 12-13. An interview with the Giorgio Joyce family.

Kain, Richard M., "Two Book Reviews by James Joyce," *PMLA,* LXVII (March 1952), 291-94. Discovery of Joyce's early literary activity.

Kelly, Robert G. "James Joyce: A Partial Explanation," *PMLA,* LXIV (March 1949), 26-39. Finds the seeds of Joyce's peculiarities in the psychological difficulties of his adolescence.

Kerr, Alfred. "Joyce en Angleterre," *Les Nouvelles litteraires,* January 11, 1936, p. 6. An interview with Joyce.

McAlmon, Robert. *Being Geniuses Together: An Autobiography,* London: Secker and Warburg, 1938. Mainly anecdotes of Joyce's night life in Paris.

Morris, Lloyd. *A Threshold in the Sun.* New York: Harper and Brothers, 1943. Another view of Joyce in Paris after the publication of *Ulysses.*

Murphy, Maurice. "James Joyce and Ireland," *The Nation,* CXXIX (October 16, 1929), 426. An apology for Joyce's life of writing rather than soldiering.

Noel, Lucie. *James Joyce and Paul L. Léon: The Story of a Friendship.* New York: The Gotham Book Mart, 1950. Information concerning Joyce's life in the thirties by the wife of his late friend and adviser.

Paul, Elliot. "Farthest North," *The Bookman,* LXXV (May 1932), 156-63. Joyce in Paris.

Slocum, John J., and Herbert Cahoon. "A Note of Joyce Biography," *The Yale University Library Gazette,* XXVIII (July 1953), 44-50. A list of biographical sources.

Spoerri, James F. "James Joyce: Books and Pamphlets Relating to the Author and His Works," *News Sheet,* Bibliographical Society of the University of Virginia, No. 34 (October 1955). Lists sixty-seven titles.

Stephens, James. "The Joyce I Knew," *The Irish Digest,* XXVIII (July 1947), 38-41. Amusing memories of Stephens's slight acquaintance with Joyce.

Straumann, Heinrich. "Last Meeting with Joyce," *A James Joyce Yearbook,* ed. Maria Jolas. Paris: Transition Press, 1949.

"Svevo, Italo" (Ettore Schmitz). *James Joyce: A Lecture Delivered in Milan in 1927 by His Friend Italo Svevo,* trans. Stanislaus Joyce. Norfolk, Conn.: New Directions, 1950. Interesting information not available elsewhere.

Troy, William. "Stephen Dedalus and James Joyce," *The Nation,* CXXXVIII (February 14, 1934), 187-88. Stresses the often forgotten idea that, though Stephen is very much like young Joyce, no absolute identification should be attempted.

Poetry

"M.A." "Lyrics of James Joyce," *New Republic,* XVIII (March 8, 1919), 191. A review of the American publication of *Chamber Music.*

Golding, Louis. *James Joyce.* London: Thornton Butterworth, Ltd., 1933. The first chapter hazards an explanation of the sentimentality in Joyce's poetry.

Kerrigan, Anthony. "News of Mrs. Bloom," *Poetry,* LXXXV (1954), 109-12. A review of the Tindall edition.

Joyce, James. *Chamber Music,* ed. William York Tindall. New York: Columbia University Press, 1954. A collated edition, with full editorial apparatus.

Zabel, Morton D. "The Lyrics of James Joyce," *Poetry,* XXXVI (1930), 206-13. A sensitive appreciation.

"Dubliners"

"Advent in America of a New Irish Realist," *Current Opinion,* LXII (April 1917), 275. Interesting collection of early critical opinions of *Dubliners.*

Aldington, Richard. "The Influence of Mr. James Joyce," *The English Review,* XXXII (April 1921), 333-41. Comment on Joyce chiefly as a naturalist writer.

Bates, H. E. *The Modern Short Story: A Critical Survey.* London: Thomas Nelson and Sons, Ltd., 1941. An excellent discussion of contemporary short fiction and of the place of *Dubliners* in that genre.

Brooks, Cleanth, Jr., and Robert Penn Warren. *Understanding Fiction.* New York: F. S. Crofts and Company, 1943. Contains an analysis of "Araby."

Colum, Padraic. "Introduction" to *Dubliners.* New York: The Modern Library, n.d.

Daiches, David. *The Novel and the Modern World.* Chicago: The University of Chicago Press, 1939. A keenly sensitive analysis of *Dubliners* as a piece of writing.

Hendry, Irene. "Joyce's Epiphanies," in *James Joyce: Two Decades of Criticism,* ed. Seon Givens. New York: Vanguard Press, 1948. A study of Joyce's artistic method.

Hudson, Richard B. "Joyce's Clay," *The Explicator,* VI, Item 30 (March 1948).

Joyce, Stanislaus. *Recollections of James Joyce by His Brother.* New York: The James Joyce Society, 1950.

———. "The Background to 'Dubliners,'" *The Listener,* LI (March 25, 1954), 526-27. An attack on symbolic analyses of Joyce's early works with information concerning the environment in which several of the stories were written.

Levin, Richard, and Charles Shattuck. "First Flight to Ithaca," in *James Joyce: Two Decades of Criticism,* ed. Seon Givens. New York: Vanguard Press, 1948. Introduces the theory that *Dubliners,* like *Ulysses,* is based on structural parallels with the *Odyssey.*

Magalaner, Marvin. "Joyce, Nietzsche, and Hauptmann in James Joyce's 'A Painful Case,'" *PMLA,* LXVIII (March 1953), 95-102. A study of Joyce's use of sources.

Mercanton, Jacques. *Poètes de l'univers.* [Paris]: Éditions Albert Skira, [1947]. A French view of *Dubliners.*

Pearson, Norman Holmes. "Joyce's Clay," *The Explicator,* VII, Item 9 (October 1948). A reply to the article by Richard B. Hudson.

Pound, Ezra. *Pavannes and Divisions.* New York: Alfred A. Knopf, 1918. The essay first appeared in *The Egoist* as a review of *Dubliners.*

———. "A Curious History," *The Egoist,* I (January 15, 1914), 26-27. A protest against the censorship of Joyce's stories in Ireland.

Pritchett, V. S. "Current Literature," *The New Statesman and Nation,* XXI (February 15, 1941), 162. A dissenting view on the stories.

Tate, Allen. "Three Commentaries: Poe, James, and Joyce," *The Sewanee Review,* LVIII (Winter 1950), 1-15. A study of the symbolism of "The Dead."

"A Portrait of the Artist as a Young Man"

Anderson, C. G. "The Sacrificial Butter," *Accent,* XII (Winter 1952) 3-13. Clever analysis of the Christian symbolic pattern of Chapter 5.

Corcoran, T. *The Clongowes Record: 1814-1932.* Dublin: Browne and Nolan, Ltd., n.d. Background of life at Clongowes College, as well as lists of teachers and classmates of Stephen-Joyce.

F. H. (Francis Hackett). "Green Sickness," *New Republic,* X (March 3, 1917), 138-39. A short but perceptive early review of *A Portrait.*

Farrell, James T. "Joyce's 'A Portrait of the Artist as a Young Man': with a Postcript on 'Stephen Hero,'" in *James Joyce: Two Decades of Criticism,* ed. Seon Givens. New York: Vanguard Press, 1948. A discussion of Stephen Dedalus as a social being.

Gordon, Caroline. "Some Readings and Misreadings," *The Sewanee Review,* LXI (Summer 1953), 384-407. States the thesis that *A Portrait* is not "primarily a picture of the artist rebelling against constituted authority. It is, rather, the picture of a soul that is being damned for time and eternity caught in the act of foreseeing and foreknowing its damnation."

Hueffer (now Ford), Ford Madox. "A Haughty and Proud Generation," *Yale Review,* XI (July 1922), 703-17.

Huneker, James G. *Unicorns.* New York: Charles Scribner's Sons, 1917. On *A Portrait* as a work of truth and realism.

Kenner, Hugh. "The Portrait in Perspective," in *James Joyce: Two Decades of Criticism,* ed. Seon Givens. New York: Vanguard Press, 1948. A brilliant analysis of the method and ideas of *A Portrait.*

Kunkel, Frank L. "Beauty in Aquinas and Joyce," *Thought Patterns,* II (1951), 61-68. On Joyce's use of the teachings of Aquinas.

McLuhan, Herbert Marshall. "Joyce, Aquinas, and the Poetic Process," *Renascence: A Critical Journal of Letters,* IV (Autumn 1951), 3-11.

Pound, Ezra. *Instigations of Ezra Pound.* New York: Boni and Liveright, 1920.

Tindall, William York. *The Literary Symbol.* New York: Columbia University Press, 1955. Contains an excellent discussion of how symbols and associated images operate to enrich *A Portrait.* The book is valuable also for its contribution to an understanding of Joyce's use of symbol in all his works.

Van Ghent, Dorothy. *The English Novel: Form and Function,* New York: Rinehart and Company, 1953. A deeply penetrating study of Joyce's use of, and interest in, words in *A Portrait,* which presents the book in a new light.

Wells, H. G. "James Joyce," *New Republic,* X (March 10, 1917), 158-60. The famous early review that praises the talent of the writer of *A Portrait* but deplores his "cloacal obsession."

"Exiles"

Colum, Padraic. "James Joyce as a Dramatist," *The Nation,* CVII (October 12, 1918), 430. A notable early review.

———, ed. *James Joyce's "Exiles."* New York: The Viking Press, 1951. Contains Joyce's notes.

Farrell, James T. "*Exiles* and Ibsen," in *James Joyce: Two Decades of Criticism,* ed. Seon Givens. New York: Vanguard Press, 1948. Social and political backgrounds of the two dramatists.

Fergusson, Francis. "A Reading of *Exiles,*" in Joyce, *Exiles* ("New Classics Series.") Norfolk, Conn.: New Directions, 1945. An unusually sensitive interpretation.

Kelleher, John. Review of Colum edition, *Furioso,* VII (Spring 1952), 65-67. Relates the work to Joyce's career.

Kenner, Hugh. "Joyce's *Exiles,*" *The Hudson Review,* V (1952), 389-403. An unusual and provocative but debatable reading.

Macleod, Vivienne Koch. "The Influence of Ibsen on Joyce," *PMLA,* LX (1945), 879-98. See comment under next item.

———. "The Influence of Ibsen on Joyce: Addendum," *PMLA,* LXII (1947), 578-80. A complete analysis, the second article covering *Stephen Hero.*

"Ulysses"

Aldington, Richard. "Mr. James Joyce's 'Ulysses,'" in *Literary Studies and Reviews.* New York: Dial Press, 1924. A reprinting of the important early discussion in *The English Review,* XXXII (April 1921), 333-41.

Barker, George. "James Joyce, Heretic," *The Nation,* CLIV (1942), 236-37. A review of Levin, emphasizing the need to consider religious motivations.

Bennett, Arnold. "James Joyce's 'Ulysses,'" in *Things That have Interested Me.* New York: George H. Doran and Company, 1936. Reprint of review in *Outlook,* April 29, 1922, and *The Bookman,* LV (August 1922).

Blackmur, R. P. "The Jew in Search of a Son," *Virginia Quarterly Review,* XXIV (Winter 1948), 96-116. *Ulysses* as a symptom of the disintegration of modern culture.

Budgen, Frank. *James Joyce and the Making of "Ulysses."* London: Grayson and Grayson, Ltd.; New York: Harrison Smith and Robert Haas, 1934. The best introduction to Joyce as a friend and artist.

Colum, Mary. "The Confessions of James Joyce," *Freeman,* V (July 19, 1922), 450-52; reprinted in *The Freeman Book.* New York: B. W. Huebsch, 1924. Emphasizes personal tensions in Joyce's work.

Colum, Padraic. "'Ulysses' in Its Epoch," *The Saturday Review of Literature,* X (January 27, 1934), 433. Re-creation of Dublin background.

Connolly, Cyril. "The Position of Joyce," in *The Condemned Playground.* London: Routledge, 1945. Pp. 1-15. A reprint from *Life and Letters,* II (April 1929), 273-90. A sensible interpretation.

Curtius, Ernst. *James Joyce und Sein "Ulysses."* Zurich: Neue Schweizer Rundschau, 1929. A partial translation in *transition,*

June 1929. An early analysis of the use of motifs, with a nihilistic interpretation.

Damon, S. Foster. "The Odyssey in Dublin," in *James Joyce: Two Decades of Criticism,* ed. Seon Givens. New York: Vanguard Press, 1948. From *Hound & Horn,* III (1929), 7-44. Ingenious symbolic and mystical insights.

Den Haan, J. *Joyce: Mythe van Erin.* Amsterdam: De Bezige Bij, 1948. A witty search for the true Joyce, reviewing Gorman, Levin, and Kain. Unfortunately not translated.

Dujardin, Édouard. *Le Monologue intérieur: son apparition, ses origines, sa place dans l'oeuvre de James Joyce.* Paris: Messein, 1931. A study of the stream-of-consciousness technique by its originator. See also the Stuart Gilbert translation of Dujardin's novel, *We'll to the Woods No More.* New York: New Directions, 1938.

Duncan, Edward. "Unsubstantial Father: A Study of the *Hamlet* Symbolism in Joyce's *Ulysses,*" *University of Toronto Quarterly,* XIX (1950), 126-40. A valuable supplement to Damon and Gilbert, showing applications of the paternity theme.

Eliot, T. S. "'Ulysses,' Order, and Myth," in *James Joyce: Two Decades of Criticism,* ed. Seon Givens. New York: Vanguard Press, 1948. Reprinted from *Dial,* LXXV (November 1923), 480-83. Emphasizes the revolutionary import of the mythical structure.

Envoy: An Irish Review of Literature and Art (Dublin), ed. John Ryan, V (April 1951). An entertaining and shrewd series of assessments by Brian Nolan, Patrick Kavanagh, Denis Johnston, Andrew Cass, Niall Montgomery, and others.

Fehr, Bernhard. "James Joyce's 'Ulysses,'" *Englische Studien,* LX (1925), 180-205. *Ulysses* as a comic version of the philosophy of relativity.

Fowlie, Wallace. *The Clown's Grail.* London: Dennis Dobson, Ltd., 1947. Joyce as an exemplar of the artist's symbolic quest.

Frank, Joseph. "Spatial Form in Modern Literature," *The Sewanee Review,* LIII (1945), 221-40, 433-56, 643-53; reprinted in part by Schorer, Miles, McKenzie, eds., *Criticism: The Foundations of Modern Literary Judgment* (New York: Harcourt, Brace and Company, 1948); by Robert W. Stallman, ed. *Critiques and Essays in Criticism, 1928-1948* (New York: The Ronald Press, 1949), and by John W. Aldridge, *Critiques and Essays on Modern Fiction, 1920-1951* (New York: The Ronald Press, 1952). An important study of the metaphysical concepts of space and time underlying the work of Proust and Joyce.

Gilbert, Stuart. *James Joyce's "Ulysses."* London: Faber and Faber, Ltd., 1930; New York: Alfred A. Knopf, 1931. Rev. ed., New York: Alfred A. Knopf, 1952. Recently reprinted in paperback by Vintage Books. The standard guide to the basic symbolic structures in *Ulysses.* The revised edition adds only a brief chapter on Joyce's literary backgrounds, particularly his affinities to Walter Pater and Father Rolfe.

Givens, Seon, ed. *James Joyce: Two Decades of Criticism.* New York: Vanguard Press, 1948. A useful collection, mainly valuable for its inclusion of the essays by Hugh Kenner on *A Portrait,* and those of S. Foster Damon and Philip Toynbee on *Ulysses.*

Gorman, Herbert. *James Joyce: His First Forty Years.* New York: B. W. Huebsch, 1924. The best of many general and unpretentious guides to Joyce, not superseded by Charles Duff, *James Joyce and the Plain Reader* (London: Harmsworth, 1932), Louis Golding, *James Joyce* (London: Thornton Butterworth, Ltd., 1933), or W. Powell Jones, *James Joyce and the Common Reader* (Norman: University of Oklahoma Press, 1955).

Hall, Vernon, Jr. "Joyce's Use of Da Ponte and Mozart's *Don Giovanni,*" *PMLA,* LXVI (1951), 78-84. An interesting example of Joyce's use of thematic material.

Hanley, Miles L., and Others. *Word-Index to James Joyce's 'Ulysses.'* Madison: University of Wisconsin Press, 1937. A concordance.

Jung, C. G. "Ein Monolog," *Europaische Revue,* VIII (1932), 547-68. Later in *Wirklichkeit der Seele . . .* (London, 1933) and translated by W. Stanley Dell, Analytical Psychology Club of New York, 1949. A stimulating personal, philosophical, and psychological reading.

Kain, Richard M. *Fabulous Voyager: James Joyce's "Ulysses."* Chicago: The University of Chicago Press, 1947. A detailed study of the realistic aspects, notably of Joyce's use of local newspapers and directories.

Kenner, Hugh, "The Trivium in Dublin," in *English Institute Essays,* New York: Columbia University Press, 1952. Pp. 208-28. Dublin as a lost, decayed example of classical civilization.

———. "Joyce's 'Ulysses': Homer and Hamlet," Essays in Criticism, II (January 1952), 85-104. Joyce as a moral satirist of modern society.

———. "Baker Street to Eccles Street: The Odyssey of a Myth," *The Hudson Review,* I (Winter 1949), 481-99. Holmes and Watson, like Dedalus and Bloom, symbolize the split in modern culture.

Klein, A. M. "The Black Panther—A Study of Joyce," *Accent,* X (Spring 1950), 139-53. Analysis of liturgical echoes in Episode I.

———. "The Oxen of the Sun," *Here and Now,* III (1949), 28-48. Ingenious, sometimes oversubtle, symbolic exegesis.

———. "A Shout in the Street," *New Directions,* XIII (1951), 327-45. Viconian references.

Larbaud, Valéry. "James Joyce," *La Nouvelle revue française,* XXIV (April 1922), 385-409. Translated in *Criterion,* I (October 1922), 94-103. The pioneer explanation of the structure.

Levin, Harry. *James Joyce: A Critical Introduction.* Norfolk, Conn.: *New Directions,* 1941; London: Faber and Faber, Ltd., 1944. The basic introduction, especially important for its placing of Joyce in the modern European literary tradition.

Lewis, Wyndham. *Time and Western Man.* London: Chatto and Windus, 1927. An important attack.

MacCarthy, Desmond. "James Joyce," in *Memories.* London: Oxford University Press, 1953. Reprinted from *Sunday Times* (London), January 19, 1941. A final appraisal by the opponent most highly respected by literary London.

McLuhan, Herbert Marshall. "Joyce, Aquinas, and the Poetic Process," *Renascence,* IV (1951), 3-11. Background of Joyce's aesthetic theory.

———. "Joyce, Mallarmé, and the Press," *The Sewanee Review,* LXII (1954), 38-55. Like Kenner, McLuhan proceeds from the position of orthodox theology, relating symbolism to medieval literary and Scholastic patterns and interpreting Joyce as a moral critic of modern civilization.

———. "James Joyce: Trivial and Quadrivial," *Thought,* XXVIII (Spring 1953), 75-98. Scholastic roots of symbolism.

Miller, Henry. "The Universe of Death," *The Cosmological Eye* (Norfolk, Conn.: New Directions, 1939). Pp. 107-34. From *The Phoenix,* Spring 1938. Joyce as a nihilist.

Miller-Budnitskaya, R. "James Joyce's 'Ulysses,'" *Dialectics,* No. 5 (1938), 6-26. An intelligent Soviet attack, not always accurate.

Moholy-Nagy, L. *Vision in Motion.* Chicago: P. Theobald, 1947. A modern artist sees Joyce's relationships to cubism and abstractionism.

More, Paul Elmer. "James Joyce," *American Review,* V (May 1935), 129-57. *In On Being Human* (Princeton: Princeton University, 1936), pp. 69-96. An intelligent humanist attack, though it blames the patient for the disease.

Pound, Ezra. *Literary Essays of Ezra Pound,* ed. T. S. Eliot. Norfolk, Conn.: New Directions, 1954. Contains important early reviews of *Dubliners* (1914), *Portrait* (1918), and *Ulysses* (1922).

———. "James Joyce et Pécuchet," *Mercure de France,* CLVI (June 1, 1922), 307-20. Translated by Fred Bornhauser, *Shenandoah,* III (Autumn 1952), 9-20. An important early reading of *Ulysses* as a satire.

Prescott, Joseph. "Notes on Joyce's *Ulysses,*" *Modern Language Quarterly,* XIII (1952), 149-62. An indication of Joyce's multifarious knowledge and his artistic use of the flotsam of mass culture.

Rogers, H. E. "Irish Myth and the Plot of 'Ulysses,'" *E.L.H.,* XV (1948), 306-27. An approach into unexplored territory.

Russell, Francis. *Three Studies in Twentieth Century Obscurity,* Aldington, Ashford, Kent: Hand and Flower Press, 1954. An intelligent attack.

Savage, Derek. *The Withered Branch.* London: Eyre and Spottiswoode, 1950, An orthodox attack: Joyce as pantheist.

Slocum, John J., and Herber Cahoon, *A Bibliography of James Joyce: 1882-1941.* New Haven: Yale University Press; London: Rupert Hart Davis, 1953. An invaluable account of the complex tale of suppression, piracy, and variant editions, together with a listing of unpublished and uncollected materials.

Stonier, G. W. *Gog, Magog . . . ,* London: J. M. Dent and Sons, Ltd., 1933. Appraises *Ulysses* as an important symptom of modern society.

Strong, L. A. G. "James Joyce," in *English Novelists,* ed. Derek Vershoyle. New York: Harcourt, Brace and Company, 1936. An early assessment of the religious influences.

Tindall, William York. *Forces in Modern British Literature.* New York: Alfred A. Knopf, 1947. Shows Joyce's affinities with his contemporaries.

———. *James Joyce: His Way of Interpreting the Modern World.* New York: Charles Scribner's Sons, 1950. Stresses symbolism and reveals Joyce's preoccupation with human themes.

Toynbee, Philip. "A Study of James Joyce's 'Ulysses,'" in *James Joyce: Two Decades of Criticism,* ed. Seon Givens. New York: Vanguard Press, 1948. Pp. 243-84. Well-reasoned doubts concerning Joyce's achievement, by an experimental novelist.

Troy, William. "Stephen Dedalus and James Joyce," *The Nation,* CXXXVIII (February 14, 1934), 187-88. A valuable review.

Ussher, Arland. *Three Great Irishmen: Shaw, Yeats, Joyce.* New York: The Devin-Adair Company, 1952. A seasoned appraisal by an experienced writer who relates Joyce to his famed compatriots and to his native background.

Von Abele, Rudolph. "'Ulysses,' the Myth of Myth," *PMLA,* LXIX (1954), 358-64. A counterattack by an antisymbolist.

West, Alick. *Crisis and Criticism.* London: Lawrence and Wishart, 1937. An intelligent Marxist attack.

West, Rebecca. *The Strange Necessity.* London: Jonathan Cape, 1927. Excited, confused, and enthusiastic; hence a fair sample of the reactions of the British reading public.

Wilder, Thornton. *James Joyce, 1882-1941.* Aurora: Wells College Press, 1944. From *Poetry,* March 1941. A fine tribute.

Wilson, Edmund. *Axel's Castle: A Study in the Imaginative Literature of 1870-1930.* New York: Charles Scribner's Sons, 1931. The best brief introduction to *Ulysses.* Minimizes symbolic aspects.

"Finnegans Wake"

Atherton, J. S. "Lewis Carroll and 'Finnegans Wake,'" *English Studies,* XXXIII (1952), 1-15.

———. "Finnegans Wake: "The Gist of Pantomime,'" *Accent,* XV (Winter 1955), 14-26.

Beckett, Samuel, and Others. *Our Exagmination. . . .* London: Faber and Faber, Ltd. (1929). A book of essays by Joyce's friends and admirers, attempting to orient the reader to *Finnegans Wake.* Later published by New Directions under the title *An Exagmination of James Joyce.*

Bishop, John Peale. "Finnegans Wake," *The Southern Review,* V (Winter 1940), 439-52. An important early review.

Budgen, Frank. "Joyce's Chapters of Going Forth by Day," in *James Joyce: Two Decades of Criticism,* ed. Seon Givens. New York: Vanguard Press, 1948. From *Horizon,* September 1941.

Campbell, Joseph. "Finnegan the Wake," in *James Joyce: Two Decades of Criticism,* ed. Seon Givens. New York: Vanguard Press, 1948. The article appeared first in *Chimera* in Spring 1946. It deals with the oriental mythology of the *Wake.*

———, and Henry Morton Robinson. *A Skeleton Key to "Finnegans Wake."* New York: Harcourt, Brace and Company, 1944. Page by page redaction of Joyce's novel.

Fadiman, Clifton. "Don't Shoot the Book-Reviewer; He's Doing the Best He Can," *The New Yorker,* XV (May 6, 1939), 88-91. A frankly puzzled review expressing the bewilderment of the ordinary reader.

Fowlie, Wallace. "Masques du héros littéraire" (Ut. II: "Le Sort de l'artiste comme héros: Proust et Joyce") in *Les Oeuvres Nouvelles.* New York: La Maison Française, 1944. *Finnegans Wake* as a modern *Purgatorio.*

Gillet, Louis. "M. James Joyce et son nouveau roman," *Revue des deux mondes,* Année 100 (August 15, 1931), 928-39. A translation of this article appeared in *transition,* XXI (March 1932), 263-72.

Halper, Nathan. "James Joyce and the Russian General," *Partisan Review,* XVIII (July-August 1951), 424-31. A fascinating working out of one motif of the *Wake,* illustrating the type of analysis that must be done in order to obtain fruitful results with such a book.

Hodgart, M. J. C. "Work in Progress." *The Cambridge Journal,* VI (October 1952), 23-39.

Hoffman, Frederick J. "Infroyce," in *James Joyce: Two Decades of Criticism,* ed. Seon Givens. New York: Vanguard Press, 1948. This article is from Hoffman's *Freudianism and the Literary Mind* (Baton Rouge: Louisiana State University Press, 1945). On Joyce's adaptation of Freudian psychology.

Kelleher, John. "Joyce Digested," *Accent,* V (Spring 1945), 181-86.

Leavis, F. R. "Joyce and 'The Revolution of the Word.'" *Scrutiny: A Quarterly Review,* II (September 1933), 193-201. Finds Joyce's use of a new language contrived, boring, and formless—not at all like Shakespeare's innovations with language.

McGuire, Owen B. "Finnegans Wake," *The Commonweal,* XXX

(September 1, 1939), 436-37. Attack on the book as unfit for Catholic readers.

Morse, J. Mitchell. "Cain, Abel and Joyce," *E.L.H.*, XXII (March 1955), 48-60.

———. "Jacob and Esau in 'Finnegans Wake,'" *Modern Philology*, LII (November 1954), 123-30.

Powys, J. C. "Finnegan's [*sic*] Wake," in *Modern Reading*, ed. Reginald Moore. No. 7. London: Wells Gardner, Darton and Company, 1943. A dithyramb of praise.

Stoll, Elmer Edgar. *From Shakespeare to Joyce: Authors and Critics; Literature and Life*. Garden City, N. Y.: Doubleday, Doran and Company, Inc., 1944. One of the more influential conservative attacks on Joyce and his experimental work.

Strong, L. A. G. *The Sacred River: An Approach to James Joyce*. New York: Pellegrini and Cudahy, 1951.

Tindall, William York. *James Joyce: His Way of Interpreting the Modern World*. New York: Charles Scribner's Sons, 1950. Very good exegesis of the meanings of mythical and symbolic patterns, especially in *Finnegans Wake*.

transition. The student will find much of interest in the issues of this little magazine during the 1920's and 1930's. They should be examined for a better understanding of the literary atmosphere in which Joyce wrote during his later years.

Troy, William. "Notes on Finnegans Wake," in *James Joyce: Two Decades of Criticism*, ed. Seon Givens. New York: Vanguard Press, 1948. The article appeared in *Partisan Review*, Summer 1939.

Ussher, Arland. "James Joyce: Doubting Thomist and Joking Jesuit," in *Three Great Irishmen: Shaw, Yeats, Joyce*. New York: Devin-Adair Company, 1953. Ways of looking at the *Wake*.

Wilson, Edmund. "The Dream of H. C. Earwicker," in *James Joyce: Two Decades of Criticism*, ed. Seon Givens. New York: Vanguard Press, 1948. It may also be found in Wilson's *The Wound and the Bow* (New York: Oxford University Press, 1947). A penetrating early study that avoids extremes of adulation and exasperated frustration.

Index

The following topics relating to Joyce are grouped here for the reader's convenience. A glance at the categories will reveal both the range of Joyce's achievement and the diversity of critical interpretation.